Eclipse in Action

Eclipse in Action

A GUIDE FOR JAVA DEVELOPERS

DAVID GALLARDO
ED BURNETTE
ROBERT MCGOVERN

With contributions to appendixes by
STEVEN HAINES

M

MANNING

Greenwich
(74° w. long.)

Manning Publications Co.   Copyeditor: Tiffany Taylor
209 Bruce Park Avenue   Typesetter: Denis Dalinnik
Greenwich, CT 06830   Cover designer: Leslie Haimes

ISBN 1-930110-96-0

Printed in the United States of America
1 2 3 4 5 6 7 8 9 10 – VHG – 08 07 06 05 04 03

To my wife Eni and my son Alejandro
D.J.G.

To Lisa, Michael, and Christopher
E.B.B.

To my wife Roberta for putting up with this insane trip
R.M.

brief contents

PART 1 USING ECLIPSE 1

    1 ▪ Overview   3

    2 ▪ Getting started with the Eclipse Workbench   13

    3 ▪ The Java development cycle: test, code, repeat   39

    4 ▪ Working with source code in Eclipse   79

    5 ▪ Building with Ant   103

    6 ▪ Source control with CVS   143

    7 ▪ Web development tools   177

PART 2 EXTENDING ECLIPSE 217

    8 ▪ Introduction to Eclipse plug-ins   219

    9 ▪ Working with plug-ins in Eclipse   249

contents

foreword   *xvii*

preface   *xxi*

acknowledgments   *xxiii*

about this book   *xxv*

about the title   *xxix*

about the cover illustration   *xxx*

PART 1   USING ECLIPSE 1

1 Overview   3

1.1   Where Eclipse came from   4

   A bit of background   *5* ▪ *The Eclipse organization*   *5*
   Open source software   *6*

1.2   What is Eclipse?   7

   The Eclipse architecture   *8* ▪ *Language and*
   platform neutrality   *10*

1.3   What's next   11

1.4   Summary   11

ix

2 *Getting started with the Eclipse Workbench* 13

   2.1   Obtaining Eclipse   14

   2.2   Eclipse overview   15

        Projects and folders   15 ▪ The Eclipse Workbench   16

   2.3   The Java quick tour   20

        Creating a Java project   20 ▪ Creating a Java class   22
        Running the Java program   25 ▪ Debugging the Java
        program   27 ▪ Java scrapbook pages   30

   2.4   Preferences and other settings   31

        Javadoc comments   32 ▪ Format style   33 ▪ Code generation
        templates   33 ▪ Classpaths and classpath variables   35
        Exporting and importing preferences   36

   2.5   Summary   37

3 *The Java development cycle: test, code, repeat* 39

   3.1   Java development tools methodology   40

        Testing is job 1   41 ▪ A sample application and working sets   41

   3.2   The JUnit unit testing framework   43

        Method stubs and unit tests   44 ▪ Creating test cases   49
        How much testing is enough?   54 ▪ Implementing the
        public methods   58

   3.3   Further adventures in debugging   62

        Setting breakpoint properties   64
        Finding and fixing a bug   66

   3.4   Logging with log4j   68

        Loggers, appenders, and pattern layouts   69 ▪ Configuring
        log4j   73 ▪ Using log4j with Eclipse   75

   3.5   Summary   77

4 *Working with source code in Eclipse* 79

   4.1   Importing an external project   80

   4.2   Extending the persistence component   83

        Creating a factory method   84 ▪ Creating the unit test class   84
        Working with the astronomy classes   85 ▪ The Star test case   88
        Creating a test suite   89 ▪ Implementing the
        ObjectManager class   90

4.3   Refactoring   95

    Renaming a class   96 ▪ Extracting an interface   99
    Future refactoring   101

4.4   Summary   102

5 Building with Ant   103

5.1   The need for an official build process   104

    Creating the build directory structure   105

5.2   Make: A retrospective   109

5.3   The new Java standard: Ant   112

    A very brief introduction to XML   113 ▪ A simple Ant
    example   115 ▪ Projects   118 ▪ Targets   119 ▪ Tasks   119
    Properties   126 ▪ File sets and path structures   128
    Additional Ant capabilities   131

5.4   A sample Ant build   131

    Creating the build file, build.xml   132 ▪ Performing a
    build   136 ▪ Debugging the build   138

5.5   Summary   140

6 Source control with CVS   143

6.1   The need for source control   144

6.2   Using CVS with Eclipse   146

    Sharing a project with CVS   146 ▪ Working with CVS   153
    Versions and branches   170

6.3   Summary   174

7 Web development tools   177

7.1   Developing for the Web   178

    The web, HTML, servlets, and JSP   178 ▪ JSP overview   179
    Servlet overview   181

7.2   Tomcat and the Sysdeo Tomcat plug-in   181

    Installing and testing Tomcat   182 ▪ Installing and setting up
    the Sysdeo Tomcat plug-in   183 ▪ Creating and testing a JSP
    using Eclipse   185 ▪ Creating and testing a servlet in
    Eclipse   187 ▪ Placing a Tomcat project under
    CVS control   190

7.3 Building a web application   191

The web application directory structure   191 ▪ Web application design and testing   192 ▪ Programming with servlets and JSPs   197

7.4 Wrapping up the sample application   210

7.5 Summary   215

PART 2 EXTENDING ECLIPSE 217

8 Introduction to Eclipse plug-ins   219

8.1 Plug-ins and extension points   220

Anatomy of a plug-in   220 ▪ The plug-in lifecycle   221 Creating a simple plug-in by hand   222

8.2 The Plug-in Development Environment (PDE)   223

Preparing your Workbench   224 ▪ Importing the SDK plug-ins   224 ▪ Using the Plug-in Project Wizard   226

8.3 The "Hello, World" plug-in example   228

The Plug-in Manifest Editor   230 ▪ The Run-time Workbench   231 ▪ Plug-in class (AbstractUIPlugin)   233 Actions, menus, and toolbars (IWorkbenchWindowActionDelegate)   237 ▪ Plug-ins and classpaths   241

8.4 The log4j library plug-in example   242

Attaching source   244 ▪ Including the source zip in the plug-in package   244

8.5 Deploying a plug-in   246

8.6 Summary   247

9 Working with plug-ins in Eclipse   249

9.1 The log4j integration plug-in example   250

Project overview   252 ▪ Preparing the project   253

9.2 Editors (TextEditor)   254

Preparing the editor class   255 ▪ Defining the editor extension   255 ▪ Adding an icon   259 ▪ Adding color   261 Token manager   268 ▪ Content assist (IContentAssistProcessor)   271 ▪ Putting it all together   275

9.3   Views (ViewPart)   279
*Adding the view   280 ▪ Modifying perspective defaults   281
View class   282 ▪ Table framework   289 ▪ Label providers
(LabelProvider)   296 ▪ Models   298 ▪ Receiver thread   300*
9.4   Preferences (FieldEditorPreferencePage)   301
Main preference page   302 ▪ Editor preference page   303
9.5   Plugin class   304
9.6   Summary   305

A   **Java perspective menu reference   307**

B   **CVS installation procedures   323**
B.1   Installing CVS on UNIX and Linux   324
*Creating the CVS repository   325 ▪ Setting up SSH remote
access   326 ▪ Setting up pserver remote access   327*
B.2   Installing CVS on Mac OS X   328
B.3   Installing CVSNT on Windows   329
B.4   Installing Cygwin CVS and SSH on Windows   330
B.5   Troubleshooting the CVS installation   332
B.6   Backing up the CVS repository   332

C   **Plug-in extension points   333**

D   **Introduction to SWT   343**
D.1   What is the Standard Widget Toolkit?   344
D.2   SWT architecture   345
Widget creation   346 ▪ Resource disposal   346
D.3   SWT and events   347
D.4   SWT and threads   348
D.5   Building and running SWT programs   350
D.6   Using SWT   353
*The BasicFramework class   353 ▪ The MainApp class   356
Trying the example   359*

E **Introduction to JFace   361**

E.1   Architecture   362

E.2   Building a JFace application   363

JFaceExample class   364 ▪ ExitAction class   366

index   369

foreword

Imagine my surprise when the editors asked me to write this foreword. I'm not a guru, just a programmer who has used Eclipse every day for the last couple of years. The biggest difference between you and me is that when I started, there weren't any books like this, so I had to dig a lot of the material you find here out of the source code. A character-building exercise, to be sure, but I'd much rather have had the book!

This book will help you come up to speed fast on a great, free Java development tool. The chapters on JUnit, Ant, and Team (CVS) integration in particular address areas where newcomers often have questions and need a little boost to become productive. If you're not already using these tools, you should be. If you are, you'll find out how Eclipse makes it easier to use them. The nuts and bolts of programming—creating and maintaining projects, editing source code, and debugging—are not neglected, and the section on refactoring will introduce you to features that, if your previous tool didn't have them, you will soon wonder how you ever lived without.

Eclipse has its own GUI framework called the Standard Widget Toolkit (SWT), which is portable across all major platforms, runs fast, and looks native. You can use SWT to develop your own applications, the same way you might use AWT/Swing. A smaller framework named JFace, built on top of SWT, adds dialogs, wizards, models, and other essentials to the basic SWT widgets. These are discussed in useful but not excruciating detail in appendixes you can also use for reference.

The book will be even more helpful if you have ambitions to go beyond using Eclipse to extending it. I'm one of those people. For a long time there was no good introduction to plug-in writing, which made it tough to get started; but now there is. I hope you will give the chapters on extending Eclipse a fair chance to excite you with the possibilities.

I don't know about you, but I'm never quite satisfied with the development tools I use. No matter how great they are, something is always missing. I think most developers are like that. We tend to fall in love with our favorite editor or IDE, defend it staunchly in the newsgroups, and evangelize our friends relentlessly. Yet, in our fickle hearts, we realize its many blemishes and shortcomings. That's why most developers are latent tool-builders. As Henry Petroski observed in *The Evolution of Useful Things*, the mother of invention is not necessity, it is irritation.

But usually our tool-building urges remain dormant, because of the great effort required to duplicate the hundreds of things about our favorite tool that are perfectly fine in order to fix the handful of things we find wanting. An open source development tool like Eclipse, built from the ground up by extending a very small nucleus with plug-ins, allows us to give vent to our frustrations in the most productive way possible. By writing plug-ins, we can improve and extend an already rich IDE, keeping all that is good about it. Moreover, we can readily share our efforts with other users of the tool and take advantage of their efforts, by virtue of the common platform that underlies all.

I speak of irritation, but I wouldn't write a plug-in for a tool I didn't like much. Eclipse has a lot to like. I won't rattle off features; you will discover these for yourself in the pages of this book or on your own. I'll just mention one thing that strikes me as extraordinary, even unique: the excellent technical support provided in the Eclipse newsgroups by the actual people who wrote the code. I know of no commercial product whose support is nearly as good, and no other open source project whose developers are so committed to answering any and all questions thrown at them. In many cases, questions are answered with source code written and tested for the occasion. For a programmer, it doesn't get much better than that.

Taking advantage of these resources, people like you and me have written or are in the process of writing a wide spectrum of plug-ins, ranging from hacks to features to entire subsystems. One guy didn't like the way the toolbar icons were laid out, so he wrote a plug-in that arranged them as he preferred; it turned out quite a few people agreed with him. I wrote an XML editor because there wasn't a decent one available at the time. Others are fitting in new programming languages, graphical editors, GUI builders. Developers in large companies are using plug-ins to tailor Eclipse to corporate ways, like the source control system the VP standardized on that no other tools seem to support. Graduate students are using Eclipse as the platform for their thesis projects. The list goes on, and it is always incomplete.

You can even make money extending Eclipse. Eclipse is free, but its license allows you to charge for your Eclipse-based extensions. (For complete licensing details, use the Legal Stuff link on the eclipse.org web page.) There are four ways to do this:

- You can take Eclipse as a whole, strip out the parts you don't want, add the extensions you do want, and sell the result as your own product.

- You can select parts of Eclipse, such as SWT and JFace (described in this book), and use them to build your own applications that don't necessarily have anything to do with development tools.

- You can sell individual plug-ins to the Eclipse community. (As you might imagine, it takes a lot of added value to get people to pay for extensions to free software, but I know of several projects underway, including my own, that intend to test the waters.)

- You can, with little extra effort, target your Eclipse plug-ins at the IBM WebSphere Application Developer (WSAD) add-on market. WSAD is based on Eclipse and is intentionally very compatible with it. (WSAD is Enterprise-with-a-big-E software; customers are accustomed to paying.)

The only catch to all this generosity is you have to know how to take advantage of it. This book will get you off and running. I heartily recommend it. I've been writing Eclipse plug-ins since 2001, and this book taught me things I didn't know. The only negative thing I can think to say is that I'm a little envious that readers will come up to speed so much faster than I did.

Bob Foster
http://www.xmlbuddy.com/

preface

This book began with a single author, David Gallardo, and a single purpose: to introduce Java developers to Eclipse. Initial feedback from early reviewers made it apparent that there was also a lot of interest in developing plug-ins to extend Eclipse and in using Eclipse's graphics libraries in other projects. The March 2003 release of Eclipse 2.1, which the book targeted, was approaching quickly, so the call went out for help.

Ed Burnette, who was interested in the potential of technologies behind Eclipse and the applications they could power, was recruited to expand the coverage of Eclipse plug-ins. Robert McGovern, the technical editor (who seemingly needs no sleep), stepped up to the plate to produce two appendixes on SWT and JFace, using source material graciously provided by Steven Haines. The expanded team permitted us to cover both using and extending Eclipse more thoroughly than would otherwise have been possible.

In the spirit of agile development, the first sample application—a file-based persistence component—was begun with little up-front design. The first part of the book accurately depicts its evolution, warts and all. The source code for each stage of the application is available on this book's web site (http://www.manning.com/gallardo), including a final version that corrects the flaws that appear when it is extended to support a database.

Although we introduce and demonstrate the tools and techniques for agile development, and we recommend this approach, this isn't an agile development primer. The material, like Eclipse itself, is equally applicable to other methodologies—or no methodology at all.

Eclipse includes a lot of information to cover. One of the big debates we had in creating the book was how to balance the information in the book with the online documentation. Where practical, we avoid duplicating information that is readily available in the online documentation (for example, we considered—but dropped—a list of all the SWT widgets). We feel that a concise guide is more useful (and readable!) than an 800-page behemoth any day.

We learned a lot while writing *Eclipse in Action*—about Eclipse, about ourselves, and about the effects of sleep deprivation. Overall, we had great fun doing it. We hope you'll find the book helpful in whatever projects you create, and that you have as much fun reading it as we did writing it!

acknowledgments

The authors would like to acknowledge and thank all the people who helped make this book a reality:

The staff at Manning who gave us this opportunity: Marjan Bace, Susan Capparelle, Dave Roberson, and in memoriam, Ted Kennedy. The production staff took our raw words, worked their magic, and transformed them into the book you now hold: Gil Schmidt, Tiffany Taylor, Denis Dalinnik, Syd Brown, Mary Piergies, Helen Trimes, Leslie Haimes, and Iain Shigeoka.

Our reviewers, Christophe Avare, Dan Dobrin, Bob Donovan, Bob Foster, Phil Hanna, Carl Hume, Michiel Konstapiel, Jason Kratz, James Poli, Eric Rizzo, and Cyril Sagan, provided invaluable guidance in focusing on the right topics and in getting the technical details right. We would also like to acknowledge the valuable contribution that Steve Haines made to our coverage of SWT and JFace.

The Eclipse community, particularly those members participating in the Eclipse newsgroups, provided valuable assistance and technical insight. The Straight Talking Java list provided us a more collegial environment to discuss matters technical and topical, a sort of virtual watercooler. We would also like to thank the Eclipse team for creating an incredible product.

David and Ed would like to thank Robert McGovern, who first came on board as a reviewer of the manuscript in its early stages and then did the technical editing of the code and text, before finally jumping in to help write the appendixes that were falling behind schedule. The many late nights he dedicated to the project and his excellent insights and comments are much appreciated, and resulted in a much better book than we could otherwise have hoped for.

David Gallardo would like to thank Ed Burnette for the expertise, careful eye, and insight Ed provided in his reviews and for the consistency and coherence Ed established in his own work; Tiffany Taylor for the fine job she did in pruning his prose; and Mary Piergies for keeping him on track. Most of all, David would like to thank his wife Eni for her patience.

Ed Burnette would like to thank his wife Lisa for keeping the house together and putting up with his late nights, Duane Ressler and Paul Kent for providing a constructive work environment that allows for exploration, and Clay Andres for inviting him along for the ride.

Robert McGovern would like to thank David and Ed for letting him join in the fun and games, Mary Piergies for leading him through, and the rest of the fantastic team at Manning. Special thanks to Joy, Kieran, Samuel, and finally to Roberta, his wife, for her understanding and encouragement.

about this book

This book is designed to help you use Eclipse to its fullest potential. Its primary focus is using Eclipse as a Java IDE, but for more advanced developers, additional information is provided to help you extend Eclipse for other languages and applications.

How the book is organized

This book has two parts, nine chapters, and five appendices. Part 1 is for those who want to develop Java code using Eclipse as an IDE:

- Chapter 1 provides an introduction to the Eclipse project, how it got started, how it's designed, and where it's headed.
- Chapter 2 covers how to obtain and install Eclipse, how to use it to create and debug Java programs, and some of the most important options and preferences.
- Chapter 3 delves into best practices of Java development supported by Eclipse, including unit testing, debugging, and logging.
- Chapter 4 uses an example application to show you how to arrange your project and use the Java toolkit's impressive refactoring support.
- Chapter 5 talks about Ant, the open source building tool. You'll learn some background about what Ant is and how it's integrated into Eclipse.

- Chapter 6 discusses CVS, a source code repository supported by Eclipse. You'll learn how to share projects, check projects in and out, and deal with conflicts when more than one person makes a change to the source.
- Chapter 7 shows you how Eclipse supports JSP and servlet web development through third-party plug-ins such as Sysdeo and XMLBuddy. An example web site is carried through the stages of design, development, debugging, and testing.

Part 2 is for those wanting to extend Eclipse with new functionality:

- Chapter 8 introduces Eclipse plug-ins and the Plug-in Development Environment. You'll learn how to create simple plug-ins and deploy them so others can use them.
- Chapter 9 explores the code of a more advanced plug-in, showing you how to create a custom editor, a viewer, and preference pages.

The appendixes provide more detailed information that supports the rest of the book:

- Appendix A is a quick reference to Eclipse's Java-related menus.
- Appendix B discusses installing a CVS server on different operating systems.
- Appendix C has a table of all extension points provided by the Eclipse Platform.
- Appendix D covers the Standard Widget Toolkit used as the basis of the Eclipse user interface.
- Appendix E introduces JFace, a higher-level user interface toolkit built on SWT.

Who should read this book

Eclipse in Action is for Java programmers at all levels who would like to learn how to use and extend Eclipse or use Eclipse technologies in their own projects. Beginning and intermediate programmers will appreciate the advice on unit testing, logging, and debugging, and the clear, step-by-step instructions on using the Java tools provided within Eclipse. Advanced developers will relish the detailed plug-in examples. Even people who have been using Eclipse for some time will find numerous tricks and tips they didn't know before.

How to use this book

If you are new to Eclipse, you should begin with chapters 1–6. This section of the book will take you through the process of learning about Eclipse and commonly accepted best practices regarding tools and programming techniques. You may find appendixes D and E useful if you want to build a standalone program that uses the Eclipse GUI toolkits instead of Swing. When you feel confident about your Eclipse Java skills, you should move on to chapter 7, where you will learn how to do web development in Eclipse.

If you've used Eclipse before but you want to extend its functionality, then you should read chapters 8 and 9. There you will be taken through the process of developing, integrating, and running a plug-in. If the plug-in you are developing needs to interact with Eclipse's user interface, then you should examine appendixes D and E to understand a little about the technologies that make up the Eclipse UI. You will also find that appendix C is a handy reference that lists in one table all the places you can extend Eclipse.

Source code

This book contains extensive source code examples of normal Java programs, Eclipse plug-ins, and standalone SWT/JFace programs. All code examples can be found at the book's web site at http://www.manning.com/gallardo.

Typographical conventions

The following conventions are used throughout the book:

- *Italic* typeface is used to introduce new terms.
- **Bold type** indicates text that you should enter.
- `Courier` typeface is used to denote code samples, as well as elements and attributes, method names, classes, interfaces, and other identifiers.
- Bold face **`Courier`** identifies sections of code that differ from previous, similar code sections.
- Code annotations accompany many segments of code. Certain annotations are marked with bullets such as ❶. These annotations have further explanations that follow the code.
- The → symbol is used to indicate menu items that should be selected in sequence.
- Code line continuations use the ➡ symbol.

Other conventions: plug-in or plugin?

Look for the word on Google and you will see that most people use "plugin." Our publisher would have preferred us to have used the unhyphenated form of the word—a printed page looks more peaceful to the eye without the hyphens disturbing the flow of letters and words, and it's quicker to type. However, the hyphenated form is used in the product itself, and, in a tip-of-the-hat to the preferences of the creators of Eclipse, we have consistently used it in this book when referring to plug-ins in general. We do use "plugin" in a few cases, when referring to specific filenames and directories that don't include the hyphen—for example, the plugins directory in which Eclipse plug-ins are installed, and the plugin.xml manifest file.

Online resources

Several excellent resources are available:

- Manning's Author Online forum provides a venue where readers can ask questions of the authors and discuss the book with the authors and with other readers. You can register for the *Eclipse in Action* forum at http://www.manning.com/gallardo.
- The Eclipse project web site is http://www.eclipse.org. It contains a number of articles and examples on using and extending Eclipse. You can also find a bug database where you can report bugs and feature requests or vote for your favorites, as well as a searchable index.
- Eclipse newsgroups are hosted on the news.eclipse.org server. To help prevent spam, the groups are password protected. For further instructions, including how to get the password, see http://www.eclipse.org/newsgroups.
- EclipseWiki (http://eclipsewiki.swiki.net) is a useful site that contains a lot of information about the Eclipse project and its many subprojects. It is loaded with tips and tricks, many of them gleaned from the Eclipse newsgroups.

about the title

By combining introductions, overviews, and how-to examples, Manning's *In Action* books are designed to help learning *and* remembering. According to research in cognitive science, the things people remember are things they discover during self-motivated exploration.

Although no one at Manning is a cognitive scientist, we are convinced that for learning to become permanent it must pass through stages of exploration, play, and, interestingly, retelling of what is being learned. People understand and remember new things—which is to say they master them—only after actively exploring them. Humans learn *in action*. An essential part of an *In Action* guide is that it is example-driven. It encourages the reader to try things out, to play with new code, and explore new ideas.

There is another, more mundane, reason for the title of this book: our readers are busy. They use books to do a job or to solve a problem. They need books that allow them to jump in and jump out easily and learn just what they want just when they want it. They need books that aid them *in action*. The books in this series are designed for such readers.

about the cover illustration

The figure on the cover of *Eclipse in Action* is a "Iudio de los estados Mahomentanos," a Jewish trader from the Middle East. The illustration is taken from a Spanish compendium of regional dress customs first published in Madrid in 1799. The book's title page states:

Coleccion general de los Trages que usan actualmente todas las Nacionas del Mundo desubierto, dibujados y grabados con la mayor exactitud por R.M.V.A.R. Obra muy util y en special para los que tienen la del viajero universal

which we translate, as literally as possible, thus:

General collection of costumes currently used in the nations of the known world, designed and printed with great exactitude by R.M.V.A.R. This work is very useful especially for those who hold themselves to be universal travelers

Although nothing is known of the designers, engravers, and workers who colored this illustration by hand, the "exactitude" of their execution is evident in this drawing. The "Iudio de los estados Mahomentanos" is just one of many figures in this colorful collection. Their diversity speaks vividly of the uniqueness and individuality of the world's towns and regions just 200 years ago. This was a time when the dress codes of two regions separated by a few dozen miles identified people uniquely as belonging to one or the other. The collection brings to life a sense of isolation and distance of that period—and of every other historic period except our own hyperkinetic present.

Dress codes have changed since then and the diversity by region, so rich at the time, has faded away. It is now often hard to tell the inhabitant of one continent from another. Perhaps, trying to view it optimistically, we have traded a cultural and visual diversity for a more varied personal life. Or a more varied and interesting intellectual and technical life.

In spite of the current downturn, we at Manning continue to celebrate the inventiveness, the initiative and, yes, the fun of the computer business with book covers based on the rich diversity of regional life of two centuries ago, brought back to life by the pictures from this collection.

Part 1

Using Eclipse

The first part of this book will get you started developing Java code in Eclipse quickly and efficiently. Chapters 1 and 2 provide an introduction to Eclipse—its history, how to obtain and install it, and how to use it to create and debug Java projects. Chapters 3 and 4 delve into the best practices of Java development, including unit testing and refactoring. Chapters 5 and 6 are dedicated to two tools no programmer or development team should be without—Ant and CVS—and how Eclipse provides first-class integration with these tools. Finally, Chapter 7 introduces the Sysdeo Tomcat plug-in and shows how to use it for Java servlet and JSP web development. Throughout these chapters, you'll find hints and tips about using Eclipse and some best practices for developing code that the authors have discovered through their extensive programming experience.

Overview **1**

In this chapter...

- A brief history of Eclipse
- The Eclipse.org consortium
- An overview of Eclipse and its design
- A peek at the future

Many blacksmiths take pride in making their own tools. When first starting out in the trade, or when undertaking a job that has special requirements, making new tools is the first step. Using forge, anvil, and hammer, the blacksmith repeats the cycle of heating, hammering, and cooling the steel until it becomes a tool of exactly the right shape, size, and strength for the job at hand.

Software development seems like a clean and abstract process when compared to the visceral force and heat of blacksmithing. But what code has in common with metal (at least at high temperatures) is malleability: With sufficient skill and effort, you can bang code or steel into a finely honed tool or a massive architectural wonder.

Eclipse is the software developer's equivalent to the blacksmith's workshop, initially equipped with forge, anvil, and hammer. Just as the blacksmith might use his existing tools to make a new tool, perhaps a pair of tongs, you can use Eclipse to build new tools for developing software—tools that extend the functionality of Eclipse. One of Eclipse's distinguishing features is its extensibility.

But don't be put off by this do-it-yourself ethos; you don't need to build your own tools to take full advantage of Eclipse. You may not even need any new tools; Eclipse comes with a fully featured Java development environment, including a source-level debugger. In addition, because of Eclipse's popularity and its open-source nature, many specialized tools (built for Eclipse, using Eclipse) are already freely available (some of which you'll be introduced to in this book), and many more are on the way.

1.1 *Where Eclipse came from*

It would be incredible for a software development environment as full-featured and mature as Eclipse to appear out of the blue. But that is what seemed to have happened when version 1.0 was released in November 2001. Naturally, there was some carping about the approach Eclipse took and the features it lacked. Since the days of emacs, one of the two most popular sports among developers has been debating which development environment is the best. (The other is debating which operating system is the best.) Surprisingly, there was little of the usual contentiousness this time. The consensus seemed to be that Eclipse was almost, but not quite there yet; what version 1.0 product is?

Some companies are famously known for not getting things right until version 3.0 (and even then you're well advised to wait for 3.1, so the serious bugs get shaken out). But though Eclipse 1.0 lacked some features and didn't quite accommodate everyone's way of working, it was apparent that Eclipse got things right.

Best of all, it was a free, open source project with a lot of resources. It was also apparent that Eclipse's developers were listening to the users—indeed, the developers themselves were the biggest users of Eclipse. When version 2.1 arrived in March 2003, it met or surpassed almost everyone's high hopes—so many people rushed to download it that it was nearly impossible to get a copy for the first week of release.

1.1.1 A bit of background

Eclipse wasn't a happy accident of engineering, of course; IBM reportedly spent more than $40 million developing it before giving it away as open source software to a consortium, Eclipse.org, which initially included Borland, IBM, Merant, QNX Software Systems, Rational Software, Red Hat, SuSE, TogetherSoft, and Webgain. Other companies that have since joined include Hewlett Packard, Fujitsu, Oracle, and Sybase. IBM continues to take the lead in Eclipse's development through its subsidiary, Object Technologies International (OTI), the people who developed Eclipse in the first place.

OTI is a distinguished developer of object-oriented development tools, with a history going back to 1988, when the object-oriented language of choice was Smalltalk. OTI, acquired by IBM in 1996, was the force behind IBM's Visual Age products, which set the standard for object-oriented development tools. Many concepts pioneered in Smalltalk were applied to Java, making Visual Age for Java (VA4J) a unique environment. For example, it had no concept of a file; versioning took place at the method level. Like the other Visual Age products, VA4J was originally written in Smalltalk.

Eclipse is essentially a rewrite of VA4Java in Java. Smalltalk-like features, which made VA4J seem quirky compared to other Java IDEs, are mostly gone. Some OO purists are disappointed, but one of the things that has made Java popular is its willingness to meet practicalities halfway. Like a good translation, Eclipse is true to the spirit of its new language and strikes a similar balance between ideology and utility.

1.1.2 The Eclipse organization

The Eclipse project is managed and directed by the consortium's Board of Stewards, which includes one representative from each of the consortium's corporate members. The board determines the goals and objectives of the project, guided by two principal objectives that it seeks to balance: fostering a healthy open source community and creating commercial opportunities for its members.

At the operational level, the Eclipse project is managed by the Project Management Committee (PMC), which oversees the project as a whole. The Eclipse project is divided into three subprojects:

- The Platform
- The Java Development Toolkit (JDT; notably led by Erich Gamma, who is well-known for his work on design patterns and agile development methodology)
- The Plug-in Development Environment (PDE)

Each of these subprojects is further subdivided into a number of components. For example, the Platform subproject includes over a dozen components such as Compare, Help, and Search. The JDT subproject includes three components: Debug (which provides debug support for Java), UI, and Core. The PDE subproject includes two components: UI and Core.

Contributions to the project are not limited to IBM and consortium members. As is true with any other open source project, any individual or company is welcome to participate and contribute to the project.

1.1.3 *Open source software*

Many commercial ventures are concerned about the growing influence of open source development and have done their best to spread fear, uncertainty, and doubt about this trend. One particularly misleading claim is that open source licenses are viral in nature—that by incorporating open source code in a commercial product, a company risks losing rights to its proprietary code.

Open source, by definition, is software that grants certain rights to users, notably the right to the obtain source code and the right to modify and redistribute the software. These rights are guaranteed by reversing the purpose of copyright protection. Rather than merely reserving rights for the creator, an open source license prohibits distribution unless the user is granted these rights. This use of a copyright is sometimes called a *copyleft*—all rights reversed.

Although some open source licenses are viral and require that all software bundled with the open source software be released under the same license, this is not true of all open source licenses. A number of licenses have been designed to support both open source and commercial interests and explicitly allow proprietary software that is bundled with open source software to be licensed under a separate, more restrictive license.

Eclipse, specifically, is distributed under such as license: the Common Public License (CPL). According to the license, it "is intended to facilitate the commercial use of the Program." The CPL is certified as meeting the requirements of an open source license by the Open Software Initiative (OSI). For more information about open source licenses, including the CPL, you can visit the OSI web site at http://www.opensource.org.

Many open source advocates are wary that commercial interests are co-opting the purpose of the open source movement, and are cynical of companies such as IBM that are materially aiding open source projects. There is no doubt, however, that open source software gains legitimacy from the backing of a major corporation such as IBM. This legitimacy helps dispel some of the weaker claims of opponents (particularly subjective attacks such as the notion that the software is hobbyware) and force the argument to remain focused on more substantial issues, such as performance and security.

A number of projects, including Mozilla, Apache, and now Eclipse, demonstrate that both commercial and free software can benefit from being open source. There are several reasons, but in particular, a successful open source project creates value for everyone.

In the case of Eclipse, there is another, more tangible reason: Eclipse creates an entire new market. Making Eclipse the best-designed open and extensible framework is like building a town market. Vendors and buyers large and small will be drawn together on market day.

1.2 *What is Eclipse?*

So far we've alluded to Eclipse in metaphorical terms, comparing it to a black-smith's shop, where you can not only make products, but also make the tools for making the products. In practical terms, that's probably a fair comparison. When you download the Eclipse SDK, you get a Java Development Toolkit (JDT) for writing and debugging Java programs and the Plug-in Development Environment (PDE) for extending Eclipse. If all you want is a Java IDE, you don't need anything besides the JDT; ignore the PDE, and you're good to go. This is what most people use Eclipse for, and the first part of this book focuses entirely on using Eclipse as a Java IDE.

The JDT, however, is an addition to Eclipse. At the most fundamental level, Eclipse is the *Eclipse Platform*. The Eclipse Platform's purpose is to provide the services necessary for integrating software development tools, which are implemented as Eclipse *plug-ins*. To be useful, the Platform has to be extended with plug-ins such as the JDT. The beauty of Eclipse's design is that, except for a small runtime kernel, everything is a plug-in or a set of related plug-ins. So, whereas the Eclipse SDK is like the blacksmith's shop, the Eclipse Platform it is based on is more like an empty workshop, with nothing but electrical, water, and gas hook-ups. If you'd rather be a potter than a blacksmith, then install a kiln and a potter's wheel, get some clay, and start throwing pots. If you only want to use Eclipse for C/C++ development, then replace the JDT with the C Development Toolkit (CDT).

This plug-in design makes Eclipse extensible. More important, however, the platform provides a well-defined way for plug-ins to work together (by means of extension points and contributions), so new features can be added not only easily but seamlessly. As you perform different tasks using Eclipse, it is usually impossible to tell where one plug-in ends and another begins.

1.2.1 The Eclipse architecture

In addition to the small platform runtime kernel, the Eclipse Platform consists of the Workbench, workspace, help, and team components. Other tools plug in to this basic framework to create a usable application. (See figure 1.1.)

The Platform runtime

The primary job of the Platform runtime is to discover what plug-ins are available in the Eclipse plug-in directory. Each plug-in has an XML manifest file that lists the connections the plug-in requires. These include the extension points it provides to other plug-ins, and the extension points from other plug-ins that it requires. Because the number of plug-ins is potentially large, plug-ins are not loaded until they are actually required, to minimize start-up time and resource

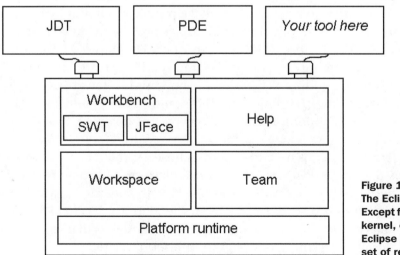

Figure 1.1
The Eclipse architecture.
Except for a small runtime kernel, everything in Eclipse is a plug-in or a set of related plug-ins.

requirements. The second part of this book focuses on the architecture of plug-ins, additional details about how they work, and how to develop them using the PDE.

The workspace

The workspace is responsible for managing the user's resources, which are organized into one or more projects at the top level. Each project corresponds to a subdirectory of Eclipse's workspace directory. Each project can contain files and folders; normally each folder corresponds to a subdirectory of the project directory, but a folder can also be linked to a directory anywhere in the filesystem.

The workspace maintains a low-level history of changes to each resource. This makes it possible to undo changes immediately, as well as revert to a previously saved state—possibly days old, depending on how the user has configured the history settings. This history also minimizes the risk of losing resources.

The workspace is also responsible for notifying interested tools about changes to the workspace resources. Tools have the ability to tag projects with a *project nature*—as a Java project, for example—and can provide code to configure the project's resources as necessary.

The Workbench

The Workbench is Eclipse's graphical user interface. In addition to displaying the familiar menus and toolbars, it is organized into perspectives containing views and editors. These are discussed in chapter 2.

One of the Workbench's notable features is that, unlike most Java applications, it looks and feels like a native application. This is the case because it is built using Eclipse's Standard Widget Toolkit (SWT) and JFace, a user interface toolkit built on top of SWT. Unlike the standard Java graphics APIs, AWT and Swing, which emulate the native graphics toolkit, SWT maps directly to the operating system's native graphics.

SWT is one of the most controversial aspects of Eclipse, because SWT must be ported to each platform that Eclipse supports. As a practical matter, this isn't a serious concern, because SWT has already been ported to the most popular platforms (including Windows, Linux/Motif, Linux/GTK2, Solaris, QNX, AIX, HP-UX, and Mac OS X).

It is possible to use SWT and JFace to create your own native-looking Java applications. An introduction to programming with SWT is found in appendix D of this book, and a brief overview of JFace is presented in appendix E. Note that Eclipse's use of SWT/JFace doesn't force you to use it in your applications; unless you are writing a plug-in for Eclipse, you can continue to program with AWT/Swing as usual.

Team support

The team support plug-in facilitates the use of a version control (or configuration management) system to manage the resources in a user's projects and define the workflow necessary for saving to and retrieving from a repository. The Eclipse Platform includes a client for Concurrent Versions System (CVS). CVS is the subject of chapter 6.

Help

Like the Eclipse Platform itself, the help component is an extensible documentation system. Tool providers can add documentation in HTML format and, using XML, define a navigation structure. Mirroring the way plug-ins connect to other plug-ins, tools documentation can insert topics into a preexisting topic tree.

1.2.2 Language and platform neutrality

Although Eclipse is written in Java and its most popular use is as a Java IDE, it is language neutral. Support for Java development is provided by a plug-in component, as mentioned previously, and additional plug-ins are available for other languages, such as C/C++, Cobol, and C#.

Eclipse is also neutral with regard to human languages. The same plug-in mechanism that lets you add functionality easily can be used to add different languages, using a special type of plug-in called a *plug-in fragment*. IBM has donated a language pack that provides support for Chinese (traditional and simplified), French, German, Italian, Japanese, Korean, Portuguese (Brazilian), and Spanish. You can download the language pack from the Eclipse downloads page at http://www.eclipse.org.

Although written in Java, which in principle allows a program to run on any platform, Eclipse is not strictly platform neutral. This is due to the decision to build Eclipse using the operating system's native graphics. Eclipse is therefore only available for those platforms to which SWT has been ported (listed earlier).

If your platform is not on the officially supported list, however, things may not be as dire as they seem. Because Eclipse is an open source project, the source code is available, and others have ported Eclipse to additional platforms; you may be able to find such a port by searching the Eclipse newsgroups. Sometimes these ports are contributed back to Eclipse and become part of the official Eclipse build. As a last resort, if you are ambitious enough, perhaps you might port Eclipse yourself.

1.3 *What's next*

One of the most frequently requested features for Eclipse is a GUI builder—a graphical tool for building user interfaces. It seems unlikely that this and other features that have a high perceived value (such as J2EE and data modeling capabilities) will ever become part of the official, free version of Eclipse, due largely to the fact that the Eclipse.org consortium must balance commercial concerns with the desires of the open source community.

Such needs are being filled in several ways: commercial offerings, such as IBM's Websphere Studio Application Developer, which (at a cost) provide these features as part of a comprehensive Eclipse-based development suite; free or low-cost commercial plug-ins, such as Lomboz for J2EE and the Sysdeo Tomcat plug-in (covered in chapter 7); and open source projects.

Planning for the next version of Eclipse, due sometime in 2004, is currently underway. Some ideas being considered include:

- Generalizing the Eclipse platform as a general application framework. It's currently possible to use the Eclipse Platform this way, but doing so requires some effort, because it is specifically designed for building IDEs.
- Adding support for Java-related languages such as JSP and providing better integration with plug-in manifest files and J2EE descriptors.
- Supporting J2SE 1.5, which is expected to include (in part) generic types and enumerations.
- Logical viewing of Java objects, such as showing `HashMaps` as tables of key-value pairs.

The Eclipse web site is the best source for additional information about Eclipse. If you are interested in discussing new features or want to learn more about existing features, visit the newsgroups page to learn how to join the newsgroups. Visit the community page to find new plug-ins. You can also report bugs or request specific features by using the bugs page.

1.4 *Summary*

If you are looking for a good, free Java IDE, you don't need to look any further than Eclipse. The Eclipse Software Development Kit (SDK), which you can download for free from the Eclipse web site, includes a feature-rich Java IDE, the Java Development Toolkit (JDT). The first part of this book (chapters 2–7) covers the use of the Eclipse JDT.

Eclipse is not just a Java IDE, however, it is actually less than that (or, depending on your point of view, more than that). It is an extensible, open source platform for development tools. For example, IDEs are available for other languages, such as C/C++, Cobol, and C#.

Eclipse's distinguishing feature is its extensibility. Fundamentally, Eclipse is nothing but a framework for plug-ins; except for a small runtime kernel, everything in Eclipse is implemented as plug-ins. Because the platform specifies the ways for plug-ins to interact with one another, new features integrate seamlessly with the existing features.

In addition to the JDT, the Eclipse SDK also includes a Plug-in Development Environment (PDE). The PDE makes it easy to develop plug-ins for Eclipse. The second part of this book (chapters 8 and 9) covers the use of the PDE and shows you how to build a tool that adds new logging capabilities to Eclipse.

Although Eclipse is open source, it's managed and directed by a consortium of software development companies with a commercial interest in promoting Eclipse as a shared platform for software development tools. Eclipse is licensed under the Common Public License, which, unlike some open source licenses, is not viral—that is, it does not require that software incorporating Eclipse technology be licensed under an open source license as well. By creating and fostering an open source community based on Eclipse, IBM and the other companies in the consortium hope the result will be symbiosis, rather that conflict, resulting in a large new marketplace for both free and commercial software that is either based on Eclipse or extends Eclipse.

Whether you use Eclipse as a development platform for developing your own software or as the basis for building free or commercial tools, you will find that it has much to offer. As you explore its many features in the chapters that follow, we will guide you in using Eclipse effectively throughout the development process. Along the way, we will point out many of the ways it can help you to be a more productive Java developer.

Getting started with the Eclipse Workbench

2

In this chapter...

- Downloading and installing Eclipse
- Essential Eclipse Workbench concepts, including perspectives, views, and editors
- Creating, running, and debugging a Java program
- Customizing Eclipse preferences and settings, including code format style and classpath variables
- Creating and modifying code generation templates

Getting started is often the hardest part of a journey. Mostly this isn't due to any real obstacle, but rather to inertia. It's easy to get set in your ways—even when you know that adventure waits. Eclipse is the new land we'll be exploring here. After downloading Eclipse and getting your bearings, you'll find that you'll soon be on your way, coding and debugging with ease.

2.1 *Obtaining Eclipse*

The first step toward getting started with Eclipse is to download the software from the Eclipse.org web site's download page at http://www.eclipse.org/downloads. Here you'll find the latest and the greatest versions—which are not usually the same things—as well as older versions of Eclipse. Basically, four types of versions, or *builds*, are available:

- *Release*—A stable build of Eclipse that has been declared a major release by the Eclipse development team. A release build has been thoroughly tested and has a coherent, well-defined set of features. It's equivalent to the shrink-wrapped version of a commercial software product. At the time of this writing, the latest release is 2.1, released March 2003; this is the release we will be using throughout this book.

- *Stable build*—A build leading up to a release that has been tested by the Eclipse development team and found to be relatively stable. New features usually first appear in these intermediate builds. These builds are equivalent to the beta versions of commercial software products.

- *Integration build*—A build in which Eclipse's individual components are judged to be stable by the Eclipse developers. There is no guarantee that the components will work together properly, however. If they do work together well, an integration build may be promoted to stable build status.

- *Nightly build*—A build that is (obviously) produced every night from the latest version of the source code. As you may guess, there are absolutely no guarantees about these builds—in fact, you can depend on their having serious problems.

If you are at all risk-averse (perhaps because you are on tight schedule and can't afford minor mishaps), you'll probably want to stick to release versions. If you are a bit more adventurous, or must have the latest features, you may want to try a stable build; the stable builds immediately before a planned release build usually offer the best feature-to-risk ratio. As long as you are careful to back up your workspace directory, these are a fairly safe bet. You can find out more about the

Eclipse team's development plans and the development schedule at http://
www.eclipse.org/eclipse/development/main.html.

After you choose and download the best version for you, Eclipse installation
consists of unzipping (or untarring, or whatever the equivalent is on your platform) the downloaded file to a directory on your hard disk. Eclipse, you'll be
happy to learn, won't infect your system by changing your registry, altering your
environment variables, or requiring you to re-boot. The only drawback is that
you'll have to navigate your filesystem searching for the Eclipse executable to
start it. If you don't want to do this each time you use Eclipse, you can create a
shortcut to it, or put it on your path. For example, in Windows, after you find the
Eclipse executable (eclipse.exe) using the Windows Explorer, right-click on it and
select Create Shortcut. Doing so will create a shortcut in the Eclipse directory
that you can drag to your desktop or system tray. On UNIX and Linux platforms,
you can either add the Eclipse directory to your path or create a symbolic link
(using `ln -s`) for the executable in a directory already in your path (for instance,
/home/*<user>*/bin).

2.2 Eclipse overview

The first time you start Eclipse, it will ask you to wait while it completes the installation. This step (which only takes a moment) creates a workspace directory underneath the Eclipse directory. By default, all your work will be saved in this directory.
If you believe in backing up your work on a regular basis (and you should), this is
the directory to back up. This is also the directory to take with you when you
upgrade to a new version of Eclipse.

You need to check the release notes for the new release to make sure it supports workspaces from prior versions; but barring any incompatibility, after you
unzip the new version of Eclipse, simply copy the old workspace subdirectory to
the new Eclipse directory. (Note that all your preferences and save perspectives
will also be available to you, because they are stored in the workspace directory.)

2.2.1 Projects and folders

It's important to know where your files are located on your hard disk, in case you
want to work with them manually, copy them, or see how much space they take
up. However, native filesystems vary from operating system to operating system,
which presents a problem for programs that must work consistently on different
operating systems. Eclipse solves this problem by providing a level of abstraction
above the native filesystem. That is, it doesn't use a hierarchy of directories and

subdirectories, each of which contains files; instead, Eclipse uses projects at the highest level, and it uses folders under the projects.

Projects, by default, correspond to subdirectories in the workspace directory, and folders correspond to subdirectories of the project folder; but in general, when you're working within Eclipse, you won't be aware of the filesystem. Unless you perform an operation such as importing a file from the filesystem, you won't be exposed to a traditional file open dialog box, for example. Everything in an Eclipse project exists within a self-contained, platform-neutral hierarchy.

2.2.2 *The Eclipse Workbench*

Eclipse is made up of components, and the fundamental component is the Eclipse Workbench. This is the main window that appears when you start Eclipse. The Workbench has one simple job to do: to allow you to work with projects. It doesn't know anything about editing, running, or debugging Java programs; it only knows how to navigate projects and resources (such as files and folders). Any tasks it can't handle, it delegates to other components, such as the Java Development Tools (JDT).

Perspectives, views, and editors

The Eclipse Workbench is a single application window that at any given time contains a number of different types of panes called *views* plus one special pane, the *editor*. In some cases, a single pane may contain a group of views in a tabbed notebook. Depending on the perspective, one pane might contain a console window while another might contain an outline of the currently selected project. The primary component of every perspective, however, is the editor.

Just as there are different types of documents, there are different types of editors. When you select (or create) a document in Eclipse, Eclipse does its best to open the document using the most appropriate editor. If it's a simple text document, the document will be opened using Eclipse's built-in text editor. If it's a Java source file, it will be opened using the JDT's Java editor, which has special features such as the ability to check syntax as code is typed. If it's a Microsoft Word document on a Windows computer and Word is installed, the document will be opened using Word inside Eclipse, by means of object linking and embedding (OLE).

You don't directly choose each of the different views in the Workbench or how they are arranged. Instead, Eclipse provides several preselected sets of views arranged in a predetermined way; they are called *perspectives*, and they can be customized to suit your needs.

Every perspective is designed to perform a specific task, such as writing or debugging a Java program, and each of the views in the perspective is chosen to allow you to deal with different aspects of that task. For example, in a perspective for debugging, one view might show the source code, another might show the current values of the program's variables, and yet another might show the program's output.

The first time you start Eclipse, it will be in the Resource perspective (see figure 2.1). You might think of this as the home perspective. It is a general-purpose perspective useful for creating, viewing, and managing all types of resources—whether a resource is a Java project or a set of word-processing documents doesn't matter in this perspective, apart from which editor is used to open specific documents in the editor area.

The panel at upper left is called the Navigator view; it shows a hierarchical representation of your workspace and all the projects in it. At first this view will

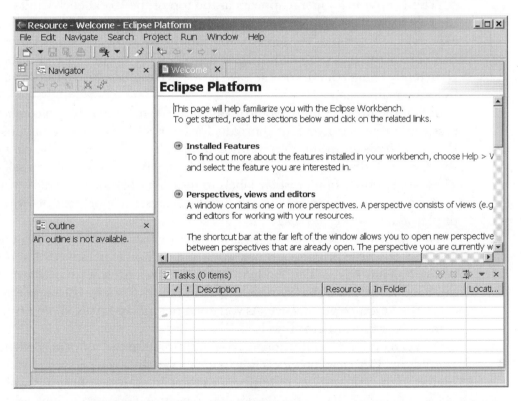

Figure 2.1   The initial view of Eclipse is the Resource perspective—a general-purpose perspective for creating, viewing, and managing all types of resources.

be empty, of course; but, as you'll see, it is the starting point for creating projects and working with Eclipse.

Within the Workbench, as you work, you can choose among the different perspectives by selecting Window→Open Perspective. Eclipse will also change the perspective automatically, when appropriate—such as changing from the Java perspective to the Debug perspective when you choose to debug a program from the Eclipse menu.

Menus and toolbars

In addition to perspective, views, and editors, several other features of the Workbench user interface (UI) are worth mentioning: the main menu, the main toolbar, and the shortcut toolbar. Like the views and editors in a perspective, the Workbench's menu and toolbar can change depending on the tasks and features available in the current perspective.

The Eclipse main menu appears at the top of the Workbench window, below the title bar (unless you are using a Macintosh, in which case the menu appears, Mac style, at the top of the screen). You can invoke most actions in Eclipse from the main menu or its submenus. For example, if the document HelloWorld.java is currently being edited, you can save it by selecting File→Save HelloWorld.java from the main menu.

Below the main menu is a toolbar called the main toolbar, which contains buttons that provide convenient shortcuts for commonly performed actions. One, for example, is an icon representing a floppy disk, which saves the contents of the document that is currently being edited (like the File→Save menu selection). These tool buttons don't display labels to indicate what they do unless you position the mouse pointer over them; doing so causes a short text description to display as a hovering *tool tip*.

Along the left side of the screen is another toolbar called the shortcut toolbar. The buttons here provide a quick way to open a new perspective and switch between perspectives. The top button, Open a Perspective, is an alternative to the Window→Open Perspective selection in the main menu. Below it is a shortcut to the Resource perspective. As you open new perspectives, shortcuts to those perspectives appear here, as well.

You can optionally add another type of shortcut to the shortcut toolbar: a *Fast View* button. Fast Views provide a way to turn a view in a perspective into an icon—similar to the way you can minimize a window in many applications. For example, you may find that in the Resource perspective, you need to look at the Outline view only occasionally. To turn the Outline view into a Fast View icon, click on the Outline icon in the view's title bar and select Fast View from the menu that appears. The Outline view is closed, and its icon appears in the shortcut toolbar. Clicking on the icon alternately opens and closes the view. To restore the view in its previous place in the perspective, right-click on the Fast View icon and select Fast View.

In addition to the Workbench menu and toolbars, views can also have menus. Every view has a menu you can select by clicking on its icon. This menu lets you perform actions on the view's window, such as maximizing it or closing it. Generally this menu is not used for any other purpose. Views can also have a view-specific menu, which is represented in the view's title bar by a black triangle. In the Resource perspective, the Navigator view has a menu that lets you set sorting and filtering options.

Some views also have a toolbar. In the Resource perspective, the Outline view has tool buttons that let you toggle various display options on or off.

Changing perspectives

As you work in the Eclipse Workbench, you'll occasionally find that the different views aren't quite the right size for the work you're doing—perhaps your source code is too wide for the editor area. The solution is to click on the left or right window border and drag it so the window is the right size.

Sometimes you may want to supersize a view temporarily by double-clicking on the title bar; this will maximize it within the Eclipse Workbench. Double-clicking on the title bar again will reduce it back to its regular size.

You can also move views around by dragging them using their title bars. Dragging one view on top of another will cause them to appear as a single tabbed notebook of views. Selecting a view in a notebook is like selecting a document in the editor pane: Click its tab at the top or bottom of the notebook. Dragging a view below, above, or beside another view will cause the views to dock—the space occupied by the stationary view will be redistributed between the stationary view and the view you are dragging into place. As you drag the window you want to move, the mouse pointer will become a black arrow whenever it is over a window boundary, indicating that docking is allowed. For example, if you want to make the editor area taller in the Resource perspective, drag the Task view below the Outline view so the Navigator, Outline, and Task views share a single column on the left side of the screen.

In addition to moving views around, you can remove a view from a perspective by selecting Close from the view's title bar menu. You can also add a new view to a perspective by selecting Window→Show View from the main Eclipse menu.

Eclipse will save the changes you make to perspectives as you move from perspective to perspective or close and open Eclipse. To restore the perspective to its default appearance, select Window→Reset Perspective.

If you find that your customized perspective is particularly useful, you can add it to Eclipse's repertoire of perspectives. From the Eclipse menu, select Window→Save Perspective As; you will be prompted to provide a name for your new perspective.

2.3   The Java quick tour

Eclipse is installed, and you understand how the different views in perspectives work together to allow you to perform a task. Let's take Eclipse out for a spin by writing, running, and debugging a traditional "Hello, world" program.

2.3.1   Creating a Java project

Before you can do anything else in Eclipse, such as creating a Java program, you need to create a project. Eclipse has the potential to support many kinds of projects using plug-ins (such as EJB or C/C++), but it supports these three types of projects as standard:

- *Plug-in Development*—Provides an environment for creating your own plug-ins for Eclipse. This approach is great if you want to extend Eclipse to do new and wonderful things—but we'll get to that later. For now, you'll use Eclipse just the way it is.
- *Simple*—Provides a generic environment, which you might use for documentation.
- *Java*—Obviously, the choice for developing a Java program. Choosing this type of project sets up an environment with various Java-specific settings, including a classpath, source directories, and output directories.

To create a new Java project, follow these steps:

1   Right-click in the Navigator view to bring up a context menu and select New→Project.

2   In the New Project dialog box, Eclipse presents the project options: Java, Plug-in Development, and Simple. Because you want to create a Java program, select Java on the left side of the dialog box.

3   Select Java Project on the right. If you've installed other types of Java development plug-ins, various other types of Java projects may potentially be

listed here (EJBs and servlets, for example). But the JDT that comes standard with Eclipse only offers support for standard Java applications, so you must choose the Java Project option.

4 Click Next to start the New Java Project Wizard. (A *wizard* is a set of dialog boxes that prompts you through a set of well-defined, sequential steps necessary to perform a specific task. This feature is used extensively throughout Eclipse.)

5 The first dialog box prompts you for a project name. This is a simple "Hello, world" example, so enter **Hello**. Clicking Next would take you to a dialog box that lets you change a number of Java build settings, but for this example you don't need to change anything.

6 Click Finish.

7 Eclipse notifies you that this kind of project is associated with the Java perspective and asks whether you want to switch to the Java perspective. Check the Don't Show Me This Message Again box and click Yes.

The perspective changes to a Java perspective (see figure 2.2). Notice that the view in the upper-left corner is no longer the Navigator view; it is now the Package Explorer view, and it displays the new Hello project. The Package Explorer is similar to the Navigator, but it's better suited for Java projects; for one thing, it understands Java packages and displays them as a single entry, rather than as a nested set of directories. Notice also that a new icon has appeared on the left edge of the Workbench: a shortcut for the Java perspective.

At the bottom of the window is a Tasks view. It is useful for keeping track of what needs to be done in a project. Tasks are added to this list automatically as Eclipse encounters errors in your code. You can also add tasks to the Task view by right-clicking in the Tasks view and selecting New Task from the context menu; this is a convenient way to keep a to-do list for your project.

Finally, notice the Outline view on the right side of the screen. The content of this view depends on the type of document selected in the editor. If it's a Java class, you can use the outline to browse class attributes and methods and move easily between them. Depending on whether the Show Source of Selected Element button in the main toolbar is toggled on or off, you can view your source as part of a file (what is sometimes referred to as a *compilation unit*) or as distinct Java elements, such as methods and attributes.

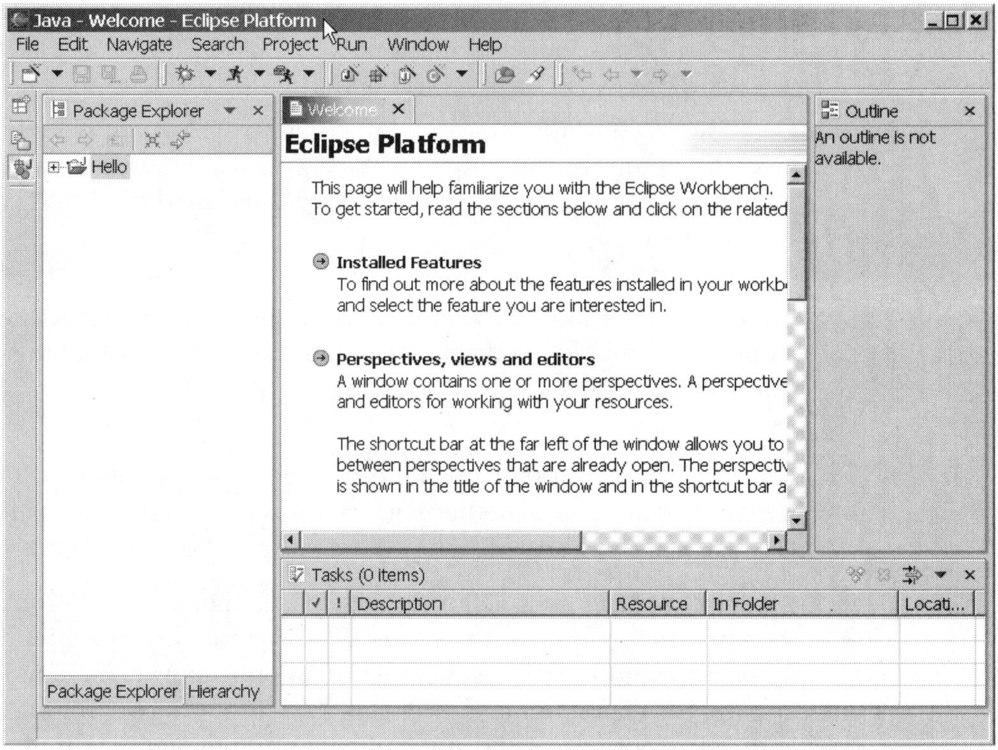

Figure 2.2   The Java perspective includes the Package Explorer view. This perspective is better suited for Java projects because it displays Java packages as a single entry instead of a nested set of directories.

2.3.2   *Creating a Java class*

Once you've created a project for it to live in, you can create your first Java program. Although doing so is not necessary, it's a good practice to organize your Java classes into packages. We'll put all packages in this book in the hierarchy starting with the Java-style version of the domain name associated with this book, `org.eclipseguide` (which of course is the reverse of the Internet style). Using domain names reduces the likelihood of name collisions—that is, more than one class with exactly the same name. You can use a registered domain name if you have one, but if not, you can use any convenient, unique, ad hoc name, especially for private use. Finally, add a name for this particular project: `hello`. All together, the package name is `org.eclipseguide.hello`.

Follow these steps to create your Java program:

1 Right-click on the project and select New→Class to bring up the New Java Class Wizard.

2 The first field, Source Folder, is by default the project's folder—leave this as it is.

3 Enter **org.eclipseguide.hello** in the Package field.

4 In the class name field, enter **HelloWorld**.

5 In the section Which Method Stubs Would You Like to Create?, check the box for `public static void main(String[] args)`. The completed New Java Class dialog box is shown in figure 2.3.

6 Click Finish, and the New Java Class Wizard will create the appropriate directory structure for the package (represented in the Navigator by the entry `org.eclipseguide.hello` under the Hello project) and the source file HelloWorld.java under this package name.

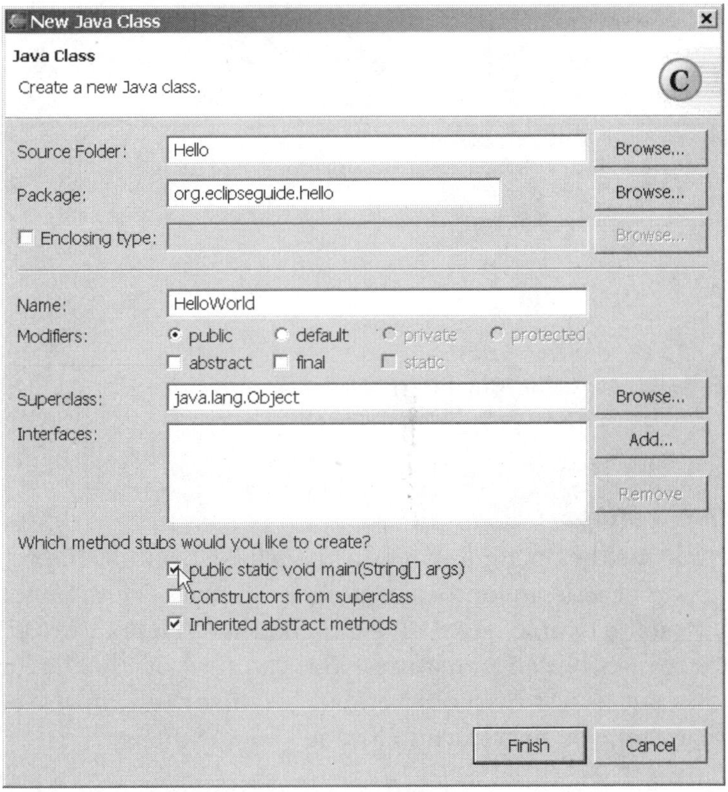

**Figure 2.3
Creating the
`HelloWorld` class
using the New Java
Class Wizard**

If you examine the workspace directory in the native filesystem, you will find that there is not a single directory named org.eclipseguide.hello, but rather the series of directories that Java expects. If you've installed Eclipse in C:\Eclipse, the full path to your new source file will be C:\Eclipse\workspace\org\eclipseguide\hello\ HelloWorld.java. Normally, though, you only need to deal with the visual representation that Eclipse provides in the Package Explorer view.

In the editor area in the middle of the screen, you see the Java code generated by the wizard. Also notice that tabs now appear at the top of the editor area, which allow you to select between the Welcome screen that first appeared and this new HelloWorld.java file. (You don't need the Welcome screen anymore, so you can click on the Welcome tab and click the X in the tab to make it go away.) You may also want to adjust the size of your windows and views to get a more complete view of the source code and the other views.

The code that's automatically generated is just a stub—the class with an empty method. You need to add any functionality, such as printing your "Hello, world!". To do this, alter the code generated by Eclipse by adding a line to `main()` as follows:

```
/*
 * Created on Feb 14, 2003
 *
 * To change this generated comment go to
 * Window>Preferences>Java>Code Generation>Code and Comments
 */
package org.eclipseguide.hello;

/**
 * @author david
 */
public class HelloWorld {

    public static void main(String[] args) {
        System.out.println("Hello, world!");
    }
}
```

Code completion features

Notice that as you type the opening parenthesis, Eclipse helpfully inserts its partner, the closing parenthesis, immediately after the cursor. The same thing happens when you type the double quote to begin entering **"Hello, world!"**. This is one of Eclipse's code-completion features. You can turn off this feature if you find it as meddlesome as a backseat driver, but like many of Eclipse's other features, if you live with it, you may learn to love it.

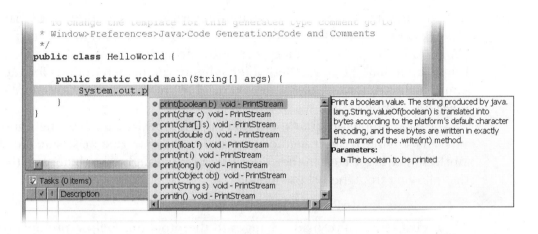

```
 * Window>Preferences>Java>Code Generation>Code and Comments
 */
public class HelloWorld {

    public static void main(String[] args) {
        System.out.p
    }
}
```

● print(boolean b) void - PrintStream	Print a boolean value. The string produced by java.
● print(char c) void - PrintStream	lang.String.valueOf(boolean) is translated into
● print(char[] s) void - PrintStream	bytes according to the platform's default character
● print(double d) void - PrintStream	encoding, and these bytes are written in exactly
● print(float f) void - PrintStream	the manner of the .write(int) method.
● print(int i) void - PrintStream	**Parameters:**
● print(long l) void - PrintStream	**b** The boolean to be printed
● print(Object obj) void - PrintStream	
● print(String s) void - PrintStream	
● println() void - PrintStream	

Tasks (0 items)

√ ! Description

Figure 2.4   The Eclipse code assist feature displays a list of proposed methods and their Javadoc comments. Scroll or type the first letter (or more) to narrow the choice, and then press Enter to complete the code.

Depending on how quickly you type, you may see another code-completion feature called *code assist* as you type **System.out.println**. If you pause after typing a class name and a period, Eclipse presents you with a list of proposals—the methods and attributes available for the class, together with their Javadoc comments. You can find the one you want by either scrolling through the list or typing the first letter (or more) to narrow the choice; pressing Enter completes the code (see figure 2.4). This is most useful when you can't remember the exact name of the method you're looking for or need to be reminded what parameters it takes; otherwise you'll find that it's usually faster to ignore the proposal and continue typing the method name yourself.

You can also invoke code completion manually at any time by pressing Ctrl-Space. The exact effect will depend on the context, and you may wish to experiment a bit with this feature to become familiar with it. It can be useful, for example, after typing the first few letters of a particularly long class name.

Eclipse's code-generation feature is powerful and surprisingly easy to customize, because it is implemented using simple templates. You'll see it in greater depth when we examine Eclipse's settings and preferences.

2.3.3   *Running the Java program*

You're now ready to run this program. There are several things you might want to consider when running a Java program, including the Java runtime it should use, whether it will take any command-line parameters, and, if more than one class has a `main()` method, which one to use. The standard way to start a Java program in Eclipse is to select Run→Run from the Eclipse menu. Doing so brings up a dialog box that lets you configure the launch options for the program; before running a program, you need to create a launch configuration or select an existing launch configuration.

For most simple programs, you don't need a special launch configuration, so you can use a much easier method to start the program: First make sure the HelloWorld source is selected in the editor (its tab is highlighted in blue) and then do the following from the Eclipse menu:

1   Select Run→Run As→Java Application.

2   Because you've made changes to the program, Eclipse prompts you to save your changes before it runs the program. Click OK.

3   The Task view changes to a Console view and displays your program output (see figure 2.5).

You may wonder why no separate step is required to compile the .java file into a .class file. This is the case because the Eclipse JDT includes a special incremental compiler and evaluates your source code as you type it. Thus it can highlight things such as syntax errors and unresolved references as you type. (Like Eclipse's other friendly features, this functionality can be turned off if you find it annoying.) If compilation is successful, the compiled .class file is saved at the same time your source file is saved.

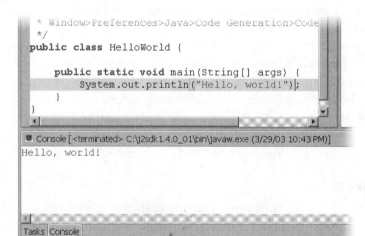

Figure 2.5
The Eclipse Console view displays the output from the HelloWorld program.

2.3.4 Debugging the Java program

If writing, compiling, and running a Java program were all Eclipse had to offer, it probably wouldn't seem worth the bother of setting up a project and using perspectives, with their shifting views, to get around; using a simple text editor and compiling at the command line is at least as attractive. As you learn how to use Eclipse more effectively, it will become increasingly obvious that Eclipse does have much more to offer, largely because it interprets the code in a more comprehensive way than a simple editor can—even an editor that can check syntax.

Eclipse's ability to run the code interactively is one major benefit. Using the JDT debugger, you can execute your Java program line by line and examine the value of variables at different points in the program, for example. This process can be invaluable in locating problems in your code.

Before starting the debugger, you need to add a bit more code to the Hello-World program to make it more interesting. Add a `say()` method and change the code in the `main()` method to call `say()` instead of calling `System.out.println()` directly, as shown here:

```java
public class HelloWorld {

    public static void main(String[] args) {
        say("Hello, world!");
    }
    public static void say(String msg) {
        for (int i = 0; i < 3; i++) {
            System.out.println(msg);
        }
    }
}
```

To prepare for debugging, you also need to set a breakpoint in your code so the debugger suspends execution and allows you to debug—otherwise, the program will run to completion without letting you do any debugging. To set a breakpoint, double-click in the gray margin on the left side of the editor, next to the call to `say()`. A blue dot will appear, indicating an active breakpoint.

Starting the program under the debugger is similar to running it. Eclipse provides two options: Use the full-service Run→Debug menu selection to use a launch configuration, or use the express Run→Debug As→Java Application selection if the default options are OK. Here, as before, you can use the latter.

Make sure the source for HelloWorld is selected in the editor and select Run→Debug As→Java Application from the main menu. Eclipse will start the program, change to the Debug perspective, and suspend execution at the breakpoint (see figure 2.6).

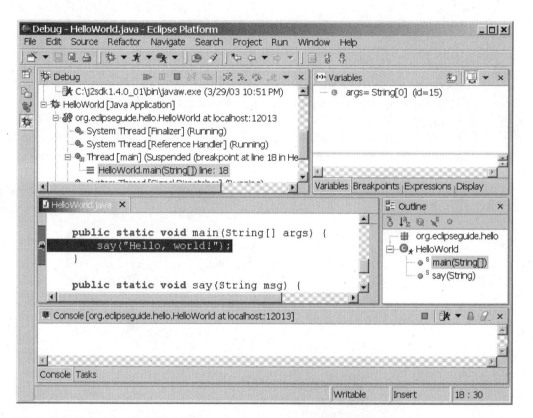

Figure 2.6   Debugging HelloWorld: Execution is suspended at the first breakpoint.

The Debug perspective includes several new views that are, not surprisingly, especially useful for debugging. First, at top left, is the Debug view (not to be confused with the Debug perspective to which it belongs), which shows the call stack and status of all current threads, including any threads that have already run to completion. Your program, which Eclipse started, has hit a breakpoint, and its status is shown as Suspended.

Stepping through code
In the title bar of the Debug view is a toolbar that lets you control the program's execution. The first few tool buttons, which resemble the familiar controls of electronic devices such as CD players, allow you to resume, suspend, or terminate the program. Several buttons incorporate arrows in their design; these allow you to step through a program a line at a time. Holding the mouse over each button in turn will cause tool tips to appear, identifying them as Step With Filters, Step

Into, Step Over, and Step Return. (There are several other buttons that we'll ignore for now; we'll look at them in chapter 3, "The Java Development Cycle: Test, Code, Repeat," when we examine debugging in greater detail.)

For example, click the second step button, Step Into. Doing so executes the line of code that is currently highlighted in the editor area below the Debug view: the call to the `say()` method. Step Into, as the name suggests, takes you into the method that is called: After clicking Step Into, the highlighted line is the first executable line in `say()`—the `for` statement.

The Step With Filters button works the same as Step Into, but it's selective about what methods it will step into. You normally want to step only into methods in your own classes and not into the standard Java packages or third-party packages. You can specify which methods Step Filter will execute and return from immediately by selecting Window→Preferences→Java→Debug→Step Filtering and defining *step filters* by checking the packages and classes listed there. Taking a moment to set these filters is well worth the trouble, because Step With Filters saves you from getting lost deep in unknown code—something that can happen all too often when you use Step Into.

Evaluating variables and expressions

To the right of the Debug view is a tabbed notebook containing views that let you examine and modify variables and breakpoints. Select the Variables tab (if it isn't already selected). This view shows the variables in the current scope and their values; before entering the `for` loop, this view includes only the `say()` method's `msg` parameter and its value, "Hello, world!". Click either Step Over or Step Into to enter the `for` loop. (Both have the same effect here, because you don't call any methods in this line of code.) The Variables view will display the loop index `i` and its current value, 0.

Sometimes a program has many variables, but you're interested in only one or a few. To watch select variables or expressions, you can add them to the watch list in the Expression view. To do this, select a variable—`i`, for instance—by double-clicking on it in the editor, and then right-click on the selection and choose Watch from the context menu. The variable (and its value, if it's in scope) will appear in the Expressions view.

One significant advantage of watching variables in the Variables and Expressions views over using `print` statements for debugging is that you can inspect objects and their fields in detail and change their values—even normally immutable strings. Return to the Variables view and expand the `msg` variable to show its attributes. One of these is a `char` array, `value`, which can be expanded to reveal the individual characters in the `msg` `String`. For example, double-click on the character *H*, and you will be prompted to enter a new value, such as **J**.

The Display view is in the same tabbed notebook. It allows you to enter any variables that are in scope, or arbitrary expressions including these variables. Select Display view and enter the following, for example:

```
msg.charAt(i)
```

To immediately evaluate this expression, you must first select it and then click the second Display view tool button (Display Result of Evaluating Selected Text), which displays the results in the Display view. It's usually better to click the first tool button (Inspect Result of Evaluating Selected Text), because it adds the expression to the Expressions view. Either way, the value displayed is not automatically updated as the variables in the expression change; but in the Expressions view, you have the option of converting the expression into a *watch expression*, which is updated as you step through the code. To do this, change to the Expressions view. Notice that the Inspect icon (a magnifying glass) appears next to the expression. Click on the expression and select Convert to Watch Expression from the context menu. The icon next to the expression will change to the Watch icon.

Let's go back to stepping through the code. You previously left the cursor at the call to `System.out.println()`. If you want to see the code for `System.out.println()`, you can click Step Into; otherwise click Step Over to execute the `System.out.println()` method and start the next iteration of the `for` loop.

Below the editor area is another tabbed notebook, which includes a Console view. Program output appears here; if you made the earlier change to the variable `msg`, the line "Jello, world!" will appear. You can either continue to click Step Over until the loop terminates or, if you find this process tedious, click Step Return to immediately finish executing the `say()` method and return to the `main()` method. Or, just click the Resume button to let the program run to the end.

2.3.5 *Java scrapbook pages*

When you're writing a program, you sometimes have an idea that you're not sure will work and that you want to try before going through the trouble of changing your code. Eclipse provides a simple but slick alternative to starting a new project (or writing a small program using a simple editor for execution at a command prompt): Java *scrapbook pages*. By virtue of its incremental compiler, you can enter arbitrary Java code into a scrapbook page and execute it—it doesn't need to be in a class or a method.

To create a Java scrapbook page, change to the Java perspective, right-click on the HelloWorld project, and select New→Scrapbook Page from the context menu. When you're prompted for a filename, enter **Test**. Enter some Java code, such as the following example:

```
for(int i = 1; i < 10; i++)
{
      HelloWorld.say(Integer.toString(i));
}
```

To execute this code, you first need to import the `org.eclipseguide.hello` package, as follows:

1   Right-click inside the editor pane and select Set Imports from the context menu.

2   In the Java Snippet Imports dialog box that appears, select Add Packages.

3   In the next dialog box, type **org.eclipseguide.hello** in the Select the Packages to Add as Imports field. (You don't have to type the complete name—after you've typed one or more letters you can choose it from the list that Eclipse presents.)

4   Click OK.

Now you can execute the previous code snippet:

1   Highlight the code by clicking and dragging with the mouse.

2   Right-click on the selected code and select Execute from the context menu.

3   As with a regular Java program, the output from this code snippet appears in the console view below the editor.

This code doesn't require any additional imports; but if you used `StringTokenizer`, for example, you could import the appropriate package (`java.util.*`) as described. In such a case, however, it's easier to import the specific type by selecting Add Types in the Java Snippet Imports dialog box and typing in **StringTokenizer**. Eclipse will find the appropriate package and generate the fully qualified type name for you.

2.4 *Preferences and other settings*

So far, you've been using Eclipse with all its default settings. You can change many things to suit your taste, your working style, or your organization's coding conventions, by selecting Window→Preferences. Using the dialog that appears, you can change (among numerous other settings) the fonts displayed, whether tabs appear at the top or bottom of views, and the code formatting style; you can also add classpath entries and new templates for generating code or comments. In this section, we'll look at a few of the settings you might want to change.

2.4.1 Javadoc comments

First, let's edit the text that appears when you create a new class. You'll remove the placeholder text, *To change this generated comment…*, and expand the Javadoc comments a bit. You'll also provide a reminder that you need to type in a class summary and a description. Follow these steps:

1 Select Window→Preferences→Java→Code Generation.

2 Click the Code and Comments tab on this page.

3 Select Code→New Java files, and click the Edit button.

4 Change the text to the following:

```
/* ${file_name}
 * Created on ${date}
 */
${package_declaration}

${typecomment}
${type_declaration}
```

5 Click OK in the Edit Template dialog box.

In addition to changing the template used whenever a new Java file is created, you need to change one of the templates it includes: the typecomment template. This is found on the same page, Code and Comments, under Comments:

1 Select Comment→Types and click the Edit button.

2 Change the text to the following:

```
/**
 * Add one sentence class summary here.
 * Add class description here.
 *
 * @author ${user}
 * @version 1.0, ${date}
 */
```

Notice that when you edit the template text, you don't need to type **${date}**— you can select it from the list of available variables by clicking the Insert Variable button. Appropriate values for the two variables in this template (${user} and ${date}) will be inserted when the code is generated.

To see your changes, create a new class called `Test` in the `org.eclipseguide.hello` package. Note how all the variables have been filled out.

2.4.2 *Format style*

Two general styles are used to format Java code. The most common places an opening brace at the end of the statement that requires it and the closing brace in the same column as the statement, like this:

```
for(i = 0; i < 100; i++) {
    // do something
}
```

This is the default style that Eclipse uses when you right-click on your source code and select Format from the context menu.

The other style places the opening and closing braces in the same column as the statement. For example:

```
for(i = 0; i < 100; i++)
{
    // do something
}
```

To change to this style, do the following:

1 Select Java→Code Formatter in the Preferences dialog.

2 In the Options area, select the first tab, New Lines.

3 Check the first selection, Insert a New Line Before an Opening Brace. When you click to enable this option, the sample code shown in the window below the options is updated to reflect your selection. You may want to experiment with some of the other options to see their effects.

One of this book's authors prefers to enable Insert New Lines in Control Statements and Insert a New Line in an Empty Block, because he finds that doing so makes the structure of the code more obvious. But the important point (beyond one author's personal preference) is that the Eclipse Java editor makes it easy to change styles and reformat your code. If you are working as part of a team with established conventions and your personal preference doesn't conform, this feature lets you work in the style of your choice and reformat according to the coding convention before checking in your code.

2.4.3 *Code generation templates*

You saw earlier that when editing source code in the Java editor, pressing Ctrl-Space invokes Eclipse's code-generation feature. Depending on the context, this key combination causes a template to be evaluated and inserted into the source code at that point.

You've already seen one example of a template: the code-generation template the New Class Wizard uses to add comments when it creates a new class file. In addition to this and the other code- and comment-generation templates, another set of templates is used to create boilerplate code such as flow control constructs; these templates are found in preferences under Java→Editor→Templates.

Let's create a template to simplify typing System.out.println():

1 Select Windows→Preferences→Java→Editor→Templates.

2 Click the New button.

3 In the New Template dialog that appears, enter **sop** as the name, ensure that the context is Java, and enter **Shortcut for System.out.println()** as the description.

4 Enter the following pattern for the template:

```
System.out.println("${cursor}");
```

5 Click OK in the New Template dialog box (see figure 2.7).

6 Click OK in the Preference dialog to return to the Workbench.

The ${cursor} variable here indicates where the cursor will be placed after the template is evaluated and inserted into the text.

To use the new template in the Java editor, type **sop** and press Ctrl-Space (or type **s**, press Ctrl-Space, select *sop* from the list that appears, and press Enter).

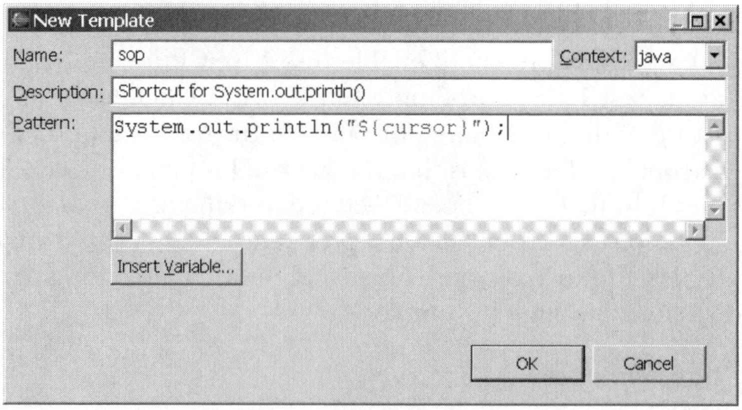

Figure 2.7   Creating a shortcut for System.out.println() **using a Java editor template**

The letters *sop* are replaced with the `System.out.println()` method call, and the cursor is replaced between the quotation marks, ready for you to type the text to be printed.

Let's create one more template to produce a `for` loop. There are already three `for` loop templates; but the template you'll create is simpler than the existing ones, which are designed to iterate over an array or collection:

1 Select Windows→Preferences→Java→Editor→Templates.
2 Click the New button.
3 Enter **for** as the name, **Simple for loop** as the description, and the following pattern:

```
for(int ${index}=0; ${index}< ${cursor}; ${index}++})
{
}
```

4 Click OK in the New Template dialog box.
5 Click OK in the Preference dialog to return to the Workbench.

Notice that this example uses a new variable, `${index}`, which proposes a new index to the user. By default, this index is initially `i`; but the cursor is placed on this index, and anything you type (such as **j** or **foo**) replaces the `${index}` variable everywhere in the template.

Try this new template by typing **for** and pressing Ctrl-Space. From the list that appears, select the entry Simple For Loop. Type a new name for the index variable, such as `loopvar`, and notice that it automatically appears in the test and increment clauses. You might also notice that the index variable has a green underline, indicating a link; pressing Tab will advance the cursor to the next link. In this case, pressing Tab takes you to the `${cursor}` variable. At this point, you can type a constant, variable, or other expression, as appropriate.

2.4.4 *Classpaths and classpath variables*

There are several ways you can add a directory or a JAR file to a project's classpath: when you create the class using the New Class Wizard, by editing your project options, or by creating a launch configuration for your project. In each case, you can either enter the path to the JAR file or directory you wish to add, or you can use a classpath variable. If you are only adding a JAR file for testing purposes, or if the JAR file is one you'll use only in this project, it's easiest to add the path and filename explicitly. But if it's something you are likely to use in many of your projects (for example, a JDBC driver), you may wish to create a classpath variable. Besides being easier to type, a classpath variable provides a single location to specify the JAR files used by your projects. This makes it easier to manage your JAR files. When you want to upgrade to a new version of a JAR, a single change will update all your projects.

Suppose you will be using the MySQL database and that the full path and filename of your JDBC driver is c:\mysql\jdbc\lib\mm.mysql-2.0.14-bin.jar. To create a classpath variable for this JAR file, open the Window→Preferences dialog and select Java→Classpath Variables. Click New and enter **MYSQL_JDBC** as the name; either browse for the JAR file by clicking the File button or type the path and filename manually. Click OK twice to save and return to the Workbench.

Now, when you need to add the MySQL JDBC JAR to a project, you don't have to search your hard drive for it; MYSQL_JDBC is one of the available classpath variables you can select. To add it to your Hello project, for example, right-click on the project name and select Properties from the context menu. Select Java Build Path on the left side of the dialog box that appears and then select the Libraries tab on the right. You could add the JAR explicitly by selecting Add External Jars, but instead select Add Variable, click MYSQL_JDBC (see figure 2.8), and click OK.

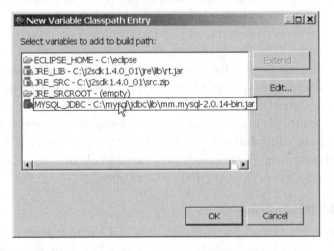

Figure 2.8
Creating a new classpath variable.
Classpath variables make it easier
to manage your classpath and
provide flexibility as well.

2.4.5 *Exporting and importing preferences*

Eclipse's preferences and settings are numerous, and you can spend a lot of time customizing it to your taste and needs. Fortunately, there is a way to save these settings so you can apply them to another Eclipse installation or share them with your friends, or, more importantly, so you have a backup in case the file they are stored in (the Eclipse metadata file) gets corrupted.

The Windows→Preferences box has two buttons at the bottom: Import and Export. To save your preferences, click the Export button, type in a filename, and click Save to create an Eclipse preference file. To restore preferences from a preference file, click the Import button, locate the file, and click Open.

2.5 *Summary*

Many different versions of Eclipse are available—you aren't limited to using only a stable, officially released version. This is one of the most interesting features of open source software. Deciding which one to use requires balancing stability with features. If you need a rock-solid product, you may wish to stick to a release version. If you are a little more daring or you absolutely require a specific new feature, you may wish to try the latest stable release. If you're just curious to see what's new, you can try an integration build. In this book, we're using the official 2.1 release, but most of the material will remain largely applicable to future releases.

The first key to using Eclipse effectively is understanding its organizational concepts of perspectives, views, and editors. The Eclipse Workbench—the window that appears on your screen when you start Eclipse—contains a number of different panes called *views*. The different views that appear at one time on the Workbench are especially selected to enable you to accomplish a specific task, such as working with Java source files. The title bar of each view has a window menu and, optionally, a view-specific menu, a toolbar, or both.

In addition to views, most perspectives have an *editor* as their central component. The specific editor that appears at any given time depends on the resource being edited. A Java source file, for example, will be opened automatically using the JDT Java editor. The Workbench also has a number of other UI elements beside views and an editor: a main menu bar at the top, a main toolbar below that, and a shortcut toolbar along the left side. Because a perspective is a collection of these views, menus, toolbars, and their relative positions, all of these elements can change as the perspective changes. The best way to learn how to use these features is to perform basic tasks, beginning with creating a Java project. (Eclipse is not limited to creating Java projects, but the Java Development Toolkit that is included is powerful, easy to use, and the most popular reason for using Eclipse.) Writing a program, running it, and debugging it provides a good introduction to Eclipse's features.

Eclipse is also highly customizable. You can modify many settings and preferences using the Windows→Preferences selection from the main menu. Preferences can be saved and restored using the Windows→Preferences Import and Export buttons; if you spend a lot of time customizing Eclipse, it's a good idea to export your changes to an Eclipse preference file for backup.

The Java development cycle: test, code, repeat

In this chapter...

- A brief introduction to agile development and test-driven development
- The JUnit unit testing framework
- Further debugging techniques
- The log4j logging framework

Eclipse's JDT provides a powerful, flexible environment for writing, running, and debugging Java code, but developing quality software requires more than that. Depending on the type of software you are developing and the size of your project, you may find that you need additional tools, either to support your development process or to add functionality to your product. Because of its open and extensible nature, Eclipse easily accommodates tools of all sorts. In this chapter, we'll examine two such tools: Eclipse's integral testing framework, JUnit; and a logging framework, log4j. In Chapter 8 you'll learn how to develop a log4j plug-in that integrates with Eclipse, but here we will use log4j simply as an external package.

3.1 *Java development tools methodology*

Although this book is primarily about a software development tool and not about software development methodology per se, the two topics are unavoidably related. Eclipse provides tools that are well suited for certain styles of programming. This doesn't mean you must program in a certain style when you use Eclipse, or that Eclipse is inappropriate for other styles of programming. It just means that if you program in the style used by the people who develop Eclipse, you'll find that many of your needs have been anticipated.

Currently, the most fashionable programming style is XP: eXtreme Programming. One of the most unique and controversial approaches advocated by XP's proponents is *pair programming*: At all times, two developers sit at a single terminal while writing code. Largely because of this requirement, more developers are probably talking about XP than doing it. Apart from this aspect, however, XP is similar to a number of other methodologies, which together are often called *agile* or *lightweight* methodologies.

In contrast to more traditional methods (often called *monumental* or *waterfall* methodologies), which emphasize developing a complete functional specification of the software up front and then following a long, well-defined development process with several distinct, waterfall-like phases, agile methodologies emphasize an iterative process. Developers work with the customer to identify a small, well-defined set of features, build it, and deliver it. They then repeat this process with another set of features, and keep repeating until the job's done. Because the agile approach eliminates surprises late in the game and provides quick feedback from the customer, what is built is more likely to meet the customer's needs. It's also more likely to just plain work.

3.1.1 Testing is job 1

All agile methods emphasize testing, but XP is the most emphatic in this regard; it puts testing first in the development process. This approach seems backward at first—how can you test something you haven't built yet? But it's not really backward. Writing the tests sets the goals for coding, helps define how the class's API will work, and provides examples of how to use the class. The tests, in effect, embody the programming requirements.

The most extreme proponents of test-driven development go so far as to say that the code should be developed with an eye to doing only what is necessary to pass the tests and no more. *Test-driven development* forces the tests to be comprehensive in order to elicit all the necessary code. Assuming the tests, in fact, test everything the program does, a code that passes all tests is, by definition, 100% correct.

3.1.2 A sample application and working sets

In this chapter, you will begin developing a sample application: a lightweight persistence component that allows you to save data in files. (As you may know, *persisting* data means saving it, using some form of more-or-less permanent storage, so you can retrieve it later.) This component will let you develop applications in later chapters that might otherwise require you to use a database. The first step in building a new application or component in Eclipse is to create a new project:

1. Select File→New→Project from the Eclipse menu.
2. Select Java→Java Project in the New Project dialog box and click Next.
3. Enter **Persistence** as the name for the project, and then click Finish.

Of course, you don't want to develop a complete database—that wheel's already been invented too many times. You just want something that does a basic job of saving and retrieving data. We'll design it in such a way that you can later replace it with a real database when you want to improve performance and add functionality.

For the moment, we'll keep this goal of being database-compatible in mind as we decide what this functionality should look like, but we won't make this compatibility a requirement. You could, for example, make an abstract class or an interface that enforces this compatibility, but we'll postpone that step until compatibility becomes a clear requirement (keeping in line with the notion of doing only what is necessary). You'll call the class `FilePersistenceServices`. It has four public methods that allow you to create a record, retrieve a record, modify an existing record, and delete a record. The signatures for these methods are as follows:

```
public static boolean write(String tableName, int key, Vector v);
public static Vector read(String tableName, int key);
public static boolean update(String tableName, int key, Vector v);
public static boolean delete(String tableName, int key);
```

The methods are defined as static, because there is no compelling reason to treat the underlying file as an object—specifically, there is no state information that needs to be stored between invocations. Requiring a client application to instantiate `FilePersistenceServices` would make the client code a little more complicated and a little less efficient. Some people feel, quite justifiably, that as a matter of object-oriented principle, if a method can be either a static method or an instance method, the latter should always be chosen. You may need to reconsider this choice later, but for now, you'll take the simplest approach and use static methods.

Defining and selecting a working set

Although it's not a problem yet, your Eclipse environment will eventually get cluttered as you work on more projects. One way to manage this situation is to define *working sets* that let you restrict what appears in the Package Explorer to a single project, a set of projects, or any arbitrary set of files within your projects. To make this new Persistence project your current working set, ensure that you are in the Java perspective and then do the following:

1   Open the Package Explorer menu by clicking the black triangle in the view's title bar.

2   Select Working Set.

3   The Select Working Set dialog box has no working sets defined initially, so you have to create one by clicking the New button. You'll be prompted to select a working set type. Select Java and click Next.

4   In the New Working Set dialog box, enter a name such as **Persistence**.

5   Select the working set content from the available resources, which are currently the two Java projects you've defined so far. Expand each one by clicking the boxes with plus signs. You can select any file or folder (and its children, if it has any) that you want to appear in this working set by clicking the checkbox next to it. To define the Persistence project as the current working set, check the box next to Persistence and click Finish.

6   Click OK.

You'll notice that the Package Explorer view no longer shows the Hello project from the previous chapter. If you want to see all the projects again later, select Deselect Working Set from the Package Explorer menu.

3.2 *The JUnit unit testing framework*

Given the importance of testing in current development methodologies, it should come as no surprise that a tool is available to make this job easier. JUnit is an open-source testing framework written by Kent Beck, the principal popularizer of XP, and Erich Gamma, the lead developer of the Eclipse JDT. Given this background, it should come as even less of a surprise that JUnit is included in Eclipse as a well-integrated plug-in.

To use JUnit in your code, the first step is to add the JUnit JAR file to your classpath. In Chapter 2, you saw that you can do so two ways: by adding the JAR explicitly or by defining a classpath variable and adding it to your classpath. The latter method is preferred for adding things you plan to use often in your projects. So, let's create a variable for JUnit. You saw in the last chapter that you can do so using the Window→Preferences dialog box; but to make it easier to create a variable at the time you need it, you can also use the project's Properties dialog box (which is where you need to go, anyway, to set the project's classpath).

First you define the class variables using the Package Explorer as follows:

1 Right-click on the project name and select Properties from the context menu.

2 In the Properties dialog that appears, select Java Build Path in the right pane and select the Libraries tab.

3 On this page, click the Add Variable button.

4 On the next page, click Edit. This will take you to the Classpath Variables dialog box you saw in section 2.4.4.

5 Click New, Enter **JUNIT** for the variable name, and click the File button to browse for the JUnit JAR file under the Eclipse plugins directory; this may be, for example, c:\eclipse\plugins\org.junit_3.8.1\junit.jar. Click Open to select the JAR from the file dialog box, and then click OK to accept the new variable.

6 Next you'll add a variable for the source JAR for JUnit, in case you need it for debugging. Click New again, and this time enter **JUNIT_SRC** as the name. Click File and locate the junitsrc.zip file under the JDT source directory; for example, c:\eclipse\plugins\org.eclipse.jdt.source_2.1.0\src\org.junit_3.8.1\junitsrc.zip. Click Open and then click OK to return to the Classpath Variables dialog.

7 Click OK to return to the New Variable Classpath Entry box.

Now you'll add the JUNIT variable to your classpath and associate the source JAR with it, using the JUNIT_SRC variable:

1 Click on the JUNIT classpath variable and click OK.

2 Make sure you are on the Java Build Path page in the Properties dialog box, and click the plus sign next to the JUNIT entry. You will see that there is no Javadoc and no source attached.

3 Double-click on Source Attachment and enter the variable name **JUNIT_ SRC**. Click OK and verify that the source JAR (for example, c:\eclipse\ plugins\org.junit_3.8.1\src.jar) is now attached.

4 Click OK to save the classpath changes and dismiss the Properties dialog box.

Note that a JUNIT library is now listed in the Package Explorer. If you open the library (by clicking the plus sign), you can explore the contents of the library.

3.2.1 *Method stubs and unit tests*

Although you'll write the code for your tests first, you can save a little work if you begin by creating the class you'll be testing (FilePersistenceServices) with method stubs, because Eclipse has a wizard you can use to create test cases from existing classes. This wizard is especially helpful when you're taking an existing project and adding unit tests for it.

Create the FilePersistenceServices class as follows:

1 Right-click on the Persistence project in the Package Explorer view in the Java perspective.

2 Select New→Class from the context menu and enter the package name **org.eclipseguide.persistence**.

3 Enter the class name **FilePersistenceServices**.

4 Make sure the checkbox for generating a main() is unchecked, and click Finish.

Add the two method stubs to the code that is generated, as shown here:

```
package org.eclipseguide.persistence;

/**
 * File-based persistence class
 * Provides methods for maintaining records using files
 *
 * @author david
 * @version 1.0 Dec 30, 2002
 */
```

```
public class FilePersistenceServices
{
   public static boolean write(String fileName, int key, Vector v)
   {
      return false;
   }

   public static Vector read(String fileName, int key)
   {
      return null;
   }
}
```

After you finish typing the code, you may notice several red marks on the right side of the editor and, on the left, yellow light bulbs with a red X. These symbols are Eclipse's way of letting you know that your code has a problem. The red square at the top right is a general indication, whereas the hollow red rectangles indicate all problems in the file; if this were a longer file, where some problems were off the screen, clicking on one would take you to that particular problem. The indicators on the left are aligned with the text in the editor; in this instance, both lines containing references to Vector are tagged because there is no import statement for the Vector class. The easiest way to add it (especially if you've forgotten what package Vector is in) is to let Eclipse's Quick Fix feature type it in for you. To get a Quick Fix:

1   Click on one of the light bulbs.
2   Double-click on the suggested fix: Import java.util.Vector.

This class should now be error-free, with not a red mark in sight. Tidy up and save the file:

1   Right-click in the editor area and select Source→Format from the context menu.
2   Right-click in the editor area and click Save.

These last two steps aren't really necessary, but they're a good habit to get into because they will help keep your files in sync with each other and make some of Eclipse's automated features work better.

Finally, if you saved the code after typing it in, not only did you get the warnings on either side of the editor window, but the task list also contained information about the problems as a helpful reminder.

The JUnit wizard

You're ready to create your first unit tests. To do so, you need to create a class that extends the JUnit `TestCase` class. It's normal to have one test class for every class in the program that you want to test, and to name them by adding `Test` to the class name. So, for the `FilePersistenceServices` class, you will create a class called `FilePersistenceServicesTest`. You could create it the normal way in Eclipse by right-clicking in the Package Explorer, selecting New→Class from the context menu, and setting `junit.framework.TestCase` as the superclass—but you won't do that.

The easiest way to create test case classes is to use the JUnit wizard:

1   Right-click on the file for which you want to create test cases—`FilePersistenceServices`—and select New→Other from the context menu.

2   Notice that in the New dialog box, you can expand the Java selection on the left by clicking the plus sign. Doing so reveals a selection for JUnit.

3   Select JUnit on the left to present the choices TestCase and TestSuite on the right.

4   Select TestCase (see figure 3.1). Click Next.

5   In the box that follows, accept the default values provided for the folder, package, test case, test class, and superclass. Later, especially for larger projects, you may consider putting tests in their own package, but keeping unit tests in the same package as the code they test has the advantage of giving them access to methods that have package access.

6   In addition to the default test entries, click the options to create method stubs for `setUp()` and `tearDown()` (see figure 3.2). Click Next.

7   In the next dialog box, you are presented with the option to create method stubs to test each of the methods in the `FilePersistenceServices` class and its superclass `Object`. Check the boxes for the `FilePersistenceServices` `read()` and `write()` methods (see figure 3.3). (If you don't see the `read()` and `write()` methods, you probably didn't save the `FilePersistenceServices` class after adding them. Click Cancel and try again.)

8   Click Finish.

These steps create the class shown in listing 3.1 with empty method stubs `testRead()` and `testWrite()` for testing, respectively, `read()` and `write()`.

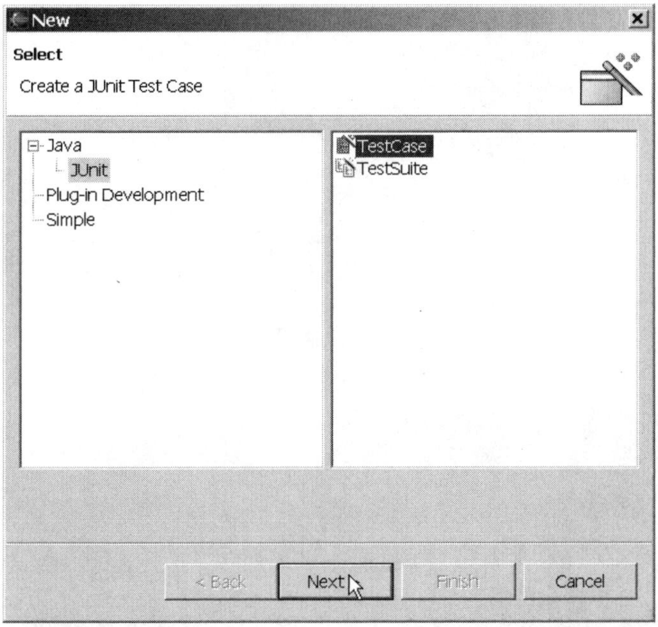

**Figure 3.1
Creating a JUnit test case with
the New JUnit Test Case Wizard**

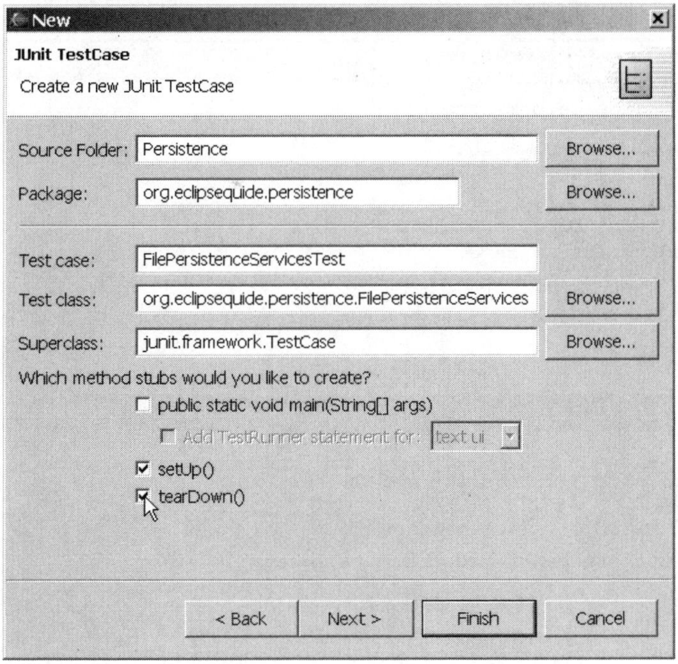

**Figure 3.2
Defining the test case and
the test class. The JUnit
wizard can also provide
method stubs for** setup()
and teardown() **methods.**

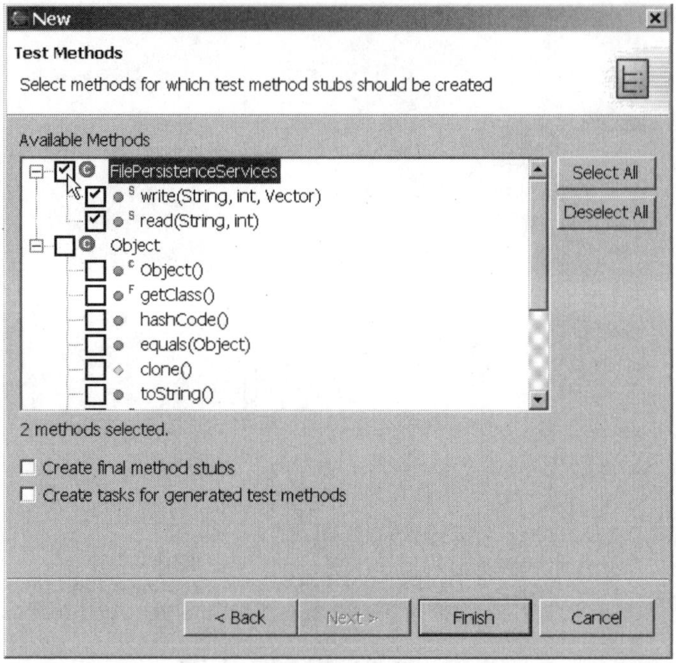

Figure 3.3
Adding test methods. Check the boxes for the test case methods you want to test.

Listing 2.1   FilePersistenceServicesTest.java—the test class for FilePersistenceServices

```java
package org.eclipseguide.persistence;

import junit.framework.TestCase;

/**
 * Enter one sentence class summary here.
 * Enter class description here.
 *
 * @author david
 * @version Jan 3, 2003
 */
public class FilePersistenceServicesTest extends TestCase
{

    /**
     * Constructor for FilePersistenceServicesTest.
     * @param arg0
     */
    public FilePersistenceServicesTest(String arg0)
    {
        super(arg0);
    }

    /**
```

```
 * @see TestCase#setUp()
 */
protected void setUp() throws Exception
{
    super.setUp();
}

/**
 * @see TestCase#tearDown()
 */
protected void tearDown() throws Exception
{
    super.tearDown();
}

public void testWrite()
{
}

public void testRead()
{
}
}
```

3.2.2 *Creating test cases*

Now that you have tests in place, you're ready to add some code to the test method stubs. First you need to add code to create a test object, a `Vector`, that you'll persist. The JUnit term for data and objects you create for use in a test case is *fixture*. The methods `setUp()` and `tearDown()` are provided, as you might guess, to set up or clean up fixtures as required. These are run, respectively, before and after each test method in your test case class.

Create the `Vector` as a class variable by adding the following to the beginning of the class (remember to either add the `Vector` import statement yourself or use the Quick Fix light bulb):

```
Vector v1;
```

Add code to the `setUp()` method to populate the `Vector` as follows:

```
protected void setUp() throws Exception
{
    super.setUp();

    v1 = new Vector();
    v1.addElement("One");
    v1.addElement("Two");
    v1.addElement("Three");
}
```

You're finally ready to add some tests. JUnit's primary tools for testing are a variety of overloaded assert methods for testing an expression or pair of expressions. These include the following:

- `assertEquals(x, y)`—Test passes if *x* and *y* are equal. *x* and *y* can be primitives or any type that has an appropriate `equals()` method.
- `assertFalse(b)`—Test passes if boolean value *b* is false.
- `assertTrue(b)`—Test passes if boolean value *b* is true.
- `assertNull(o)`—Test passes if object *o* is null.
- `assertNotNull(o)`—Test passes if object *o* is not null.
- `assertSame(ox, oy)`—Test passes if *ox* and *oy* refer to the same object.
- `assertNotSame(ox, oy)`—Test passes if *ox* and *oy* do not refer to the same object.

When you run a test case including these methods, JUnit reports the number of assertions that failed. For now, you'll test just the most basic functionality: whether the `read()` and `write()` methods return reasonable values. The `write()` method should return true if it succeeded in writing the values stored in the `Vector` you passed as an argument to a file, so you'll use the `assertTrue()` method:

```
public void testWrite()
{
    assertTrue(FilePersistenceServices.write("TestTable", 1, v1));
}
```

Because you ensured that the `read()` method returns a `Vector` (because that's its type), it's sufficient to test for a nonnull value with `assertNotNull()`. You can also test the number and value of the individual elements returned in the `Vector` by comparing them to the original `Vector`. With this code added, the `testRead()` method looks like this:

```
public void testRead()
{
    Vector w = FilePersistenceServices.read("TestTable", 1);
    assertNotNull(w);
    assertEquals(w, v1);
}
```

Running the JUnit tests in Eclipse is similar to running a Java application. First, make sure the test case class you want to run is selected—in this case, `FilePersistenceServicesTest`—either in the editor pane or in the Package Explorer view. From the Eclipse menu, select Run→Run As→JUnit Test.

Figure 3.4
The JUnit test view.
Keep an eye on the colored bar!

Running JUnit tests automatically adds the JUnit view to the tabbed notebook on the left side of the screen, covering the Package Explorer view. The JUnit view has two sections (see figure 3.4). The most notable feature in the top section is a red bar, which turns green once your class passes all the unit tests successfully. In addition, there are two tabbed pages: The Failures tab lists each test that has failed, marked with a black X if it failed an assertion test or a red X if failed due to a compilation or runtime error; the Hierarchy tab shows each test with either a green checkmark if it passed or a black or red X if it failed. After viewing the test results, you can click on the Package Explorer view's tab at the bottom left of the Workbench to return this view to the top.

You can get a little instant gratification by changing the return value of the `write()` method in the `FilePersistenceSevices` class from false to true and commenting out the `testRead()` method in the `FilePersistenceServicesTest` class. (Eclipse provides an easy way to comment out a section of code: Select the code to be commented out by clicking and dragging over it, and then either select Source→Comment from the main menu or press Ctrl-/.) Running the JUnit tests with these changes will give you a preview of what you can expect once your persistence class is implemented and passes all its tests. Eclipse keeps track of the

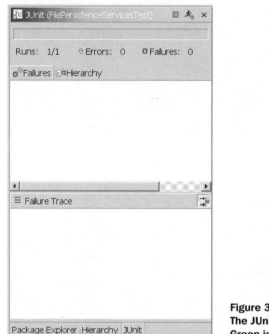

Figure 3.5
The JUnit test view.
Green is good to go.

last thing you ran, so you can run the tests by clicking the Run button (with the running person icon) in the main toolbar. For the results, see figure 3.5.

Local history

It's easy to make experimental changes and then back them out, because Eclipse keeps track of your changes and lets you compare the current version of source code with previous versions you've saved. The changes you made to fool the tests in the previous section were minor, and you can probably undo them manually using Eclipse's Undo feature (choose Edit→Undo from the main menu or press Ctrl-Z); but instead, let's try Eclipse's compare and replace feature. It's usually safer to return to a known working state this way, because it's easy to introduce errors when making changes by hand.

To compare the current version of the file with a previous version, do the following:

1 Right-click on the file in the Package Explorer.
2 Select Compare With→Local History.

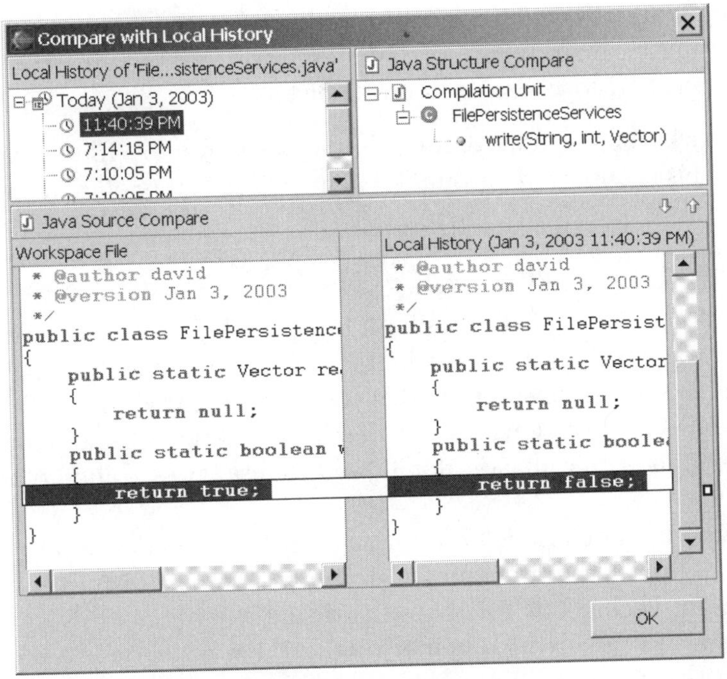

Figure 3.6
Comparing the current code with a previous version in the local history

Doing so brings up a dialog box that lets you select the previous version by date and time and then scroll through the source to see what has changed between the two versions. (This technique can be invaluable in finding out why code has inexplicably broken.) When you compare the different versions of `FilePersis-tenceServices` there is only one difference, of course: The return value of `write()` has changed from false to true (see figure 3.6).

You can let Eclipse change the source code to a previous version in much the same way:

1. Right-click on the filename in the Package Explorer view.
2. Select Replace With→Local History.

Doing so brings up a dialog box nearly identical to the one in figure 3.6 that lets you compare the current and previous versions, but this one has a Replace button you can use to revert to the previous version you select. Do the following:

1. Verify that the previous version has the original return value (false) and click Replace.
2. Remove the comment marks from the `testRead()` method in `FilePer-sistenceServicesTest`. You can do this by deleting the comment marks,

by using Undo, by highlighting the code and selecting Source→Uncomment from the main menu (or pressing Ctrl-\), or by using the Replace With→Local History feature—your choice.

You should be back where you were: two minimal tests and zero functionality. But don't despair—this is important, groundbreaking work. You're off to a great start, and things will move quickly from here.

3.2.3 *How much testing is enough?*

It's often difficult to decide what to test and how detailed tests should be. So far, you've written two tests that only test whether your persistence class can write a `Vector` out to a file successfully and whether it can retrieve that `Vector` from a file unchanged. At this level, you don't test any details of how the class does this. These tests may be enough—after all, you don't need to test Java's ability to read and write to files.

However, although not strictly necessary, it may help you develop functionality if you test at a finer level of detail. For example, you may wish to ensure that what is written out is correctly formatted and that what is read in is correctly parsed. To do so, you can create a helper method that converts a `Vector` into a formatted string rather than include this functionality directly in the `write()` method, and you can create another method that parses a formatted string and creates a `Vector`, rather than include this in the `read()` method. Doing so allows you to create tests for this functionality. As mentioned previously, you don't need to make these methods public; because the tests are in the same package as the code they are testing, you can give them the default package access.

You'll store the data in a file using comma-separated values; CSV is a common data-exchange format. More precisely, you'll enclose strings in quotes, separate fields with commas, and separate records by giving each record its own line. For example, you could represent several book records as follows:

```
"1","Ai","Cruelty","Houghton Mifflin","1973"
"2","Ted Hughes","Crow","Crow","HarperCollins","1971"
"3","Gary Snyder","Turtle Island","New Directions","1974"
```

Note that in addition to the author, title, and other book information, you precede each record with a unique number—a key you can use to locate a specific record. You need to add this arbitrary bit of information because none of the other fields are guaranteed to be unique by themselves. You'll deal with this key automatically later, but for now you'll provide the number yourself together with the rest of the information.

In keeping with the test-first philosophy, let's write the test first:

1 Re-use the existing fixture, the `Vector` `v`, and add the string representation you expect to see to the test class's attributes:

```
String s1 = "\"1\",\"One\",\"Two\",\"Three\"";
```

2 Assuming the method you'll create will be called `vector2String()`, add the following test case—a method called `testVector2String()`—to `FilePersistenceServicesTest`:

```
public void testVector2String()
{
    assertEquals(s1, FilePersistenceServices.vector2String(v1, 1));
}
```

3 Add the method `vector2String()` to `FilePersistenceServices` (remember, you can use the simple `for` template you created in Chapter 2—type **for**, press Ctrl-space, and select the `for` template from the list):

```
static String vector2String(Vector v, int key)
{
    String s = null;
    StringBuffer buffer = new StringBuffer();
    // start with key
    buffer.append("\"" + Integer.toString(key) + "\",");
    // add comma, quote delimited entry for each element in v
    for (int i = 0; i < v.size(); i++)
    {
        buffer.append("\"");
        buffer.append(v.elementAt(i));
        buffer.append("\"");
        if (i != (v.size() - 1))
        {
            buffer.append(",");
        }
    }
    s = buffer.toString();
    return s;
}
```

4 Run the tests again. The first two still fail, but the new third test passes. To see this, click on the Hierarchy tab at the top of the JUnit view (see figure 3.7).

Add the following test method, `String2Vector()`, to `FilePersistenceServicesTest`:

```
public void testString2Vector()
{
    assertEquals(FilePersistenceServices.string2Vector(s1), v1);
}
```

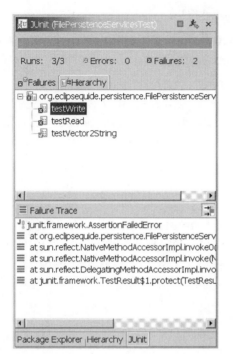

Figure 3.7
Not a complete success, but the
`testVector2String()` **test method passes**

The easiest way to implement `string2Vector()` is to use Java's `StringTokenizer` class to parse the string for you and add each token it returns to a `Vector` as follows:

```
static Vector string2Vector(String s)
{
    Vector v = new Vector();
    // use comma and double quotes as delimiters
    StringTokenizer st = new StringTokenizer(s, "\",");
    while(st.hasMoreTokens())
    {
        v.addElement(st.nextToken());
    }
    return v;
}
```

When you run the unit test, however, you'll discover a slight problem with this implementation: The test fails, because as the Failure Trace indicates, the comparison expected `"1"` but the value returned was `"One"`. This result is due to the fact that you added `"1"` as the key for the record. You need to decide: Should `string2Vector()` throw this value away? Or should your test expect this result? The answer is that at the client level, you deal with the keys independently of the record, so the actual representation of the key is best left as an internal issue for the `FilePersistenceServices` class. In this method, which is concerned only with returning data in the form of a `Vector`, you simply throw away the first token. The method should instead look like this:

```
static Vector string2Vector(String s)
{
    Vector v = new Vector();
    // use comma and double quotes as delimiters
    StringTokenizer st = new StringTokenizer(s, "\",");
    int count = st.countTokens();
    if (count >= 2)
    {
        st.nextToken();
        for (int i = 1; i < count; i++)
        {
            v.addElement(st.nextToken());
        }
    }
    return v;
}
```

Run the test again, and you will see that it now passes.

Although the key is not part of the data you want to return from the record, you need the key to locate a particular record. To facilitate this process, let's add another method that returns just the key from the string that represents a record. This is the test:

```
public void testGetKey()
{
    assertEquals(1, FilePersistenceServices.getKey(s1));
}
```

And this is the method:

```
static int getKey(String s)
{
    int key = -1;
    StringTokenizer st = new StringTokenizer(s, "\",");
    if(st.hasMoreTokens())
    {
        key = Integer.parseInt(st.nextToken());
    }
    return key;
}
```

After running the tests to make sure all your utility methods work as expected, you are ready to begin implementing your class's public methods.

3.2.4 *Implementing the public methods*

Breaking out pieces of functionality into helper methods that you can test independently makes the job of creating higher-level methods much easier. Because you know the component parts work, you can have more confidence that whole will work as well.

The `write()` method uses the `vector2String()` method to convert the `Vector` it is passed into a string, open a file, append the string, and close the file:

```
public static boolean write(String fileName, int key, Vector v)
{
   boolean success = false;

   String s = vector2String(v, key);
   try
   {
      BufferedWriter out =
         new BufferedWriter(new FileWriter(fileName, true));
      out.write(s);   // write record
      out.newLine(); // end with newline
      out.close();
      success = true;
   }
   catch (IOException e)
   {
      success = false;
   }
   return success;
}
```

> **TIP** You can avoid having to use the Quick Fix tool by using the Content Assist function (press Ctrl-space or choose Edit→Content Assist). If you begin typing **Buff** and use Ctrl-space, you can scroll through the list and select the `BufferedWriter` class. When you do this, Eclipse quietly helps by adding the `import` statement for the class if it is not already there.

The `read()` method reads lines from the file until it finds the one matching the given key. Then it calls the `string2Vector()` method to convert the matching line to a `Vector`:

```
public static Vector read(String fileName, int key)
{
   Vector v = null;
   try
   {
      // Open file for reading
```

```
        FileReader fr = new FileReader(fileName);
        BufferedReader in = new BufferedReader(fr);
        String str;
        boolean found = false;
        while ((str = in.readLine()) != null
                && !(found = (getKey(str) == key)))
        {
        }
        in.close();

        if (found) // record with key found
        {
            v = string2Vector(str);
        }
    }
    catch (IOException e)
    {
    }
    return v;
}
```

If you run the tests now, everything looks fine; but you need to think about some of the things that could go wrong, and add tests to make sure you handle them correctly. What if you add different records with the same key? What if you try to retrieve a nonexistent record? You need to extend your tests to cover these situations.

Add another `Vector` and `String` pair to your test fixture:

```
Vector v1, v2;
String s1, s2;
```

Change the `setUp()` method accordingly:

```
protected void setUp() throws Exception
{
    super.setUp();
    v1 = new Vector();
    v1.addElement("One");
    v1.addElement("Two");
    v1.addElement("Three");

    v2 = new Vector();
    v2.addElement("A");
    v2.addElement("B");
    v2.addElement("C");

    s1 = "\"1\",\"One\",\"Two\",\"Three\"";
    s2 = "\"1\",\"A\",\"B\",\"C\"";
}
```

In general, you should only add tests and not remove any (unless, of course, requirements change). First, let's decide what should happen if you try to add multiple records with the same key. Doing so would obviously be a problem, because it would mean you could add records you can't retrieve; you should not allow this. So, let's add more assertions to the `testWrite()` method—one that tries to add the same record a second time (which should fail and return false), and another that adds a different record (which should succeed):

```
public void testWrite()
{
    assertTrue(FilePersistenceServices.write( "TestTable", 1, v1));
    assertFalse(FilePersistenceServices.write("TestTable", 1, v1));
    assertTrue(FilePersistenceServices.write( "TestTable", 2, v2));
}
```

To makes these tests pass, you need to add a check to the `write()` method to make sure a record with the same key does not already exist. All you need to do is call the `read()` method:

```
public static boolean write(String fileName, int key, Vector v)
{
    boolean success = false;
    // make sure record with this key doesn't already exist
    if(read(fileName, key)!= null)
    {
        return success;
    }
    // etc.
```

There's one problem, however: The first assertion now fails, because you already have a record with a key of 1 from running the tests earlier. You can either change the keys or delete the existing records. The latter is good functionality to implement, because you will want it anyway. In fact, two such methods are left to implement: `drop()`, which deletes the entire table; and `delete()`, which deletes a single record.

You can test a `drop()` method by adding some records to the table, verifying that you can retrieve them, dropping the table, and then verifying that you can no longer retrieve any of the records. Here is the test method:

```
public void testDrop()
{
    FilePersistenceServices.write( "TestTable", 1, v1);
    FilePersistenceServices.write( "TestTable", 2, v2);
    assertNotNull(FilePersistenceServices.read("TestTable", 1));
    assertNotNull(FilePersistenceServices.read("TestTable", 2));
    assertTrue(FilePersistenceServices.drop("TestTable"));
    assertNull(FilePersistenceServices.read("TestTable", 1));
    assertNull(FilePersistenceServices.read("TestTable", 2));
}
```

The method to delete a file is smaller than the test:

```
public static boolean drop(String fileName)
{
    File f = new File(fileName);
    return f.delete();
}
```

Deleting a record is a little trickier. To do this, you need to open the file as a random access file in read/write mode, advance through it until you find the record you're looking for, back up to the start of the record, and mark the record as deleted by changing its key value to 0. (This is a rule we just made up: Records are only allowed to have keys greater than 0. Records with a key equal to 0 should be ignored. To be thorough, you may also want to add a check to the `write()` method to prevent such records from being written along with the corresponding test.) First, here is the test for the `delete()` method:

```
public void testDelete()
{
    FilePersistenceServices.write( "TestTable", 1, v1);
    FilePersistenceServices.write( "TestTable", 2, v2);
    assertNotNull(FilePersistenceServices.read("TestTable", 1));
    assertNotNull(FilePersistenceServices.read("TestTable", 2));
    assertTrue(FilePersistenceServices.delete("TestTable",1));
    assertNull(FilePersistenceServices.read("TestTable", 1));
    Vector w = FilePersistenceServices.read("TestTable", 2);
    assertEquals(w, v2);
}
```

As you can see, it's similar to the previous test. You add a couple of records, delete one, and then verify that the record you deleted can no longer be retrieved, whereas the other can still be retrieved.

Try this code for the `delete()` method:

```
public static boolean delete(String fileName, int key)
{
    String buffer = null;
    try
    {
        RandomAccessFile file = new RandomAccessFile(fileName, "rw");

        boolean cont = true;

        // find record by key
        while (cont)
        {
            // remember start of line
            long fp = file.getFilePointer();
            buffer = file.readLine();
```

```
            if (buffer != null)
            {
                if (getKey(buffer) == key)
                {
                    // return to beginning of line to delete
                    file.seek(fp);
                    file.writeChars("\"0\"");
                    cont = false;
                }
            }
            else
            {
                cont = false;
            }
        }
        file.close();
    }
    catch (FileNotFoundException e)
    {
    }
    catch (IOException e)
    {
    }
    return (buffer != null);
}
```

When you run the unit tests, the `testDelete()` method will fail. Clicking on the Hierarchy tab and then clicking on `testDelete` displays the Failure Trace (see figure 3.8). It reveals that the problem occurred in the Java `Integer.parseInt()` method. Reading down the trace, you can see that this method was called (recursively) by `Integer.parseInt()`, which was called in line 171 of the `FilePersistenceServices` class in the `getKey()` method. This method in turn was called by `read()`. This is curious, because you haven't made any changes to these methods. To investigate further, you'll need to use the debugger.

3.3 *Further adventures in debugging*

The debugger is one of the most valuable tools that Eclipse provides, but using it effectively requires a bit of practice. It's easy to find yourself stepping fruitlessly through code, trying to find some clue to what's gone wrong. When that happens, it's best to step back and devise a strategy to zero in on the problem. One common difficulty is the inability to find where the problem occurs; you only see a later consequence, such as a null pointer error, and you need to work backward to find out where the pointer went null (or check your assumption that it was valid to begin with).

**Figure 3.8
Clicking on the
`testDelete()`
method in the JUnit
test view displays
the failure trace.**

Let's begin by looking at the line where the problem first appears: line 166 in
`FilePersistenceServices`. (Note that you can make the editor show line numbers by selecting Windows→Preferences→Java→Editor from the main menu and checking the Show Line Numbers box, or you can watch the line number in the lower-right corner of the Workbench as you move the cursor to find a specific line. Your numbers may vary.) Here is the line in question:

```
key = Integer.parseInt(st.nextToken());
```

To investigate what's going on in more detail, first break this line in two, so you can see the return value from `st.nextToken()` by putting it into a variable:

```
String token = st.nextToken();
key = Integer.parseInt(token);
```

Next, set a breakpoint by double-clicking in the left margin next to the second line. To begin debugging, do the following:

1 Select the test case class `FilePersistenceServicesTests` in either the Package Explorer or the editor pane.

2 Select Run→Debug As→JUnit Test from the main menu.

Assuming no other breakpoints have been inadvertently set (this is easy to do by accidentally double-clicking instead of single-clicking when using the Quick Fix feature), the program will run until it reaches the breakpoint in the `getKey()` method. (If you encounter other breakpoints on the way, you can clear them by double-clicking on them. Then click Resume in the Debug view title bar to continue.) The value of `token` appears in the Variables view in the upper-left pane of the Workbench. If you click the Resume button on the Debug view title bar repeatedly, you'll see that the value of `token` is either 1 or 2 for a while, until a strange value appears—a single quote.

3.3.1 *Setting breakpoint properties*

Debugging can be tedious like this, when you hit a breakpoint many times before a problem occurs. There are often ways to avoid this type of tedium. Sometimes, for example, you know that a problem occurs on a specific iteration, so you can set the breakpoint to stop only on a specific hit count. To do so here, right-click on the breakpoint and select Breakpoint Properties. Check the Enable Hit Count option and enter a number in the Hit Count field (see figure 3.9).

Other times—as is the case here—you don't know how many times the breakpoint must be hit before the problem occurs, but you can watch for specific conditions. In this case, you're apparently having a problem parsing the key, which you know should only be 0, 1, or 2. You can set the breakpoint to suspend execution if the key takes on another value. To do so, right-click on the breakpoint, select Breakpoint Properties, check the Enable Condition option, and enter the following condition:

```
!token.equals("1") && !token.equals("2")
```

If the debugger is still running (possibly paused on a breakpoint), click the Terminate button and start the debugger again; the program will stop when token is assigned an unexpected value. When this happens, click on the variable name `token` in the Variable view and click the Show Detail Pane button (the second button) in the Variables view title bar to see the value in more detail (see figure 3.10). The value appears as a box signifying an undisplayable character. You can see even more detail by looking into the complete string that it came from, `s`. Click on the plus sign next to `s` to expand it, and then click on the `value` attribute. You'll see that it begins with the character box, followed by double quotes, box, 0, box, and

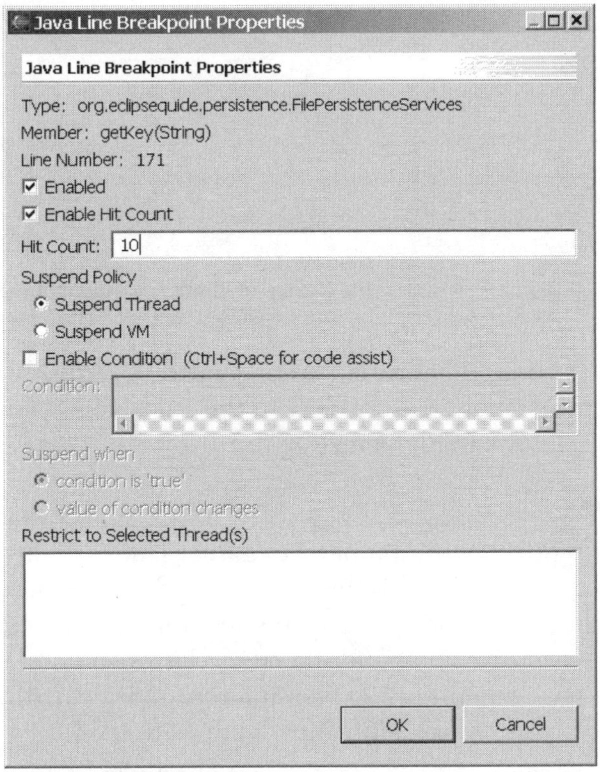

Figure 3.9
Breakpoint properties allow you to set a breakpoints based on count or on a conditional expression.

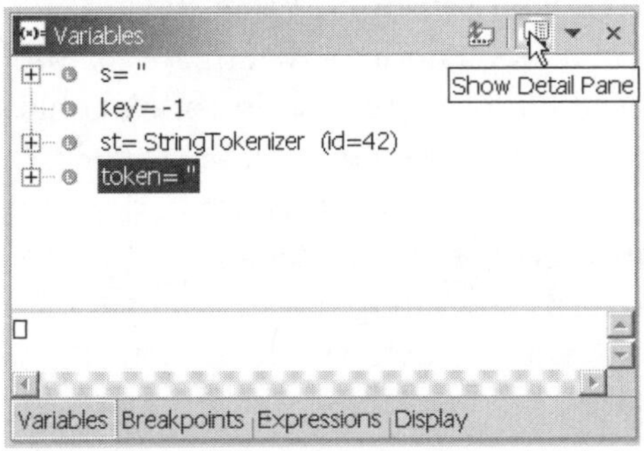

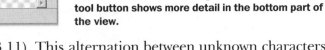

Figure 3.10
The Variables view. Clicking the Show Detail Pane tool button shows more detail in the bottom part of the view.

double quotes (see figure 3.11). This alternation between unknown characters and valid characters suggests that you somehow got a string that uses double-byte characters when you were expecting single-byte characters.

As you might deduce, your new `delete()` method appears to have botched up the database file when it tried to replace an existing key with 0 using `RandomAccessFile`'s `writeChars()` method. You can verify this problem by opening the

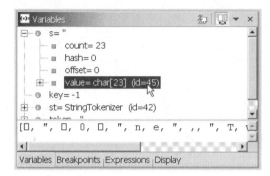

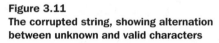

Figure 3.11
The corrupted string, showing alternation between unknown and valid characters

TestTable file. (To make this new file appear, you may need to refresh the Package Explorer view: Select the Persistence project in the Package Explorer, and then select File→Refresh from the main menu.)

3.3.2 *Finding and fixing a bug*

Finding a bug is like playing detective: You need to gather clues and investigate all the likely suspects. Here, the observation that the data in the file is getting corrupted is an important clue that should spur you into looking more carefully into the documentation for `RandomAccessFile` and the other classes you are using for file access—especially because you are using two different APIs, which is a little suspicious. You'll discover that there is an incompatibility between Java's `RandomAccessFile` and the `BufferedReader` and `BufferedWriter` classes. `RandomAccessFile` doesn't provide the same degree of character set support that the `BufferedWriter` and `BufferedReader` classes provide. On a U.S. Windows system, for example, `BufferedWriter` and `BufferedReader` use a single-byte Western European character set by default. With `RandomAccessFile`, you have two choices: `writeChars()`, which writes a string as a sequence of two-byte Unicode characters; and `writeBytes()`, which writes a string as a sequence of single-byte characters. If you aren't aware of the difference between these two methods, and aren't aware that `BufferedReader` and `BufferedWriter` are writing using a single-byte character set, it's easy to be tempted into making a wrong selection.

The quick fix is to use the `RandomAccessFile`'s `writeBytes()` method instead of `writeChars()`. Another more comprehensive solution is to eliminate the possibility of character set incompatibilities by using only random access to read and write to the file. However, this approach would require a lot of work to implement, and you can't be sure it wouldn't introduce new problems, such as poor performance.

Ultimately, you don't need to worry about the incompatibility between single-byte character sets in this situation. You will only be changing a number enclosed in quotes to another number enclosed in quotes, and these characters are the same in virtually all single-byte character sets—so the quick fix is good enough, at least for now. Here is the corrected code in the `delete()` method:

```
// ...
if (getKey(buffer) == key)
{
    // return to beginning of line
    file.seek(fp);
    file.writeBytes("\"0\""); // not writeChars()!
    cont = false;
}
// ...
```

Unfortunately, this fix still doesn't make your failures in the unit tests go away, because the file is botched and your program continues to fail. One quick fix is to delete the botched file manually and start over. Another is to delete the file at the start of your tests, perhaps in the `setUp()` method, like this:

```
protected void setUp() throws Exception
{
    super.setUp();
    FilePersistenceServices.drop("TestTable");
```

This approach causes another problem, however, because the `setUp()` method is run before every test method. If you delete the table every time, the `testRead()` method can't depend on the results of the `testWrite()` method. You can either replace the tests with a single method that tests both the `read()` and `write()` methods, or you can make the tests independent of each other. The second choice is the best option. You can leave the `testWrite()` method as it is, but you need to expand `testRead()` as follows:

```
public void testRead()
{
    FilePersistenceServices.write( "TestTable", 1, v1);
    FilePersistenceServices.write( "TestTable", 2, v2);
    Vector w;
    w = FilePersistenceServices.read("TestTable", 1);
    assertEquals(w, v1);
    w = FilePersistenceServices.read("TestTable", 2);
    assertEquals(w, v2);
}
```

After these changes, if the unit tests still fail with a `NumberFormatException`, it's possible the `setUp()` method was unable to delete the database file because an

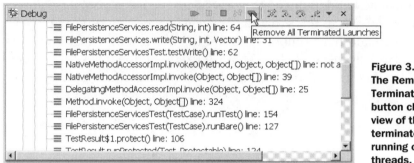

Figure 3.12
The Remove All Terminated Launches tool button clears the Debug view of threads that have terminated, leaving only running or suspended threads.

instance of the unit tests is still running—perhaps you abandoned an instance by leaving it paused at a breakpoint in the debugger. You can see if this is the case by looking in the Debug view's main panel for suspended threads (in particular, threads named `main`). If nothing is running, clicking Remove All Terminated Launches should clear all the entries in this list (see figure 3.12). If threads are still running, keep clicking the Terminate button followed by Remove All Terminated Launches until none are left.

3.4 *Logging with log4j*

A tried and true alternative to the techniques you've just seen for testing and debugging code is to use print statements. For example, it's common in Java to put a `main()` method inside a class that instantiates the class, runs various tests, and prints the results using `println()` statements.

You can create unit tests by putting code like the following in your `FilePersistenceServices` class instead of using JUnit:

```
public class FilePersistenceServices
{

    public static void main(String[] args)
    {
        FileIO.drop("TestTable");

        Vector v = new Vector();
        v.addElement("One");
        v.addElement("Two");
        v.addElement("Three");
        boolean b = FileIO.write("TestTable", 1, v);
        Vector w = FileIO.read("TestTable", 1);
        System.out.print("Count: " + w.size());

        v = new Vector();
        v.addElement("A");
```

```
      v.addElement("B");
      v.addElement("C");
      v.addElement("D");
      b = FileIO.write("TestTable", 2, v);
      w = FileIO.read("TestTable", 2);
      System.out.print("Count: " + w.size());

      // etc.
   }

// etc.
```

Likewise, for debugging, instead of delving into the code using the debugger, you can include print statements that print out suspect variables at different points in the program. Although they are good in a pinch, print statements don't have the power and flexibility that dedicated tools have. The same is true about print statements used for maintaining a transaction journal or writing errors to a log: Tools created specifically for logging provide far more options and can be configured at runtime, in a way print statements cannot.

Unlike print statements, logging tools are not limited to sending output to a console or a file. For instance, they can also write to a database or send email messages. One such tool is the logging API that has been included in Java since JDK 1.4. However, because not everyone uses JDK 1.4, the best option is to use the tool on which the Java API is based: log4j. Even though it is a little more difficult to set up initially than the JDK version, it has the virtue of being useable on JDK 1.1, 1.2, 1.3, and 1.4. Therefore, log4j is what we'll examine here.

3.4.1 *Loggers, appenders, and pattern layouts*

If print statements are like using a fax machine, log4j is like using a messenger service. You have many more options than simply printing directly to a destination such as the console or a file. To enable this flexibility, three actions must happen dynamically (normally, based on a configuration file) before a message can be delivered:

- The message is assigned a priority and filtered according to that priority.
- The message's destination (or destinations) is determined dynamically.
- The message is formatted appropriately for each destination.

In order to follow how log4j performs these three actions, you need to understand three key log4j concepts: *loggers*, *appenders*, and *pattern layouts*.

Loggers

A logger is used in an application just like `System.out` is used for print statements. It is an object you use to send messages.

Loggers exist in a hierarchy. The root logger is anonymous and exists automatically. You can get this logger by using the `Logger.getRootLogger()` static method. It's preferable, however, to instantiate your own named logger (which inherits from the root logger) by calling the `Logger.getLogger()` method. Assuming everything is properly configured, you can obtain a logger named `myLogger` as follows:

```
logger = Logger.getLogger("myLogger");
```

Loggers do not have simple methods like `print()` and `println()`; instead they have methods that indicate the priority of the message. The five methods, in ascending order of priority, are as follows:

- `debug()`
- `info()`
- `warn()`
- `error()`
- `fatal()`

These methods all formally accept type `Object`; but whatever the object is, it will be converted to a `String` by calling the object's `toString()` method before it's delivered to its destination.

As an example, you can send information that is useful for debugging purposes using the `debug()` method:

```
logger.debug("Entering method");
```

On the other hand, you probably want to log exceptions (such as `IOExceptions`) at a higher priority. For example, you might have the following `catch` clause in your code:

```
catch (IOException e)
{
    logger.error("Caught:" + e);
}
```

The priority determines whether a message is sent to its destination. This control is important, because you want your programs to provide different levels of information depending on the circumstances. For example, if you are testing a program, you may want to be able to look through a log and see everything the program did: every method it entered, every user who logged in, and so on. But if you are running the program in production, you don't want to log potentially sensitive information like usernames and passwords. You also don't want performance degraded by excessive logging. You can ignore debug and info messages, and instead log all errors to a file and fatal errors to both a file and the console. log4j lets you change the level of logging without recompiling by using a configuration file, where a level is assigned to each logger.

Appenders

An appender is an object that performs actual output. The simplest appender is the ConsoleAppender, which corresponds to System.out. Obviously, it writes output to the console.

Appenders are available to write to files, to write to databases using JDBC, and to send email, among other things. Table 3.1 lists some of the appenders included with log4j.

Table 3.1   Appenders, which perform output in log4j

Appender	Description
ConsoleAppender	Logs to the console
FileAppender	Logs to a file
RollingFileAppender	Logs to a file and creates a backup when the file reaches a specified size
DailyRollingFileAppender	Logs to a file, which is rolled over to a backup file at a specified time
JDBCAppender	Logs to a database
NTEventLogAppender	Logs to the Windows event log (available only on Windows)
SMTPAppender	Logs using the SMTP mail server (sends email)
SocketAppender	Logs to a TCP socket

A logger can be associated with one or more appenders. If a logger is associated with the ConsoleAppender and a RollingFileAppender, for example, messages will be sent both to the console and to the file, providing they meet or exceed the level to which the logger has been set.

Layout

A layout is an object that formats the message according to a format string, which can contain both regular text and special patterns called *conversion specifiers*. Regular text is printed as is. Conversion specifiers print different types of data dif-

ferent ways, depending on the specifier and its options. (If you have used the
printf() function's format specifiers in C, conversion specifiers will be familiar.)

A conversion specifier begins with a percent sign (%) followed by, at minimum,
one other character (usually a letter) indicating what is to be printed. (Note that
the specifier characters are case sensitive, so *m* is different than *M*.) For example,
the specifier character *m* refers to the message passed to the logger; to print the
message alone, the pattern layout is %m. Typically, however, you include additional
information, such as the date and time, and, for debug information, perhaps the
filename and line number. Table 3.2 lists some generally useful specifiers. The first
eight (up to %%) can be safely used without incurring a serious performance cost.
The last four (%C, %F, %l, and %L) provide information about the code that logged
the message, and should be used carefully because they are more costly to execute.

Table 3.2   log4j conversion specifiers that print data in different ways

Specifier	Description
%c	Name of the logger. (In previous versions of log4j, loggers were called *categories*; hence the abbreviation.)
%d	Date and time. The default format is ISO8601.
%m	Message passed by the logger.
%n	Platform-dependent new line string. (Depending on the platform, it may be "\r\n", "\n", or "\r".)
%p	Priority of the message.
%r	Elapsed time, in milliseconds, since the application was started.
%t	Name of the thread.
%%	Percent sign.
%C	Fully qualified name of the class.
%F	Filename.
%l	Location information. Depending on the JVM, may include the fully qualified name of the method, the source filename, and the line number. If this is the last specifier before %n in a layout, the message provides a hotlink to the source code in the Eclipse Console view.
%L	Line number.

You can also add other formatting characters to conversion specifiers between
the percent sign and the specifier character. All are optional, but if any appear,
they must appear in the following order:

- - (dash)—Left justify. (Default is right justify.)
- n (number)—Minimum width. Data is padded with spaces if necessary.
- m—Maximum width. Data is truncated from the left if necessary.

To limit the length of a message to 50 characters, for example, you can use the following:

```
%50m%n
```

To display the file, line number, and message in aligned columns, you can use the following:

```
%-20.20F %-5.5L: %50m%n
```

Several conversion specifiers can be followed by an additional option enclosed in braces. For example, the date specifier can be followed by a *date format specifier.* The date format specifier accepts a pattern string using the same syntax as the standard Java `SimpleDateFormat`, but log4j has several formats predefined that perform significantly better. Table 3.3 lists the log4j formats, the corresponding `SimpleDateFormat` style pattern, and an example of what their printout looks like.

Table 3.3   log4j date formats

log4j format	`SimpleDateFormat` **style pattern**	Sample printout
ABSOLUTE	hh:mm:ss,SSS	18:16:10,432
DATE	dd MMM YYYY hh:mm:ss,SSS	08 Jan 2003 18:16:10,432
ISO8601	YYYY-mm-dd hh:mm:ss,SSS	2003-01-08 18:16:10,432

Here is an example of a date specifier using the ABSOLUTE date format:

```
%d{ABSOLUTE}
```

The next example uses a `SimpleDateFormat` pattern:

```
%d{MMM d, YYYY hh:mm:ss a}
```

This would display the following, for example:

```
Jan 8, 2003 6:16:10 PM
```

3.4.2   *Configuring log4j*

Although it is possible to configure log4j programmatically—that is, assign appenders to loggers and layouts to appenders using various methods in the log4j API—the best way to do this is to use a configuration file. Doing so makes it possible to change the configuration easily, without having to recompile the application. This file can be in the form of a Java properties file or an XML file. You'll use a properties file here, because this is the traditional format and most log4j documentation and examples use it.

By default, log4j looks for a configuration file called log4j.properties in the classpath. In a basic configuration file, you just need to set up the root logger with an appender or two. The named loggers that you instantiate in your code will inherit all their properties from this root logger. You need to do the following:

1   Specify the priority level for the root logger.
2   Specify, using arbitrary names as keys, which appenders are to be associated with the root logger.
3   Set properties, such as the pattern layout, for each appender you named.

Specifying the root logger

You specify the information for the root logger (priority level and appenders) using the following format:

```
log4j.rootLogger=PriorityLevel, Appender1 [, Appender2 [, etc.]]
```

The *PriorityLevel* can be any of the values DEBUG, WARN, and so on. *Appender1*, *Appender2*, and *etc.* can be any name you choose to give your appenders; these names are used as keys throughout the rest of the configuration file. The following line sets the root logger's priority to DEBUG and associates two appenders named myConsole and myLogFile with the root logger:

```
# Set root logger to DEBUG and assign two appenders
log4j.rootLogger=DEBUG, myConsole, myLogFile
```

The remaining lines in the configuration file, which assign properties to appenders, are key=value pairs having this basic format:

```
log4j.appender.KeyName[.Property[.Property[.etc]]={Class|Value}
```

Adding appenders

The first thing you need to define for each appender is a class. This then determines what properties are applicable. For example, a console appender will not have a filename associated with it, but a file appender will. If this property in turn is a class, it too may have properties you can set. (Refer to the log4j Javadoc for specific information about each of the appender classes.)

The following lines specify that the `myConsole` appender is of type `ConsoleAppender` and set its layout property to the `PatternLayout` class. You then assign a conversion pattern to the layout.

```
# Console appender
log4j.appender.myConsole=org.apache.log4j.ConsoleAppender
log4j.appender.myConsole.layout=org.apache.log4j.PatternLayout
log4j.appender.myConsole.layout.ConversionPattern=%5p [%t] (%F:%L)
    - %m%n
```

Next, you configure the `myLogFile` appender as a `RollingLogFileAppender`. You specify that it should create a backup file when its size exceeds 100KB and that it should keep two backups at a time. As you did for the console appender, assign it `PatternLayout` and specify a conversion pattern:

```
# Rolling file appender
log4j.appender.myLogFile=org.apache.log4j.RollingFileAppender
log4j.appender.myLogFile.File=mylog.log
log4j.appender.myLogFile.MaxFileSize=100KB
log4j.appender.myLogFile.MaxBackupIndex=2
log4j.appender.myLogFile.layout=org.apache.log4j.PatternLayout
log4j.appender.myLogFile.layout.ConversionPattern=
    %d{MMM d, yyyy hh:mm:ss a}: %p [%t] %m%n
```

Because the root logger's priority is set to `DEBUG`, all messages with a priority of `DEBUG` or higher—which is to say, all messages—are logged. You override this default for individual appenders by setting the `threshold` property. Let's set the priority for the log file to `WARN` by adding the following line, so that `DEBUG` and `INFO` messages are ignored:

```
log4j.appender.myLogFile.threshold=WARN
```

With all these preliminaries out of the way, you are finally ready to use log4j inside Eclipse.

3.4.3 *Using log4j with Eclipse*

Let's try out log4j by adding logging to the persistence class. The first step is to obtain the log4j JAR file and add it to your project's classpath. Because log4j does not come with Eclipse, you must download it from the Apache Software Foundation at http://www.apache.org, where it is part of the Jakarta project. You have a choice of downloading it in either Zip or tar format; depending on your system, one may be more convenient than the other.

After downloading, unzip or untar the file to a directory such as C:\log4j. Doing so will install the complete log4j distribution, which includes the log4j JAR file, documentation, examples, and source code in a version-specific subdirectory.

Assuming you installed version 1.2.8 of log4j according to the earlier example, the log4j JAR file is C:\log4j\ jakarta-log4j-1.2.8\dist\lib\log4j-1.2.8.jar.

Because you will probably use this tool in most of your projects, create a classpath variable for it in the Workbench's Java preferences, such as LOG4J, and use this variable to add log4j to the Persistence project's classpath in the project properties. (See Chapter 2 for complete instructions.)

Next, create the log4j configuration file. Right-click on the Persistence project and select New→File, make sure the Persistence folder is selected, enter **log4j.properties** as the filename, and click Finish. The empty file will appear in the editor pane. Type in the configuration file described in the previous section.

Now you can add logging code to your FilePersistenceServices class. First add a logger. It's a common practice to add a logger to each class using the class name like this:

```
public class FilePersistenceServices
{
    static Logger logger =
                Logger.getLogger(FilePersistenceServices.class);

    // etc.
```

As you might expect, entering this code will cause Eclipse to complain and display the familiar Quick Fix light bulb in the left margin. Click on the bulb to bring up a list of suggestions. If you are using JDK 1.4 or greater, this list will include the option to import java.util.logging.Logger—do not select this option! If log4j is properly installed and included in the classpath, the list should also include the option to import org.apache.log4j.Logger; choose this class instead.

It's time to add messages to your methods. Let's use the read() method as an example. Add a debug() method at the top, to log when the method is entered:

```
public static Vector read(String fileName, int key)
{
    logger.debug("Entering read()");
    Vector v = null;
    // etc.
```

Logging when methods are entered and exited is sometimes useful, but doing so usually only leads to a lot of useless information. Setting the priority of these types of messages to debug makes it easy to turn them off while letting other, more important messages through.

Let's add another message, using the warn() method, to report when the read() method fails to find a record. Add the following else clause after the if statement near the bottom of the method:

```
 Console [<terminated> C:\j2sdk1.4.0_01\jre\bin\javaw.exe (1/8/03 10:50 PM)]        □  ⌀  ×
WARN  [main]  (FilePersistenceServices.java:50)  - Failed to find key: 2  ▲
DEBUG [main]  (FilePersistenceServices.java:28)  - Entering read()
DEBUG [main]  (FilePersistenceServices.java:28)  - Entering read()
DEBUG [main]  (FilePersistenceServices.java:28)  - Entering read()
DEBUG [main]  (FilePersistenceServices.java:28)  - Entering read()
WARN  [main]  (FilePersistenceServices.java:50)  - Failed to find key: 2
DEBUG [main]  (FilePersistenceServices.java:28)  - Entering read()
DEBUG [main]  (FilePersistenceServices.java:28)  - Entering read()
DEBUG [main]  (FilePersistenceServices.java:28)  - Entering read()
DEBUG [main]  (FilePersistenceServices.java:28)  - Entering read()
DEBUG [main]  (FilePersistenceServices.java:28)  - Entering read()
DEBUG [main]  (FilePersistenceServices.java:28)  - Entering read()
WARN  [main]  (FilePersistenceServices.java:50)  - Failed to find key: 2
DEBUG [main]  (FilePersistenceServices.java:28)  - Entering read()
DEBUG [main]  (FilePersistenceServices.java:28)  - Entering read()
DEBUG [main]  (FilePersistenceServices.java:28)  - Entering read()
WARN  [main]  (FilePersistenceServices.java:50)  - Failed to find key: 1
DEBUG [main]  (FilePersistenceServices.java:28)  - Entering read()   ▼
◄                                                                    ►
 Tasks  Console
```

Figure 3.13   Log messages in the console. The console appender inherits the root logger's priority threshold, which is set to `debug`**, so all messages are displayed here.**

```
if (found) // record with key found
{
    v = string2Vector(str);
}
else
{
    logger.warn("Failed to find key: " + key);
}
```

Run the unit tests. The console will display all messages (see figure 3.13), whereas the log file, whose threshold is set to WARN, will contain only the messages from the warn method. To view the log file, right-click on the Persistence project in the Package Explorer view and select Refresh from the context menu; doing so updates the Files view to include the newly created file. Double-click on it to open it in the text editor. Here are the first few lines from mylog.log:

```
Jan 8, 2003 10:47:22 PM: WARN [main] Failed to find key: 1
Jan 8, 2003 10:48:10 PM: WARN [main] Failed to find key: 2
Jan 8, 2003 10:48:10 PM: WARN [main] Failed to find key: 2
Jan 8, 2003 10:48:10 PM: WARN [main] Failed to find key: 2
```

3.5 *Summary*

Eclipse is a rich environment for developing Java applications. Because of its extensible nature, many tools are available that promote a good development methodology, such as the JUnit framework for testing.

JUnit encourages you to build tests up front, to set the bar for your coding efforts. It may feel awkward, or even backward at first, but once you become comfortable with test-driven development, you may find that you are producing better quality code in a shorter period of time.

Because of the way JUnit and other plug-ins integrate seamlessly, it's often difficult to tell where one ends and the other begins. This integration lets you work more smoothly when you need to switch from one tool, such as JUnit, to another, such as the JDT's debugger.

In this chapter we also looked at another tool that can change the way you work: log4j. Although we didn't explore its use in much detail, dwelling instead on how to set it up, you are encouraged to get into the habit of using log4j where you would ordinarily use print statements. You'll find its flexibility (not to mention the ability to easily turn it off and on) a refreshing change from using `System.out.println()` statements—and it's less ugly, too.

Working with source code in Eclipse

4

In this chapter...

- Importing an external project
- Adding a new package to the Persistence component
- Refactoring

One of the benefits of pair programming is that it provides the opportunity to see in depth how someone else works—how he approaches a problem and thinks things through, whether she uses the mouse to click on menus or uses keyboard shortcuts, whether he writes a little or a lot of code before testing, and so on. It's quite common to learn something that surprises you, which could have made your life much easier in the past. This chapter is an attempt at providing a similar experience: As you continue to develop the program you began in chapter 3, you'll be introduced to some of Eclipse's key features that make the job easier.

4.1 *Importing an external project*

Unless you've been working exclusively with Eclipse for a long time, you'll occasionally find that you have source code you created with another tool or editor, which you now want to move into Eclipse—either to start a new project or to incorporate into an existing project. Suppose, for example, that as an exercise you created a class hierarchy representing stars, planets, and moons (see figure 4.1). Now, you want to use the persistence class you developed in chapter 3 to store the astronomy data. Assume your astronomy Java source files are in a Java package called `org.eclipseguide.astronomy` and are located in the following directory structure:

```
C:\ASTRONOMY
+---org
    +---eclipseguide
        +---astronomy
                CelestialBody.java
                Moon.java
                OrbitingBody.java
                Planet.java
                Star.java
```

There are several ways you can bring this code into Eclipse. You can use Eclipse's Import feature to copy the source code into your workspace directory, either as a new project or as a new folder in an existing project. Either way, the original files are only copied and otherwise are left untouched. In some situations you need to work directly with files outside of Eclipse's workspace directory; usefully, Eclipse provides a way to add a link to this external directory to an Eclipse project. Links of this type will be covered in chapter 7. Here you will use the Import feature.

To import these files and their directory structure into Eclipse, follow these steps:

1   Right-click on the Persistence project in the Package Navigator and select Import from the context menu.

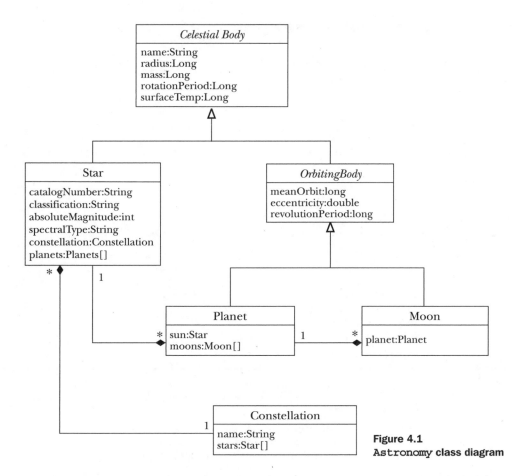

Figure 4.1
Astronomy class diagram

2 In the Import dialog box that appears, select File System and click Next.

3 In the next dialog box, either click Browse to browse for your source files or type the directory (**c:\astronomy**) directly into the From Directory text box. The box below From Directory shows a directory tree from which you can select the directories and folders you want to import. (If you typed in the directory name in the previous step, you will need to press Tab or click in this box to force it to update and show this tree.) In this case, you want to import the entire source tree, so select the checkbox next to Astronomy (see figure 4.2).

4 Below this are several options; accept the default selection, Create Selected Folders Only.

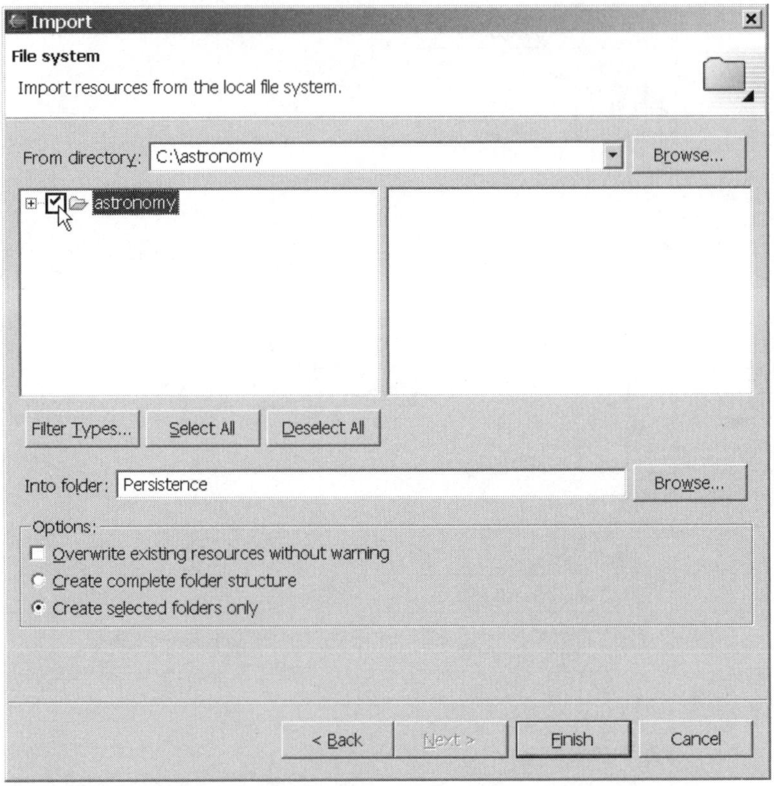

Figure 4.2   Importing the `astronomy` source code. The box below From Directory lets you explore the directory tree and select directories and files for importing. Here astronomy and all its subdirectories are selected.

5   Click Finish to complete the import. Figure 4.3 shows the Package Explorer with the `org.eclipseguide.astronomy` package added.

After the Import, you can select File→Save All from the Eclipse main menu and examine the changes made to your workspace directory structure. The Java source files are found in the following directories:

```
C:\ECLIPSE\WORKSPACE\PERSISTENCE
|
+---org
    +---eclipseguide
        +---astronomy
        |       CelestialBody.java
        |       Moon.java
        |       OrbitingBody.java
        |       Planet.java
```

```
        |           Star.java
        |
        +---persistence
                FilePersistenceServices.java
                FilePersistenceServicesTest.java
```

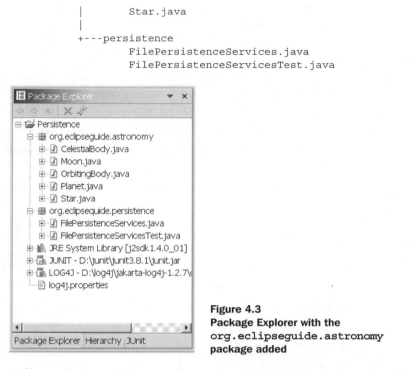

Figure 4.3
Package Explorer with the
`org.eclipseguide.astronomy`
package added

Eclipse also provides another way of importing code: using drag-and-drop. If you open a Windows Explorer window and locate the astronomy directory, you can click on the org folder, and then drag it and drop it on the Persistence project name.

4.2 *Extending the persistence component*

In this chapter you'll create a class that allows you to save instances of any of the concrete astronomy classes: Star, Planet, or Moon. This is a fairly elaborate example, but it will let us cover issues addressed by some of Eclipse's refactoring tools more realistically, and we hope it will be more interesting and less contrived than a smaller example.

Because the FilePersistenceServices class expects vectors, the job of this new class will be to map between objects and vectors. You'll call this class Object-Manager, and it will have the following methods, paralleling the methods in FilePersistenceServices:

```
public Object get(int key)
public boolean save(Object o, int key)
public boolean update(Object o, int key)
```

```
public boolean delete(int key)
public boolean dropObjectTable()
```

4.2.1 *Creating a factory method*

The `ObjectManager` class is specifically designed for use with the `FilePersistence-Services` class, but in the future, as mentioned previously, you may want to provide additional options—in particular, the ability to use a database. This change should not affect a client class using the `ObjectManager` class. To ensure this, you'll provide a factory method that returns an `ObjectManager` object, rather than letting the client class instantiate the `ObjectManager` directly. This way, you can change the type of the object that is returned—to a subclass of `ObjectManager`, for example. We'll consider this topic in a bit more detail when we look at refactoring later in this chapter.

The signature of the factory method for `ObjectManager` looks like this:

```
public static ObjectManager createObjectManager(Class type);
```

You can require that clients use this method by adding a private do-nothing constructor, which prevents them from instantiating the class directly:

```
private ObjectManager(){}
```

You also need to create the stubs for your methods; this is an example of what the `get()` method looks like at first:

```
public Object get(int key)
{
    return null;
}
```

The stubs for the rest of the methods—`save()`, `update()`, `delete()`, and `dropObject()`—are omitted here in the interest of saving space, but they should all return false.

4.2.2 *Creating the unit test class*

With these methods defined (but not implemented), you can begin to write some JUnit tests. You'll put both the `ObjectManager` class and its test class in the `org.eclipseguide.persistence` package. Follow these steps:

1 Right-click on the package name and select New→Other to bring up the New dialog box.

2 If the Java selection on the left side of the screen hasn't been expanded yet, click on the plus sign to do so. Select JUnit on the left, select TestCase on the right, and click Next.

3 Verify that the package name is correct. If you right-clicked on Persistence instead of the package, this box will be empty and you'll need to type in the name.

4 Skip the Test Case field, and type the name of the class you'll be testing (**ObjectManager**) in the Test Class field instead; notice that Eclipse automatically fills in the Test Case as you type.

5 Your test case this time is one all-inclusive test, so you won't require any method stubs; make sure none of the boxes under Which Method Stubs Would You Like To Create are checked. Click Finish.

4.2.3 *Working with the astronomy classes*

The unit tests basically let you prototype how you'd like to be able to use the ObjectManager class. You'll use one of the concrete astronomy classes, Star, for your tests. Let's first take a look at Star.java:

```
package org.eclipseguide.astronomy;

import java.util.Vector;

public class Star extends CelestialBody
{

    public String catalogNumber;
    public double absoluteMagnitude;
    public String spectralType;
    public String constellation;
    public String galaxy;
}
```

Note that the class has been simplified slightly by making the constellation field a string and omitting the field planets, because the Persistence class does not support nested classes.

```
package org.eclipseguide.astronomy;

abstract public class CelestialBody
{
  public String name;
  public long radius;
  public long mass;
  public long rotationPeriod;
  public long surfaceTemperature;
}
```

These classes allow other classes to directly read and set their attributes. In many cases, you want to limit access by making the fields private and using get*XXX*()

and set*XXX*() methods to read or set them. For reasons you'll see shortly, you need to leave these attributes public; but should you ever need getter and setter methods, Eclipse can generate them for you automatically:

1   Click on the source code and select Source→Generate Getter and Setter from the context menu. Doing so brings up the Getter and Setter dialog box.

2   Click Select All to generate both get*XXX*() and set*XXX*() methods for all attributes, and then click OK.

In your data model, however, these classes represent a type of object called a *value object* that needs to work intimately with your ObjectManager class. You'll use the reflection API to access the object's values; doing so multiplies the cost of indirection that getter and setter methods introduce, because it's much harder to determine a class's methods and their signatures and then call the methods than it is to access attributes directly.

Also, because the astronomy classes are in a separate package, the classes themselves need to be public in order for ObjectManager to access them. For reasons such as these—making access easy and efficient—it's typical for value objects to have public attributes. (Because they're usually used in multitier situations, they're also typically serializable, but that's a topic for another time.)

If you tried the Generate Getter and Setter feature as described previously, you need to revert to the original file by using Eclipse's Undo feature. Either select Edit→Undo from the menu twice (once to undo the Generate Getter and Setter function and once to undo the change from public to private) or use the keyboard shortcut Ctrl-Z.

You need to make one change to your astronomy classes. To support JUnit, you must implement an equals() method that allows JUnit to test if two objects are equivalent. This method needs to compare each field in the object to the fields in another object that is passed in as a parameter. Here is the method for Star:

```
// ...
public class Star extends CelestialBody
{

    //...

    public boolean equals(Object o)
    {
        boolean equal = false;

        if (o instanceof Star)
        {
```

```
        Star star = (Star) o;
        equal = cmpStrings(catalogNumber, star.catalogNumber)
                && absoluteMagnitude == star.absoluteMagnitude
                && cmpStrings(spectralType, star.spectralType)
                && cmpStrings(constellation, star.constellation)
                && cmpStrings(galaxy, star.galaxy);
        equal = super.equals(o) && equal;
      }
      return equal;
    }
  }
```

Notice two things. First, `equals()` uses the method `cmpStrings()` to compare strings. This helper method, found in the `CelestialBody` superclass, helps simplify the logic; comparing strings is a little messy, because it is valid for them to be null, in which case the `String` `equals()` method fails due to a null pointer error. Second, notice that `Star`'s `equals()` method calls the superclass `equals()` method.

Here are the `CelestialBody` `equals()` method and the `cmpStrings()` helper method:

```
// ...
abstract public class CelestialBody
{
  // ...
  public Object get(int key)
  {
    return null;
  }

  public boolean equals(Object o)
  {
    boolean equal = false;

    if (o instanceof CelestialBody)
    {
      CelestialBody body = (CelestialBody) o;
      equal = cmpStrings(name, body.name)
            && radius == body.radius
            && mass == body.mass
            && rotationPeriod == body.rotationPeriod
            && surfaceTemperature == body.surfaceTemperature;

    }
    System.out.println("leaving CelestialBody equals()");
    return equal;
  }

  public static boolean cmpStrings(String a, String b)
  {
    if (a == null && b == null) // both null
```

```
    {
        return true;
    }
    if (a == null || b == null) // one null
    {
        return false;
    }
    return a.equals(b); // ok to test
    }
}
```

4.2.4 *The Star test case*

Begin your test method by obtaining an `ObjectManager` for the `Star` class and then calling the `dropObjectTable()` method to delete any data that may have been left over from a previous test run:

```
public void testStar()
{
    // start fresh by dropping old table
    ObjectManager starMgr =
        ObjectManager.createObjectManager(Star.class);
    starMgr.dropObjectTable();
```

Now you're ready to create a `Star` object and populate it with data:

```
Star s = new Star();

// fields in Star
s.catalogNumber = "HD358";
s.absoluteMagnitude = 2.1;
s.spectralType = "B8IVp";
s.constellation = "Andromeda";
s.galaxy = "Milky Way";  // (Just a guess...)

// fields in superclass CelestialBody
s.name = "Alpheratz";
s.radius = 5;
s.mass = 0;
s.rotationPeriod = 0;
s.surfaceTemperature = 9100;
```

As usual, when you type in this code, Eclipse alerts you that the type `Star` is unresolved and offers some suggested ways to fix this situation. Choose to import `org.eclipseguide.astronomy.Star`. Note that if you had chosen to import the `astronomy` classes into another project, you would instead need to add the classes to the project's classpath.

Save this star by calling the `save()` method, wrapped with a JUnit `assertTrue()` method:

```
// save it
assertTrue(starMgr.save(s, 1));
```

Next, make sure you can retrieve it, and check that it has the same values you put in:

```
// make sure we can retrieve it correctly;
Star newStar = (Star) starMgr.get(1);
assertNotNull(newStar);
assertEquals(s, newStar);
```

In addition, test to make sure that duplicates are rejected, that you can modify objects, and that you can delete them. Here is the rest of the `testStar()` test method:

```
// modify and update
newStar.absoluteMagnitude = 123;
newStar.radius = 500;
starMgr.update(newStar, 1);

// make sure changes are ok; verify it's a different object
Star modStar = (Star) starMgr.get(1);
assertNotSame(newStar, modStar);

// try deleting
assertTrue(starMgr.delete(1));
assertNull(starMgr.get(1));
}
```

4.2.5 *Creating a test suite*

Once you have two or more test case classes, you want to create a test suite that runs all the tests at once. To do this:

1 Right-click on the `org.eclipseguide.persistence` package.

2 Select Right→New→Other.

3 Click on the plus sign to expand the choices for Java and select JUnit on the left side of the dialog box.

4 Select TestSuite on the right and click Next.

5 In the next dialog box, the name of the test suite class is `AllTests`; the test cases `FilePersistenceServicesTest` and `ObjectManagerTest` are included in the suite (see figure 4.4). This and the other defaults are acceptable; click Finish.

Running a test suite is identical to running a test case: Make sure the test suite class, in this case `AllTests`, is selected. Select Run→Run As→JUnit Test from the main menu.

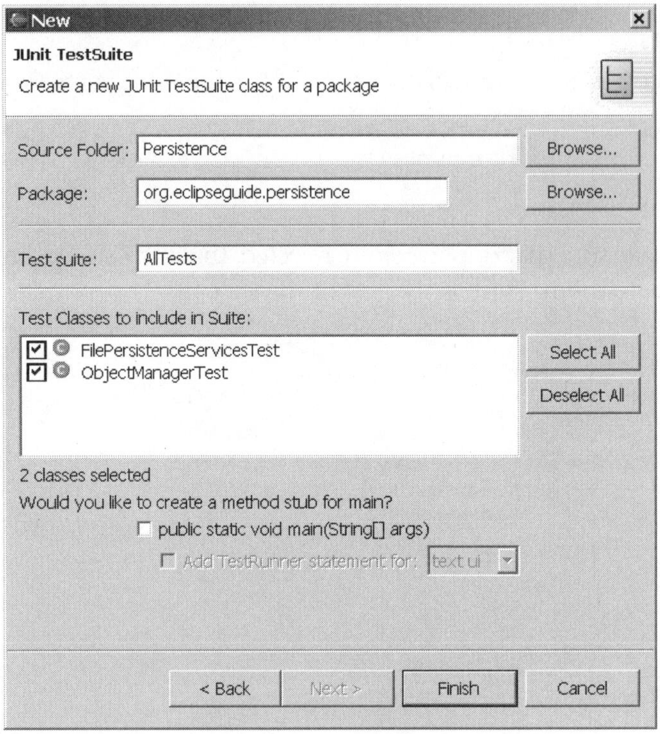

Figure 4.4
Creating the test suite class. The JUnit wizard automatically locates and includes all the test cases in the package.

4.2.6 *Implementing the ObjectManager class*

Now you're prepared to implement the ObjectManager class. By using the Java reflection API, this class will be able to create and modify objects of types determined dynamically at runtime. This functionality is briefly described here, but for more information, please refer to Sun's Reflection Tutorial at http://java.sun.com/docs/books/tutorial/reflect/. The important point is that you understand the overall functionality, not necessarily the details.

You'll begin by implementing the createObjectManager() factory method. This method instantiates, initializes, and returns an ObjectManager object that can manage value objects of a specific class, such as Star. Its single parameter is of type Class. You need the Class to obtain information about the value object type, such as its name and attributes, and, later, to instantiate the class.

First, though, here are the private attributes of the ObjectManager class that createObjectManager() is responsible for setting:

```
// ...
public class ObjectManager
```

```
{
    Collection fieldMap = null;
    Class classType = null;
    String className = null;
    static Logger logger = Logger.getLogger(ObjectManager.class);
```

Here is the code for the `ObjectManager` factory method:

```
public static ObjectManager createObjectManager(Class type)
{
    ObjectManager om = new ObjectManager();
    om.classType = type;
    om.className = type.getName();
    om.setFieldMap();
    return om;
}
```

The first three lines are fairly straightforward: They instantiate `ObjectManager` and save the class type and fully qualified class name in instance variables. (If you call this method with Star.class, for example, `getName()` will return `org.eclipseguide.astronomy.Star`.) The next line, which calls the `setFieldMap()` method, does the most important work.

In order to put the value object's values in a vector or vice versa, `ObjectManager`'s `save()`, `get()`, and `update()` methods need to know the attributes of the value object—specifically, their name and type. In an implementation that uses a database, this method would also need to map the attributes (or fields) to the corresponding database table's columns. Here, where you are using a file-based implementation, you only need to know what type each attribute is so you can perform appropriate conversions to and from strings.

You obtain information about the value object's attributes by using the `Class` method `getFields()`, which returns an array of `Fields`; each `Field` in the array corresponds to one of the value object's attributes. These are not guaranteed to be in any particular order, so to make sure you read and write the attributes consistently, you use the `TreeMap` class to store the information you obtain; using the attribute name as the key ensures that the attribute information (which you store in an object called a `FieldMapEntry`) is in alphabetical order.

Here is the `setFieldMap()` method:

```
void setFieldMap()
{
    Field[] f = classType.getFields();
    TreeMap map = new TreeMap();
    for (int i = 0; i < f.length; i++)
    {
        FieldMapEntry entry = new FieldMapEntry();
        entry.attributeName = f[i].getName();
```

```
        entry.attributeType = f[i].getType();
        map.put(entry.attributeName, entry);
    }
    fieldMap = map.values();
}
```

As you will have noted, `FieldMapEntry` is underlined, and there is a light bulb.
Click the light bulb and then select Create Class FieldMapEntry. In the new class
file, add the following to the attributes and then save:

```
String attributeName;
Class attributeType;
```

The `save()` method is straightforward: After making sure it's been passed the right
kind of object, it calls the method `object2Vector()` to convert the object to a vector
and then uses `FilePersistenceServices` to write it to a file. Notice that you use
className as the filename:

```
public boolean save(Object o, int key)
{
    boolean success = false;
    if (!(classType.isInstance(o)))
    {
        return success;
    }

    Vector v = object2Vector(o);

    if (v.size() > 0)
    {
        success = FilePersistenceServices.write(className, key, v);
    }
    return success;
}
```

The heavy lifting is in the `object2Vector()` method, which uses the field map to
pull values out of the value object in order and put them in the vector:

```
Vector object2Vector(Object o)
{
    Vector v = new Vector();
    for (Iterator iter = fieldMap.iterator(); iter.hasNext();)
    {
        FieldMapEntry entry = (FieldMapEntry) iter.next();
        Field field;
        try
        {
            field = classType.getField(entry.attributeName);
            v.addElement(field.get(o));
        }
        catch (NoSuchFieldException e)
```

```
            {
            }
        catch (IllegalAccessException e)
            {
            }
        }
    return v;
    }
```

Note that you preserve the type of each object when you add it to the vector; it's the responsibility of `FilePersistenceServices` to perform whatever conversion is needed in order to store it.

The complementary method to `save()` is `get()`. It receives a vector from `FilePersistenceServices` and uses it to populate an object that it instantiates on the fly. Because every element of the vector is a string, you need to call a method, `typeMap()`, to convert it to the appropriate type (which you determine from the `fieldMap`):

```
public Object get(int key)
{
    Object o = null;
    try
    {
        Vector v = FilePersistenceServices.read(className, key);
        Field field = null;
        int size;
        if (v != null
            && (size = fieldMap.size()) == v.size()
            && size > 0)
        {
            o = classType.newInstance();
            Iterator vIter = v.iterator();
            Iterator mIter = fieldMap.iterator();
            for (int i = 0; i < size; i++)
            {
                FieldMapEntry entry = (FieldMapEntry) mIter.next();
                field = classType.getField(entry.attributeName);
                Class fieldType = field.getType();
                Object value = typeMap(fieldType, vIter.next());
                field.set(o, value);
            }
        }
    }
    catch (Exception e)
    {
        logger.warn(e);
    }
    return o;
}
```

Here is the typeMap() method. To keep things simple, only a few data types are supported: String, double for all floating-point values, long for large integer values, and integer for small integer values:

```
Object typeMap(Class type, Object val)
{
    Object o = null;
    String typeName = type.getName();
    String valString = val.toString();
    if (typeName.equals("java.lang.String"))
    {
        if (((String)valString).equals("null"))
        {
            o = null;
        }
        else
        {
            o = valString;
        }
    }
    else if (typeName.equals("long"))
    {
        o = Long.valueOf(valString);
    }
    else if (typeName.equals("int"))
    {
        o = Integer.valueOf(valString);
    }
    else if (typeName.equals("double"))
    {
        o = Double.valueOf(valString);
    }
    return o;
}
```

The remaining methods are not very interesting:

```
public boolean update(Object o, int key)
{
    boolean success = false;
    if (!(classType.isInstance(o)))
    {
        return success;
    }
    Vector v = object2Vector(o);
    if (v.size() > 0)
    {
        success = FilePersistenceServices.write(className, key, v);
    }
    return success;
}
```

```
    public boolean delete(int key)
    {
        return FilePersistenceServices.delete(className, key);
    }
    public boolean dropObjectTable()
    {
        return FilePersistenceServices.drop(className);
    }
}
```

What's missing

In the interest of brevity, we've skipped over several things. First, no unit tests for the helper methods in `ObjectManager` have been shown. Also, you may have noticed that you included a log4j logger in the class; it would be a good idea to use this logger to at least log some of the exceptions, for example.

Also note that exception handling is spotty and not very robust; this isn't a good practice. There is a large general problem here: Many of the errors you might get from the classloader, from the filesystem, and potentially from the database, should not be passed to the client, but instead mapped to a set of your own exceptions that represent a restatement of these more specific errors in persistence terms. For example, rather than return a boolean error, `FilePersistence-Services.write()` might instead throw one of several errors, such as `Duplicate-RecordException` or `StoreDoesNotExist`, which your `ObjectManager update()` method could pass up to the client.

Other errors/exceptions (such as those thrown by the `Field` methods) are more problematic, because they shouldn't occur if your code is correct. This isn't something you can explain to the client as a persistence-related failure; it's a general application failure, and it should probably be fatal. You should log the exception information and return some sort of generic `ObjectManager` exception, such as `ClassMappingFailure`, which is returned when the code can't get or save an object for reasons unrelated to the underlying data store.

Dealing properly with exceptions in Java is an important topic, but it's beyond the scope of the basic design and coding issues we're considering here.

4.3 *Refactoring*

Agile programming methods recommend that you build applications incrementally, adding a small, well-defined set of features at a time. This approach has the consequence that you are occasionally forced to reconsider previous design choices to meet new requirements. Often, before implementing a new requirement, you need to change the structure of your code to accommodate the new features. At the same time, you must be careful not to break the existing features. Changing the structure of a program without changing the functionality is called *refactoring*.

A number of development tools help make refactoring code painless and foolproof enough that you can consider refactoring a valid and valuable tool in the development process, rather than a penalty you must pay for lack of foresight. You've seen one tool that supports refactoring indirectly: the exhaustive unit testing provided by a test framework such as JUnit. Having a comprehensive set of tests is a safety net that allows you to aggressively change your code, because it ensures that you have the same functionality before and after the alterations. Another important tool is automated refactoring. Eclipse has excellent support for refactoring and currently provides over a dozen different types of common, well-defined transformations. We'll look at a couple in detail in this section; all refactorings are covered with examples in Appendix A.

4.3.1 *Renaming a class*

One relatively simple refactoring is to change the names of methods, fields, classes, or packages to better reflect a new design. Renaming a method, field, or class by hand can be tedious when it is referenced in many other methods or classes, and using an editor to find and replace all instances can be error-prone; because editors are not semantically aware, they can't distinguish between like-named methods from different classes, for example. In the case of changing a package name, not only must changes be made to the files in the package, and files in other packages that reference it, but the directory structure must be changed as well. As you'll see, Eclipse's Rename feature handles each of these tasks adroitly.

In the previous section you developed an `ObjectManager` that directly uses your file-based persistence class. Now, suppose you add another class like `ObjectManager` that uses a database for persistence instead of files. If you call it `DatabaseObjectManager`, then for consistency shouldn't you also call your old `ObjectManager` something like `FileObjectManager`? This approach also lets you re-use the name `ObjectManager` for an abstract class (or, alternatively, an interface) that specifies what methods concrete classes such as `FileObjectManager` and `DatabaseObjectManager` must provide. Figure 4.5 gives an overview of this new extended object model.

The first refactoring you'll do is changing the name of the `ObjectManager` class. Notice that because factoring is specifically a JDT feature, Refactor appears in the Eclipse main menu only if you are in the Java perspective. So, in the Java perspective, do the following:

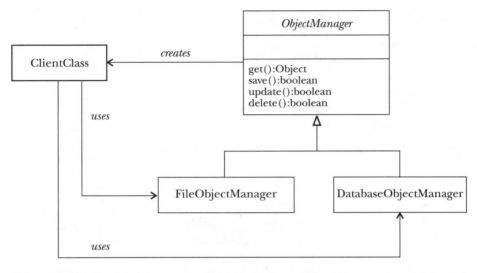

Figure 4.5   The Persistence component's class diagram. `ObjectManager` is an abstract class created from the concrete `FileObjectManager` class.

1   Select ObjectManager.java in the Package Explorer view. Right-click on it and select Refactor→Rename from the context menu.

2   The Rename dialog box opens. Enter the new name: **FileObjectManager**.

The Rename dialog box also presents a number of options; one, allowing you to change references, is selected by default. If you don't leave this option checked, Eclipse will change only the class name, the filename, and the names of any constructors (see figure 4.6). It will not change references to the class in this or any other file. (The other options, to change references in Javadoc comments, comments, and strings aren't applicable for your code.)

If you check the option to rename references and click OK, in addition to changing the class name, filename, and constructor names, Eclipse will also change references in this and any other files, including your unit tests in Object-ManagerTest.java. Although this is a great feature, you don't want that to happen now, because you're going to create an abstract `ObjectManager` class and you want the unit tests to use this abstract class; you want to hide specific concrete classes from your unit tests and other client classes.

To change all references in one file but not the other, you need to exercise more precise control over what refactoring will do:

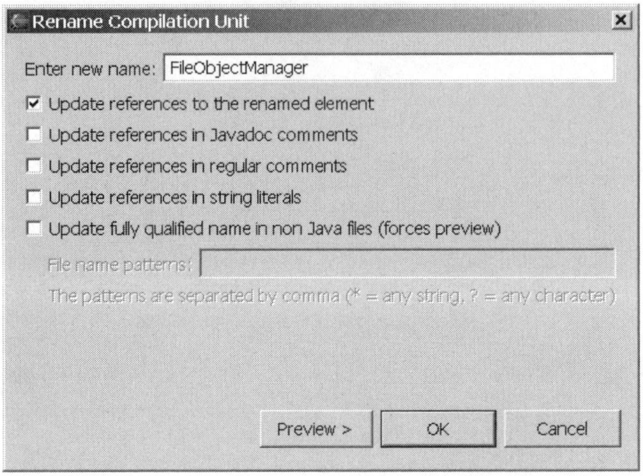

Figure 4.6
Renaming a class. When renaming an element such as a class name, Eclipse can automatically update all references to the element in the project.

1 Click the Preview button to open a dialog box that allows you to view and veto individual changes (see figure 4.7). The top section of the box contains a list of the proposed changes with a checkbox for each change, so you can choose which to accept. Two files (ObjectManager.java and Object-ManagerTest.java) are listed, plus the proposed filename change.

2 Clicking on a file displays a side-by-side comparison of the file before and after the proposed changes in the bottom section of the dialog box. You only want to accept the changes to the `ObjectManager` class and filename, so make sure the boxes next to ObjectManager.java and the Rename proposal are both checked and the box next to ObjectManagerTest.java is not.

3 Click OK to perform the refactoring.

After refactoring, it's important to review the results carefully, because only one refactoring can be undone and this is possible only if no other changes are made to the affected files. (Considering that Eclipse may need to make a large number of changes to a large number of files, it's somewhat surprising that it's even possible to undo a refactoring.) Note that undoing a refactoring is slightly different than a regular undo; you must select Refactor→Undo from the main menu (rather than Edit→Undo).

There are now problems with the unit tests, of course, as indicated by the red X next to `ObjectManagerTest` in the Package Explorer; this is the case because the tests refer to a now–nonexistent `ObjectManager` class—but you expected that problem, and you'll fix it soon.

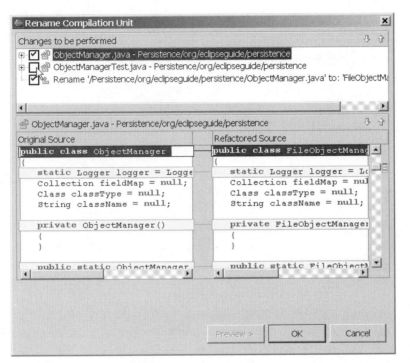

Figure 4.7
The Rename preview. Here you can approve or veto individual changes.

4.3.2 *Extracting an interface*

Eclipse doesn't offer an option to create an abstract class based on an existing concrete class, but it does provide a refactoring that extracts an interface from an existing class. This refactoring is close to what you want, so you'll begin with it. After making sure `FileObjectManager` is selected in the Package Explorer, do the following:

1. Select Refactor→Extract Interface from the main menu.
2. Enter **ObjectManager** as the interface name.
3. Select the checkbox to change references to the class `FileObjectManager` into references to the interface.
4. Eclipse presents a list of methods you can add to the interface—all the public methods in the class. Click Select All on the right side of the screen (see figure 4.8) and then click Preview.

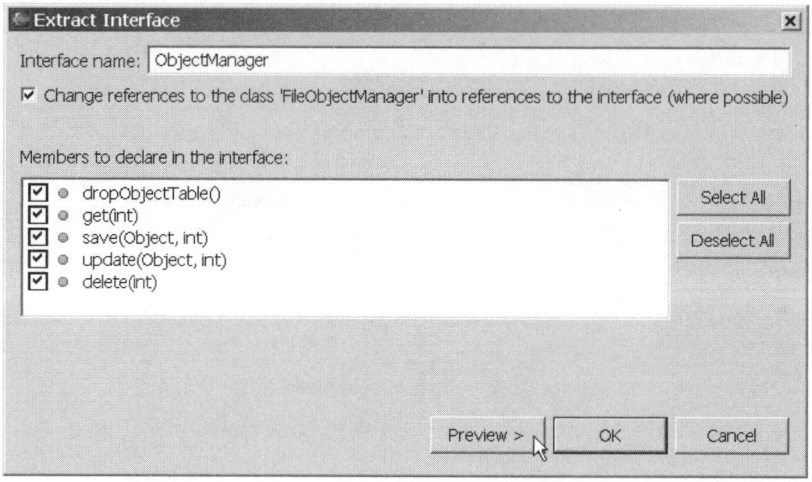

Figure 4.8 Extracting an interface from a class. Here you select the methods to be included in the interface.

Again, this approach gives you the opportunity to view individual changes and veto them case by case. In particular, you might wonder what references to `File-ObjectManager` Eclipse proposes to change to `ObjectManager`. It turns out that Eclipse only wants to change the return value of the `createObjectManager()` method to `ObjectManager`, which is what you want; click OK to accept the refactoring.

Now you need to manually change the interface to an abstract class and add a static factory method. (You need an abstract class rather than an interface because you can't have a static method in an interface.) This is the interface Eclipse produced:

```
public interface ObjectManager
{
    boolean dropObjectTable();
    Object get(int key);
    boolean save(Object o, int key);
    boolean update(Object o, int key);
    boolean delete(int key);
}
```

And this is how you change it to an abstract class with a factory method:

```
public abstract class ObjectManager
{
    abstract boolean dropObjectTable();
    abstract Object get(int key);
    abstract boolean save(Object o, int key);
```

```
    abstract boolean update(Object o, int key);
    abstract boolean delete(int key);

    public static ObjectManager createObjectManager(Class type)
    {
        return FileObjectManager.createObjectManager(type);
    }
}
```

This always returns a `FileObjectManager` object, because that's the only concrete persistence class implemented so far. But you can imagine that as you implement other types, such as a `DatabaseObjectManager`, there would be a switch mechanism of some sort—perhaps based on a configuration file—that determines which type to instantiate.

The final change you need to make is to the `FileObjectManager` class; you need to change from implementing an interface to extending an abstract class. This is the corrected class declaration:

```
public class FileObjectManager extends ObjectManager
```

After you make this change to FileObjectManager.java and save it, ObjectManagerTest.java should no longer be marked with a red X. You're ready for the moment of truth: It's time to run the unit tests again. And, of course, they pass with the big green JUnit stripe.

4.3.3 *Future refactoring*

As we've mentioned several times, in the future you may want to use a database to provide persistence. What you've done here—making `ObjectManager` abstract and providing a specialized `FileObjectManager` subclass that uses file-based persistence—is a step in the right direction.

A better alternative, however, would be to provide an abstract class or interface for the persistence layer, perhaps called `PersistenceServices`, and leave `ObjectManager` as a concrete class that uses this interface. This approach makes for a simpler object model—which would become obvious when you began to implement the database version of `ObjectManager` and realized it had a lot in common with what the file-based version needs to do, especially if the databased persistence object also represented data using vectors.

Creating an abstract `PersistenceServices` class would require making the methods in `FilePersistenceServices` nonstatic, because you can't specify abstract static methods in either an interface or an abstract class. Doing so also lets you simplify your method signatures, because instead of passing the table or filename with each method call, the name can be an attribute of the `Persistence-Services` object, which can be set when the object is instantiated.

When `PersistenceServices` is subclassed, each concrete subclass can manage whatever resources it needs in the manner that is most appropriate for the type of persistence it's using. Whereas a file-based implementation may want to open and close files with each method call, a database implementation may want to keep database connections open for the life of the object, because database connections are expensive in terms of time and resources. If you expect to have a lot of objects, you may want the objects to share a single connection or use a pool of connections. These are all details the `ObjectManager` layer doesn't need to know about.

Until you need to provide database-based persistence, correcting this design flaw doesn't provide any clear benefit—and, in fact, doing so may have a cost in terms of performance and complexity. For now, make a note of it and defer making the change until it's necessary.

4.4 *Summary*

Eclipse provides many tools for working with source code. After importing source code and extending the sample application you began in chapter 3, you've seen one of the consequences of implementing features incrementally: the need to change your design to accommodate the new features. At the same time, the functionality must not change, because it must still support your old features. This process of changing design without changing functionality is called refactoring.

One of Eclipse's greatest strengths is its support for refactoring, with over a dozen types of automated refactorings available. We took a look at two here: renaming a class and extracting an interface. In both cases, Eclipse can make semantically aware changes to all affected files in the project; but by using the refactoring preview feature, you can review and select the changes it applies.

In extending and refactoring the persistence project, you once again saw the benefits of unit testing. Because your classes have unit tests to verify that they are working, you can be confident when coding and fearless when refactoring. This fearlessness extends to the design decisions you make: You can concentrate on making decisions based on simplicity and short-term needs, because you know you can easily and safely correct shortcomings as your project grows.

Building with Ant

In this chapter...

- What a formal build process can accomplish
- Organizing a project for a formal build
- A retrospective look at an old standard: Make
- The new standard Java build tool: Ant
- Ant projects, targets, tasks, and properties
- A sample Ant build file

Although programming—writing and compiling code—is the most obvious part of software development, it's by no means the only part. Testing is important too, as you've seen. But many more steps are necessary to deliver a finished product: You also need to document, package, and deploy the software you develop. Performing these steps by hand is tedious, repetitious, and error-prone. This is a task begging to be automated.

5.1   *The need for an official build process*

You've gone through the cycle of testing and coding, testing and coding, and you finally have something people can actually use. How do you deliver that functionality?

The next step is to identify in concrete terms what the product is. Is it an API? An executable with a GUI? Is it packaged in a JAR file? Does it include documentation? Sample code? Does all of this get burned onto a CD-ROM, or is it zipped together for delivery over the Internet?

Once you've made a decision, Eclipse makes it easy to perform any of these steps. As soon you save your source code, everything is compiled; you can run the unit tests, use the Javadoc wizard to create the documentation (assuming that's adequate for your audience), export your classes to a JAR, and put the whole thing into a zip file. This process is fine if you want to informally give a friend the latest version of the game you've been working on, but you wouldn't want to do this if you're delivering a product to a client or to the public. There are just too many things that can go wrong: forgetting to refresh the source tree, forgetting to run unit tests, overlooking a failed test, selecting the wrong options when generating the Javadoc, forgetting to copy over resource files, mistyping the zip filename—the possible problems are endless. These issues become even more complicated when more than one person is working on a project.

One of the main purposes for a separate build process is reproducibility. Ideally, you want to be able to type one command at a workstation; the machine should then churn its hard disk for awhile and, in the end (if all goes well and unit tests have run successfully), spit out a zip file or CD-ROM. Reducing human intervention decreases the likelihood of error in the build process, and any errors that do occur can be permanently corrected.

Because it's difficult to automate processes using a GUI, build procedures are usually designed to be run at a command prompt. That way they can be kicked off by a simple command or automatically at a specific time of day, using the UNIX or Linux `chron` command or the Windows `at` command.

One additional benefit of using an external, independent build process is that it can free developers to use the development environment of their choice. This may not seem like a critical requirement, but forcing developers—especially the most experienced ones—to abandon the tools they've mastered can be detrimental to productivity.

5.1.1 *Creating the build directory structure*

Before we look at specific build tools, let's consider the task of planning and organizing the build process, using the file-based Persistence component you began to develop in previous chapters as an example. Imagine that for some reason you (or your management) have decided it's a viable product. The first step in formalizing the build process is to organize your files so a clear separation exists between source files and other resources, temporary files, and deliverables.

Separating the source and build directories

When you created the Persistence project, you didn't stop to consider the directory structure. You simply accepted the default that Eclipse gave you: The project folder is equivalent to the source folder. This structure results in source files, test classes, and compiled class files being mixed together:

```
C:\ECLIPSE\WORKSPACE\PERSISTENCE
|
+---org
    +---eclipseguide
        +---astronomy
        |       *.java
        |       *.class
        |
        +---persistence
                *.java
                *.class
```

Because there is no clean separation between source files and generated files, deleting the generated files before starting a new build would require you to delete certain files in certain directories. That's not difficult, but it's much easier and more reliable to use a separate directory so you can blow away the whole directory before starting a build—thus avoiding the possibility of outdated files accidentally contaminating the build and causing mysterious problems.

A better design than having the source files and class files mixed is to create separate directories for each within the project folder, like this:

```
C:\ECLIPSE\WORKSPACE\PERSISTENCE
+---bin
```

```
|     +---org
|          +---eclipseguide
|               +---astronomy
|               |         *.class
|               |
|               +---persistence
|                         *.class
|
+---src
     +---org
          +---eclipseguide
               +---astronomy
               |         *.java
               |
               +---persistence
                         *.java
```

Eclipse is quite flexible about a project's structure. If you had known from the beginning that you needed a formal build process, you could have specified src as the source directory when you created the project. Instead of accepting the defaults and clicking Finish immediately after entering the project name, you could've clicked Next to move to another dialog box that provides the option of adding a new source folder; clicking Add Folder on the Source page lets you create the new source folder name (see figure 5.1).

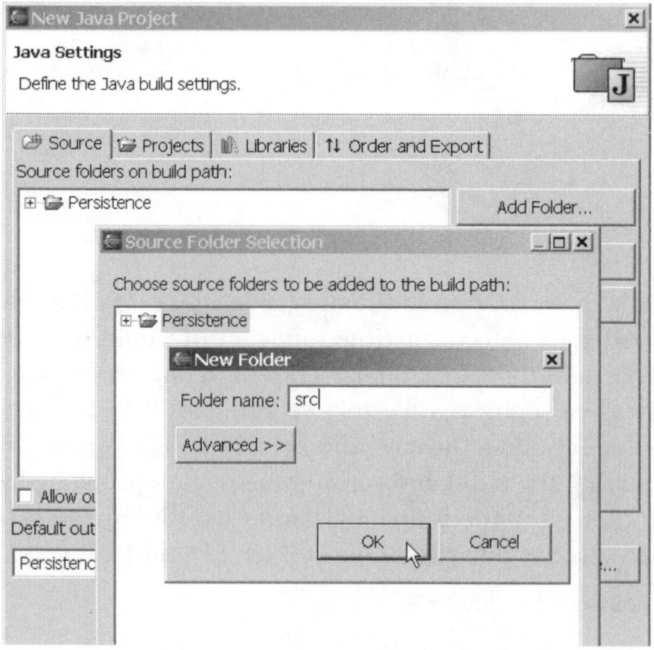

Figure 5.1
New source folder. You can define a separate source folder when creating a new project, and Eclipse will offer to create a separate output folder.

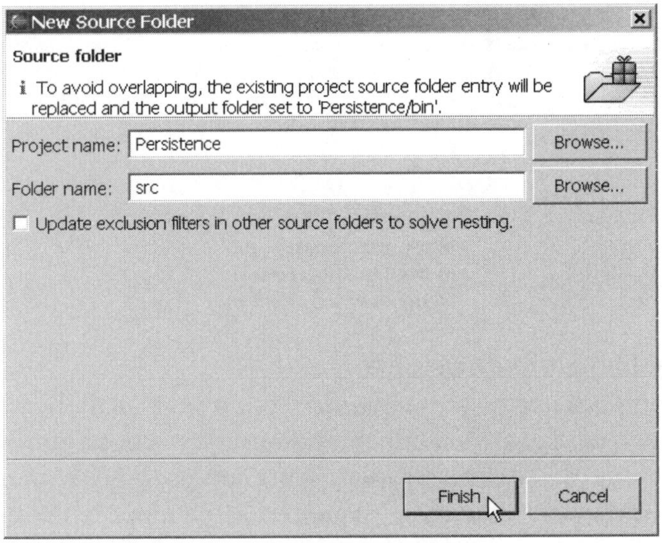

Figure 5.2
Adding a source folder to an existing project. Eclipse automatically creates a new output directory.

But not to worry—you don't have to go back all the way to square one and start over. Agile development is all about incremental changes—taking things a step at a time and never doing anything the hard way if you don't have a good reason. As you might expect by now, Eclipse makes this change a breeze. All you need to do is create a new source folder (src) and move your source code into it. Eclipse takes care of creating the new separate output folder (bin) and its subdirectories. (In addition, when you build with Eclipse it puts all the class files in the right place.)

In the Java perspective, right-click on the project name (Persistence), select New→Source Folder, and enter **src** as the folder name (see figure 5.2). Notice the note at the top of the dialog box: *To avoid overlapping, the existing project source folder entry will be replaced and the output folder set to 'Persistence/bin'*. This is exactly what you want, so click Finish. (If you don't want to name the output folder bin— if you want to name it build, for example—you can change the default later by selecting Properties→Java Build Path→Source from the project's context menu.)

Now, to move the source files into the new src directory, right-click on the top-level source directory (org), select Refactor→Move, and select the src directory under Persistence (see figure 5.3). (You can safely disregard the warning that references to the default package will not be updated.) Or—even easier— click on the org folder in the Package Explorer and drag-and-drop it onto the src folder.

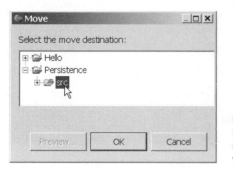

Figure 5.3
More refactoring:
moving the source tree
to the new src directory

Creating a directory for distributable files

Creating a separate output directory is a good start, but it's not all there is to delivering software. A bunch of classes in a bunch of directories is not a product. You need to decide which pieces to deliver to your clients and package them neatly in a JAR file. Any good software product also requires documentation; because your product is a software component intended for developers, it will probably be sufficient to include just the Javadoc. (We've been lax about including Javadoc comments in the code in the previous chapters, a situation you should think about fixing—but for now, let's leave it as an exercise for you, the reader.)

Assume the Persistence component is the only part that is of general interest. You need to separate the persistence classes from the astronomy classes and test classes. Keeping in mind that you still need to build all the classes in order to test the persistence classes, a good way to do that is to create yet another directory, where you gather together just the pieces that make up the deliverable product. You'll call it dist (for *distribution*), and it will include the Persistence component JAR file and the Javadoc:

```
C:\ECLIPSE\WORKSPACE\PERSISTENCE
+---bin
+---src
+---dist
    +---doc
    |       *.html
    +---lib
            persistence.jar
```

Eclipse automatically keeps the class files in the bin directory up to date as you make changes to the Java source files in the src directory, but you need to do everything beyond that. As mentioned, you can do this manually using Eclipse; but for reliability and consistency, it's much better to automate the process using a build tool.

5.2 *Make: A retrospective*

Before we consider Ant, the de facto Java standard build tool, let's take a quick retrospective look at the traditional build tool—Make—to provide some perspective on the advantages offered by Ant. Many different flavors of Make are available, including various UNIX varieties, Gnu make, and Microsoft's NMAKE (New Make), but they are all more or less alike.

Make accepts a make file that contains a list of targets, each followed by a script that is run when the target is invoked. (By default, Make looks for a file with a specific name, usually makefile, but you can usually explicitly specify a file with another name on the command line.) A target and its commands are sometimes called *rules*.

A target can have *dependencies*; these are other targets that must be evaluated first. When Make runs, it finds the first target's dependencies to see if they exist. If the target is a file, and the dependency is a file, Make compares their timestamps; if the dependency is newer than the target, Make executes the rule to bring the target up to date.

This is the general format of a make file rule:

```
TARGET:  dependencies ...
    commands
    ...
```

A small, simple make file to build an application from two C source files might look like this:

```
myapp.exe: main.obj aux.obj
    link main.obj aux.obj -o myapp.exe

main.obj: main.c
    cc main.c

aux.obj: aux.c
    cc aux.c
```

If you aren't familiar with C, don't worry about the details, except to note that two steps are normally required to create an executable program from C source code: compiling source code into object files (the .obj files in this example) and linking all the object files into a single executable file (the .exe file in this example).

The first target, myapp.exe, is a rule that prescribes how to build the executable by linking together two object files. By default, the first target in a make file is the one Make executes. Make evaluates the chain of dependencies to make sure everything in this chain is up to date. The first time you run this make file, it first compiles aux.obj and main.obj, and then builds the application myapp.exe by linking them.

If you then change aux.c and run Make again, main.obj will still be up to date. So, Make only compiles aux.obj before linking the new aux.obj and the existing main.obj to make myapp.exe.

In addition to a target that builds the application, you can add other targets that perform special tasks, such as removing all the generated files in order to force a complete rebuild. You might add these two targets at the end of the file:

```
CLEANALL: CLEAN
    del *.exe
    echo Deleted executable

CLEAN:
    del *.obj
    echo Deleted object files
```

Because they do not identify a real object to build, targets like these are usually called *pseudo-targets*. These two targets are not included in the default target's chain of dependencies, so the only way to execute them is to explicitly specify them on the command line when Make is started.

Specifying CLEAN deletes the intermediate object files. Specifying CLEANALL first deletes the intermediate object files because of its dependency on the CLEAN target, and then deletes the executable—a dependency used in this way has an effect similar to a method call.

In addition to rules, a make file can also make variable assignments and access environment variables. Because this section is only intended to provide an overview of Make, we won't cover these topics here.

As this example demonstrates, Make provides several significant advantages over a batch file or shell script:

- *Make reduces build time*—Make can evaluate which build targets are older than their sources and build only those that are necessary to bring the build targets up to date. When you're working with a large system that may take a long time to compile completely, this can be a huge timesaver.

- *Make is declarative*—You don't need to tell it how to build, step by step. Instead, you only specify what needs to be built as a set of related goals. The order of execution, or flow of control, is not normally explicitly stated—although you can use pseudo-targets to perform a sequence of commands in order, when necessary.

■ *Make is extensible*— Commands are executed by the shell, so if you need any functionality that shell commands don't provide, you can write your own utility programs—using C, for example.

Aside from some quirks (like the finicky distinction between spaces and tabs that's driven every Make user nuts at least once), Make is a perfectly serviceable build tool. But the example was in C for a reason: to better demonstrate Make's ability to build incrementally. Using Make with Java doesn't provide nearly as much benefit in this regard, because most Java compilers automatically evaluate dependencies. Suppose you have a Java class, `HelloWorld`:

```
// HelloWorld.java

public class HelloWorld
{
    public static void main(String[] args)
    {
        Printer printer = new Printer();
        printer.out("Hello, world");
    }
}
```

It uses this Java class, `Printer`:

```
// Printer.java

public class Printer
{
    void out(String s)
    {
        System.out.println(s);
    }
}
```

You can compile these two classes with a single command:

```
javac HelloWorld.java
```

The Java compiler, javac, evaluates HelloWorld.java and determines that it uses Printer.java. If Printer.java hasn't been compiled yet, or if Printer.java is newer than Printer.class, javac compiles Printer.java. In other words, this single command is essentially equivalent to the first part of the make file you saw earlier for the C program—that is, the first three rules that specify how to build the application.

Because incremental compilation is the biggest advantage Make offers over a batch file or shell script, the ability of the Java compiler to determine dependencies may seem to diminish the need for a Make utility in Java development. It doesn't eliminate the need for some type of build tool altogether, however, because object types aren't always known at compile time. Classes that contain a collection cause problems because a collection can hold any type of object; for example, a `Company` class may contain a `Vector` of `Employee`, but the compiler may not be able to determine this at compile time. If you want reliable incremental compilation, you still need some type of build utility.

Finally, and most importantly, compilation isn't the only thing build tools do. As shown in the example, traditional make files typically also perform simple housekeeping tasks such as deleting old files. Java projects often require additional steps, such as generating Javadocs and archiving packages.

5.3 *The new Java standard: Ant*

Using a traditional Make utility for Java has one serious drawback: These utilities execute shell commands, which differ from platform to platform. This fact defeats one of the main reasons for developing in Java: the ability to write once and run anywhere. The obvious solution is to implement a tool comparable to Make in Java. Ant, an open-source build tool from the Apache Software Foundation, takes this approach. In addition to being a better cross-platform solution than Make, Ant updates the syntax of the make files to use a standard declarative format: XML. For these reasons, Ant has quickly become the standard build tool for Java and has been tightly integrated with Eclipse; this integration includes a special editor for working with Ant build scripts.

NOTE   Up until now, because you've been using Eclipse to compile your Java source code, you haven't needed a separate Java compiler. As noted previously, Eclipse includes its own special, incremental compiler; all you need to add is a Java Runtime Environment (JRE).

To build using Ant, especially at a command prompt, you need to have a complete Java Development Kit (JDK). Depending on your platform, you may have a number of choices; but at a minimum you should use JDK 1.3.x (preferably JDK 1.4.x), whether from Sun or another company. Make sure the JDK's bin directory precedes any other directories that contain a JRE in your `PATH` environment variable. Also make sure to remove any references to old JDKs and JREs from your `CLASSPATH` environment variable. You don't need to include any of the JDK's standard directories or JARs in the classpath, because these are located automatically based on the executables for the Java compiler (javac.exe in Windows) and Java virtual machine (java.exe).

5.3.1 *A very brief introduction to XML*

XML (Extensible Markup Language) has become the *lingua franca* for representing data of all kinds, so you've probably encountered it for one or another of its many uses. If you haven't used it, or if you've used it but aren't familiar with some of its terminology, this introduction will make it easier to follow the discussion of Ant build files that follows.

XML has its roots in SGML (Standard Generalized Markup Language), like HTML (Hypertext Markup Language), which it resembles closely. Both use tags, which are identifiers enclosed by angle brackets, like this:

```
<TITLE>
```

But there are a few important differences between HTML and XML. Because HTML is designed to serve a limited purpose—describing how to display data as a web page—it defines a standard set of tags. TITLE is a valid HTML tag, but ORDER_NUMBER is not. XML, on the other hand, is open-ended. The application you are using defines which tags are valid. In an application that uses XML to represent data in an online store, ORDER_NUMBER may very well be a valid tag.

A tag such as <TITLE> is called an *opening tag*; it marks the beginning of a piece of data. Opening tags generally require a closing tag, which are tags having the same name as the opening tag, preceded by a slash. The following defines the title for a web page:

```
<TITLE>A very brief introduction to XML</TITLE>
```

HTML is pretty lax about syntax. Opening tags don't always require closing tags. For example, the <P> tag is supposed to mark the beginning of a paragraph, and </P> should mark the end. In practice, however, you can simply use <P> to indicate spacing between sections of text on a web page. This is absolutely not true for XML—every opening tag *must* have a closing tag.

Sometimes in HTML you can get away with improperly nesting opening and closing tags; in XML you cannot. The following is invalid XML because of improper nesting:

```
<B><I>This is not valid in XML!</B></I>
```

One last difference between HTML and XML is that XML is case sensitive. In HTML, <TITLE> and <title> are both valid and equivalent. In XML, depending on the application, they are both potentially valid, but are not equivalent.

Elements and attributes

An opening tag and a closing tag define an *element*. Every XML document must have one root element (or document element) that encloses all other elements in the document.

The opening tag of each element may contain additional information about the element in the form of name-value pairs called *attributes*. The value must always be enclosed by quotation marks. Depending on the tag, certain attributes may be required or may be optional. For example, Ant defines a `<target>` tag for identifying build targets. The `target` tag accepts several attributes, such as `depends` and `description`, but only the `name` attribute is required:

```
<target name="Compile" depends="Init">
   <!-- do compilation stuff here-->
</target>
```

(Notice that, as in HTML, you can insert comments beginning with `<!--` and ending with `-->`.)

Sometimes elements don't have any content. For example, the Ant tag to run a Java program, `<java>`, allows you to specify all the information you need as attributes. If you have a class file Hello.class, you can run it inside a target like this:

```
<target name="SayHello">
   <java classname="Hello.class"></java>
</target>
```

As a shortcut, empty elements like the one formed here with the `<java>` and `</java>` tags can be written by ending the opening tag with `/>` and omitting the closing tag. The following is equivalent to the previous example:

```
<target name="SayHello">
   <java classname="Hello.class"/>
</target>
```

Representing data with attributes and nested elements

Both attributes (such as the `name` attribute in the `<target>` tag) and nested elements (such as the text enclosed by the `<TITLE>` and `</TITLE>` tags) can be used to specify data in XML. The choice is left up to the application. Sometimes the application supports both formats and leaves the choice to the user. Ant sometimes provides attributes for selecting single options (like `classname`) and nested elements for more complex things, such as sets of files, or combinations of paths and individual files.

The `<java>` tag, to take one example, lets you specify the classpath using either an attribute or nested elements. You can use the `classpath` attribute to set the path to the predefined property `java.class.path` (which Ant sets to your environment's classpath) like this:

```
<target name="SayHello">
    <java classname="Hello.class" classpath="${java.class.path}"/>
</target>
```

Or, equivalently, you can use a nested `classpath` element:

```
<target name="SayHello">
    <java classname="Hello.class">
        <classpath path="${java.class.path}"/>
    </java>
</target>
```

Nested elements can in turn contain nested elements. For example, you can replace the `path` attribute in the `<classpath>` tag with one or more nested `<pathelement>` elements, as well as other elements:

```
<target name="SayHello">
    <java classname="Hello.class">
        <classpath>
            <pathelement path="${java.class.path}"/>
            <pathelement location="c:/junit/lib/junit.jar"/>
        </classpath>
    </java>
</target>
```

Sometimes Ant and other applications that use XML can be confusing because they allow multiple options like this. Nested elements provide much more flexibility than attributes, which are limited to a single value. When a single value is all you need, it's convenient to have the option to use the simpler syntax.

Extending options this way, by using nested elements, exemplifies the main problem with XML: its verbosity. Each bit of data that you include adds another pair of opening and closing tags. Fortunately (or by necessity), most XML-based applications provide tools that make the job of writing XML easier.

5.3.2 *A simple Ant example*

Before delving into the details of Ant and its build scripts, let's look at the mechanics of using Ant inside Eclipse with the Ant equivalent of "Hello, world." The same way that Make automatically assumes a make file's name is makefile, Ant assumes the name of the build script is build.xml. As with Make, you can override this default by specifying a file explicitly when you invoke Ant. However, it's most common to stick to this convention, especially because Eclipse also assumes the build script's name is build.xml and automatically opens files with this name using the Ant script editor. (You can change this behavior by going to the Window→

Preferences→Workbench→File Associations dialog, but it's not a good idea to change it so that it opens all .xml files—in the future, you'll encounter other types of XML files that will benefit from other specialized editors. If you don't want to call your build script build.xml, enter each individual build script name in the File Associations dialog box to use the Ant editor with it.)

Create the build file by right-clicking on an existing project, such as your old Hello project, and selecting New→File from the context menu. Enter **build.xml** as the filename and click Done. If the editor does not automatically open build.xml for you, then double-click on the build.xml file. Type in the following:

```
<?xml version="1.0"?>
<project name="Hello" default="print message">
   <target name="print message">
      <echo message="Hello from Ant!"/>
   </target>
</project>
```

The Ant editor isn't as helpful as the Java editor, but it provides some basic conveniences, such as a code-completion feature you can invoke at any time by pressing Ctrl-Space. Outside of a tag, it shows you available tags; inside of a tag, it shows you the valid attributes for that tag. (The latter feature is especially useful because the attribute names are not consistent from tag to tag.) The Ant editor also provides syntax highlighting and an outline view.

To run this script, first save it, and then right-click on build.xml in the Package Explorer and select Run Ant from the context menu. Doing so opens a dialog box with the default target selected (see figure 5.4).

Click the Run button at the bottom of the dialog box to produce the following output in Eclipse's Console view:

```
Buildfile: c:\eclipse\workspace\hello\build.xml

print message:
     [echo] Hello from Ant!
BUILD SUCCESSFUL
Total time: 2 seconds
```

Running Ant outside of Eclipse

In addition to running this Ant script inside Eclipse, you can use the build script outside of Eclipse. To do so, you need to download and install the complete Ant distribution from the Apache Software Foundation (the Ant project can be found at http://ant.apache.org). If the current version is not identical (or at least compatible) with the one included with Eclipse, you need to either locate and download the older version or upgrade the version in Eclipse.

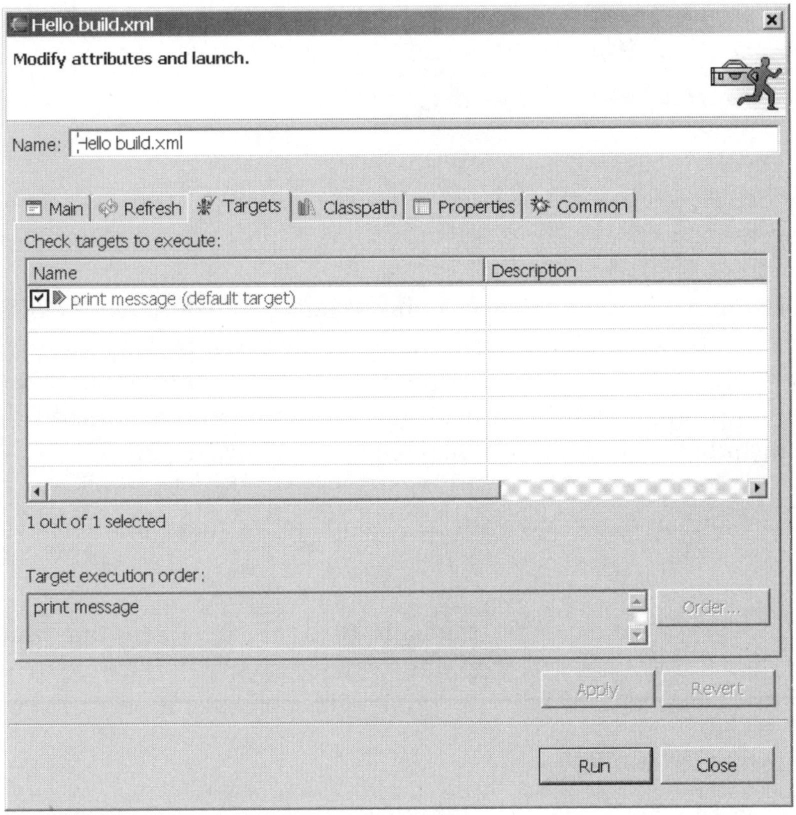

**Figure 5.4
Running an Ant
file. The default
target is
automatically
selected.**

To upgrade the version of Ant that Eclipse uses, select Window→Preferences→
Ant→Runtime from the main Eclipse menu. Then, remove the classpaths for 1.5.2
ant.jar and optional.jar, and add the paths to the new versions of those JAR files.

After downloading the appropriate zip file (or tar file) for your system and
decompressing it, add the bin directory to your path and the lib directory to your
classpath. If you installed Ant on Windows in the c:\jakarta-ant-1.5.2 directory,
you can add these directories to your path by typing the following commands at
a command prompt:

```
SET PATH=c:\jakarta-ant-1.5.2\bin;%PATH%
SET CLASSPATH=c:\jakarta-ant-1.5.2\lib;%CLASSPATH%
```

This change will affect only the current command-prompt window. A more permanent option is to modify these settings using the Systems applet in the Control Panel on Windows NT, 2000, or XP, or the autoexec.bat file on Windows 95, 98,
or ME; any command-prompt window you open afterward will be set properly

for Ant. Having performed either of these steps, you can now change to the c:\eclipse\workspace\Hello directory and run Ant by entering **ant**:

```
C:\eclipse\workspace\Hello>ant
Buildfile: build.xml

print message:
     [echo] Hello from Ant!

BUILD SUCCESSFUL
Total time: 2 seconds
```

If you are using Ant for your project's official build but continue to use Eclipse's automatic compilation for your day-to-day work (which is pretty convenient), you may want to occasionally run the `ant` build either inside Eclipse or, preferably, at the command prompt. Doing so will ensure you haven't broken the official build and have included in the build any files you've recently created.

Before you tackle building a larger build file, let's first look in more detail at the important tags and attributes that make up an Ant make file.

5.3.3 *Projects*

The required document element for a build file is the `<project>` tag, which must specify a default target, and which optionally may also specify a name. In addition, it may identify a base directory for the project. Its attributes appear in table 5.1.

Table 5.1 `<project>` tag attributes

Attribute	Description	Required?
default	The default target to run	Yes
name	The name of the project	No
basedir	The base directory	No
description	A description of the project	No

The `basedir` attribute lets you specify either a relative or an absolute path; in either case, this is resolved to an absolute path that other tags can use. Using a relative path is preferable, however, because it makes the build more portable. Other developers' machines and the official build machine don't have to be set up just like yours in order to run a build. The following example sets the `basedir` attribute to the current path (.)—which is to say, the directory in which build.xml is located:

```
<project name="Hello" default="compile" basedir="."
     description="Hello, world build file">
```

The `<project>` tag can have the following nested elements:

- `<description>`—You can include a description of the project as a nested element instead of an attribute if you want it to extend over more than one line. Having a description is highly recommended.
- `<target>`—Described in the section 5.3.4.
- `<property>`—Described in section 5.3.6.

5.3.4 Targets

A target is a container tag for a task or a group of related tasks and can be compared (roughly) to a method. It can have the attributes listed in table 5.2.

Table 5.2 `<target>` tag attributes

Attribute	Description	Required?
name	The name of the target	Yes
depends	List of dependencies	No
if	Execute only if the specified property is set	No
unless	Execute only if the specified property is not set	No
description	Description of the target	No

Giving your main targets a description is a good idea because Ant provides a `-projecthelp` option that lists all targets with `description` as main targets. This option makes your build file self-documenting to a degree.

Here's an example:

```
<target name="compile" depends="init"
    description="Compile all sources">
```

5.3.5 Tasks

If a target can be compared to a method, a task can be compared to a statement in that method. Ant provides numerous tasks—more than 100, if you count both core and optional tasks.

One of the great advantages of Ant is that it takes care of cross-platform issues transparently. For example, in UNIX, a file path is written using forward slashes (/) between directories and filenames, whereas in Windows, a backslash (\) is used. In Ant, you can use either, and Ant will provide the correct format for the system you are using. The same is true of classpaths. In UNIX, the different paths on a classpath are separated by a colon, whereas in Windows a semicolon is used; you can use either one, and leave the rest to Ant.

The following are a few common tasks together with a basic set of their attributes—enough to understand the examples and to begin writing your own build files. For a complete description of all tasks and their options, refer to the Ant documentation available at http://ant.apache.org/manual/index.html.

<buildnumber>

This task reads the build number from a file, sets the property `build.number` to that number, and writes the value `build.number`+1 back to the file. It has the single attribute listed in table 5.3.

Table 5.3   `<buildnumber>` task attribute

Attribute	Description	Required?
file	File to read (default: `build.number`)	No

Here's an example:

```
<buildnumber file="buildnum.txt"/>
```

<copy>

This task copies a file or set of files. To copy a single file, use the `file` attribute. To copy multiple files, use a nested `<fileset>` element instead.

Normally, this task performs the copy only if the destination file doesn't exist or if the destination file is older than the source, but you can override this behavior by setting the `overwrite` attribute to `true`. The `<copy>` task's attributes are listed in table 5.4.

Table 5.4   `<copy>` task attributes

Attribute	Description	Required?
file	Source filename	Yes, unless `<fileset>` is used instead
tofile	Target filename	Yes, unless `todir` is used instead
todir	Destination directory	Yes, if more than one file is being copied
overwrite	Overwrite newer destination files	No; default=`false`
includeEmptyDirs	Copy empty directories	No; default=`true`
failonerror	Stop build if file not found	No; default=`true`
verbose	List files copied	No; default=`false`

A `<fileset>` nested element can be used to specify more than one file. (See section 5.3.7.)

Here's an example:

```
<copy file="log4j.properties" todir="bin"/>
```

<delete>

This task deletes a file, a set of files, or a directory. To delete a single file, use the `file` attribute. To delete multiple files, use a nested `<fileset>` element instead. To delete a directory, use the `directory` attribute. The `<delete>` task's attributes are listed in table 5.5.

Table 5.5 `<delete>` task attributes

Attribute	Description	Required?
file	File to delete	Yes, unless `dir` or nested `<fileset>` is used instead
dir	Directory to delete	Yes, unless `file` or nested `<fileset>` is used instead
verbose	List files deleted	No; default=`false`
failonerror	Stop build on error	No; default=`true`
includeEmptyDirs	Delete directories when using `<fileset>`	No; default=`false`

A `<fileset>` nested element can be used to specify more than one file. (See section 5.3.7.)

Here are two examples:

```
<delete file="ant.log"/>
<delete dir="temp"/>
```

<echo>

This task writes a message to System.out (the default), a file, a log, or a listener. Its attributes are listed in table 5.6.

Table 5.6 `<echo>` task attributes

Attribute	Description	Required?
message	Text to write	Yes, unless text is used as the element content
file	Output file	No
append	Append to (rather than overwrite) file	No; default=`false`

Here are some examples:

```
<echo message="Hello"/>
<echo>
    This is a message from Ant.
</echo>
```

<jar>

This task compresses a set of files into a JAR file. Options allowed are shown in table 5.7.

Table 5.7   `<jar>` task attributes

Attribute	Description	Required?
destfile	JAR filename	Yes
basedir	Base directory of files to be JARred	No
includes	Pattern list of files to be JARred	No
excludes	Pattern list of files to be excluded	No

Pattern lists are comma- or space-separated lists of file-matching patterns. `<jar>` accepts the same nested elements as a `<fileset>` element. (See section 5.3.7.)

Here are some examples:

```
<jar destfile="dist/persistence.jar"
     basedir="bin"
     includes=
  "org/eclipseguide/persistence/**, org/eclipseguide/astronomy/**"
     excludes="*Test*.class"/>

<jar destfile="dist/persistence.jar">
   <include name="**/*.class"/>
   <exclude name="**/*Test*"/>
</jar>
```

<java>

The `java` task invokes a class using a JVM. By default, the JVM is the same one Ant is using. If you are calling a stable custom build utility, this can save time; but if you are using it to run untested code, you risk crashing not just the bad code but the build process as well. You can invoke a new JVM by setting the `fork` option to `true`. The task's attributes are listed in table 5.8.

Table 5.8 `<java>` **task attributes**

Attribute	Description	Required?
classname	Name of the class to run	Yes, unless `jar` is specified instead
jar	Name of the executable JAR to run	Yes, unless `classname` is specified instead
classpath	Classpath to use	No
fork	Runs the class or JAR with a new JVM	No; default=`false`
failonerror	Stop the build if an error occurs	No; default=`false`
output	Output file	No
append	Append or overwrite the default file	No

The `<java>` task can use these nested elements:

- `<classpath>`—Can be used instead of the `classpath` attribute
- `<arg>`—Can be used to specify command-line arguments

Here are some examples:

```
<java classname="HelloWorld"/>
<java classname="Add" classpath="${basedir}/bin">
   <arg value="100"/>
   <arg value="200"/>
</java>
```

<javac>

This task compiles a Java file or set of files. It has a complex set of options (see table 5.9), but it's easier to use than you might expect, because many of the options are provided to allow you to control compiler options. The Ant-specific options are oriented toward working with directories, rather than a single Java file, which makes building projects easier.

Table 5.9 `<javac>` **task attributes**

Attribute	Description	Required?
srcdir	Base of the source tree	Yes, unless nested `<src>` is used instead
destdir	Output directory	No
includes	Pattern list of files to compile	No; default=include all .java files
excludes	Pattern list of files to ignore	No
classpath	Classpath to use	No
debug	Include debug information	No; default=`false`

Table 5.9   `<javac>` **task attributes** *(continued)*

Attribute	Description	Required?
`optimize`	Use optimization	No; default=`false`
`verbose`	Provide verbose output	No
`failonerror`	Stop the build if an error occurs	No, default=`true`

By default, `<javac>` will not compile with debug information. This behavior is usually appropriate for a build that will be used in a production environment. You may wish to have a way of turning this option on or off, perhaps by having separate targets for a debug build and a release build.

`<javac>` can have these nested elements:

- `<classpath>`—Can be used instead of the `classpath` attribute.

- `<jar>`—Accepts the same nested elements as a `<fileset>` element. (See section 5.3.7.)

Here are some examples:

```
<javac srcdir="src" destdir="bin"/>

<javac srcdir="${basedir}" destdir="bin"
      includes="org/eclipseguide/persistence/**"
      excludes="**/*Test*">
  <classpath>
    <pathelement path="${java.class.path}"/>
    <pathelement location=
        "D:/log4j/jakarta-log4j-1.2.8/dist/lib/log4j-1.2.8.jar"/>
  </classpath>
</javac>
```

<javadoc>

The `<javadoc>` task produces Javadoc from Java source files. The options for selecting which files to include should be familiar from the `jar` and `java` tasks. The principal options specific to `javadoc` specify which Javadoc comments to include; see table 5.10.

The `<javadoc>` task can have these nested elements:

- `<fileset>`—Can be used to select sets of files. Ant automatically adds `**/*.java` to each set.

- `<packageset>`—Can be used to select directories. The directory path is assumed to correspond to the package name.

- `<classpath>`—Can be used to set the classpath.

Table 5.10 `<javadoc>` task attributes

Attribute	Description	Required?
sourcepath	Base of the source tree	Yes, unless `sourcefiles` or `sourcepathref` is specified instead
sourcepathref	Reference to a path structure specifying the base of the source tree	Yes, unless `sourcepath` or `sourcefiles` is specified instead
sourcefiles	Comma-separated list of source files	Yes, unless `sourcepath` or `sourcepathref` is specified instead
destdir	Destination directory	Yes, unless `doclet` has been specified
classpath	Classpath	No
public	Show only public classes and members	No
protected	Show protected and public classes and members	No; default=`true`
package	Show package, protected, and public classes and members	No
private	Show all classes and members	No
version	Include `@version` information	No
use	Include `@use` information	No
author	Include `@author` information	No
failonerror	Stop the build process on error	No; default=`true`

Here are some examples:

```
<javadoc destdir="doctest"
      sourcefiles=
          "src/org/eclipseguide/persistence/ObjectManager.java"/>

<javadoc destdir="doc"
      author="true"
      version="true"
      use="true"
      package="true">
   <fileset dir="${src}/org/eclipseguide/astronomy/">
      <include name="**/*.java"/>
      <exclude name="**/*Test*"/>
   </fileset>
   <classpath>
      <pathelement path="${java.class.path}"/>
      <pathelement location=
          "D:/log4j/jakarta-log4j-1.2.8/dist/lib/log4j-1.2.8.jar"/>
   </classpath>
</javadoc>
```

<mkdir>

This task creates a directory. It has the single attribute listed in table 5.11. If a nested directory is specified, the parent directories are also created if necessary.

Table 5.11 `<mkdir>` task attribute

Attribute	Description	Required?
dir	The directory to create	Yes

Here's an example:

```
<mkdir dir="dist/doc"/>
```

<tstamp>

This task sets the properties DSTAMP, TSTAMP, and TODAY. A nested element, `<format>`, can be used to change their formats using the patterns defined by the Java `SimpleDateFormat` class, but by default, these formats are as follows:

```
DSTAMP    yyyyMMdd
TSTAMP    hhmm
TODAY     MMM dd yyyy
```

Please refer to the Ant documentation for more information about `<tstamp>` and the `<format>` element.

5.3.6 *Properties*

Properties are name-value pairs you can use as symbolic constants inside a build file. The value of a property is referenced by enclosing the name with ${ and }. For example, if a property `junit_home` has been defined with the value `D:/junit/junit3.8.1`, you can use this property to add the junit JAR file to the classpath when you compile:

```
<javac srcdir="src" destdir="bin"
       classpath="${junit_home}/lib/junit.jar"/>
```

Properties can be defined several ways:

- Predefined by Ant
- On the Ant command line, using the -D option (for example, `ant -Djunit_home=D:/junit/junit3.8.1`)
- Inside a build file with the `<property>` task

The properties predefined by Ant include all the standard Java system properties, including the following:

- java.class.path
- os.name
- os.version
- user.name
- user.home

Properties specific to Ant include:

- ant.version
- ant.file
- ant.project.name

<property> and the name attribute

The most common way to set properties inside an Ant build file is to use the `<property>` task with the `name` attribute and either the `value` attribute or the `location` attribute. The `value` attribute is used to set a literal value:

```
<property name="jar_name" value="myapp.jar"/>
<property name="company" value="Acme Industrial Software Inc."/>
```

The `location` attribute is used to set an absolute path or filename. If you specify a relative path, Ant converts it to an absolute path by assuming it is relative to the `basedir` property and resolving it. In addition, file path separators are converted to the appropriate character (/, \, or :) for the platform. For example:

```
<property name="junit_home"  location="D:/junit/junit3.8.1"/>
<property name="src" location="src"/>
```

The first of these examples is left unchanged (except for the file path separators), because it represents an absolute path. The second example is expanded, because it's a relative path; assuming the `basedir` is c:\eclipse\workspace\persistence, ${src} will evaluate to c:\eclipse\workspace\persistence\src.

<property> and the file attribute

You can use the `file` attribute to read properties from a file using the standard Java properties file format. Assume that a file build.properties exists in the base directory or on the classpath:

```
# build.properties
junit_home=D:/junit/junit3.8.1
log4j_home=D:/log4j/jakarta-log4j-1.2.8
```

You can read these properties using the following tag:

```
<property file="build.properties"/>
```

<property> and the environment attribute

It's also possible to read environment variables as properties by assigning a prefix to the environment using the `environment` attribute The following assigns the prefix `myenv` to the environment:

```
<property environment="myenv"/>
```

After this, you can access environment variables as properties with the prefix `myenv`. For example, if `JUNIT_HOME` is defined in the environment, you can obtain its value with `${myenv.JUNIT_HOME}`.

You should use this technique with caution, because it's not supported on all operating systems. Also, property names in Ant are case sensitive even if the underlying operating system treats them as though they are case insensitive. This behavior can cause problems for the unwary in versions of Windows that preserve the case of environment variables but perform comparisons in a case-insensitive way.

For example, if a variable `CLASSPATH` already exists with the value `c:\mylibs`, the following will not create a new variable `classpath` nor change the case of the existing `CLASSPATH`:

```
set classpath=%classpath%;c:\anotherlib
```

Rather, this will update the existing `CLASSPATH` to `c:\mylibs;c\anotherlib`. To ensure that the case is what you expect, you can unset the variable and redefine it. The following lines at the command prompt or in a batch file force `classpath` to lowercase:

```
set tmpvar=%classpath%
set classpath=
set classpath=%tmpvar%;c:\anotherlib
```

If you're going to set environment variables for Ant using Windows batch files, you should consider programming defensively in this way—especially if the batch files will be used on other systems.

5.3.7 *File sets and path structures*

Because of the nature of Ant, many Ant tasks, such as `<javac>` and `<jar>`, require that you specify paths and sets of files. Ant provides elements that allow you to specify them with as much as detail as necessary, either by explicitly selecting files and directories or by using patterns to include or exclude groups of files or directories. Because these elements don't do anything, but rather refer to objects, they are called *types*. You use only two types here: `<fileset>` and `<classpath>`.

<fileset>

As the name suggests, the `<fileset>` element allows you to select sets of files. The only required attribute for a `<fileset>` is the base directory. If you don't specify anything else, all files in this directory and its subdirectories are selected—with the exception of certain temporary files and files generated by certain tools such as CVS. (Such files generally have unusual filenames that begin or end with a tilde [~] or #, or have specific names and extensions such as CVS and SCCS; it's unlikely they will coincide with the typical files in a typical project. For a complete list of the patterns Ant uses for its default excludes, please refer to the Ant documentation.)

You can also select or exclude files that match patterns you provide. Patterns can include the following wildcards:

?	Match any one character
*	Match zero or more characters
**	Match zero or more directories

Consider these two common examples: You can use the pattern `**/*.java` with the `include` attribute to include all Java source files, and you can use the pattern `**/*Test*` with the `exclude` attribute to exclude test cases. Together, they specify all Java files except test cases.

The `<fileset>` element's attributes are listed in table 5.12.

Table 5.12   `<fileset>` element attributes

Attribute	Description	Required?
dir	Base of the directory tree	Yes
defaultexcludes	Exclude common temporary and tool files	No; default=`true`
includes	Pattern list of files to include	No
excludes	Pattern list of files to exclude	No
followsymlinks	Use files specified by symbolic links	No

The `<include>` and `<exclude>` nested elements can be used in place of the attributes `includes` and `excludes`, respectively.

Here are some examples:

```
<fileset dir="src/org/eclipseguide/astronomy"
    includes="**/*.java"
    excludes="**/*Test*"/>

<fileset dir="src/org/eclipseguide/astronomy/">
   <include name="**/*.java"/>
   <exclude name="**/*Test*"/>
</fileset>
```

<classpath>

The <classpath> element allows you to specify which directories and JAR files an application should search for the classes it needs to run (or, in the case of the Java compiler, to compile). By default, Ant inherits the environment classpath, but you often need to add additional directories or JAR files for specific applications such as JUnit. Tasks that use a classpath provide a classpath attribute, but sometimes it's more convenient to use a <classpath> nested element—especially when the classpath is long. Paths can include multiple files or directories separated by either a semicolon or a colon; Ant will convert the separator to the appropriate character for the operating system.

Table 5.13 lists the <classpath> element's attributes.

Table 5.13   <classpath> element attributes

Attribute	Description	Required?
path	Colon- or semicolon-delimited path	No
location	Single file or directory	No

One or more <pathelement> elements can be nested to build a longer classpath. <pathelement> accepts the same attributes as <classpath>: path and location.

In addition, a <fileset> can be used to specify files.

Here are some examples:

```
<classpath path="bin"/>

<classpath>
   <pathelement path="${java.class.path}"/>
   <pathelement location="${junit_path}"/>
   <pathelement location="${log4j_path}"/>
</classpath>
```

5.3.8 *Additional Ant capabilities*

The basics covered here should be enough to get you started working with Ant, without being overwhelming. As you work more with Ant, you'll probably come across a situation—finding that you're using the same `<filelist>` over and over, perhaps—and wonder if there isn't a more elegant solution than cut and paste. In general, you'll find that almost nothing is impossible with Ant.

One way to reduce redundant code is to use references. Every element in Ant can be assigned an ID, for example; and (depending on the types of elements involved) you can use this ID to reference the element elsewhere in the build file. For example, you can assign an identifier to a `<classpath>` using the `id` attribute:

```
<classpath id="common_path">
    <pathelement path="${java.class.path}"/>
    <pathelement location="${junit_path}"/>
    <pathelement location="${log4j_path}"/>
</classpath>
```

This classpath can then be referenced elsewhere using the `refid` attribute:

```
<javac srcdir="src" destdir="bin">
    <classpath refid="common_path"/>
</javac>
```

Ant provides tasks and types that let you filter files as you copy, replacing tokens with text so you can include version information in your build—for example, by using the `<copy>` task with a `<filterset>`. It lets you select files based on complex criteria using selector types such as `<contains>`, `<date>`, and `<size>`. In the rare instances that Ant doesn't have a task to do something you need, you'll find it's pretty easy to write your own Ant tasks.

5.4 *A sample Ant build*

These are the principal steps your build process needs to do:

- Compile the application, placing the output in the bin directory
- Run unit tests in the bin directory
- Generate Javadoc, placing output in the dist/doc directory
- Package the application's class files in a JAR file in the dist directory

Because you may want to be able to do all these things individually, they will be separate targets in the Ant build file. Normally, however, you'll want to perform all these steps at one time, so you also need a target that has these separate targets as dependencies.

Often the separate targets have common setup requirements. You can create an initialization target that performs this setup, which the separate targets can then include as a dependency. Because this is a relatively simple example, all you'll do here is initialize the properties DSTAMP, TSTAMP, and TODAY to the current date and time by calling the tstamp task, and print the date and time.

5.4.1 *Creating the build file, build.xml*

To create the build file, follow these steps:

1 Right-click on Persistence in the Package Explorer and select New→File.
2 Enter **build.xml** in the New File dialog box and click Finish.

Before you define any targets, let's create some properties to use as symbolic constants, instead of littering the build file with hard-coded values. This approach will make the build file much easier to maintain. Here is the start of build.xml:

```
<?xml version="1.0"?>
<project name="Persistence" default="BuildAll" basedir=".">

    <description>
        Build file for persistence component,
        org.eclipseguide.persistence
    </description>

    <!-- Properties -->
    <property name="bin" location="bin"/>
    <property name="src" location="src"/>
    <property name="dist" location="dist"/>
    <property name="doc" location="${dist}/doc"/>
    <property name="jardir" location="${dist}/lib"/>
    <property name="jarfile" location="${jardir}/persistence.jar"/>
    <property name="logpropfile" value="log4j.properties"/>
    <property name="relpersistencepath" value=
        "org/eclipseguide/persistence"/>
    <property name="alltests" value=
        "org.eclipseguide.persistence.AllTests"/>
    <property name="junit_path" location=
        "D:/junit/junit3.8.1/junit.jar"/>
    <property name="log4j_path" location=
        "D:/log4j/jakarta-log4j-1.2.8/dist/lib/log4j-1.2.8.jar"/>
```

As you may expect, directories are generally specified using the location attribute, which Ant expands to the absolute path based on the project's base directory. There is one exception, relpersistencepath, which is a relative path you'll use in a couple of different contexts, starting at different directories; to keep Ant from turning it into an absolute path, you set it using the value attribute.

Notice also that you provide several classpaths explicitly. This isn't the best way—because it means the build will only work if a machine is set up in a particular way—but it is the easiest. You may wonder if you can instead use the `class-path` variables you set up in Eclipse. The answer is yes, it's possible to do so using a custom third-party Ant task; but that would mean you could only use this build process inside Eclipse. (If you don't mind this limitation, you can find the code for a custom Ant task that does this by searching the eclipse.tools newsgroup.)

Apart from this approach, especially when you build outside Eclipse at a command prompt, you can set these classpaths several other ways. The first, and probably easiest, is to add them to the environment's CLASSPATH variable using a command as follows:

```
set CLASSPATH=%CLASSPATH%;D:/junit/junit3.8.1/junit.jar;D:/log4j/
➥ jakarta-log4j-1.2.8/dist/lib/log4j-1.2.8.jar
```

The second is to pass them in to Ant on the command line using the -D option explicitly:

```
ant -Djunit_path=D:/junit/junit3.8.1/junit.jar -Dlog4j_path=
➥ D:/log4j/jakarta-log4j-1.2.8/dist/lib/log4j-1.2.8.jar
```

A bit better is to store these paths in their own environment variables. You can read them inside the build file using the following property tags:

```
<property environment="env"/>
<property name="junit_path" value="${env.JUNIT_HOME}/lib"/>
<property name="log4j_path" value="${env.LOG4J_HOME}/lib"/>
```

Or pass them in like this in the command line:

```
ant -Djunit_path=%JUNIT_HOME%\lib -Dlog4j_path=%LOG4J_HOME%\lib
```

Finally, another option is to use a properties file. You might have a build.properties file that includes the following lines:

```
junit_path=D:/junit/junit3.8.1/junit.jar
log4j_path=D:/log4j/jakarta-log4j-1.2.8/dist/lib/log4j-1.2.8.jar
```

To use the values in this file, include the following tag in build.xml:

```
<property file="build.properties"/>
```

After setting your properties, you include the main targets. You aren't required (as you are with Make) to put the default target first, but you will do so because it's a special target—it doesn't do anything except link together the other targets as a sequence of dependencies:

```
!-- Main targets -->
<target name="BuildAll"
       depends="-Init, -Prep, Compile, Test, Javadoc, Jar"
       description=
  "Complete rebuild. Calls Init, Compile, Test, Javadoc, Package">
    <echo message="Build complete."/>
</target>
```

You may want to include the rest of the main targets in the order they are called by `BuildAll`, in which case next the `Compile` target is next. Notice that by identifying the source directory as org, you can compile everything in both the `org.eclipseguide.persistence` and `org.eclipseguide.astronomy` packages, including unit tests. This is also a good place to copy over any resources that are required—in this case, the log4j.properties file:

```
<target name="Compile"
       depends="-Init"
       description="Compile all Java classes">
    <!-- Compile org.* (${src}) -->
    <javac srcdir="${src}" destdir="${bin}">
       <classpath>
           <pathelement path="${java.class.path}"/>
           <pathelement location="${junit_path}"/>
           <pathelement location="${log4j_path}"/>
       </classpath>
    </javac>
    <!-- Copy log4j.properties files -->
    <copy file="${logpropfile}" todir="${bin}"/>
    <echo message="Compiled."/>
</target>
```

The next target runs the unit tests. To run JUnit tests outside of Eclipse, you need to use one of the JUnit `TestRunner` classes. Because you want to be able to run this build file at a command prompt and log to a file, you need to use the text-based `TestRunner`, `junit.textui.TestRunner`, rather than the fancy graphical version. To launch it as a Java application, use Ant's `java` task. To make sure it doesn't crash and bring down your build process with it, you need to specify that it should use a separate JVM by setting the `fork` attribute to `true`. You must also provide a few other values as nested values, including the name of the test class `TestRunner` should run and the classpath it needs to use:

```
<target name="Test"
       depends="-Init"
       description="Run JUnit tests">
    <!-- Run test suite using separate JVM -->
    <java fork="yes" classname="junit.textui.TestRunner"
          taskname="junit" failonerror="true">
```

```
            <arg value="${alltests}"/>
            <classpath>
                <pathelement path="${java.class.path}"/>
                <pathelement location="${bin}"/>
                <pathelement location="${log4j_path}"/>
                <pathelement location="${junit_path}"/>
            </classpath>
        </java>
        <echo message="Tested!"/>
    </target>
```

The `Javadoc` target includes the most complicated task you're using here. First,
you specify the `packagename` and the Javadoc comments you want to include as
attributes in the `javadoc` tag. Then, because you want to exclude the unit tests,
you use a nested `<fileset>`, which in turn includes nested `<include>` and
`<exclude>` tags:

```
    <target name="Javadoc"
            depends="-Init"
            description="Create Javadoc">
        <!-- Javadoc, only for persistence classes -->
        <javadoc destdir="${doc}"
                author="true"
                version="true"
                use="true"
                package="true">
            <fileset dir="${src}/${relpersistencepath}">
                <include name="**/*.java"/>
                <exclude name="**/*Test*"/>
            </fileset>
            <classpath>
                <pathelement path="${java.class.path}"/>
                <pathelement location="${junit_path}"/>
                <pathelement location="${log4j_path}"/>
            </classpath>
        </javadoc>
        <echo message="Javadoc complete."/>
    </target>
```

The `Jar` target is fairly straightforward. As you did for the `javadoc` task, you use a
`<fileset>` here to specify that test files should be excluded. You also copy the
log4j.properties file, because users need it to use the Persistence package:

```
    <target name="Jar" depends="-Init">
        <!-- Jar for persistence classes -->
        <jar destfile="${jarfile}"
            basedir="${bin}"
                includes="${relpersistencepath}/*.class"
                excludes="**/*Test*"
        />
```

```
      <echo message="${bin}${relpersistencepath}/**"/>
      <!-- Copy log4j.properties to provide a sample -->
      <copy file="log4j.properties" todir="${dist}"/>
      <echo message="Packaging complete"/>
   </target>
```

Finally, you come to the internal targets: -Init and -Prep. (Their names begin with a hyphen to discourage their being used directly. This isn't a requirement, but it's a good practice because it makes your intentions explicit.) -Init prints out the time. It is a dependency of all the main targets:

```
   <!-- Internal targets -->
   <target name="-Init"> <!-- private target, omit description-->
      <!-- Set timestamp and print time -->
      <tstamp/>
      <echo message="Build time: ${TODAY} ${TSTAMP}"/>
   </target>
```

-Prep is called only when you specify the BuildAll target. It deletes everything—specifically, the bin and dist directories—from previous builds:

```
   <target name="-Prep">
      <!-- Delete output directories -->
      <delete dir="${bin}"/>
      <delete dir="${dist}"/>
      <delete dir="${jardir}"/>
      <!-- Create output directories -->
      <mkdir dir="${bin}"/>
      <mkdir dir="${dist}"/>
      <mkdir dir="${jardir}"/>
   </target>

</project>
```

5.4.2 Performing a build

Running the Ant build file is the same as before—right-click on build.xml and select Run Ant. But now you have more options, because you have more targets. Notice that the default target BuildAll is automatically selected, but you can select other targets using the checkboxes provided. You could, for example, select Compile and Javadoc (see figure 5.5).

You can also set the order in which these targets are executed by clicking the Order button to open the dialog box shown in figure 5.6. Click on a target and click Up or Down to change its place in the build order. Once you've made these selections, click OK and then click Run to start the build.

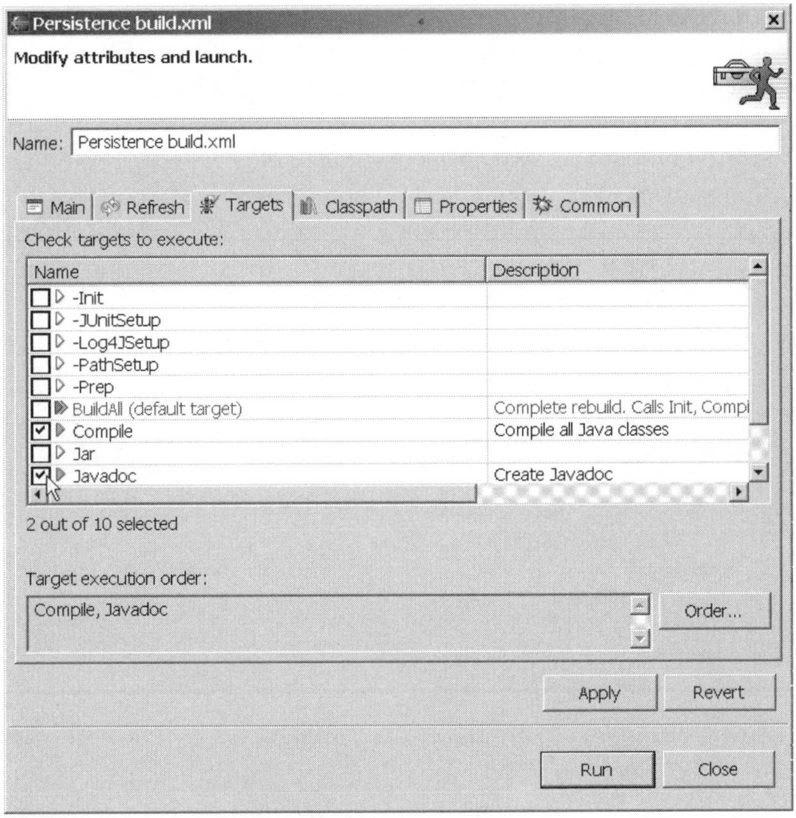

Figure 5.5
You can select targets explicitly in the Ant build dialog box.

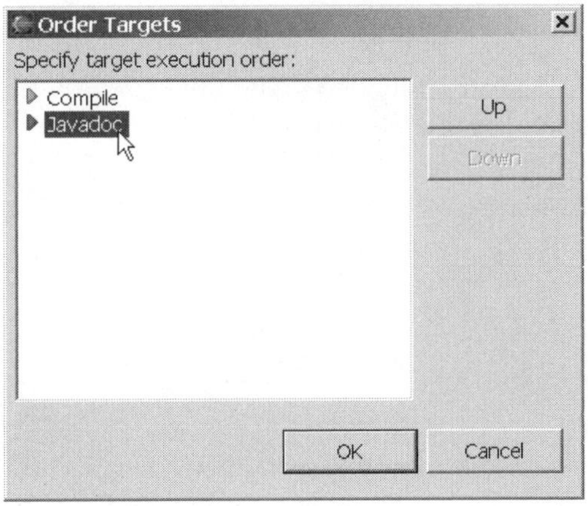

Figure 5.6
Order Targets dialog box. Here you can modify the order in which selected targets are executed.

As before, the output appears in the Console view. Different types of messages appear in different colors: Ant's status messages appear in blue, <echo> messages appear in orange, and errors—should there be any—appear in red.

If you've been careful and not made assumptions that are true only for the Eclipse environment (such as relying on classpath settings that are unique to your Eclipse configuration), you should also be able to build at a command prompt. To do this, type **ant** at a command prompt, as you did in the Hello example.

You've been careful to include descriptions for the project and the main targets, so others will find it easier to use your build file because they can type **ant -projecthelp** at the command prompt. Doing so produces the following output:

```
C:\eclipse\workspace\persistence>ant -projecthelp
Buildfile: build.xml

Build file for persistence component,
org.eclipseguide.persistence

Main targets:

 BuildAll  Complete rebuild. Calls Init, Compile, Test, Javadoc, Pa
 Compile   Compile all Java classes
 Javadoc   Create Javadoc
 Test    Run JUnit tests

Default target: BuildAll
```

There are some advantages to running the build file in Eclipse, however—especially when you are first developing it, because of the way Ant and Eclipse are integrated.

5.4.3 *Debugging the build*

Although Eclipse and Ant don't provide a debugger for Ant, they can help identify and correct the different types of errors that can occur. The first line of defense against errors, of course, is the syntax highlighting provided by the editor. In the Ant editor, comments are normally in red, text content in black, tag and attribute names in blue, and attribute values in green. If things are not the color they should be (such as several lines of code appearing in red), it's obvious, and you know something is wrong.

The Ant editor's syntax highlighting isn't intended to identify all errors, however; aside from missing quotation marks and closing tags on comments, you need to save your build file in order to have it parsed properly. After you save the file, errors are identified in the outline view next to the Ant editor and in the right margin of the editor. Clicking on the red box in the margin will take you to the error (see figure 5.7).

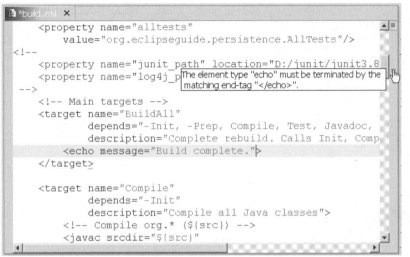

```
<property name="alltests"
    value="org.eclipseguide.persistence.AllTests"/>
<!--
<property name="junit_path" location="D:/junit/junit3.8
<property name="log4j_p
-->
<!-- Main targets -->
<target name="BuildAll"
        depends="-Init, -Prep, Compile, Test, Javadoc,
        description="Complete rebuild. Calls Init, Comp
        <echo message="Build complete.">
</target>

<target name="Compile"
        depends="-Init"
        description="Compile all Java classes">
    <!-- Compile org.* (${src}) -->
    <javac srcdir="${src}"
```

The element type "echo" must be terminated by the matching end-tag "</echo>".

Figure 5.7
The Ant editor identifies a syntax error in the right margin.

Some errors aren't identified until you run the build file. This can happen if you use an invalid attribute, for example. Suppose you remember that `<javac>` uses a superset of the attributes and nested elements `<fileset>` uses, and you write the following:

```
<javac dir="${src}" destdir="${bin}"/>
```

Actually it's almost true that `<javac>` has all the attributes `<fileset>` does; the only difference is that `<javac>` uses `srcdir` where `<fileset>` uses `<dir>`. Running the build file with this error causes the following problem to appear in the console window when Ant tries to execute this task:

```
[javac] BUILD FAILED: file:C:/eclipse/workspace/persistence/
    build.xml:38: The <javac> task doesn't support the "dir" attribute.
```

Clicking on this error also results in Ant attempting to take you to the offending code when you click on the text `[javac]`—this time successfully. (Clicking on any of the task names in square brackets, not just those with errors, will take you to the corresponding code in the build file.)

Of course, once you've ironed out a few initial problems with the build process and build file, build problems usually involve the source code. This is where Ant's integration with Eclipse really shines, because clicking on a compile error takes you to the source file where the problem occurred.

For example, assume you misspelled the variable name `type` as `typo` in the parameter list of the `createObjectManager()` method in the `FileObjectManager` class. When you compile, you get an unresolved symbol error (see figure 5.8).

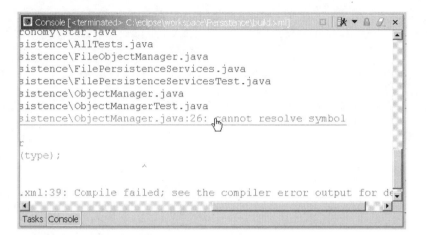

Figure 5.8 Ant console output. Clicking on an error takes you to the corresponding line in the source code.

Clicking on the error message in the console opens the corresponding source file in the editor, with the cursor on the line where the error occurred.

5.5 *Summary*

Team development introduces new requirements to the development process. One of these is the need to pull together the work of the different developers on the team and produce an official build. Because this should be a reproducible process, it isn't enough to simply produce an ad hoc build. The traditional way of performing an official build has been to use a command-line tool called Make; different versions of this tool with a wide range of capabilities exist on different platforms, but they all share a common format and slightly arcane syntax.

You could certainly use Make to build Java products, but Java has slightly different requirements than traditional programming languages such as C/C++; chief among them is that Java strives seriously to be a cross-platform language, which makes Make less than ideal. Ant has been developed in large part to fill this need. While remaining true to the spirit of Make, it also introduces several new features, including XML syntax and extensibility using Java classes.

Because of its integration with Eclipse, an Ant build process can be run both inside Eclipse and outside at the command prompt. Thus the official process, run at the command prompt, can be completely independent of Eclipse. This ability provides the additional benefit that developers can potentially use any development environment they are comfortable with.

Although team development makes a build tool a requirement, Ant's use isn't restricted to teams. Individuals can also benefit from using Ant, even in an environment such as Eclipse that compiles code automatically and provides easy-to-use wizards for producing Javadocs, JAR files, and zip files. A build process consisting of multiple steps, however easy, can be tedious and consequently error-prone, so spending a little time automating the process with Ant is an investment worth considering.

Source control with CVS

In this chapter...

- The benefits of source control
- Introduction to source control with CVS
- Using CVS with Eclipse
- The CVS workflow process: updating, synchronizing, and committing
- Creating and applying patches
- Creating versions and branches

Things that are nice to have when you're working solo become must-haves when you are working with other people. You've already seen this to an extent with regard to building a product. You can get away with an informal build-and-release process for a small project, but once a project becomes more complex and includes other developers, you need to use a build tool to keep things under control. The same considerations apply to the way you manage your source files. When you are working independently on a small project, making an occasional backup may be sufficient; but when more files and more people are involved, you need a source control tool to manage and coordinate the changes to your source code. In this chapter we'll discuss Eclipse's source control tool: Concurrent Versions System (CVS).

6.1 *The need for source control*

The need for source control becomes obvious as soon as two or more people begin working together on a single set of files. If they don't coordinate changes somehow, eventually two people will make changes to the same source file at nearly the same time, and one set of changes will get lost in the process—the last one in wins. The most rudimentary type of source control is to simply coordinate the team's development efforts through communication: email, meetings, and instant messaging.

Source control systems (also called *version control systems*) cannot (and should not) replace communication, but they help support and enhance the process of managing source code in two major ways: by controlling access to the source code, using a locking system to serialize access; and by keeping a history of the changes made to every file, so that previous versions can be reconstructed and retrieved.

The ability to preserve a file's complete history is a remarkably powerful feature. If a new bug is discovered, you can trace back through different revisions to see when the problem first appeared. Version control also allows you to enter comments when you check in your code, so you can see what was changed in the faulty revision. In addition, version control can help when you decide, after radically reworking a file, that you've gone down a wrong path, because you can easily revert to a previous revision. This functionality means it's safer to make the bold and aggressive changes that agile development sometimes requires.

Version control also allows you to branch a project and develop different versions of it in parallel. By branching when you officially release a product, you can fix bugs in the release branch while simultaneously continuing development on the main branch. (Note that if you fix a bug in the release branch, you will generally need to fix it in the development tree as well.)

It's important to recognize that these benefits of version control can be advantageous to anyone, not just developers working as part of a team. For instance, those working on documentation can obtain a history of all changes that have been made in any given period of time.

Revision history is important, but the most critical job a source control system performs is maintaining the integrity of the files. It does this by carefully controlling access and making sure changes don't get lost. It can do so in one of two ways:

- *Pessimistic locking*—Only one user can retrieve a modifiable copy of a file at one time. Until that user relinquishes control by checking in the changed code (or simply releasing the lock on the file), no one else can obtain a modifiable copy. However, it is still possible to obtain a read-only version.

- *Optimistic locking*—Users are free to obtain and modify files at any time. When a file is checked back in to the repository, the version control software makes sure conflicting changes haven't been checked in by someone else in the meantime. If the version control system can merge the changes automatically, it does so; otherwise it notifies you that you must resolve the conflict manually.

Pessimistic locking works against the goals of agile development, because it's difficult to make pervasive changes quickly. Eclipse's automatic refactoring feature makes it trivial to rename a method, because it can identify and update every reference to it in a project—but this isn't possible if the developer doesn't have the ability to modify all the necessary files.

Furthermore, a strong sense of ownership goes against the principles of agile programming, which encourages collective ownership of the code. Sharing ownership means sharing responsibility. If you see something wrong anywhere, you fix it. If you find code that is unnecessarily complex, you simplify it. If more people understand more of the code, bugs will find it harder to hide, and the overall design will improve.

As you might expect, given Eclipse's other support for agile methodology, the source control tool that comes integrated with Eclipse—CVS (Concurrent Versions System)—supports optimistic locking. By choosing Eclipse, you aren't limited to this way of working, however. You can set up CVS to use pessimistic locking, but doing so isn't recommended. If you need this ability, version control tools from other vendors that are designed to support strict code ownership are available, and they integrate equally seamlessly with Eclipse via plug-ins. Here, in keeping with the agile approach that Eclipse encourages, you'll use CVS.

In this chapter, we assume you have access to a CVS server and, possibly, an administrator who can tell you the information you need to connect. If you don't, see appendix B for instructions on setting up a CVS server.

6.2 *Using CVS with Eclipse*

Using CVS for source control, as previously discussed, has obvious benefits. The only problem is that it can have a steep learning curve if you need to learn the many commands and options necessary to use it via the command line. Using a dedicated GUI client can make this curve easier to overcome, but the learning process still adds enough complexity that it may not seem worth the trouble— especially if you don't have a clear need to use source control. Fortunately, Eclipse's seamless integration with CVS provides an efficient and fairly intuitive interface. Simple operations are not much more complicated than saving or opening files.

Managing the contributions of multiple developers, however, is more complicated. Eclipse makes CVS itself easy to use, but mastering the workflow process necessary to coordinate your efforts with those of the other team members requires more effort. Like learning to communicate effectively with your team members, it's just part of working together. In the sections that follow, we'll look at these two aspects of CVS—sharing a project and working together—using the sample code developed in previous chapters.

6.2.1 *Sharing a project with CVS*

Several steps are necessary to add a project to a CVS repository using Eclipse. The first step is to enter the information that Eclipse needs to connect to the CVS repository. This information is stored as an object called a *repository location*. After you create a repository location, you create a new module in CVS corresponding to your project and, finally, add your projects files to that module.

Creating a repository location

To create a repository location, you need to know the name of your CVS server, the path of the CVS repository on it, and the protocol it is using. You also must have a valid username and password for the server or the CVS repository. Follow these steps:

1   From the main menu, select Window→Open Perspective→Other.

2   A complete list of available perspectives appears. Select CVS Repository Exploring and click OK. (Eclipse will remember this selection, and this perspective will appear directly in the Open Perspective menu in the future.)

3   In the CVS Repositories view, right-click and select New→Repository Location.

4   Enter the name of the CVS server, the repository path, the username, and the password. Note that the repository path is the full path to where the CVS repository is located (for example, /usr/local/repository).

5   Choose the protocol. If you are using pserver, you obviously need to choose pserver. If you are using SSH, you need to choose extssh, which is Eclipse's built-in support for SSH1. (The third choice, ext, lets you use an external program for remote access. You might need to use this option if your SSH server supports only SSH2 and doesn't provide backward compatibility for SSH1, or if you are using an entirely different protocol. To set the external program to use, select Window→Preferences→Team→CVS→ Ext Connection Method.)

6   Unless you've changed the CVS port for some reason, leave Use Default Port checked. Also leave Validate Connection on Finish checked. (See figure 6.1.)

7   Click Finish. The information you entered is saved, and Eclipse connects to verify the information. Eclipse will notify you only if it is unable to connect to the server; otherwise, if everything goes OK, you'll see this repository location as a new entry in the CVS Repositories view.

Sharing the project

Once you've entered the parameters you need to connect to your repository, you can add your project to the CVS repository by following these steps:

1   Change to the Java perspective, right-click on the project, and select Team→Share Project.

2   In the Share Project with CVS Repository dialog box that appears, make sure Use Existing Repository Location is checked and the repository location you entered earlier for cvsserver is selected.

3   By default, the CVS module name is the same as the Eclipse project name. If this is OK, click Finish.

If your project name has spaces, you may want to consider using something different for the repository name, especially if other users will be using CVS from

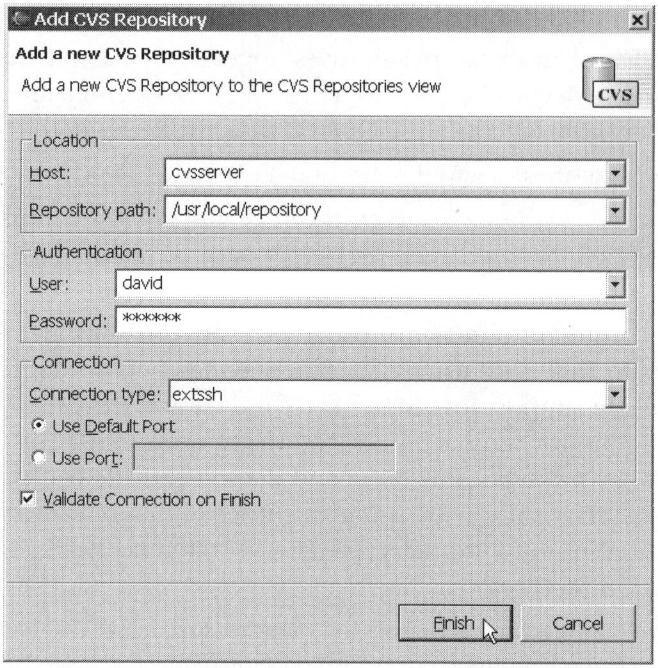

Figure 6.1
Entering repository information.
You may need to obtain some of
this information from your CVS
server's administrator.

the command line; otherwise they'll have to remember to enclose the repository name in quotes in commands. To use a different name, click Next instead of clicking Finish in the first Share Project dialog box. In the following dialog, check Use Specified Module Name, enter the new name, and click Finish.

NOTE   If attempting to share the project causes an error, indicating CVS was unable to create a directory, see the troubleshooting instructions in appendix B.

This step creates a module on the CVS server but doesn't add any files to it. Notice that Eclipse opens a CVS Synchronize view below the editor pane. This view normally lets you compare your local version of files with those in the repository; but it isn't a very interesting view when you first check in a project, because none of the files are in the repository. You'll see that it's very useful later, however, when there is something to compare.

At this point, you may wish to set Eclipse to display additional CVS information in the Package Explorer view, so you can see version and other information for shared files (see figure 6.2). The main indicators are a golden cylindrical

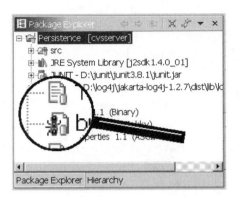

Figure 6.2
CVS label decorators indicate, among other things, which files and folders are under CVS version control, their current revision number, and whether they have been changed locally.

object decorating the resource's icon, indicating it's under version control; a greater-than sign indicating it has been changed locally; a version number; and the file type.

To display the CVS label decorators, follow these steps:

1 Select Windows→Preferences.

2 Go to Workbench→Label Decorations.

3 Check the CVS checkbox and click OK.

Another optional step you may want to take is to open a CVS console view so you can see the commands Eclipse sends CVS and the responses it receives. This view is useful if you know how to use CVS from the command line and want to see what's going on—especially when things go wrong. It can also be useful if you want to learn how to use CVS commands. To open a CVS console, select Window→Show View→Other→CVS→CVS Console from the main menu. Doing so opens another tabbed page in the existing console view.

Adding and committing files

It takes two steps to check a new file in to CVS:

1 Add the file to CVS.

2 Commit the file.

Adding the file doesn't actually cause the file to appear in CVS; it just sends a notification to CVS, which schedules the file for addition. The second step, committing the file, causes the file to appear in the CVS repository and be made available to other users.

Although you could go through your project file by file, adding individual files (by right-clicking on the file and using Team→Add to Version Control), it's much easier to let Eclipse do this for you. Eclipse lets you commit the entire project in (essentially) a single step, as follows:

1 Select the Persistence project.

2 Right-click and select Team→Commit.

Eclipse notifies you that a number of files have not yet been added to version control and asks if you want to add them. You can review and modify the list of files by clicking the Details button (see figure 6.3). Normally, Eclipse correctly identifies the files that should be placed under source, including, in this case, the Java source files in the src directory (that is, those in the `org.eclipseguide.persistence` and `org.eclipseguide.astronomy` packages), the Ant build file (build.xml), and the log4j configuration file (log4j.properties).

Two of the files Eclipse automatically includes are Eclipse specific: .project and .classpath. Whether you want to include them depends largely on the development environment the other developers on your team are using. If you've been careful to use classpath variables rather than hard-coded paths, sharing these files is helpful for the Eclipse developers on your team. On the other hand, if few developers are using Eclipse, these files (and potentially other similar files from other development environments) may be considered clutter by the rest of the team.

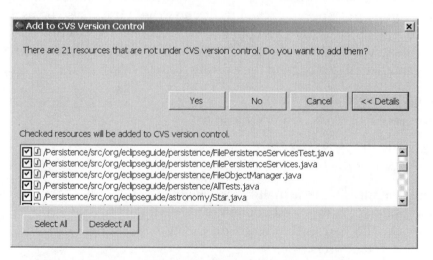

Figure 6.3   Adding files to version control. Clicking the Details button lets you review and change the files that Eclipse adds to CVS.

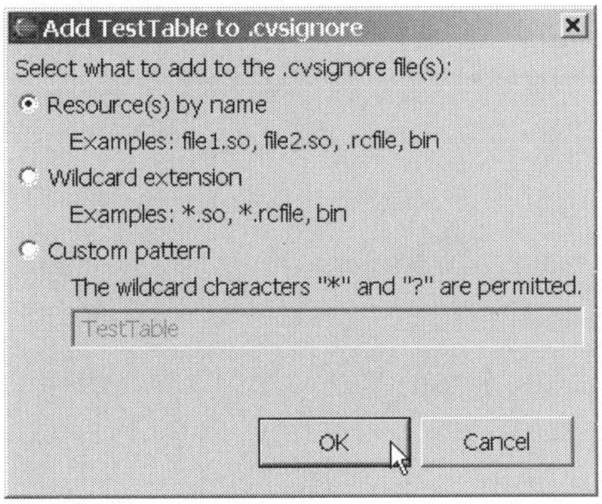

Figure 6.4
Files added to the .cvsignore file will not be checked into CVS. Here we selected a file by right-clicking on it in the Package Explorer and choosing Team→Add to .cvsignore.

You can tell CVS to ignore particular files by using a file called .cvsignore. Doing so is simple: Right-click on the file and select Team→Add to .cvsignore. A dialog appears that allows you to control what files should be ignored (see figure 6.4). The easiest option to use is Resource(s) by Name, which adds the file you've specified. (The figure shows a spurious `TestTable` table that resulted from some previous experimentation.) When you've done this, a new file called .cvsignore is generated, which you should add and commit to the CVS repository for this project. Note that you will need to swap to the Resource perspective to be able to see some files—for instance, those that start with a period (.), like .project.

You'll probably notice that Eclipse is smart enough to leave out the files and directories built by the build process, including bin and dist, and all the .class files and Javadoc files. After deciding what to do about .project and .classpath (and unchecking them if you decide not to check them in), do the following:

1 Click OK to add and commit the files to the CVS repository.

2 Enter a comment as prompted. There's usually not much to say the first time around, so **Initial revision** will suffice.

In the future, when you make revisions and are prompted for a comment, you should enter something more descriptive, of course—something that would provide a useful clue if something broke as a result of the changes you made, and that would help whoever needs to compile release notes for the next build.

Checking a project out of CVS

Let's change our point of view for a moment and see how a co-worker would obtain the project you've just made available in CVS. (Although sharing source code with team members is the most typical use of CVS, you might also do this if you want to be able to work on the code on different machines or operating systems.)

As before, the first step is to create a repository location; to do this, your co-worker switches to the Repository perspective and then follows these steps:

1 Right-click in the CVS Repository view.

2 Select New→Repository Location from the context menu.

3 Enter the host name, repository path, username, password, and connection type and click Finish.

The new repository location appears in the Repository view. Expanding the Repository location displays several entries: HEAD, Branches, and Versions. You are interested in HEAD—the main branch of development.

You can use CVS to maintain different branches of a project. Doing so is often necessary if you release a version of your project to the public, such as version 1.0. As you begin to work on adding new features for version 2.0, the code is not stable enough for release; so, if any serious bugs are discovered in version 1.0, they must be made to the original 1.0 code. CVS allows you to create a separate branch, starting with the original 1.0 code, so you can maintain this code separately from the new development continuing with the main branch, HEAD.

Versions differ from branches. A version is a snapshot of a branch at a given point in time—in other words, it's a particular set of file revisions. You need to mark versions that relate to official releases, obviously, but it's also convenient to mark versions corresponding to project milestones such as feature completion and beta releases. We'll examine versions, branches, and revisions in more detail in the sections that follow. To check out the current (and as it happens, only) Persistence project, do the following:

1 Expand the HEAD entry in the repository. Doing so shows the CVSROOT directory (CVS's administration directory) and any modules that have been checked in to this CVS repository, such as the Persistence project.

2 Select the Persistence module, right-click on it, and select Check Out As from the context menu.

3 After a short pause while Eclipse talks to the CVS server, a dialog appears that allows you to define what type of project you are going to check out. This is useful if you added .project to .cvsignore, or if you're checking out a project you know is of type Java and want to be able to use the Java perspective. Select Java and then Java Project. Click Next.

4 Enter the name of the project you wish to check the files in to.

5 Click Finish.

These steps create a new Java project named Persistence and attempt to build it.

NOTE If the Eclipse .project wasn't checked in and you chose Check Out as Project, the project won't be recognized automatically as a Java project; you will need to open a Java perspective explicitly by selecting Window→ Open Perspective→Java. In addition to checking out the CVS code, doing so will take you through the steps necessary to create a new Java project.

After checking out the project in a new Eclipse environment, the first problem you'll encounter is that the classpath variables the project requires (JUNIT and LOG4J) have not been defined. Assuming log4j and JUnit are installed, this situation is easy to fix by selecting Windows→Preferences→Java→Classpath Variables from the Eclipse main menu.

Another problem, which is potentially harder to solve, is getting the Ant build to work, because it has hard-coded paths for the required JAR files. Unless your co-workers are working on the same platform with the JARs installed in the same directories, either they need to edit the hard-coded paths (not a good solution, because doing so will cause a conflict when the code is checked in to CVS later) or you have to implement one of the solutions outlined in section 5.4.1, such as using environment variables. You should do this in such a way as not to break the build on other developers' machines.

Perhaps, after consultation with the team, you decide that one of the other developers will implement a solution that checks to see if the environment variables JUNIT and LOG4J have been defined and, if so, uses those environment variables to set the paths—otherwise the original hard-coded values are used. This may not be the best design (because it leaves arbitrary paths in the build file), but it's a reasonable compromise that ensures backward compatibility. You'll leave your co-worker to this task while you return to your own work.

6.2.2 *Working with CVS*

Once your files are under source control, you need to be more careful about how you work with them. Because CVS doesn't lock files to prevent changes by multiple developers, the longer you go without synchronizing your local copies of files with the latest versions on the CVS server, the more likely it is that you will find conflicts between your changes and other people's changes—and the harder they will be to resolve.

How long is too long time depends on how many people are working on the project and what they are doing. This timing is something you'll learn from experience, but a good start might be to get in sync at least once a day. Sometimes this frequency is inconvenient, because you also need to consider check-ins from a task-oriented point of view.

If you are adding a feature or doing a refactoring that takes significantly more than a day, you may not want the intrusion of foreign code until you have your own code working. In such a case, communication is especially important—you'll need to work out a plan with the other developers interested in changing the same code.

You should also contribute your changes to the repository as often as practical, so that others aren't surprised by the extent of your changes. A good rule to follow is to check in code that represents a sensible, integral change after making sure it compiles and passes the unit tests.

A little more refactoring

In chapter 5 we mentioned a problem with the persistence model: `FilePersistenceServices` should be a subclass of an abstract `PersistenceServices` class, and in order to do this properly, you shouldn't use static methods. First you'll change your static methods to instance methods as follows:

1 Remove the static modifier from the public `read()`, `write()`, `update()`, `delete()`, and `drop()` methods in the `FilePersistenceServices` class.

2 Remove the filename parameter from these public methods.

3 Add a constructor to `FilePersistenceServices` that takes a filename and saves it in an instance variable.

4 Make corresponding changes to the appropriate unit tests.

5 Make corresponding changes to the `FileObjectManager` class.

You need to make most of these changes manually or using the editor's find and replace feature, but Eclipse provides automated refactoring for changing the method signatures in step 2—removing the filename parameter from the `read()`, `write()`, `update()`, `delete()`, and `drop()` methods. Let's take the `read()` method as an example. It looks like this at first:

```
public static Vector read(String fileName, int key)
{
    // ...
```

After locating this method in the editor, right-click on the method name and select Refactor→Change Method Signature; this option displays a list of parameter types, names, and default values. (You may be prompted to save your files; if so, click OK. You may want to click the Always Save All Modified Resources Automatically Prior to Refactoring option to prevent this prompt in the future.)

Here you are removing a parameter, so the default value doesn't come into play; but if you were adding a parameter, this default value would be used wherever the method is called. For example, if you add a `String` parameter to a method `myMethod()`, with a default value of null, all calls to `myMethod()` are replaced with `myMethod(null)`.

To remove a parameter, follow these steps:

1   The first parameter you want to remove, `filename`, is already highlighted. Click Remove.

2   You can click Preview to view the results of the proposed change; you should do this for the first method, to understand the changes it will make.

3   In the next dialog box (whether you clicked Preview or not), Eclipse displays the problem resulting from the change: The `filename` parameter is referenced in the method, so it's left as an unresolved reference. This is OK, because you'll add an instance variable to the class to replace it. Click Continue.

4   If you chose Preview, the next screen allows you to compare before and after views of the affected files.

5   Once you are satisfied with the changes Eclipse proposes, click OK.

You probably noticed that you were not provided with an opportunity to remove the static modifier from the method signature. As long as you're here, do this manually.

After these changes, the method signature for the `read()` method looks like this:

```
public Vector read(int key)
{
    // ...
```

If you examine the other files that call this method, such as `FileObjectManager`, you'll find that they have been changed appropriately. Repeat these steps for each of the other four public methods: `write()`, `update()`, `delete()`, and `drop()`.

Next, to replace the `filename` parameter you removed from the methods, add an instance variable to the class. Doing so will resolve the unresolved references:

```
private String fileName = null;
```

Also add the following constructor to set the filename when the class is instantiated:

```
public FilePersistenceServices(String fileName)
{
    this.fileName = fileName;
}
```

After these changes, `FilePersistenceServices` should be in a consistent state and no errors should remain flagged. This won't be the case with `FileObjectManager` and `FilePersistenceServicesTest`, however, so next you need to make the corresponding changes to these classes.

Begin with the unit tests. First add an instance variable to the unit tests for the `FilePersistenceServicesTest` class and initialize it by calling the constructor:

```
public class FilePersistenceServicesTest extends TestCase
{
    Vector v1, v2;
    String s1, s2;
    FilePersistenceServices ps =
        new FilePersistenceServices("TestTable");
    // ...
```

You also need to change all the calls to public methods to instance method calls. You can do this most easily by using Eclipse's search and replace feature. Locate the first method call to `FilePersistenceServices.drop()` and double-click on the class name. Be careful that you replace only calls to the public methods, because you've left the utility methods static:

1 Select Edit→Find/Replace from the main menu.

2 The Find field is already filled in with `FilePersistenceServices`; fill in the Replace With field with the instance name, ps.

3 Notice that the Direction setting is set to Forward by default. This is what you want: You should change this text only in the code that follows and not the code you just added.

4 Click Replace/Find. Doing so changes the currently highlighted instance of `FilePersistenceServices` to ps and then locates the next instance.

5 Until you reach the end of the file, click Replace/Find wherever `FilePersistenceServices` is used with public methods such as `read()` and `write()`. Click Find wherever `FilePersistenceServices` is used to call utility methods such as `vector2String()` and `getKey()`—doing so will leave the text unchanged and locate the next instance.

These changes should correct all the problems you caused when you removed the static modifier from `FilePersistenceServices` and make the red flags go away. This is a good time to run the unit tests to verify that the changes are correct:

1   Select the `FilePersistenceServicesTest` class in either the editor or the Package Explorer.

2   Select Run→Run As→JUnit Test from the main menu.

As usual, the green bar means everything's OK.

Next, you need to change the `FileObjectManager` class in a similar way. First, add an instance variable for the `FilePersistenceServices` object, but initialize it to null, because you'll instantiate it only when you instantiate the `FileObjectManager` class (you won't know what the filename is until then). Here is the start of the class:

```
public class FileObjectManager extends ObjectManager
{
    static Logger logger
        = Logger.getLogger(FileObjectManager.class);
    Collection fieldMap = null;
    Class classType = null;
    String className = null;
    FilePersistenceServices ps = null;
    // ...
```

And here is the updated factory method (which you're using in lieu of a constructor):

```
public static ObjectManager createObjectManager(Class type)
{
    FileObjectManager om = new FileObjectManager();
    om.classType = type;
    om.className = type.getName();
    om.setFieldMap();
    om.ps = new FilePersistenceServices(om.className);
    return om;
}
```

Now you need to change all the static calls with calls to the instance methods. This is essentially the same thing you did with the unit tests; however, you don't have to worry about calls to static utility methods, so you can replace them all at once. Again, locate the first call to a `FilePersistenceServices` method (which should be a call to `drop()` in the `dropObjectTable()` method) and double-click on `FilePersistenceServices`. Then follow these steps:

1   Select Edit→Find/Replace from the main menu.

2   Verify that the Find field is filled in with `FilePersistenceServices`. Enter ps in the Replace With field.

3 Click Replace All.

4 Right-click in the editor area and select Save. All the red error flags in the project should be gone.

You should now be able to run and pass all the unit tests. You can run the unit tests for `FileObjectManager` as described earlier, but before you check in these changes, carry out a more comprehensive check by performing a complete build and test using the Ant build file:

1 Right-click on build.xml in the Package Explorer and select Run Ant from the context menu.

2 Make sure the `BuildAll` target is the only target selected in the Modify Attributes and Launch dialog box and click Run.

Assuming everything builds and tests correctly, you're ready to check your changes in to CVS. Notice that the three files that have outgoing changes are indicated by a greater-than sign (>).

Checking in to CVS

It's generally not a good idea to make changes and simply check them in to CVS. Obviously, you should first make sure your changes compile and pass the unit test, as you've just done, but you should also make sure your changes don't conflict with changes other people have made, and that your changes work together with the other changes correctly.

If you know there are no conflicting changes, Eclipse's Update feature is the easiest way to get up to date. CVS performs any necessary merges automatically and silently. This is especially useful if it's been a while since you made changes, but others have been working—perhaps because you've been working on another project or been away on vacation.

If you update and some of the changes conflict—that is, if you've changed the same lines in a file that someone else has changed—Eclipse combines the changes in a single file that you need to edit by hand (a messy and error-prone process). This situation isn't exactly a disaster; but if there is a chance it will happen, it's more convenient to perform the merge using Eclipse's Synchronize Repository feature, because this feature takes advantage of Eclipse's compare feature.

We'll examine merging shortly, but because you know from your communication with the other developers that the only other change is to the build file, you can safely use Update now. Doing so provides little feedback if everything goes smoothly, so take a moment to note the revision number of each file. At the out-

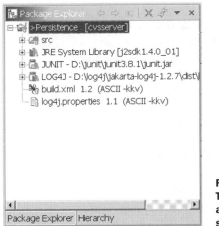

Figure 6.5
The Package Explorer
after updating. Can you
spot what changed?

set, as indicated by the CVS label decorators in the Package Explorers, all of your files are the initial version, revision 1.1. To update, select the project, right-click on it, and select Team→Update.

Suppose your co-worker, who was supposed to change the build file to support environment variables, has already checked in this change. The only indication that Eclipse provides that something was updated is the change in the revision numbers. In this case, the revision number of the build.xml file has changed from 1.1 to 1.2 (see figure 6.5). If there were many files and they had varied revision numbers, it would be virtually impossible to tell what happened.

To see what changes were made to the file, select build.xml, right-click on it, and select Team→Show in Resource History. Doing so lists each revision together with comments (see figure 6.6). If you want to know more specifically what changes have been made, you can compare the current revision with previous revisions by selecting Compare With→Local History from the file's context menu.

Revision	Tags	Date	Author	Comment
*1.2		3/4/03 11:35...	sophia	Changed build file to use environment vari...
1.1		3/4/03 11:24...	david	Initial revisions

Figure 6.6
Build file resource
history. It makes
for excellent
reading when the
project's done.

Now that you have the combination of the latest code from the repository and your changes, you should try to build and test once again by selecting the build.xml file, right-clicking on it, and selecting Run Ant from the context menu. Once the code passes this final test, you're ready to check it in as follows:

1   Select the project, right-click on it, and select Team→Commit from the context menu.

2   You are prompted to enter a comment. Do so, and then click OK.

Committing the project as a whole, as you do here, means you need to enter a comment that applies to all the changed files. If you want to enter more specific comments for each file, you must instead select each file individually and commit it. Depending on the extent of the changes, this is sometimes more appropriate; here, the changes are all directly related to making the `FilePersistenceServices` class instantiable, so a single comment will do.

Resolving conflicts in an updated file

As mentioned previously, when you select the Update feature and changes have been made to both the local version and the repository version, CVS does its best to merge the two. When it finds a conflict in a line or group of lines, it includes both versions and marks them to indicate which version came from which file, using `<<<<<<< filename` to mark the start of the local version, `=======` to mark the end of the local version and the start of repository version, and `>>>>>>> revision` to mark the end of the repository version.

Let's take a simple example using HelloWorld. Suppose the original 1.1 revision is as follows:

```
public class HelloWorld
{
    public static void main(String[] args)
    {
        System.out.println("Hello, world!");
    }

}
```

You change this code to use a separate method to print out the message as follows:

```
public class HelloWorld
{
    public static void main(String[] args)
    {
        say("Hello, world!");
    }
```

```
   public static void say(String msg)
   {
      System.out.println(msg);
   }
}
```

Before you can check in this code, someone else changes the hard-coded string in the method call to a symbolic constant and checks the change in to CVS:

```
public class HelloWorld
{
   private static final String HELLO="Hello, world!";

   public static void main(String[] args)
   {
      System.out.println(HELLO);
   }

}
```

If you update before checking in your change, you'll find that your local file is changed as follows:

```
public class HelloWorld
{
   final private static String HELLO="Hello, world!";

   public static void main(String[] args)
   {
<<<<<<< HelloWorld.java
      say("Hello, world!");
   }

   public static void say(String msg)
   {
      System.out.println(msg);
=======
      System.out.println(HELLO);
>>>>>>> 1.2
   }
}
```

Notice that the line declaring the symbolic constant HELLO is not marked in any way; because it didn't conflict with any of the changes you made, it is added as is. The remaining lines are more problematic. You clearly don't want to replace your call to System.out.println() with the 1.2 version—instead you should keep your code but replace the hard-coded "Hello, world!" parameter with the symbolic constant. Here is the merged code:

```
public class HelloWorld
{
   final private static String HELLO = "Hello, world!";

   public static void main(String[] args)
   {
      say(HELLO);
   }

   public static void say(String msg)
   {
      System.out.println(msg);
   }
}
```

Once you've resolved the conflicts CVS identified and determined that your code compiles and runs correctly, you can commit your changes as before, using Team→Commit from the project's context menu.

Synchronizing with the repository

Resolving minor conflicts in a file that CVS has merged is not usually a major problem. But when the two versions have diverged significantly and conflicts exist throughout the merged file, it can be virtually impossible to understand the purpose of the changes. It's much clearer to see a comparison of the two versions of the file with each change in its original context. You can do that by using Eclipse's Synchronize with Repository feature:

1 Select the project in the Package Explorer and right-click on it.

2 Select Team→Synchronize with Repository from the context menu.

This option opens a new Synchronize view in the Java perspective, in the area below the editor (if it's not open already). This view presents a lot of information—it's a sort of Workbench on its own—so you may want to double-click on the title bar to maximize it within the Eclipse Workbench. The upper-left corner of this view shows a Structure Compare outline view displaying files that have changed.

We'll look at the alternatives later in this section. In the current example, because the file has changed both in the repository and locally, Eclipse has automatically selected *incoming mode* and decorated the filename in the list with a double-headed red arrow. Double-clicking on the filename displays additional information, including a Java Structure Compare section to the right of Structure Compare, showing changes at the Java element level, and below that, a comparison of the two different versions of the file (see figure 6.7).

The Java Structure Compare section of this view shows that the HELLO attribute, as indicated by the blue left-pointing arrow, is a new incoming change from the

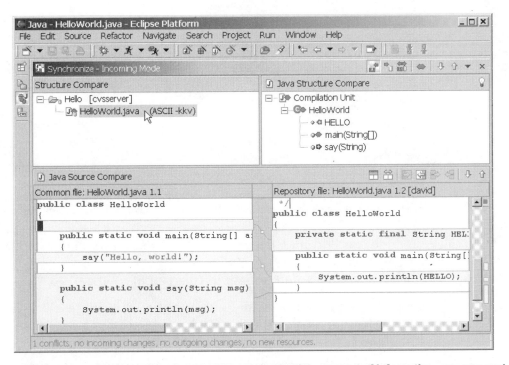

Figure 6.7 Synchronizing with the repository. Because of the amount of information, you may want to double-click on the title bar to maximize this view within the Workbench.

repository. The red double-headed arrow next to the `main()` method indicates conflicting changes.

You can explore these changes in detail using the Java Source Compare section below the structure comparisons and apply changes from one version to the other. To add the HELLO attribute to the local version, hold the pointer over the open box in the line linking the change on the right to its place on the left. A button appears, along with hover text indicating that it will copy the current change from right to left.

When you use the Synchronize view in other contexts, the link between the local code and the repository view may not contain an open box. (This would be the case if Eclipse already considers the code merged, for example.) To copy the change over in this case, select the change either by clicking on the code on the right side of the screen or by clicking on the corresponding blue rectangle in the right margin. (You can also click on the attribute name in the Java Structure Compare section to select and display only that change in the comparison.) Then,

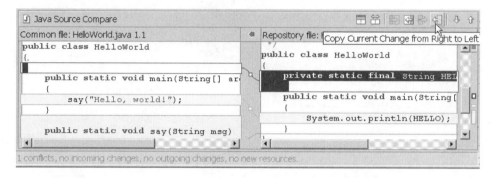

Figure 6.8 Java Source Compare. You can copy changes from the repository file on the right to the local copy of the file either by clicking on the links or by using the tool button as shown.

click on the Copy Current Change from Right to Left tool button in the Java Source Compare title bar (see figure 6.8).

To merge the changes and commit the merged file, follow these steps:

1 Copy the HELLO attribute using either method described earlier—for example, select the code on the right and click the Copy Current Change from Right to Left tool button.

2 Manually change the string in the main() method to the symbolic constant HELLO.

3 These changes should result in the same merged code shown earlier as a result of using the Update feature and editing by hand. Once you are satisfied with the merge, right-click on the filename in the Structure Compare section and select Mark as Merged to indicate that you've resolved the conflict.

4 Commit the change by right-clicking on either the filename or the project name and selecting Commit.

5 Enter a comment when prompted and click OK.

This example includes only a single file, but if there were more, you would repeat the first three steps for each file until all conflicts were resolved. You could then either commit each file individually by right-clicking on each filename, if you wanted to enter comment for each file, or you could commit the project or the individual packages by right-clicking on the project or package name if a single comment is appropriate for the project or package.

TIP   What happens if you use Update and realize you shouldn't have, because there are many unexpected incoming changes? In Eclipse, if you make a mistake, you can usually press Ctrl-Z to undo the change. However, generally speaking, you need to undo carefully when interacting with CVS, because Eclipse often issues commands to CVS behind the scenes that have an immediate and permanent effect, and these can not be undone.

If you update and then discover to your regret that CVS has made a mess of your code, you can still undo the change by selecting the file in the editor and clicking Undo. Just be aware that Eclipse treats the undo as part of your manual merge with the latest CVS revision, rather than a reversion to the previous local version. When you choose Synchronize with Repository at this point, there will be some minor differences in the options you are given, but you will still be able to merge as described earlier.

If you are at all unsure about what an update might do, you should make a backup of your project beforehand so you can return to your known working project. Sometimes it pays to be cautious.

Synchronization modes: incoming, outgoing, incoming/outgoing

As you've just seen, when you select Synchronize with Repository from the Team menu and there are changes in the repository, Eclipse opens the Synchronize view in incoming mode. This mode is one way of filtering the files that are shown; altogether there are three modes:

- *Incoming*—Lists only the files that have changed in the repository since you last synchronized your local code with the repository (by explicitly synchronizing, committing, or updating your code)
- *Outgoing*—Lists only files you have changed since you last synchronized
- *Incoming/outgoing*—List files that have changed either in the repository or locally since you last synchronized with the repository

The mode in which the Synchronize view starts depends on whether you have outgoing changes and whether there are incoming changes from the repository. If there are incoming changes, regardless of whether there are outgoing changes, the view starts in incoming mode. If there are only outgoing changes, it starts in outgoing mode. This is in keeping with the recommended CVS workflow: After making changes, you should bring your code up to date with the latest changes from the repository and then build and test with those changes before checking in your code.

To illustrate, suppose a project includes four files: ClassA, ClassB, ClassC, and ClassD. One morning, you start by updating your local source and begin working on the files. At the same time, another developer works on the same set of files. You make changes to ClassA, the other developer makes changes to ClassB, and you both make changes to ClassC. Nobody makes changes to ClassD. At the end of the day, you select Team→Synchronize with Repository from the project's context menu, after the other developer has checked in his changes. Because there are changes in the repository, the Synchronize view starts in incoming mode and shows only the files the other developer changed: ClassB and ClassC (see figure 6.9).

Incoming mode lets you examine these files one by one, so you can combine them with your code. Even though there is no conflict, you may wish to double-click on ClassB to examine the changes before accepting them. If everything looks OK, you can right-click on the filename and select Update from Repository to accept the changes.

The second file, ClassC, has one or more changes that conflict with your code, so you can't simply accept it by selecting Update from Repository—this selection is grayed out in the context menu. If, after comparing it to your version, you decide you want to discard your changes and replace your local version with the version from the repository (perhaps because the changes the other developer made supercede your changes), you can do so by right-clicking on the filename and selecting Override and Update from the context menu.

Another possibility in the case of a conflict would be to discard the other developer's changes. (Generally you want to make sure the other developer knows you are doing this, of course.) To do so, right-click on the filename and select Mark as Merged from the context menu—this option identifies your unchanged local version as the merged version even though you haven't made any changes. Once all conflicts have been resolved, you can commit your changes.

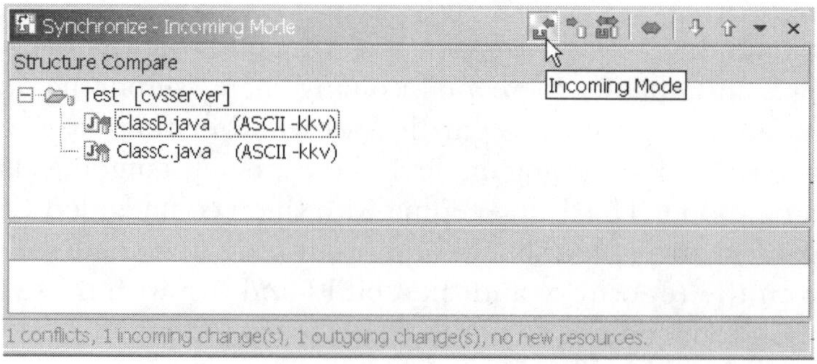

Figure 6.9
Synchronization
incoming mode, one of
four viewing modes,
shows only files that
have changed in the
repository.

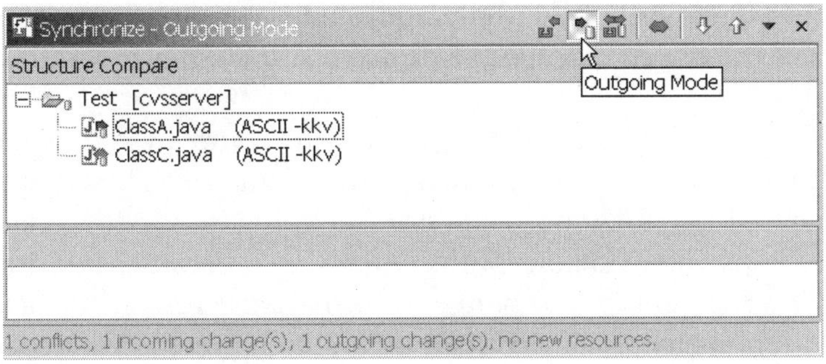

Figure 6.10
Outgoing mode shows files you have changed locally.

Whereas incoming mode is well suited to resolving conflicts before checking in code, outgoing mode is useful for reviewing your changes as a whole (perhaps for preparing release notes) because it lists all the files you've changed and lets you compare them to the version in the repository. In figure 6.10, the outgoing view shows ClassA and ClassC.

Incoming and outgoing modes provide filtering, so you can deal with smaller sets of files. The incoming/outgoing mode, in contrast, provides an overview of every file that has changed in a project. Because it shows all the files that have changed, either locally or in the repository, you can use it in place of either incoming or outgoing mode (see figure 6.11).

Creating and applying a patch

Sometimes a CVS server is set to allow certain users (such as anonymous users) read-only privileges. This is true of many public CVS servers, such as the one for Eclipse (which you can access using the repository location: :pserver:anonymous@dev.eclipse.org:/home/eclipse) and the projects on sourceforge.net.

To send changes to another developer, perhaps one who has commit privilege, you can use Eclipse to create a *patch*—a file that lists the changes that have

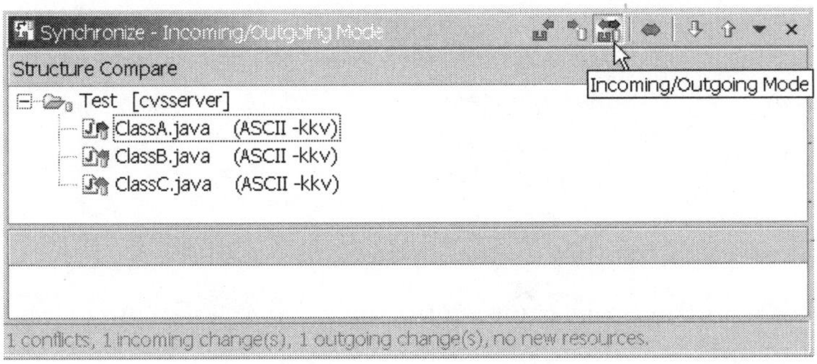

Figure 6.11
Incoming/outgoing mode shows every file that has changed.

been made to the source code, including multiple files and packages. The developer who receives the file can then use Eclipse or some other tool to review and apply the changes.

Suppose, for example, that another team in your company is using your Persistence component and extends it to work with a database. They don't want to maintain a separate branch of your code; for one thing, doing so would make it harder for them to use new versions of the component, because they would have to merge each time. Assuming the changes they make are reasonable, it's in both your interest and theirs for them to contribute their changes to your code.

In addition to creating a new `DatabaseObjectManager` class, they also change the `ObjectManager` class, adding some symbolic constants, a static method to select the `persistence` type, and a `switch` statement in the factory method that selects the appropriate concrete class:

```
public abstract class ObjectManager
{
    public final static int FILE_PERSISTENCE = 1;
    public final static int DB_PERSISTENCE = 2;
    private static int persistenceType = FILE_PERSISTENCE;

    // abstract methods ...

    public static void setPersistenceType(int persistenceType)
    {
        ObjectManager.persistenceType = persistenceType;
    }

    public static ObjectManager createObjectManager(Class type)
    {
        ObjectManager om = null;
        switch (persistenceType)
        {
            case FILE_PERSISTENCE :
                om = FileObjectManager.createObjectManager(type);
                break;
            case DB_PERSISTENCE :
                // om = DatabaseObjectManager.createObjectManager(type);
                break;
        }
        return om;
    }
}
```

After making these changes, they create a patch file as follows:

1   Right-click on the project name and select Team→Create Patch from the
    context menu.

2   Choose a place to save the patch. The choices are the clipboard, the file-
     system, and the workspace. Assuming they choose the filesystem, they
     enter a filename such as C:\patch.txt.

3   Clicking Next allows them to change the options; but the defaults are
     OK, so they click Finish.

This resulting patch file looks similar to the file the CVS Update command produces when it merges two files with conflicting changes, because the CVS `diff`
utility is used in both cases. The difference is that the patch file contains the
results of comparing multiple files and information about the files, including
path, timestamps, and version. Here is the start of the patch information for
`ObjectManager`:

```
Index: src/org/eclipseguide/persistence/ObjectManager.java
===================================================================
RCS file: /usr/local/repository/src/org/eclipseguide/
→persistence/ObjectManager.java,v
retrieving revision 1.1
diff -u -r1.1 ObjectManager.java
--- src/org/eclipseguide/persistence/ObjectManager.java    6 Apr
→2003 04:47:18 -0000    1.1
+++ src/org/eclipseguide/persistence/ObjectManager.java    6 Apr
→2003 12:43:37 -0000
@@ -1,6 +1,7 @@
 package .org.eclipseguide.persistence;

 import java.util.Collection;
+import java.util.Properties;

 /**
  * Enter one sentence class summary
@@ -11,18 +12,34 @@
  */
 public abstract class ObjectManager
 {
-    public final static int FILE_PERSISTENCE = 1;
-    public final static int DB_PERSISTENCE = 2;
-
```

An important feature of the patch file is that it is a plain text file, so it can simply
be sent to you in an email, for example. When you receive it, you can save it to
your filesystem and apply the changes to your local copy as follows:

1   Right-click on the project name and select Team→Apply Patch from the
     context menu.

2   Type in the filename or use Browse to locate the patch file. Click Next.

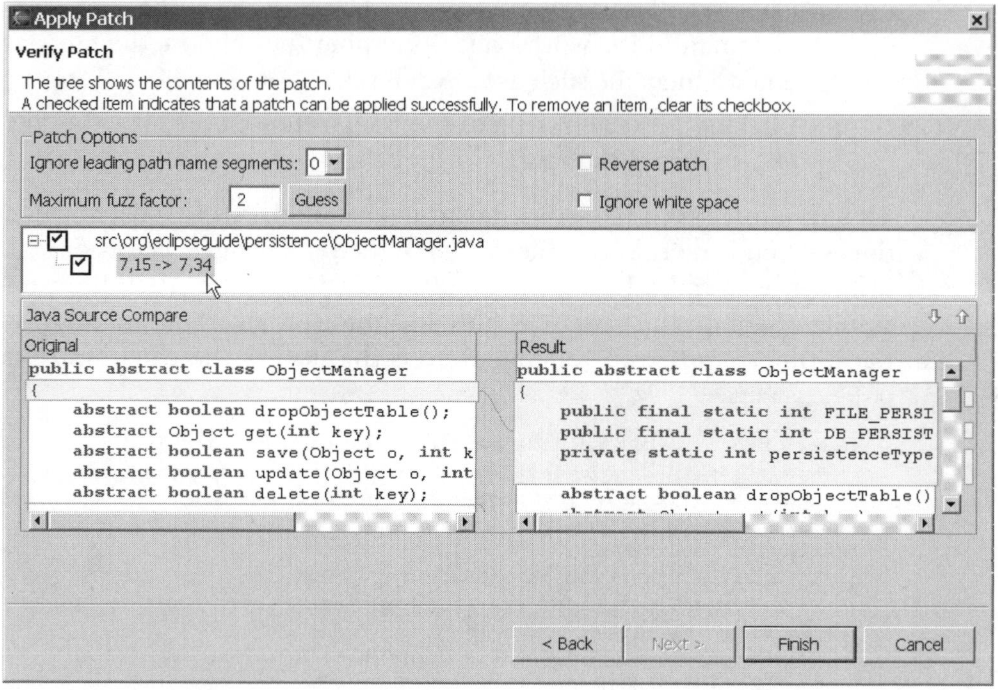

Figure 6.12   Applying a patch from the filesystem. Changes can be reviewed and individually accepted or vetoed.

3 The next dialog box lets you identify the changes in the patch and whether they can be successfully applied. You can also examine the change by double-clicking on the line ranges (see figure 6.12).

Patches work best if the contributor started out with the same version of the files you currently have on your local system. If you have also made changes to the same files in the meantime, you may encounter conflicts that CVS cannot resolve. You will need to merge those sections of code manually.

6.2.3 Versions and branches

CVS is not limited to storing a history of revisions for each file. If it were, it would be awkward to retrieve the code from a particular point in time. Some files change more quickly than others, so at any given time, different files are likely to have different revision numbers. (It's possible to retrieve files from CVS based on their date, but Eclipse doesn't permit this.) A good way to manage this situation is to assign a version label to the project, which is like taking a snapshot of the project at that point in time. You can later retrieve the project using the version label to return to that point in time.

CVS can also store multiple histories for each file. This feature allows you to branch the project—that is, pursue more than one line of development at a time. As mentioned previously, one branch might be used to provide maintenance (such as bug fixes) for a released version of a product while development for the next version continues on the head branch.

Adding a version label

Adding a version label to a project associates the revision number of each particular file with a single project-level label. When you retrieve a project using a version label, CVS provides you with the revision of each file that was current when the version was created.

You should consider tagging a project with a version label at all significant development milestones, such as a beta or an official release, or before any drastic change is undertaken. Suppose, as you continue with your efforts to make a product out of the Persistence component, you decide that the astronomy package you included as part of the project shouldn't really be included. It's easy enough to delete, but before you do that, you'll give the current source code a version label. If you later decide it was a mistake to delete the package, you can retrieve the old complete version.

To give a project a version label, first make sure your local copy of the source code has been synchronized with the repository and all your changes have been committed. Then, follow these steps:

1 Right-click on the project name and select Team→Tag as Version from the context menu.

2 Enter a label, such as **OriginalProject** (see figure 6.13). There are restriction on the name: It must start with a letter and cannot contain single quotes ('), back ticks (`), dollar signs ($), colons (:), semicolons (;), at signs (@), or pipe symbols (|).

3 Click OK.

Now you can safely delete the astronomy project by selecting the astronomy package and clicking Delete, knowing you can easily return to this point in the project's history if necessary. Once you do this, you'll discover that the ObjectManagerTest class has numerous problems because it refers to the Star class from the package you deleted. One solution is to create a new test class (omitted here in the interest of brevity) and change all references in ObjectManagerTest to the new class and its

Figure 6.13
Tagging a project with a version label provides a snapshot of a project's files at the current point in time.

attributes. (If you choose to undertake this as an exercise, remember that your new class will need to implement an `equal()` method so JUnit can compare the two instances of the class correctly.) Once you've fixed all the compilation problems resulting from this surgery and the unit tests succeed, you can synchronize and commit your changes, including the addition of the new test class file.

Retrieving a version

You can retrieve a version two ways: initially, by checking out the project from CVS using the Repository view; or, when you already have the project checked out, by selecting Replace With→Another Branch or Version from the project's context menu. You'll use the latter here, but in either case, you are presented with a tree showing the branches and versions available in the Persistence project. Follow these steps:

1   Right-click on the project name and select Replace With→Another Branch or Version from the project's context menu.

2   Click on the plus sign next to Versions to list all available versions, which in this case is only OriginalProject (see figure 6.14).

3   Select OriginalProject and click OK.

After retrieving the OriginalProject version of the project, you'll find that the `astronomy` package has been restored and any new files you've added to the main branch since tagging this version are gone. You can return to the current version by repeating these steps, selecting HEAD instead of the OriginalProject version.

Creating and using a branch

A branch is similar to a version, with the important difference that you can make changes to the files associated with a branch and commit the changes. The changes you make will, of course, appear only to you and anybody else working with that branch. Once you've started or retrieved a branch in your workspace, you do not have to do anything special; Eclipse knows which branch you are working on.

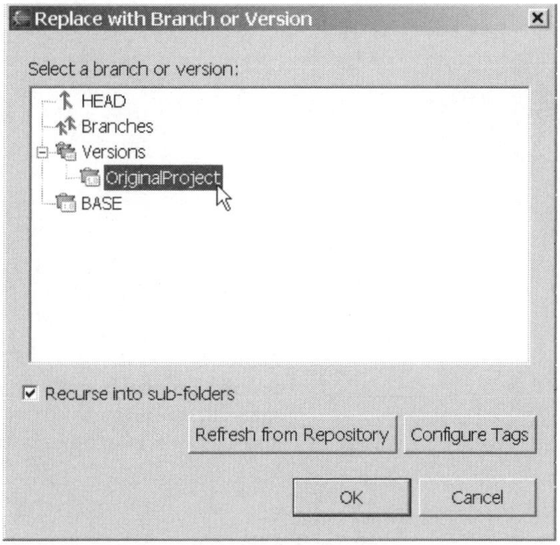

Figure 6.14
Retrieving a previously tagged version restores all the files in the project to the way they were when they were tagged.

When you create a branch, the starting point is the current version in your workspace. This can be either the head, if you intend to pursue a new line of development, or a previously tagged version. Suppose that even though the main Persistence project will not include the astronomy classes, you want to develop another application that does include these classes. After making sure Original-Project is the version in your workspace, do the following:

1 Right-click on the project name and select Team→Branch.

2 Enter a name for the branch, such as **StarList** (see figure 6.15). The branch name is subject to the same restrictions as the version name.

3 Leave the Start Working in the Branch box checked and click OK.

This scenario is similar to what might happen when you want to create a maintenance branch for an official release, because you often don't know what version will be released until after some time has passed, due to testing. When you are close to releasing, you may begin tagging your code (or have the build process tag your code) with version labels such as ReleaseCandidate1, ReleaseCandidate2, and so on. When you finally have a successful candidate, you can return to that version, add a new version label indicating its status as an official release (such as Release1.0), and create a new branch, such as Release1.

Retrieving a branch is identical to retrieving a version. You can use either the Repository view or select Replace With→Another Branch or Version from the project's context menu.

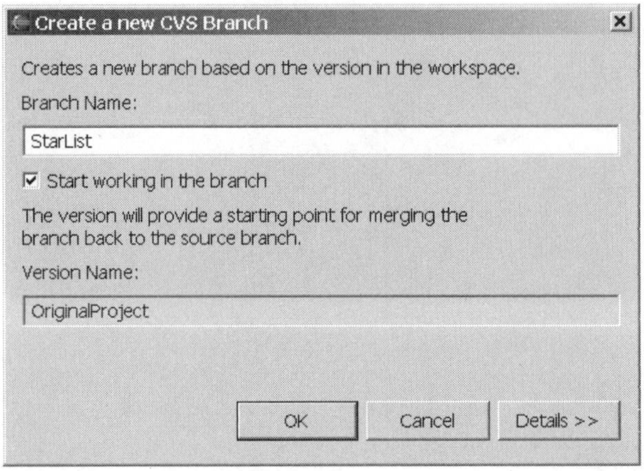

Figure 6.15
Creating a new branch. Changes made in one branch will not affect the source code in another branch.

6.3 *Summary*

Source control systems bring two principal benefits to the software development process: First, a source control system maintains a history of all revisions made to the source code; second, it controls access to the files so multiple developers can work on the same set of files without the danger of losing work or corrupting files.

Access to files can be controlled by using either pessimistic locking or optimistic locking. Pessimistic locking is the more heavy-handed approach: Once a developer locks a file, no one else can change it until she checks the file back in. Optimistic locking is the agile way: Anyone can make changes to files at any time. This approach prevents roadblocks that can slow the development process and encourages people to take greater responsibility for the source code. The keys to making optimistic locking work are communication, regular synchronization, and following the recommended workflow process.

The most popular source control system employing the optimistic locking model is CVS (Concurrent Versions System), which, like Eclipse, is an open-source project. Eclipse includes a well-integrated client for CVS, which makes the source control process easy and nearly intuitive.

Success with CVS depends on careful attention to workflow. Before checking in your code—*committing*, in CVS parlance—you should first make sure it compiles and passes the unit tests successfully. In addition, you should synchronize your source code with the most recent changes others have made (and resolve any conflicts if necessary) and make sure the resulting combination also compiles and passes the unit tests successfully.

The revision history CVS maintains allows you to retrieve any previous revision of a file (or set of files), which is invaluable when a bug or design flaw is discovered belatedly. CVS also lets you tag a project with a version, which in effect takes a snapshot of the project at a given point in time.

Another powerful CVS feature is the ability to branch a project, creating multiple revision histories. The main branch, called the head, is used for the main line of development, whereas a branch might be created to maintain a released version of the project. This way, a bug can be fixed in the released code without introducing new and unstable code.

Web development tools

7

In this chapter...

- An overview of web application design
- An introduction to JSPs and servlets
- Installing the Tomcat web server and the Sysdeo Tomcat plug-in
- Creating JSPs and servlets in Eclipse
- Building a sample web application
- Debugging JSPs and servlets, including multithreaded debugging

177

Computer applications are not very useful if they don't provide output of some sort. An easy and popular way to do this today is to use a web browser to provide a programmable graphical user interface. In this chapter we'll examine Tomcat, a web server that can be programmed using Java servlets and JavaServer Pages (JSPs); and the Sysdeo Tomcat plug-in that allows you to control Tomcat and debug programs from within the Eclipse environment.

7.1 Developing for the Web

An important goal in designing an application with a GUI is to separate the business logic from the presentation logic. There are a number of different ways to accomplish this, but one popular and successful approach is a pattern called the *MVC architecture*. This pattern divides the design into three principal components: the Model, the View, and the Controller.

In brief, the Model refers to the application's data model, the View (as you might expect) represents the presentation logic, and the Controller represents the logic that mediates between the two and allows the user to interact with the View and the Model. One of the main benefits of a properly designed MVC application is that each component is isolated to a large degree from the other components. This isolation makes it easier, for example, to change an application's interface from a web application to an application using a graphical interface such as the standard Java Swing/AWT or Eclipse's SWT. (See appendix D for more information about Eclipse's windowing library.)

In developing for the Web using Java, MVC is usually implemented as follows:

- *Model*—JavaBeans or value objects
- *View*—HTML and JSP
- *Controller*—Servlets and ordinary Java classes

Implementing a design using these components requires a kind of web server called a *servlet container*. Tomcat, from the Apache Organization's Jakarta project, is the de facto standard servlet container, as well as the official, Sun-approved, reference implementation for Java servlets and JSP. Like all Apache software, Tomcat is free and open-source.

7.1.1 The web, HTML, servlets, and JSP

It is impossible to adequately introduce a topic as large as servlets and JSP in a few short pages, but we hope to provide enough of an overview that readers unfamiliar with topic can follow the discussion. Most people are familiar with how HTML, the Web, and web browsers work: A user types a server's address (and possibly a page name) into a browser, and the web server returns a page written in HTML, which the browser then renders. In some cases the web page is simply a static file that the web server has waiting for all users that request it; in other cases, the web page is not a file, but rather, text that is generated programmatically based on a specific user's request. Apart from the greater interactivity that the latter provides, it makes no difference to the user or the user's browser how the web page was created.

A servlet container provides two ways to interact with a user's browser: JSP and servlets. (As you'll see, servlets are a special type of Java class that extend the abstract class `javax.servlet.http.HttpServlet`.) Both accept requests from a browser and both can send text (or other data) to a browser. By far the easiest to use are JSPs, because they permit you to use a scripting language in what is otherwise a standard HTML page.

7.1.2 JSP overview

JSP is a mixed blessing. It allows you to embed script commands in HTML ranging from special JSP tags to arbitrary Java code. As we mentioned, JSPs are best used for the presentation logic of an application and are best developed by people skilled in web design rather than programming. Mixing large amounts of code with HTML leads to JSPs that are hard to understand and hard for designers and developers to maintain. Sometimes this situation is unavoidable, but to the greatest extent possible, programming logic should be implemented in servlets or in JSP custom tags.

It helps to understand that JSP is not interpreted at runtime. Rather, the first time a JSP is invoked, it is converted into a Java class—a servlet, in fact—and then compiled. Within this servlet is a `service` method that is called by the servlet container. Scripting elements are converted to Java code, and static HTML is converted to `print` statements inside the `service` method.

There are four principal types of JSP scripting elements: scriptlets, expressions, tags, and directives. We'll discuss them next.

JSP scriptlets

JSP *scriptlets* are sections of Java code that are placed verbatim in a JSP between the characters `<%` and `%>`. The following example initializes two variables:

```
<% int myVar = 10;
   String message="Hello";
%>
```

Code such as this is included unchanged in the servlet's `service` method, so different scriptlets on a page can work together. A scriptlet further down can use the value of `myVar` that is declared here. The following example prints the word *Hey* ten times:

```
<% for(int i=0; i<myVar; i++) { %>
   <H2>Hey</H2>
<% } %>
```

JSP expressions

JSP *expressions*, as the name suggests, are Java expressions that can be embedded in HTML code between the characters `<%=` and `%>`. The value of the expression is included as part of the HTML that is sent to the browser; this is in effect a shortcut for printing values on a web page. The following prints the value of `myVar` defined earlier:

```
<%= myVar %>
```

JSP tags

JSP *tags* (also called *actions*) are XML tags that invoke Java code defined elsewhere. JSP includes a number of standard tags, but you can also create a custom tag library that includes your own tags.

The following three tags are particularly important:

- `<jsp:useBean id="name" class="classname" scope="scope"/>`—Attempts to obtain a reference to a JavaBean using the name `name` in the given scope. (Here we'll only consider the request scope, which is associated with a single request from a browser.) If a bean with the specified name has not yet been created, the servlet container instantiates the bean class using its no-args constructor.

- `<jsp:setProperty name="name" property="property" value="value"/>`—Sets the property `property` to the value `value` in a bean named `name` that was obtained using the `<jsp:useBean>` tag.

- `<jsp:getProperty name="name" property="property"/>`—Gets the property `property` from a bean named `name` that was obtained using the `<jsp:useBean>` tag.

These tags are useful, as you'll see soon, because you can use them to pass data in the form of JavaBeans back and forth between servlets and JSPs.

JSP directives

JSP *directives* are instructions to the JSP interpreter. In the examples, you'll use the `include` directive, which allows you to include another file inside a JSP at any point. Here you'll use it to include the standard HTML preamble plus a banner at the top of each JSP.

7.1.3 Servlet overview

In the simplest possible terms, a *servlet* is a Java class that can be invoked by the servlet container to process an HTTP request. In turn, it can respond to the request or it can forward the request to another servlet or JSP.

A servlet extends the `HttpServlet` class and, at a minimum, must implement one of two methods `doGet()` or `doPost()`, for handling GET and POST requests, respectively. Because a servlet can handle both request types identically, it's usual to implement one (`doPost()`, for example) and have the other (`doGet()`) call `doPost()`. Both of these methods take the same two parameters: a request object and a response object.

A servlet can do everything a JSP can do, and more. It can respond to a request by writing HTML, as follows:

```
public class TestServlet extends HttpServlet
{
    protected void doGet(HttpServletRequest request,
                         HttpServletResponse response)
    {
        PrintWriter out = response.getWriter();
        out.println("<HTML><HEAD>");
        out.println("<TITLE>Hello</TITLE>");
        out.println("</HEAD><BODY>");
        out.println("Hello!");
        out.println("</BODY></HTML>");
    }
}
```

Of course, this isn't good practice, because it's not easy to lay out and format a web page within `print` statements like this. Presentation is a job for JSP. The sample application in section 7.3 demonstrates some techniques for integrating JSPs and servlets that utilize the best advantages of each.

7.2 Tomcat and the Sysdeo Tomcat plug-in

Eclipse includes a Tomcat server plug-in. However, it's not the complete server, so you'll need to download the complete Tomcat binary distribution from the Apache web site; you'll find it listed under the Jakarta project. Like Eclipse, Tomcat is an open source project, so you must decide which type of build you want to use: a release version; a more recent (but possibly less stable) milestone version, such as a beta release; or—if you like to live dangerously—a nightly build. Like other Java software, there is only one version for all platforms, but you need to choose the compression format most appropriate for your platform (such as .zip for Windows or .tar.gz for Linux). In addition, you need to make sure the version of Tomcat you choose is supported by the Sysdeo Tomcat plug-in.

7.2.1 *Installing and testing Tomcat*

Installation is as simple as downloading the compressed file from Apache (or a mirror site) and decompressing it to a directory on your hard drive, such as C:\Tomcat. After you unzip Tomcat, you can run it from the command line as follows:

1 Make sure the environment variable JAVA_HOME is set. If it isn't, you can type it in at the command line before starting Tomcat, or add it to your environment in the usual way.

2 Change to the Tomcat bin directory. If you downloaded build 4.1.18 and extracted it as described, the full directory path might be: C:\Tomcat\jakarta-tomcat-4.1.18\bin, for example. At the command prompt, run the script startup.bat for Windows or startup.sh for Linux or UNIX. On Windows, this script launches Tomcat in a new window.

3 Test the installation by starting a web browser and entering **http://localhost:8080** in the address box. Doing so should bring up the default Tomcat home page, which includes the message "If you're seeing this page via a web browser, it means you've setup Tomcat successfully. Congratulations!"

You'll notice that you need to specify the HTTP port 8080 in the URL, because this is what Tomcat is initially configured to use—it's different than the default HTTP port 80. If you don't want to have to specify the port each time, you can change it in the Tomcat server.xml configuration file, providing this setting doesn't conflict with another HTTP server running on your machine.

You can also make sure Tomcat can display JSP pages by clicking on the JSP Examples link under Examples on the left side of the page and then running one or more of the examples on the page that follows. Shut down Tomcat by running either shutdown.bat on Windows or shutdown.sh on UNIX or Linux.

7.2.2 Installing and setting up the Sysdeo Tomcat plug-in

Download the Sysdeo Tomcat plug-in from http://www.sysdeo.com/eclipse/ tomcatPlugin.html. Unzip the file to the Eclipse plugins directory. If you do not have a zip utility, you can use the Java archive utility as follows:

1 The `jar` command has no option for specifying the destination directory, so you must change to the Eclipse plugins directory (for example, C:\ Eclipse\plugins).

2 Assuming the plug-in version you downloaded is named tomcatPluginV21.zip and you've downloaded it to the C:\downloads directory, enter the command `jar xf C:\downloads\tomcatPluginV21.zip`.

3 Eclipse automatically finds the plug-in the next time it starts, so stop Eclipse if necessary and then start it again.

Some plug-ins are inconsistent in the way they are packaged and must be unzipped into the Eclipse directory or higher rather than the plugins directory. If you cannot get a plug-in to work after installing it, this is the first thing you should check. To make certain that plug-ins are installed in the right directory, you may wish to unzip them to another directory first and then copy them from there—this approach has the added benefit of providing a backup of all your plug-ins, which can make it easier to upgrade to a new version of Eclipse later.

After installing the plug-in, you need to add Tomcat to the Java perspective and, optionally, to the Resource perspective. (Note that if you are working with a freshly installed Eclipse installation and you added the Tomcat plug-in before starting Eclipse the first time, you may already see Tomcat as one of the main menu selections.) Change to each perspective in turn and follow these steps:

1 Select Window→Customize Perspective from the main menu.

2 Expand the Other selection and click the box next to Tomcat. Click OK.

In addition to the new menu option, these steps add three new tool buttons to the main toolbar (see figure 7.1).

Configure the Tomcat plug-in by telling it where Tomcat is installed and which projects should be available for use in Tomcat projects, as follows:

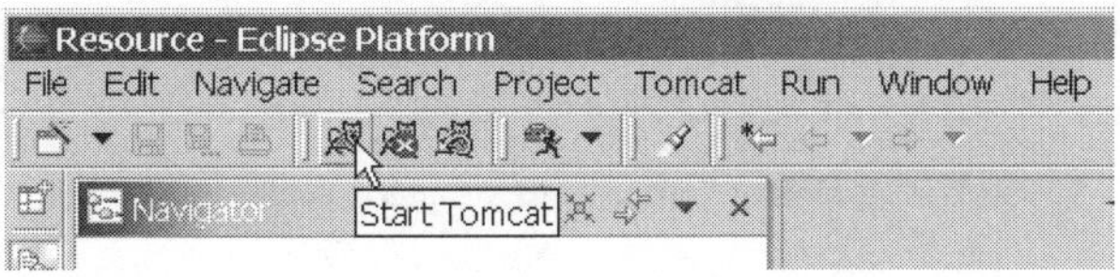

Figure 7.1
The Tomcat tool buttons. You can start or stop Tomcat using either the tool buttons or the Tomcat menu selection.

1 Select Window→Preferences→Tomcat.

2 Select the version of Tomcat you are using.

3 Enter, or click Browse to find, the Tomcat home directory. If you installed Tomcat as described earlier, this directory is C:\Tomcat\jakarta-tomcat-4.1.18. The entry for the configuration file will be updated automatically.

4 In the rest of this chapter, you will continue to use the Persistence project you began in chapter 3. So, in the Add Java Projects to Tomcat Classpath section, click the box next to Persistence. (See figure 7.2.)

5 Click OK.

You can now test the Tomcat plug-in either by clicking the Start Tomcat tool button or by selecting Tomcat→Start Tomcat from the main menu. Doing so displays startup information in the console window; once Tomcat is running, enter

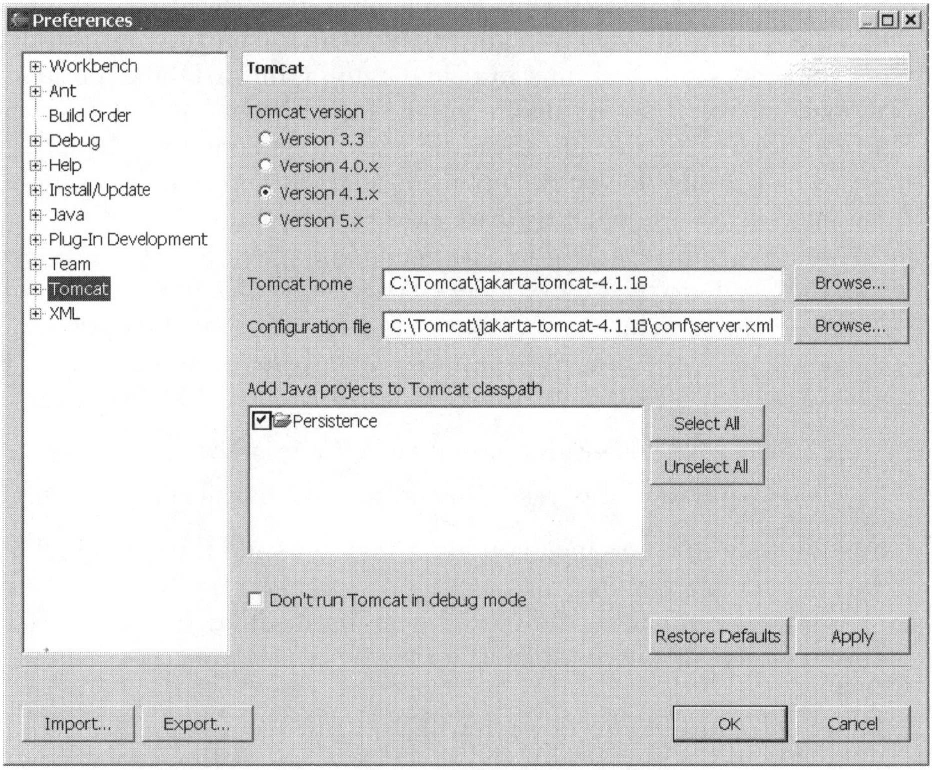

Figure 7.2   Tomcat preferences. Select the version of Tomcat you are using and enter its path here.

the URL **http://localhost:8080** in your browser's address box and verify that you get the Tomcat home page.

TIP   Although you won't need to edit much XML, you may want to install an XML editor anyway. It will provide syntax coloring and code assistance not only for XML, but also for HTML and JSP. Eclipse's Plug-in Development Environment (PDE) provides a wizard that builds a basic XML editor, but you can also download a free plug-in such as XMLBuddy from http://www.xmlbuddy.com. Installing XMLBuddy is a simple matter of unzipping and copying the plug-in to the Eclipse plugins directory.

Tomcat logging

Recent versions of Tomcat use another Apache component, Commons Logging, to provide logging services. This component is a wrapper that provides a single interface supporting different loggers, such as log4j. The wrapper locates a logging API through a somewhat complicated discovery process at runtime. If it finds the log4j configuration file that you created in chapter 3, you'll discover that Tomcat logs a lot of debug information in the Eclipse console view and takes a long time to start up.

You have two options to bring logging under control. The first is to continue to let Tomcat use your log4j configuration file, but to increase the logging threshold to filter out the numerous debug messages. To do this, open the file log4j.properties file in the bin folder under the Persistence project and change DEBUG in the second line to INFO, as follows:

```
# Assign two appenders to root logger
log4j.rootLogger=INFO, myConsole, myLogFile
```

The second option is to configure the Commons Logging component to use a different logger (or a different instance of log4j) than your Persistence component. You can find out more about this technique at the Apache web site.

7.2.3 *Creating and testing a JSP using Eclipse*

You can further test the plug-in installation by creating a Tomcat project with a simple JSP file. First create the project that you'll use later for the sample web application:

1 In the Java perspective, right-click in the Package Explorer view and select New→Project from the context menu.

2 In the New Project dialog box, select Java on the left side and Tomcat Project on the right side (see figure 7.3). Click Next.

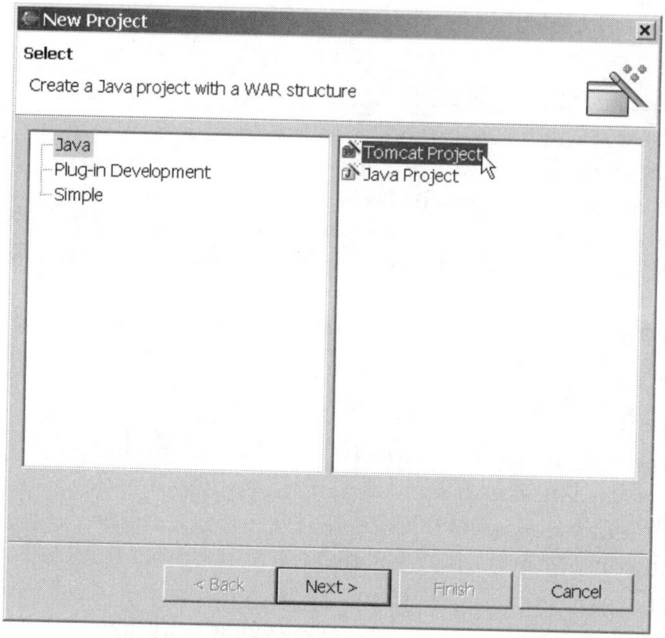

Figure 7.3
A new Tomcat project. The Sysdeo Tomcat plug-in adds a new option, Tomcat Project, to the New Project Wizard.

3   Enter a name for the project, such as **StarList**. You can set additional options by clicking Next, but in this case accept the defaults and click Finish.

Note that if you previously selected a working set that includes only the Persistence project, you may need to choose Deselect Working Set from the Package Explorer menu to get this new project to appear. You can also edit the current working set and add this project, or you can create a new working set that includes both the Persistence and StarList projects. In any case, both the Persistence and StarList projects should appear in the Package Explorer view (see figure 7.4).

Now you can create a JSP file and run it. To do this, follow these steps:

1   Right-click on the StarList project and select New→File from the context menu.

2   Enter a name for the file, such as **Testing.jsp**. If you haven't installed an XML editor, Eclipse won't recognize this type of file, so it will open the file with the default text editor.

3   Enter some HTML or JSP code, such as the following:

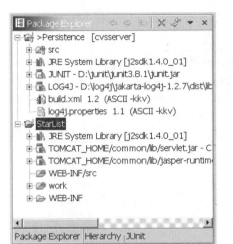

Figure 7.4
**The new Tomcat project, StarList. The Tomcat plug-in
creates the directory structure that Tomcat expects.**

```
<HTML>
<HEAD>
<TITLE>Testing</TITLE>
</HEAD>
<BODY>
Testing
<% for(int i = 1; i <= 3; i++) { %>
      <%= i%> ...
<% } %>

</BODY>
</HTML>
```

4   Right-click in the editor and select Save.

5   Start (or restart) Tomcat so that the new project is registered.

6   Start your browser. Load the JSP by entering the server address plus the web application context, which by default is the project name plus the JSP file name: **http://localhost:8080/StarList/Testing.jsp**.

If all is well, you will see a web page showing *Testing 1 ... 2 ... 3 ....*

7.2.4 *Creating and testing a servlet in Eclipse*

Let's add a servlet to accompany the JSP file you created earlier. Do this as follows:

1   Right-click on the new Tomcat project, StarList, and select New→Class.

2   In the New Java Class dialog that opens, note that the source directory is automatically set to StarList/WEB-INF/src.

3   Enter the package name **org.eclipseguide.starlist**.

4   Enter the class name **TestServlet**.

5   Enter **javax.servlet.http.HttpServlet** as the superclass. (You can do this most easily by clicking the Browse button and typing the first few letters of the unqualified classname to narrow the list of classes that appear and then selecting HttpServlet from the list.)

6   Make sure the option to create a main() method is not selected, and click Finish.

To the class that is generated, add a doGet() method. (Note that you can get Eclipse to generate the method skeleton for you by typing **doGet** and pressing Ctrl-Space.) Change the method as follows:

```
public class TestServlet extends HttpServlet
{
   protected void doGet(
      HttpServletRequest request,
      HttpServletResponse response)
      throws ServletException, IOException
   {
      PrintWriter out = response.getWriter();
      out.println("Hello from the servlet!");
   }
}
```

To test the servlet, enter the following URL in your browser: http://localhost:8080/StarList/servlet/org.eclipseguide.starlist.TestServlet. It should produce a web page with the text *Hello from the servlet!* If instead you get an error stating that the requested resource is unavailable, you may need to edit the web.xml file in the Tomcat conf directory. This is true of the most recent stable release, 4.1.18, available at the time of this writing. One way to do this is to add a link to this file to your project and use the XML editor in Eclipse to edit it.

Using a linked folder to edit web.xml

Eclipse 2.1 introduced a feature that allows a directory to be contained inside an Eclipse project logically, but remain located elsewhere physically, similar to the way links work in UNIX. If you need to manually manage the Tomcat configuration files, you can make a link to the Tomcat configuration directory as follows:

1   Right-click on the StarList project name and select New→Folder.

2   Click Advanced in the New Folder dialog box. Doing so displays the option to link to a folder.

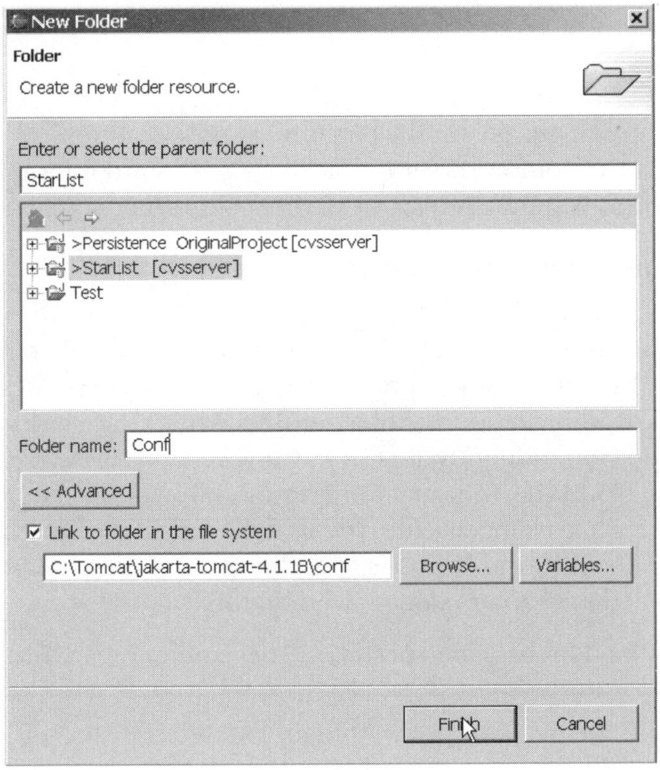

Figure 7.5
Creating a link to an external folder. Unlike the Import→File System menu selection, this option does not copy the contents into the Eclipse workspace directory.

3 Enter a name for the new folder in your project, such as **Conf**.

4 Click the Link to Folder in the File System box.

5 Type in the path to the Tomcat conf folder, or click Browse to locate it; if Tomcat is installed as described earlier, this directory is C:\Tomcat\jakarta-tomcat-4.1.18\conf (see figure 7.5).

6 Click Finish.

You can now expand the Conf folder in the Package Explorer view like any other folder in your project and edit the files in it. Note that the Conf folder has a little arrow in the bottom-right corner; this indicates that it is a shortcut and acts as a visual cue to remind you that the folder isn't part of your project tree.

Double-click on web.xml and find the following section, which is currently commented out:

```
<!--
<servlet-mapping>
```

```
      <servlet-name>invoker</servlet-name>
      <url-pattern>/servlet/*</url-pattern>
</servlet-mapping>
-->
```

To uncomment it, remove the `<!--` at the beginning and `-->` at the end. Save the file, and then restart the Tomcat server by clicking the Restart Tomcat tool button or selecting Tomcat→Restart Tomcat from the main menu.

7.2.5 *Placing a Tomcat project under CVS control*

In principal, there is no difference between placing a Tomcat project under source control and any other Java project. You need watch out for several things, though. When you check in a Tomcat project, the files that Eclipse uses to store project and classpath information (.project and .classpath) are automatically selected as candidates for adding to the Concurrent Versions System (CVS), but you need to manually add the Tomcat configuration file, .tomcatplugin. At the same time, you may wish to change its file type from binary to text (which, for historical reasons, is called ASCII in Eclipse's CVS client). Assuming you're already using CVS, as described in chapter 6, one way to do this is as follows:

1 Change to the Resource perspective. (The configuration files do not appear in the Java perspective.)
2 Right-click on the filename .tomcatplugin and select Team→Add to Version Control.
3 Right-click on the filename again and select Team→Change ASCII/Binary Property.
4 You can select either of the two ASCII options, but for consistency with the other ASCII files, choose ASCII with Keyword Substitution. Doing so presents further options; select ASCII with Keyword Expansion -kkv.
5 Click Finish.

The Tomcat plug-in configuration file is not the only file that will have the wrong file type; Eclipse doesn't recognize JSP files, so they are consequently treated as binary like all other unknown types. Rather that fix each JSP manually, it's better to add JSPs to the list of recognized file types:

1 Select Window→Preferences→Team→File Content and click the Add button.
2 You are prompted for a file extension. Enter **jsp** and click OK.

3 Verify that jsp appears in the file extension list and that its type is ASCII. If the type is incorrect, click on it and then click the Change button.

4 Click OK.

The final thing to watch for is that when you first check out a project, the Tomcat plug-in will not update the Tomcat server.xml file, so the web application (that is, the JSPs and servlets in the project) will not be recognized. You must force the plug-in to register the web application by right-clicking on the Tomcat project's name and selecting Tomcat Project→Update Context in Server XML.

7.3 *Building a web application*

Let's continue with the Persistence application you began in previous chapters by adding a simple web interface to let users list existing data and add new data. The goal is to eventually allow them to enter any kind of astronomical bodies, but for now you'll limit them to stars.

If you followed the instructions in chapter 6 to remove the `astronomy` package from the main branch in CVS and create an `OriginalProject` branch that includes the `astronomy` package, make sure you are working in the `OriginalProject` branch. This is essentially the same state you were in at the end of chapter 5, so you shouldn't have any problems if you didn't follow the examples in chapter 6.

7.3.1 *The web application directory structure*

In the same way that Java applications are packaged into an archive called a JAR file, web applications can be packaged into a WAR file, using the same standard Java archive utility, `jar`. The J2EE specification defines the directory structure a WAR file must have, and this same directory structure is generally used even when the application is not archived. One of the benefits of using the Tomcat plug-in is that it creates and maintains this WAR structure for you.

This is what the project's directory tree looks like after you create the JSP and servlet and refresh the project:

```
StarList
|   Testing.jsp
|
+---WEB-INF
|   +---classes
|   |   +---org
|   |   |   +---apache
|   |   |   |   +---jsp
|   |   |   |           Testing_jsp.class
```

```
|    |            +---eclipseguide
|    |                 +---starlist
|    |                          TestServlet.class
|    |
|    +---lib
|    +---src
|         +---org
|              +---eclipseguide
|                   +---starlist
|                            TestServlet.java
|
+---work
     +---org
          +---apache
               +---jsp
                         Testing_jsp.java
```

The significance of these directories is as follows:

- *StarList (project root)*—JSP source files. In addition, you put resources such as images and HTML files in this directory (or in subdirectories below this directory).

- *WEB-INF*—Servlets. The source code goes under the src directory, and the compiled classes go under the classes directory.

- *work*—JSP files are automatically converted to Java source files and compiled by Tomcat under this directory. As you'll see in section 7.3.3, you can use the Java source files to debug a JSP if necessary.

In addition to this development environment, you need to be aware of several files in the Tomcat environment. In particular, the web.xml files (which you've already seen) and server.xml are used to configure web applications and the Tomcat server.

7.3.2 *Web application design and testing*

So far, you have a persistence mechanism that can store and retrieve arbitrary Java objects using an arbitrary index. Let's use it (along with the star class) to build a web site you can use to enter and look up information about stars. (You may want to extend this site later so the existing information can be modified or deleted.) Figure 7.6 shows a map of the proposed web site.

NOTE   As you've continued to extend the sample application in previous chapters, in the interest of keeping the focus on developing the application, we've stressed agile techniques less and less, particularly test-driven development. The assumption has been, however, that this work continues off-stage.

As you move into building an application with multiple tiers, testing becomes significantly more difficult, and you'll find you need more tools (and more complex tools) in order to continue with the test-driven approach. One such tool is Cactus, an Apache Jakarta project that extends JUnit to support testing server-side code; we encourage you to learn more about Cactus by visiting its web site at http://jakarta.apache.org/cactus/. Another approach is to simulate the server-side environment (or parts of it) by using *mock objects*—that is, objects that imitate the behavior of the real objects your code normally calls. You can learn more about mock objects at http://www.mockobjects.com. Because of their scope, we won't cover these topics here.

The StarList home page

You'll begin with the home page; it's straightforward, because it only needs to provide users with a way to select between listing existing stars and entering new stars. This page can be straight HTML, but even if it is, you can give it a .jsp extension to add flexibility. (Most importantly, an HTML page cannot handle POST requests, so servlets can forward only GET requests to an HTML page. A JSP,

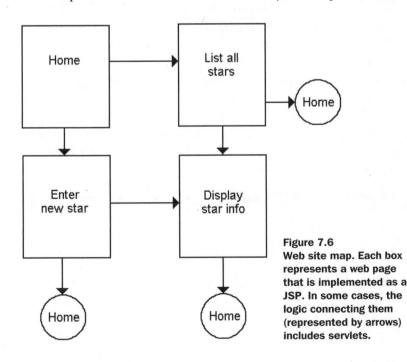

Figure 7.6
Web site map. Each box represents a web page that is implemented as a JSP. In some cases, the logic connecting them (represented by arrows) includes servlets.

however, can handle both, and there are often reasons—such as providing better security—for preferring POST requests over GET requests.) As long as it's JSP anyway, you can create a common header and banner for all your applications and use a JSP page directive to include it.

To create the header, use the New→File selection from the StarList project's context menu. It doesn't matter what you call the header, but because it includes HTML, let's call it Header.html (see listing 7.1).

Listing 7.1   Header.html

```
<!DOCTYPE HTML PUBLIC "-//W3C//DTD HTML 4.0 Transitional//EN">
<HTML>
<HEAD>
<TITLE>Star List</TITLE>
</HEAD>
<BODY BGCOLOR="000000" TEXT="E1D57E"><H1><CENTER>
<IMG SRC="/StarList/hoagsobject.jpg" ALT="Star search"></H1>
<BR><P></CENTER>
```

If you're using the XMLBuddy plug-in, you'll notice that it colorizes the text and (somewhat) helpfully generates a closing tag for every tag you enter; although closing tags are necessary for XML, they're not for HTML. After typing this code, save the file. (The banner uses an image file; you can download it from the book's web site along with the rest of this application, but it's not necessary because the ALT attribute supplies text in its place.)

Next, create the Home.jsp home page the same way, using the New→File selection from the project context menu (see listing 7.2). This page has two forms, each with a Submit button that forwards to a different page; one, labeled List All Stars, requests a servlet, StarListServlet; the other, labeled Enter a Star, requests another JSP, NewStarEntry.jsp. Notice how the home page includes the header file you created in the previous step.

Listing 7.2   Home.jsp

```
<%@ include file="Header.html" %>
<CENTER>
<P>
Welcome to the Star List home page. You can find information
about stars or enter a new star. Press one of the following
buttons to continue:
<P></P>
<FORM METHOD="POST"
    ACTION=
```

```
      "/StarList/servlet/org.eclipseguide.starlist.StarListServlet">
<INPUT TYPE="SUBMIT" NAME="ACTION" VALUE="List all stars">
</FORM>

<FORM METHOD="POST" ACTION="/StarList/NewStarEntry.jsp">
<INPUT TYPE="SUBMIT" NAME="ACTION" VALUE="Enter a star">
</FORM>
</CENTER>
</BODY>
</HTML>
```

Once you've created these two files, you can start Tomcat (if it's not running already) and view the home page by entering the URL **http://localhost:8080/ StarList/Home.jsp** in your browser. But don't click either button yet!

The new star entry form

Next let's consider NewStarEntry.jsp (listing 7.3), because it permits you to enter some data. Apart from the JSP directive to include the banner, it's mostly straightforward HTML. A form is used to allow the user to enter information about a star; this form has a Submit button that forwards the information to a servlet, StarEntryServlet. An additional form has a single button to let the user cancel out of the operation and return to the home page:

Listing 7.3 NewStarEntry.jsp

```
<%@ include file="Header.html" %>

<FORM METHOD="POST"
    ACTION="/StarList/servlet/org.eclipseguide.starlist.StarEntryServlet">
<CENTER>
<TABLE>

<TR><TD COLSPAN=2>
<CENTER><H2>New star</H2></CENTER></TD></TR><P>
Enter the star's information below and press <B>Save</B>.<P>
<TR>
    <TD>Name</TD>
    <TD><INPUT TYPE="TEXT" NAME="name"></TD>
</TR>
<TR>
    <TD>Catalog number</TD>
    <TD><INPUT TYPE="TEXT" NAME="catalogNumber"></TD>
</TR>
<TR>
    <TD>Absolute magnitude</TD>
    <TD><INPUT TYPE="TEXT" NAME="absoluteMagnitude"></TD>
</TR>
```

```
<TR>
   <TD>Spectral type</TD>
   <TD><INPUT TYPE="TEXT" NAME="spectralType"></TD>
</TR>
<TR>
   <TD>Constellation</TD>
   <TD><INPUT TYPE="TEXT" NAME="constellation"></TD>
</TR>
<TR>
   <TD>Galaxy</TD>
   <TD><INPUT TYPE="TEXT" NAME="galaxy"></TD>
</TR>
<TR>
   <TD>Radius</TD>
   <TD><INPUT TYPE="TEXT" NAME="radius"></TD>
</TR>
<TR>
   <TD>Mass</TD>
   <TD><INPUT TYPE="TEXT" NAME="mass"></TD>
</TR>
<TR>
   <TD>Period of rotation</TD>
   <TD><INPUT TYPE="TEXT" NAME="rotationPeriod"></TD>
</TR>
<TR>
   <TD>Surface temperature</TD>
   <TD> <INPUT TYPE="TEXT" NAME="surfaceTemperature"></TD>
</TR>
<TR>
   <TD COLSPAN=2>
      <CENTER>
      <INPUT TYPE="SUBMIT" NAME="ACTION" VALUE="Save">
      </CENTER>
   </TD>
</TR>
</FORM>
</TABLE>
<FORM METHOD="POST" ACTION="/StarList/Home.jsp">
   <INPUT TYPE="SUBMIT" NAME="ACTION" VALUE="Cancel">
</FORM>
</CENTER>
</BODY>
</HTML>
```

Once you've created and saved this file, you can click the Enter a Star button on the home page. Doing so displays the screen shown in figure 7.7.

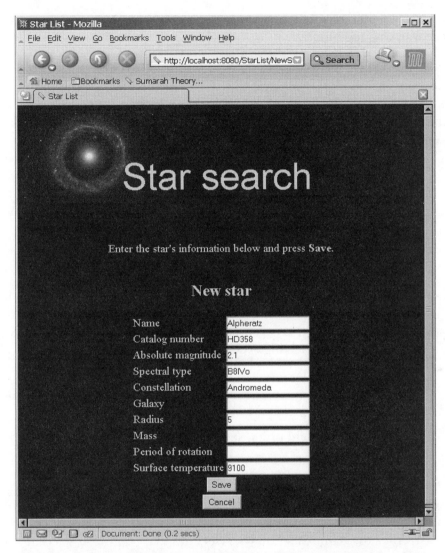

Figure 7.7 The page generated by NewStarEntry.jsp. The user enters data using a standard HTML form. (Image courtesy of NASA and the Hubble Heritage Team [STScI/AURA].)

7.3.3 *Programming with servlets and JSPs*

So far, you've built static pages. You used some JSP, but as a convenience rather than out of necessity. To proceed further, you need to do some real programming. The next step is to create a servlet that uses this information to create a `Star` object and save the information in the database; but before you can do that, you need to change some settings to get the two projects, StarList and Persistence, working together.

Multiproject build settings: build paths and build order

When you installed Tomcat, you saw that you need to add the projects you're using (in this case, Persistence and StarList) to the Tomcat classpath by selecting Window→Preferences→Tomcat from the main menu. You also need to add Persistence to the StarList project's build path as follows:

1 Select Properties from the StarList project context menu.

2 Select Java Build Path on the left of the Properties dialog box.

3 Click on the Projects tab on the right. Doing so displays a list of all the other projects in your workspace.

4 Click the box next to Persistence to add it to your build path (assuming it's not already selected) and click OK.

When one project depends on another, it's important that they get built in the right order. Because StarList depends on Persistence, and Persistence was the first project you created, this isn't an issue here; the default build order is already correct. You can verify or change the build order as follows:

1 Select Window→Preferences from the main menu.

2 Select Build Order. Projects are listed in the order they are built by Eclipse (see figure 7.8).

3 To change the build order, select a project and then click Up or Down as appropriate.

The star entry servlet

To create the star entry servlet, begin by selecting New→Class from the project context menu. Enter an appropriate package name, such as **org.eclipseguide. starlist**, enter the name **StarEntryServlet**, and make sure you select `javax.servlet.http.HttpServlet` as the superclass. In the editor, create method stubs for `doGet()` and `doPost()` by typing the first few letters of each (case doesn't matter) and pressing Ctrl-Space. You'll be handling both `POST` and `GET` requests identically, so you can either have them both call another method or have one call the other. Taking the latter approach, you can change `doGet()` as follows:

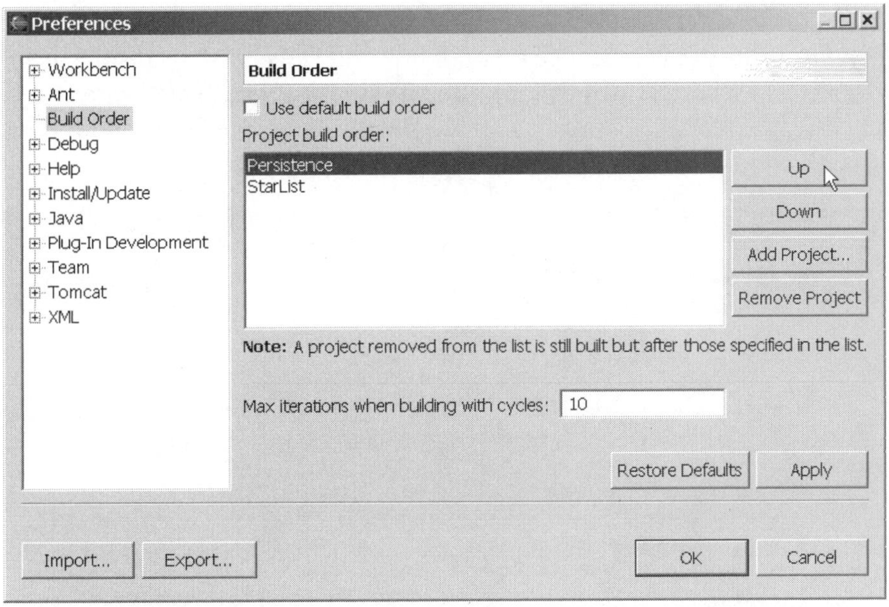

Figure 7.8   Build order. If the default build order is not correct, you can set the order manually.

```
protected void doGet(
   HttpServletRequest request,
   HttpServletResponse response)
   throws ServletException, IOException
{
   doPost(request, response);
}
```

Note that the method stub Eclipse generated included a call to the superclass's doGet() method, but it's unnecessary; we've removed it here.

Data validation and conversion

The code for creating a Star, filling in the fields, obtaining an ObjectManager, and using it to persist the Star should be familiar from previous chapters. The only new twist is that you obtain the values from the form by using the request.getParameter() method, which returns a String. In the case of numeric fields, you need to perform the proper conversion, using the methods Double.parse-Double() and Long.parseLong(). (The Star class only uses these two numeric types.) You need to be careful to validate the user's input, however, because HTML forms don't provide a way to perform validation—the user can type anything (or nothing) into any of the fields.

To provide verification, after the star information is saved, the servlet retrieves it again from the Persistence component and calls a JSP to display it to the user. Notice that a servlet can call another servlet, JSP, or HTML page by obtaining a `RequestDispatcher`. Listing 7.4 shows the `doPost()` method followed by the conversion routines.

Listing 7.4   The StarEntryServlet's doPost() method

```
protected void doPost(
   HttpServletRequest request,
   HttpServletResponse response)
   throws ServletException, IOException
{
   ObjectManager om =
      ObjectManager.createObjectManager(Star.class);
   Star star = new Star();
   star.name = request.getParameter("name");
   star.catalogNumber = request.getParameter("catalogNumber");
   star.absoluteMagnitude =
      cvtDouble(request.getParameter("absoluteMagnitude"));
   star.spectralType = request.getParameter("spectralType");
   star.constellation = request.getParameter("constellation");
   star.galaxy = request.getParameter("galaxy");
   star.radius = cvtLong(request.getParameter("radius"));
   star.mass = cvtLong(request.getParameter("mass"));
   star.rotationPeriod =
      cvtLong(request.getParameter("rotationPeriod"));
   star.surfaceTemperature =
      cvtLong(request.getParameter("surfaceTemperature"));

   int index = om.getNextKey();
   om.save (star, index);
   star = (Star) om.get(index);

   String destPage = "/DisplayStar.jsp";
   if (star == null)
   {
      destPage = "/Home.jsp";
   }
   else
   {
      request.setAttribute("star", star);
   }

   RequestDispatcher dispatcher =
      getServletContext().getRequestDispatcher(destPage);
   dispatcher.forward(request, response);
}

public double cvtDouble(String value)
{
```

```
        double number = 0;

        try
        {
           if (value != null)
           {
              number = Double.parseDouble(value);
           }
        }
        catch (NumberFormatException e)
        {
           // ignore
        }
        return number;
    }
    public long cvtLong(String value)
    {
        long number = 0;

        try
        {
           if (value != null)
           {
              number = Long.parseLong(value);
           }
        }
        catch (NumberFormatException e)
        {
           // Ignore
        }
        return number;
    }
```

Note that you need to change the visibility of the save() method in ObjectManager to public. This is an error the unit tests didn't catch because they were in the same package.

Notice that the FileObjectManager includes a new method you haven't seen before: getNextKey(). It is essentially a counter you use to obtain a new index when you want to add a new object to the data store. It uses the methods in FilePersistenceServices to store, retrieve, and increment a value in a separate file with a single entry. This isn't very efficient, but it's sufficient for now:

```
    public int getNextKey()
    {
        int key;
        String seqFileName = className + ".nextkey";
        Vector v = FilePersistenceServices.read(1);
```

```
        if (v == null)
        {
           key = 1;
           v = new Vector();
           v.add(Integer.toString(2));
           FilePersistenceServices.write(1, v);
        }
        else
        {
           try
           {
              key = Integer.parseInt((String) v.get(0));
           }
           catch (NumberFormatException e)
           {
              key = 1;
           }
           v.clear();
           v.add(Integer.toString(key + 1));
           FilePersistenceServices.update(seqFileName, 1, v);
        }
        return key;
     }
```

Note that we don't show the unit tests used to develop this method, or a method for resetting the key back to zero (required by the unit tests).

Robust string handling

You may wonder why strings are not verified. As you probably remember, data is stored in a text file in a comma- and double-quote–delimited format, which is parsed using the standard Java `StringTokenizer` class. This is simply too fragile a scheme to store any real data, and you need to fix the `FilePersistenceServices` class instead, so that no string will cause a problem.

One way to make strings safe is to escape all characters that might cause a problem. You can easily do that using the `URLEncoder` and `URLDecoder` classes that Java provides. This leaves the problem that `StringTokenizer` doesn't deal properly with null entries; you can either provide a special nonnull null entry (like the word *null*) or replace `StringTokenizer` with a more robust parser. The latter is the better option in a production environment, because `StringTokenizer` can be pretty slow (due to its being threadsafe); but you'll never use a file-based persistence component in a production environment, so you'll work around `StringTokenizer`'s limitation for this example.

The relevant method for encoding strings is `FilePersistenceServices.vector2String()`. But to begin, you should think of all the devious things users might enter, and create the appropriate test cases in `FilePersistenceServicesTest`, `testVector2String()`, and `testString2Vector()`. These tests are not shown here, but `vector2String` looks like this after it's been bulletproofed against rogue string values:

```
private static final String ENCODING = "UTF-8";

static String vector2String(Vector v, int key)
{
    String s = null;
    StringBuffer buffer = new StringBuffer();
    buffer.append("\"" + Integer.toString(key) + "\",");         Start with
                                                                  key
    for (int i = 0; i < v.size(); i++)      Add comma, quote
    {                                       delimited entry for
        buffer.append("\"");                each element in v
        String elem;
        if (v.elementAt(i) == null)
        {
            elem = "null";
        }
        else
        {
            elem = v.elementAt(i).toString();
            if (elem.equals(""))
            {
                elem = "null";
            }
        }
        try
        {

            buffer.append(URLEncoder.encode(elem, ENCODING));
        }
        catch (UnsupportedEncodingException e)
        {
            logger.fatal(                                        Unsupported
                "Programming error: Bad encoding selected");     character set
        }

        buffer.append("\"");
        if (i != (v.size()-1))
        {
            buffer.append(",");
        }
    }
    s = buffer.toString();
    return s;
}
```

The complementary changes to `string2Vector()` look like this:

```
static Vector string2Vector(String s)
{
    Vector v = new Vector();
    StringTokenizer st = new StringTokenizer(s, "\",");     Use comma
    int count = st.countTokens();                           and double
    if (count >= 2)                                         quotes as
    {                                                       delimiters
        st.nextToken();
        for (int i = 1; i < count; i++)
        {
            try
            {
                v.addElement(
                    URLDecoder.decode(st.nextToken(), ENCODING));
            }
            catch (UnsupportedEncodingException e)
            {
                logger.fatal("Bad encoding selected");
            }
        }
    }
    return v;
}
```

Note that there is no need to deal specially with null values here. Because Java supplies the string value `"null"` in certain cases, the object-mapping layer already deals with this situation correctly.

Debugging a servlet

There is nothing special about debugging a servlet—it's just another Java class. The only difference from those you've seen so far is that you cannot run it directly. Rather, the servlet is invoked automatically when the Tomcat server gets a request for it. To see this, place a breakpoint by double-clicking on the right margin next to the first line of code in the `doPost()` method. Then, using your browser, enter the URL for the home page: **http://localhost:8080/StarList/Home.jsp**. Click Enter New Star, fill in some data, and then click Save. Eclipse will automatically change to the Debug perspective, with the cursor on the first line of code in the `StarEntryServlet` class (see figure 7.9).

As usual, you can step into other classes or place breakpoints in any of the code that is executed—even in other projects, such as the modified `vector2String()` method in the `FilePersistenceServices` class.

Note, however, that when you are finished debugging, you should not click Terminate, because doing so will stop the Tomcat server. Instead, when you are finished or encounter an error, click Resume. Tomcat will return an error page to the browser, if appropriate, and continue listening for more requests.

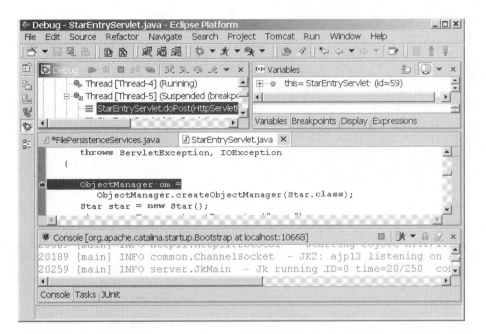

Figure 7.9 Debugging a servlet. Don't click Terminate, or you'll kill Tomcat. Instead, click Resume to stop debugging.

You don't need to stop and start Tomcat after saving a file; just remember to save, and Tomcat will recognize that the file has been recompiled. (Or, in the case of a JSP, it will recognize that it needs to convert the JSP to a Java source file and recompile.)

Using a JavaBean with JSP

Now you're ready to display the star information to the user with the first real JSP. One of the big benefits of JSPs is that they work well with JavaBeans. You can take advantage of this by adding getter methods to the Star class and its superclass, CelestialBody, which will make Star, in effect, a read-only JavaBean. To do this, follow these steps:

1 Find the Star class in the Package Explorer under the Persistence project and right-click on it.

2 In the context menu, select Source→Generate Getter and Setter.

3 Eclipse offers to generate both getXXX() and setXXX() methods for each field. Click on each of the getXXX() methods and click OK. Save Star.

4   Do the same for the `CelestialBody` class. (As you know, `Star` inherits these
methods from `CelestialBody`.) Save `CelestialBody`.

Now you can use a `<jsp:useBean>` tag to obtain and read a `Star` object in a JSP. In
the `StarEntryServlet`, you added a `Star` object to the request with the following
line of code:

```
request.setAttribute("star", star);
```

Create a new file, DisplayStar.jsp, and add the JSP code shown in listing 7.5 for
retrieving and displaying this star.

Listing 7.5   DisplayStar.jsp

```
<%@ include file="Header.html" %>

<jsp:useBean id="star" class="org.eclipseguide.astronomy.Star"
    scope="request"/>

<FORM METHOD="POST" ACTION="/StarList/Home.jsp">
<CENTER>
<H2><jsp:getProperty name="star" property="name"/></H2><P>
<TABLE>
</TR>

</TD></TR>
<TR>
    <TD>Catalog number</TD>
    <TD><jsp:getProperty name="star" property="catalogNumber"/></TD>
</TR><TR>
    <TD>Absolute magnitude</TD>
    <TD><jsp:getProperty name="star" property="absoluteMagnitude"/>
    </TD>
</TR><TR>
    <TD>Spectral type</TD>
    <TD><jsp:getProperty name="star" property="spectralType"/></TD>
</TR><TR>
    <TD>Constellation</TD>
    <TD><jsp:getProperty name="star" property="constellation"/></TD>
</TR><TR>
    <TD>Galaxy</TD>
    <TD><jsp:getProperty name="star" property="galaxy"/></TD>
</TR><TR>
    <TD>Radius</TD>
    <TD><jsp:getProperty name="star" property="radius"/></TD>
</TR><TR>
    <TD>Mass</TD>
    <TD><jsp:getProperty name="star" property="mass"/></TD>
</TR><TR>
    <TD>Period of rotation</TD>
```

```
   <TD><jsp:getProperty name="star" property="rotationPeriod"/></TD>
</TR><TR>
   <TD>Surface temperature</TD>
   <TD><jsp:getProperty name="star" property="surfaceTemperature"/>
   </TD>
</TR><TR>
   <TD COLSPAN=2><CENTER>
      <INPUT TYPE="SUBMIT" property="ACTION" VALUE="Home">
   </CENTER></TD>
</TR>
</TABLE></CENTER></FORM>
</BODY></HTML>
```

Notice how nicely the `<jsp:useBean>` and `<jsp:getProperty>` tags obviate the need to do any programming once the servlet has served up the data in a JavaBean. Unfortunately, JSPs aren't always this clean. If you want to display a list of all the stars in the database, for example, you can't obtain them easily as JavaBeans like this; at a minimum, you need some Java code that loops through, retrieving (probably with Java code) and displaying each one. But whether it's behind the scenes (as it is here) or in the open, where there's code, there are sometimes bugs.

Debugging JSPs

Debugging JSPs is no different than debugging servlets, because JSPs are converted into servlets and compiled. The only problem is that you can't debug your JSP code directly (at least, not with the Sysdeo Tomcat plug-in); you need to find the generated Java servlet in the Tomcat work directory and work with that. Fortunately, it's usually easy to correlate what's happening in the Java code with what you wrote using JSP—especially if it's Java code in the JSP.

As an example, locate the file DisplayStar_jsp.java under the work directory in the StarList project, inside the `org.apache.jsp` package, and double-click on it to open it in the editor. (You may have to refresh the project contents by right-clicking on the project and selecting Refresh.) The first thing to notice is that the class `DisplayStar_jsp` is of type `HttpJspBase`, which is a subclass of `HttpServlet`. (You can discover this, and much more about the class, its attributes, and its methods, by right-clicking on `HttpJspBase` or `DisplayStar_jsp` and selecting Open Type Hierarchy from the context menu.) The most interesting method in the class is `_jspService()`, which is where your JSP code resides. For example, here is how it instantiates and populates the `Star` object:

```
org.eclipseguide.astronomy.Star star = null;
synchronized (request) {
   star = (org.eclipseguide.astronomy.Star)
```

```
        pageContext.getAttribute("star", PageContext.REQUEST_SCOPE);
  if (star == null){
     try {
        star = (org.eclipseguide.astronomy.Star)
          java.beans.Beans.instantiate(
             this.getClass().getClassLoader(),
             "org.eclipseguide.astronomy.Star");
     } catch (ClassNotFoundException exc) {
        throw new InstantiationException(exc.getMessage());
     } catch (Exception exc) {
        throw new ServletException("Cannot create bean of class "
           + "org.eclipseguide.astronomy.Star", exc);
     }      pageContext.setAttribute("star", star,
                PageContext.REQUEST_SCOPE);
  }
}
```

One of the problems with using JSPs and servlets is that they are loosely linked. There is nothing to guarantee that you use the same name for the `Star` JavaBean in the servlet and in the JSP, for example, and no error will occur at compile time or runtime. If the names don't agree (perhaps because of a typo), whatever information you enter for a `Star` will mysteriously be lost. (If you look at the database, you'll see that the information was saved there, which only deepens the mystery.)

You may already know that the `<jsp:useBean>` tag creates a new instance of the JavaBean if one with the specified identifier doesn't already exist, but if you didn't, it's apparent from this code. If you trace into it, you'll find the call to `getAttribute()` fails, and that a new uninitialized instance of `Star` is displayed instead.

Multithreaded debugging

One of the issues you need to be aware of when working with servlets is thread safety. Tomcat only instantiates a single instance of the servlet to handle all requests, so all requests share the same instance data and data such as attributes in the application scope. This means two requests arriving at the servlet at the same time can wreak havoc on each other. You can explore this situation in the debugger by using two browser windows to send two requests to a servlet at the same time.

As it is, `StarEntryServlet` is threadsafe because the data it uses, such as the variables `star` and `index`, are method local. To wreak a little havoc, move the declaration of `Star` as follows, to make it a class instance variable:

```
public class StarEntryServlet extends HttpServlet
{
   Star star;
```

```
protected void doPost(
   HttpServletRequest request,
   HttpServletResponse response)
   throws ServletException, IOException
{
   ObjectManager om =
      ObjectManager.createObjectManager(Star.class);
   star = new Star();
   // etc...
```

Make sure you still have a breakpoint set in the first line of the doPost() method in StarEntryServlet. Then go to the New Star entry page in your browser, enter **First star** as the star's name, and click Save. As before, the debugger in Eclipse suspends execution when the breakpoint is reached. Now, click Step Over to advance the cursor to the next line in the program. Notice that the Debug view includes an entry such as Thread [Thread-5] Suspended, and that the first child entry below it indicates that it is suspended on line 34 of the method StarEntry-Servlet.doPost(). (Your line and thread numbers may differ, of course.)

Open another browser window, go to the star entry page, enter **Second star** as the name, and click Save. The debugger again suspends execution of this request at the breakpoint. Notice that you now have two arrows in the left margin of the editor, one for each suspended thread. Likewise, the Debug view shows two suspended threads (see figure 7.10). Note that threads are assigned arbitrarily from a pool, so in this case the second thread is Thread-3. You can control the execution of each thread individually by clicking on it in this view and then clicking the debug buttons in the toolbar.

You can easily demonstrate the problems that nonthreadsafe code can cause:

1 Place a breakpoint at the call to om.save().

2 Select the first thread, which in this case happens to be Thread-5, and press Resume. You now have a new Star object, star, with the value of the name attribute set to First star, which you verify in the Variables view.

3 Select the second thread, Thread-3 here, and click Resume. This assigns a new Star object to star with the name Second star, overwriting the first.

At this point it doesn't matter which thread you run next—both save a Star named Second star (with different indexes, because the index is a local variable), and the information for Second star is returned to both browsers.

After changing the code back to the way it was originally, you can repeat the steps and verify that this problem doesn't occur with star as a local variable.

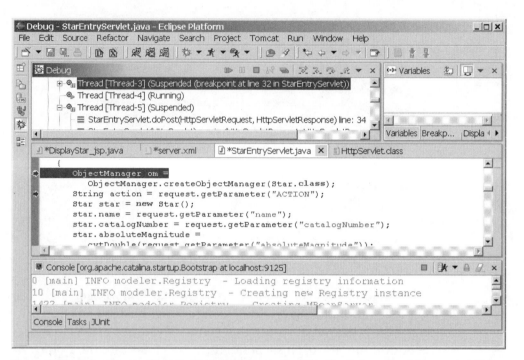

Figure 7.10 Debugging multiple threads. Selecting a thread in the Debug view lets you control its execution.

7.4 *Wrapping up the sample application*

Before bidding adieu to the sample application you've been developing in this part of the book, let's tie up a few loose ends. You've seen how keys are obtained when creating records, and you may wonder how you can get those keys to retrieve a record. You do so by creating a method to query the data in the file. For now you'll implement a simple query that returns the keys for all the records in the database, getCollection(), but in a more fully developed application you may want to have a way to specify the criteria that data must meet to be returned.

This is the method in FileObjectManager:

```
public Collection getCollection()
{

   Collection coll =
      FilePersistenceServices.getCollection(className);
   return (Collection) coll;
}
```

Most of the work is done in the `FilePersistenceServices` class, in a corresponding `getCollection()` method:

```
public static Collection getCollection(String fileName)
{
    Vector v = new Vector();
    try
    {
        FileReader fr = new FileReader(fileName);
        BufferedReader in = new BufferedReader(fr);
        String str;
        boolean found = false;

        while ((str = in.readLine()) != null)
        {
            v.add(new Integer(getKey(str)));
        }
        in.close();
    }
    catch (FileNotFoundException e)
    {
        v = null;
    }
    catch (IOException e)
    {
        v = null;
    }
    return v;

}
```

Listing 7.6 shows the `StarListServlet` servlet that calls these methods to get the star keys. Converting the collection to an array makes the JSP's job easier.

Listing 7.6   StarListServlet.java

```
public class StarListServlet extends HttpServlet
{
    protected void doPost(
        HttpServletRequest request,
        HttpServletResponse response)
        throws ServletException, IOException
    {

        ObjectManager om =
            ObjectManager.createObjectManager(Star.class);
        Collection starCollect = om.getCollection();
        if (starCollect != null)
        {
            Integer[] starKeys =
                (Integer[]) starCollect.toArray(new Integer[0]);
            request.setAttribute("starKeys", starKeys);
```

```
        }
    RequestDispatcher dispatcher =
        getServletContext().getRequestDispatcher("/ListStars.jsp");
    dispatcher.forward(request, response);
    }

    protected void doGet(
        HttpServletRequest request,
        HttpServletResponse response)
        throws ServletException, IOException
    {
        doPost(request, response);
    }

}
```

You could use these keys to look up and display each star on a JSP. But instead, you'll display the names and let the user use a radio button to select a star he wants to learn more about (see figure 7.11).

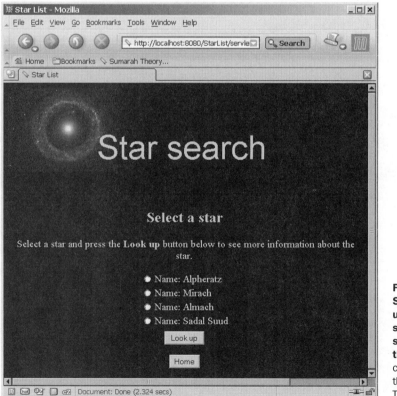

Figure 7.11
Selecting a star using a radio button sets a variable to the star's index behind the scenes. (Image courtesy of NASA and the Hubble Heritage Team [STScI/AURA].)

Listing 7.7 shows ListStars.jsp; note that the index of each star is stored in the radio button's value attribute.

Listing 7.7   ListStars.jsp

```
<%@ include file="Header.html" %>
<%@ page import="org.eclipseguide.persistence.ObjectManager" %>
<%@ page import="org.eclipseguide.astronomy.Star" %>

<CENTER>
<FORM METHOD="POST"
   ACTION=
   "/StarList/servlet/org.eclipseguide.starlist.StarEntryServlet">

<TABLE>
<%  Integer [] starList=
        (Integer [])request.getAttribute("starKeys");
    ObjectManager om =
        ObjectManager.createObjectManager(Star.class);
    boolean starsFound = true;
    if(starList!=null)
    {
%>
    <H2>Select a star</H2><P>

Select a star and press the <B>Look up</B> button below to see
 more information about the star. <P>

<%
      for(int i=0; i < starList.length; i++)
      {
         int index = starList[i].intValue();
         Star star = (Star) om.get(index);
         if(star != null)
         {
%>
      <TR><TD>
      <INPUT TYPE="radio" NAME="STAR_SELECTED"
          VALUE="<%= index %>">
      </TD>
        <TD>
      Name: <%= star.getName() %>
      </TD></TR>
<%        }
      }
   }
   else
   {
      starsFound = false;
%>
   <H2>No stars found!</H2>
<%   }
```

```
%>
<TR>
   <TD COLSPAN=2>
      <CENTER>
<% if(starsFound)
   {
%>
</TR>
</TABLE>
   <INPUT TYPE="SUBMIT" NAME="ACTION" VALUE="Look up">
</FORM>
<%  } %>

<FORM METHOD="GET" ACTION="/StarList/Home.jsp"
   <INPUT TYPE="SUBMIT" NAME="ACTION" VALUE="Home">
</CENTER>
</BODY>
</HTML>
```

This JSP defies the rule we mentioned earlier about separating display logic from business logic; but because of the need to loop through each star in preparing the form, there's no getting around the fact that you have to mingle the two here. One possible remedy that would reduce (but not eliminate) this mess would be to use custom tags, but doing so introduces additional complexity to the application.

Notice that after the user has chosen a star, the form on this JSP calls StarEntryServlet to display the information, because this servlet already has the logic for instantiating a star and forwarding the request to a JSP to display it. You need to change to the servlet so that it uses the ACTION parameter from the form on the JSP to determine whether it needs to create a new star or retrieve an existing one:

```
protected void doPost(
   HttpServletRequest request,
   HttpServletResponse response)
   throws ServletException, IOException
{
   ObjectManager om =
      ObjectManager.createObjectManager(Star.class);
   Star star = null;
   String destPage = "/DisplayStar.jsp";
   String action = request.getParameter("ACTION");
   if (action.equals("Look up"))
   {
      try
      {
         int index =
            Integer.parseInt(
               request.getParameter("STAR_SELECTED"));
```

```
        star = (Star) om.get(index);
        request.setAttribute("star", star);
    }
    catch (NumberFormatException e)      Leaves
    {                                     star==null
    }
}
else if (action.equals("Save"))
{
    star = new Star();
    star.name = request.getParameter("name");
    star.catalogNumber = request.getParameter("catalogNumber");
    // etc...
```

Not shown here is another `else` clause to deal with the case in which a valid star is not found, either because this servlet was called in error or because the user entered its URL directly in the browser. In that case, the destination page variable `destPage` is set to point to an error page.

There are additional features that would be nice to implement, such as the ability to delete a star or to edit a star's data, but we leave them as exercises for the reader.

7.5 *Summary*

In this chapter, you completed the first iteration of the sample application you began in chapter 3, by providing a web interface that allows you to use a file-based persistence component to store and retrieve data. There's more that can be done, such as adding the ability to delete and modify existing data, but the JSPs and servlets developed in this chapter provide something you can use for show-and-tell outside the confines of Eclipse.

Although Eclipse comes only with support for standard Java development, its extensibility makes possible third-party plug-ins for developing more advanced types of projects, such as web applications. One of the important design considerations for applications with GUIs is the need to separate the presentation logic from the business logic; JSPs are good for the former, and servlets are good for the latter.

You can use Eclipse's basic text editor to edit JSPs (and HTML and XML documents), but a number of other plug-ins add more features. We mentioned XML-Buddy, but you can also find more plug-ins by visiting the Eclipse Community page at http://www.eclipse.org/community.

JSPs and servlets are not standalone Java applications; they need to run in the context of a servlet container. In this chapter we also looked at the Sysdeo Tomcat plug-in for developing applications inside Eclipse using the popular and free Tomcat servlet container. As you saw, the Sysdeo plug-in conveniently lets you start and stop the Tomcat server using tool buttons in Eclipse's main toolbar. More importantly, however, it lets you debug the web application using Eclipse's powerful, multithread-aware debugger.

Whether you choose to undertake the next iteration of the sample application is up to you, but we hope this first part of the book has provided a thorough and useful introduction to the tools you need to use Eclipse effectively for this—or better yet, your own—Java project.

Part 2

Extending Eclipse

Now that you're comfortable using Eclipse for Java and web development, the second part of this book will introduce you to Eclipse's extensible plug-in architecture. Using this architecture, you can extend Eclipse with your own custom functionality, including support for other languages. Chapter 8 introduces plug-ins and walks you through the process of building simple ones with the Plug-In Development Environment provided by Eclipse. Then, chapter 9 probes deeper by taking you through a complete plug-in for log4j integration, including an editor, viewer, and properties pages.

Introduction
to Eclipse plug-ins

8

In this chapter...

- Understanding Eclipse's plug-in architecture
- Preparing your Workbench for plug-in development
- Using the Plug-in Development Environment (PDE)
- Creating simple plug-ins using the built-in wizards and templates

Up to now, you've been using Eclipse as it comes out of the box. As you'll discover in this chapter, however, the beauty of Eclipse lies in its extensible architecture. This architecture allows anyone to add features and capabilities the original designers never dreamed of.

Eclipse's loosely connected design is perfect for systems that aren't designed all at once, but instead are built up from components written for particular needs. From its earliest roots, Eclipse was designed as an "open extensible IDE for anything, and nothing in particular." The decentralization that plug-ins provide gives the Eclipse Platform the ability to morph into any application and support any language. Come with us now as we seek out that man behind the curtain and learn the secrets of Eclipse plug-ins.

8.1 Plug-ins and extension points

Imagine a giant jigsaw puzzle. A few pieces are already connected for you—these will form the core around which the rest of the puzzle is built. The boundaries between the pieces are uniquely cut to fit snugly together. If Eclipse is the puzzle, then the pieces are plug-ins. A *plug-in* is the smallest extensible unit in Eclipse. It can contain code, resources, or both.

The Eclipse Platform consists of nearly 100 plug-ins working together. The boundaries between these pieces that let plug-ins connect to one another are called extension points. An *extension point* is the mechanism by which one plug-in can add to the functionality of another.

Appendix C lists the extension points provided by the Platform. Each one can be used to add some new component such as a menu or view to the system, and is usually associated with a Java class that performs the logic for the component.

Unlike most jigsaw puzzles, though, Eclipse has no corners or straight edges. It can be extended forever, with each new plug-in defining its own extension points that other plug-ins can use. Large projects such as WebSphere Studio have hundreds of plug-ins. (Better bring a big table.)

8.1.1 Anatomy of a plug-in

Plug-ins are conceptually simple. If you look at the directory where you installed Eclipse in chapter 2, you will see a subdirectory called plugins. Inside this directory you'll find one directory for every plug-in. The name of each directory is the same as the name of the plug-in, followed by an underscore and a version number. For example:

```
C:\ECLIPSE
|
+---features
+---plugins
|    +---org.eclipse.ant.core_2.1.0
|    |    |    .options
|    |    |    about.html
|    |    |    antsupport.jar
|    |    |    plugin.properties
|    |    |    plugin.xml
|    |    |
|    |    +---lib
|    |
|    +---org.eclipse.compare_2.1.0
|    |
|    ...
+---workspace
```

The `org.eclipse.ant.core` plug-in provides the Eclipse Platform with its integration with the Ant builder (see chapter 5). In every plugins folder, including this one, you will find a *plug-in manifest* file (plugin.xml) together with some optional files. The manifest describes the plug-in—its name, its version number, and so forth. It also lists the required libraries and all the extension points used and defined by the plug-in.

The files and folders typically seen in a plugins folder are as follows:

- *plugin.xml*—Plug-in manifest
- *plugin.properties*—Contains translatable strings referenced by plugin.xml
- *about.html*—Standard location used for licensing information
- **.jar*—Any Java code needed for the plug-in
- *lib*—Directory for more JAR files
- *icons*—Directory for icons, usually in GIF format
- *(other files)*—As needed

8.1.2 *The plug-in lifecycle*

When you first start the Eclipse Platform, it scans the plugins directory to discover what plug-ins have been defined (this is a slight simplification, but close enough for this discussion). If it finds more than one version of the same plug-in, only one (typically the one with the highest version number) will be used. The list of plug-ins the Platform builds during this scan is called the *plug-in registry*. Although the Platform reads all the plug-in manifests, it doesn't actually load the plug-ins (that is, run any plug-in code) at this point. Why? To make Eclipse start up faster.

Plug-ins are loaded only when they are first used. For example, if you write a plug-in that defines a menu item, Eclipse can tell by looking at the manifest where the menu should go and what the text of the menu is. Because of the information in the manifest, Eclipse can delay loading your plug-in until it is really needed.

If you select the menu, the plug-in is loaded at that point. This behavior is especially important in large Eclipse-based products with hundreds of plug-ins. Most of the plug-ins will not be needed, because they are in specialized parts of the product that may never be run. So, any time spent loading and initializing those plug-ins would be wasted. This is sometimes referred to as *lazy loading*.

When are plug-ins unloaded? The short answer is, never. However, one of the goals of the Equinox project (http://www.eclipse.org/equinox) is to allow plug-ins to be loaded and unloaded on demand, so this situation may change in the future.

8.1.3 *Creating a simple plug-in by hand*

Eclipse plug-ins can be created without any special tools. To demonstrate, create a subdirectory in the plugins directory called org.eclipseguide.simpleplugin_1.0.0. Inside this directory, use a text editor like Notepad or vi to create a plugin.xml file containing the following lines:

```
<?xml version="1.0" encoding="UTF-8"?>
<plugin
    id="org.eclipseguide.simpleplugin"
    name="Simple Plug-in"
    version="1.0.0"
    provider-name="Eclipse in Action">
</plugin>
```

Now save the file and restart Eclipse. You won't notice anything different, because this plug-in doesn't do anything. However, you can tell it was registered by selecting Help→About Eclipse Platform and then clicking Plug-in Details. Scroll down to the bottom of this window, and you'll see the plug-in listed as shown in figure 8.1. The More Info button is grayed out because you didn't create an about.html file.

Table 8.1 describes the purpose of each line in plugin.xml.

Congratulations—you have just created your first plug-in! Next we'll look at the tools Eclipse provides to make this process manageable for more complex projects.

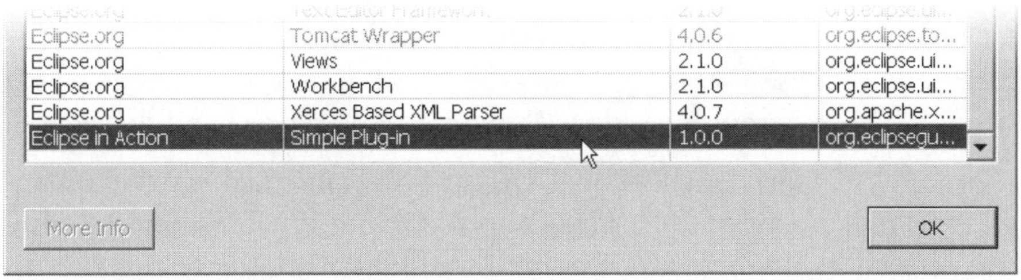

Eclipse.org	Text Editor Framework	2.1.0	org.eclipse.ui...
Eclipse.org	Tomcat Wrapper	4.0.6	org.eclipse.to...
Eclipse.org	Views	2.1.0	org.eclipse.ui...
Eclipse.org	Workbench	2.1.0	org.eclipse.ui...
Eclipse.org	Xerces Based XML Parser	4.0.7	org.apache.x...
Eclipse in Action	Simple Plug-in	1.0.0	org.eclipsegu...

More Info   OK

Figure 8.1 In the About page, you can click the Plug-in Details button to see the list of installed plug-ins. The Simple Plug-in shown here was discovered by the Eclipse Platform during startup.

Table 8.1 The plug-in manifest file (plugin.xml) for each plug-in is read when Eclipse starts, in order to build up its plug-in registry. Here is the simplest manifest possible and the meaning of each line.

Line	Purpose
`<?xml version="1.0" encoding="UTF-8"?>`	Required XML prolog; never changes
`<plugin`	Starts defining a new plug-in
`    id="org.eclipseguide.simpleplugin"`	Provides the fully qualified id for the plug-in
`    name="Simple Plug-in"`	Gives the plug-in a human-readable name
`    version="1.0.0"`	Specifies a version number
`    provider-name="Eclipse in Action">`	Provides information about the author
`</plugin>`	Finishes defining the plug-in

8.2 *The Plug-in Development Environment (PDE)*

Creating a plug-in by hand is an interesting exercise, but it would quickly become tedious in practice. Plug-in manifests can grow to be hundreds of lines long, and they need to be coordinated with names and data in various source and property files. Also, plug-ins need a fair amount of boilerplate code in order to run. That's why Eclipse provides a complete Plug-in Development Environment (PDE). The PDE adds a new perspective and several views and wizards to the Eclipse Platform to support creating, maintaining, and publishing plug-ins:

- *Plug-in Project*—A normal plug-in; the most common type
- *Fragment Project*—An addition to a plug-in (for languages, targets, and so on)
- *Feature Project*—An installation unit for one or more plug-ins
- *Update Site Project*—A web site for automatic installs of features

8.2.1 *Preparing your Workbench*

Before you start using the PDE, you should turn on a few preferences. They are off by default, because Eclipse users who are not building plug-ins don't need them. Bring up the Preferences window (Window→Preferences) and do the following:

1   Select Workbench→Label Decorations and turn on the Binary Plug-in Projects decoration. This is optional, but if you use binary plug-ins (see section 8.2.2) it will help them stand out from the rest of your projects.

2   Select Plug-In Development→Compilers and set all the messages to Warning. Doing so will provide an early indication of any problems in your plug-in manifests.

3   Select Plug-In Development→Java Build Path Control and turn on the Use Classpath Containers for Dependent Plug-ins option. This confusingly named option causes all plug-in JARs that your plug-in uses to appear in a folder of your project called Required Plug-in Entries. The nice thing about this special folder is that Eclipse dynamically manages it based on your plug-in's dependencies.

4   Click OK. A dialog will appear, stating that the compiler options have changed and asking whether you would like to recompile all the projects. Click Yes.

8.2.2 *Importing the SDK plug-ins*

As mentioned earlier, the Eclipse Platform is made up of dozens of plug-ins. Wouldn't it be nice if you could see the source code for all those plug-ins, and do searches to see how certain classes and interfaces are used internally? The API documentation is not perfect, so this is an important tool for plug-in developers. Of course, you could connect to the Eclipse CVS Repository (host **dev.eclipse.org**, path **/home/eclipse**, user **anonymous**) and download what you need, but there is a better way. It turns out that if you downloaded the Eclipse Platform SDK then all the source code is already installed, just waiting to be used.

The easiest method is to hold down the Ctrl key and hover your mouse over a class or object name in the Java editor, and then click on the name. If the source is available, Eclipse will open it. Or, using the Package Explorer, you can expand just about any JAR file and double-click on one of its class files to open it in the editor.

Sometimes, though, it's more convenient to bring these plug-ins into your workspace just like your regular projects. For example, you can search your entire workspace for references to a type, but if the type is not currently in the workspace, then it won't be found. The Required Plug-in Entries folder is searched, but it contains only the JAR files from plug-ins you are currently dependent on.

To bring installed plug-ins into your workspace, select File→Import→External Plug-ins and Fragments and then click Next (see figure 8.2). Turn off the option to Copy Plug-in Contents into the Workspace Location and click Next. Then, select the plug-ins you want to import and click Finish. This is called a *binary import*, and projects created this way are *binary plug-ins* because you didn't build them from source.

Later, if you decide you don't want them in your workspace, just delete them—doing so will not affect the Eclipse installation. You can also temporarily

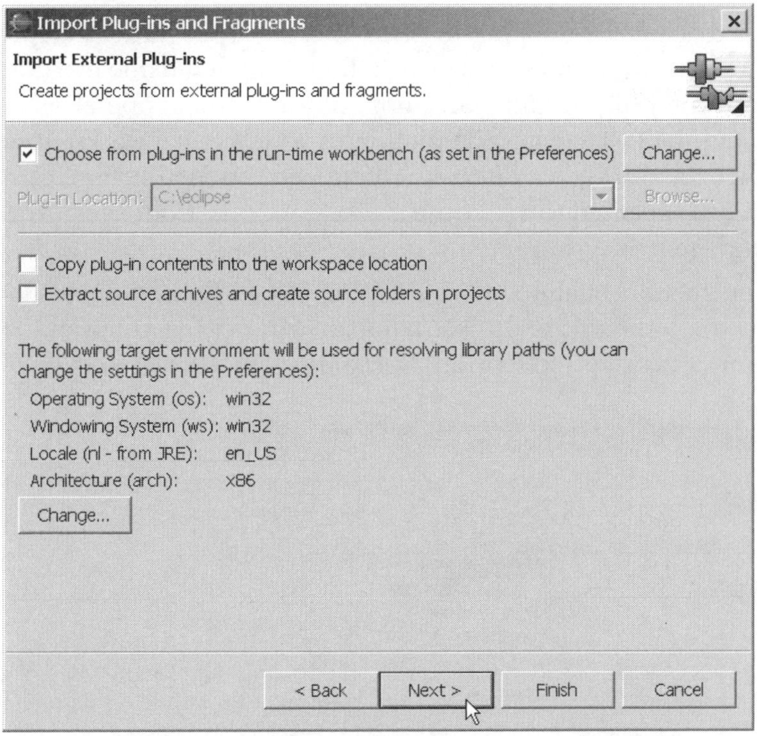

Figure 8.2 You can bring any installed plug-ins into your workspace by importing them. Doing so creates a binary plug-in project for each one and makes them available for searching and browsing. This is a great way to discover how the Eclipse Platform uses the Eclipse SDK classes and interfaces.

hide them from the Package Explorer menu: Select Filters, turn on the option to Exclude Binary Plug-in and Feature Projects, and click OK.

8.2.3 *Using the Plug-in Project Wizard*

The PDE makes it easy to create a new plug-in by providing wizards that ask a few questions and generate much of the code for you. Let's walk through a simple example:

1   Select File→New→Project to bring up the familiar New Project Wizard shown in figure 8.3.

2   Select Plug-in Development on the left-hand side to bring up the list of plug-in wizards on the right. You can use the Plug-in Project Wizard to create new plug-ins; select it and then click Next to open the first page of the wizard.

3   Enter a name for the plug-in, such as **org.eclipseguide.helloplugin** (see figure 8.4). We recommend using a fully qualified name like this so it can match the plug-in name and not collide with anyone else's name. By default, the PDE creates the plug-in in your normal workspace directory (either the workspace directory where you installed Eclipse or the directory you specified with Eclipse's -data option). Click Next to get to the next page.

4   Enter the fully qualified ID of the plug-in (see figure 8.5); by default, the ID is the same as the project name, which is what you want. Select the Create a Java Project option. Some plug-ins consist of only resources,

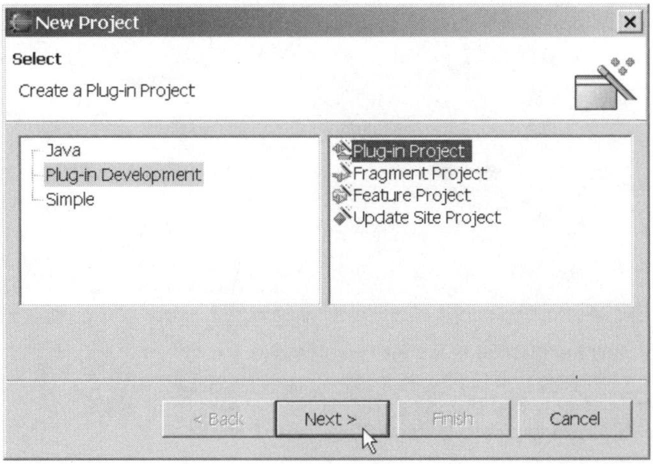

Figure 8.3
The PDE provides several wizards for creating new projects. See section 8.2 for a description of each type of project supported.

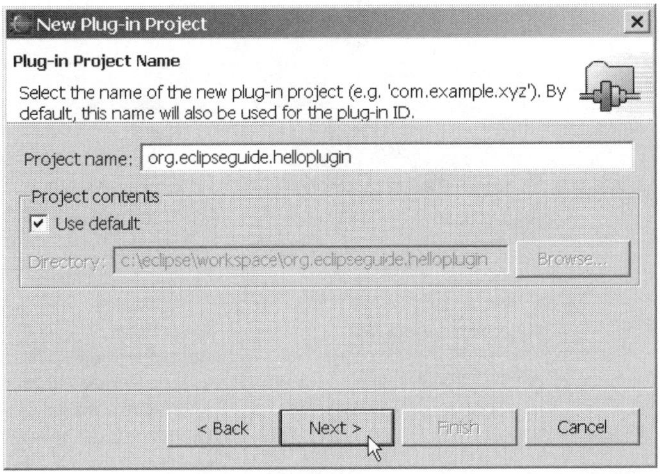

Figure 8.4
Specify the name and location of the project in the first page of the Plug-in Project Wizard.

such as a plug-in that only contains help files, but most of the time plug-ins have some Java code associated with them. The Java Builder Output option controls where the Eclipse compiler places generated .class files. The Plug-in Runtime Library is the JAR file that holds all your Java code, and Source Folder allows you to change the subdirectory that contains your .java files. The defaults for these settings are fine, so click Next to bring up the code generation page.

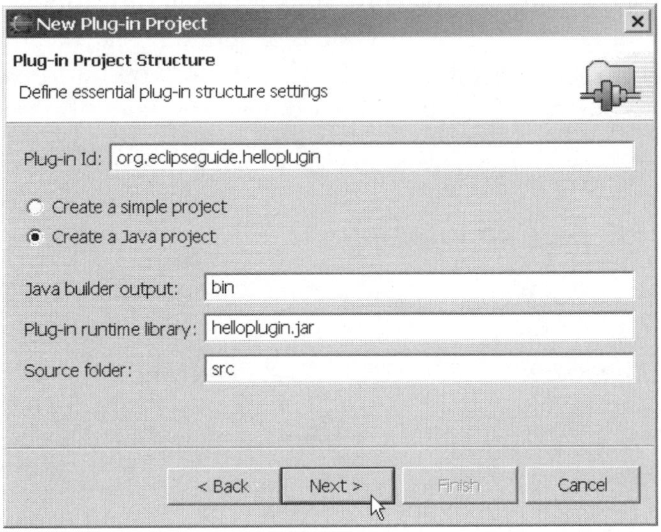

Figure 8.5
Specify the fully qualified ID of the plug-in in the second page of the New Plug-in Project Wizard. You can also control whether this plug-in will contain Java code.

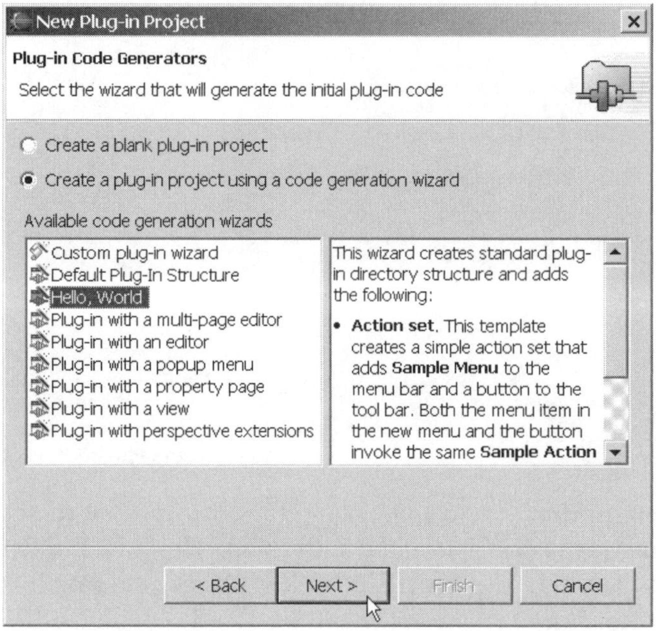

Figure 8.6
Select a code-generation wizard to quickly create a new plug-in from a template. Using the templates lessens the learning curve for Eclipse extensions and is less error-prone than creating the code from scratch. There also is an experimental feature in Eclipse 2.1 for adding your own wizards to this dialog.

5 The PDE provides several standard templates to help you quickly create some common kinds of plug-ins. A few are listed on this page (figure 8.6); you can see the rest by selecting the Custom Plug-in Wizard. The option to Create a Blank Plug-in Project makes a minimal directory with a plug-in.xml file but not much else; no code is generated. The Default Plug-in Structure Wizard creates a top-level Java class for you but does not use any extension points. It is possible to add new templates, if necessary.

You're almost done. Now you just have to decide which template to use.

8.3 *The "Hello, World" plug-in example*

It's time for another "Hello, World" example—this one for plug-ins. In the New Plug-in Project page, select the Hello, World Wizard. It creates the default plug-in structure and also uses two extension points (`org.eclipse.ui.actionSets` and `org.eclipse.ui.perspectiveExtensions`) to add an item to the menu bar and the tool bar. (These extension points and the other wizards will be discussed later). Now, follow these steps:

1 In the code-generation dialog, click Next to start the Hello, World Wizard. Set the Plug-in Name to **Hello Plug-in**, the Class Name to **org.eclipse-**

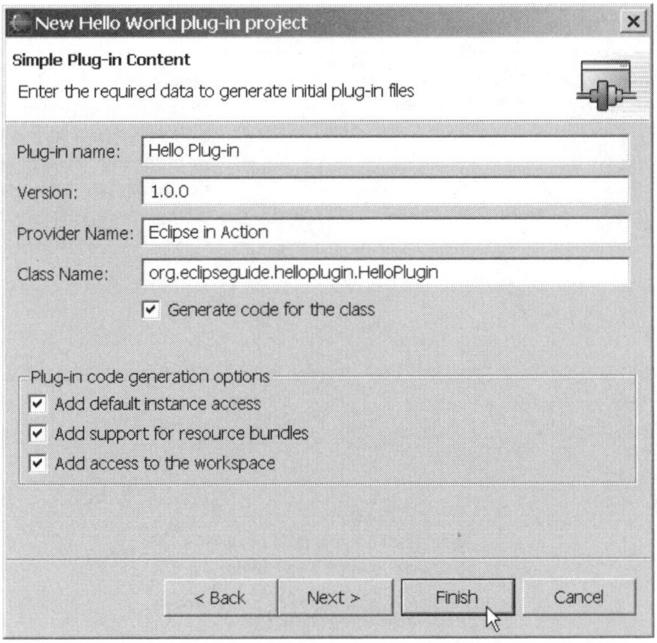

Figure 8.7
This page is common to most plug-in wizards. Use it to fill in the plug-in name and other required data.

guide.helloplugin.HelloPlugin, and the Provider Name to **Eclipse in Action** (see figure 8.7). The next page would let you control the text the example will display; however, the defaults are good, so click Finish to generate the directories, files, and classes necessary for the project.

2 You may get a dialog telling you that the wizard is enabling any needed plug-ins (figure 8.8). This is normal, so click OK.

3 Another dialog asks if you want to switch to the Plug-in perspective (figure 8.9). Click Yes.

That's it! You now have a plug-in project, as shown in figure 8.10.

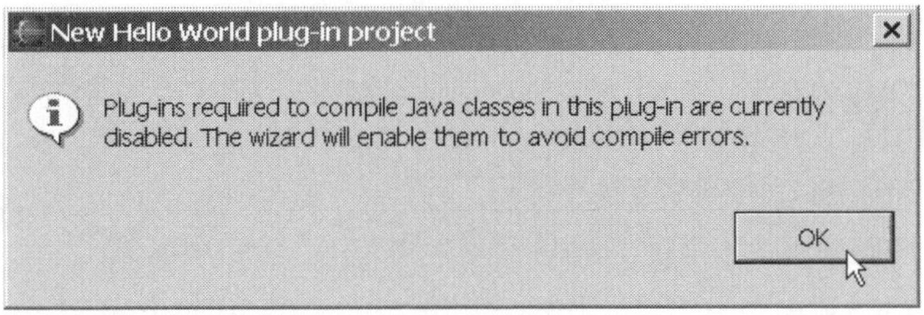

Figure 8.8
The wizard automatically enables plug-ins that this plug-in depends on. You can see the list of enabled plug-ins in the Preferences dialog under Plug-In Development→Target Platform.

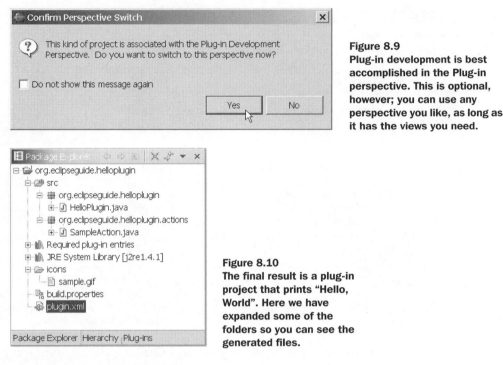

Figure 8.9
Plug-in development is best accomplished in the Plug-in perspective. This is optional, however; you can use any perspective you like, as long as it has the views you need.

Figure 8.10
The final result is a plug-in project that prints "Hello, World". Here we have expanded some of the folders so you can see the generated files.

8.3.1 *The Plug-in Manifest Editor*

The PDE automatically opens the Plug-in Manifest Editor when you first create a plug-in (see figure 8.11). You can bring it up later by double-clicking on plugin.xml. This multipage editor provides convenient access to all the different sections of the plugin.xml file.

Because you'll be spending a great deal of time in the Plug-in Manifest Editor, it's a good idea to familiarize yourself with it now. Its pages are as follows:

- *Welcome*—A quick introduction to the Manifest Editor with links to some of the most important sections. You can turn off this page once you are familiar with the editor.

- *Overview*—Summarizes the plug-in, including the name, version number, extension points consumed and provided, and other information. This is the page you will use most often.

- *Dependencies*—Specifies the plug-ins required for this plug-in.

- *Runtime*—Defines the libraries that need to be included in the plug-in's classpath and whether classes in those libraries should be exported for use by other plug-ins.

Figure 8.11
When you first open the plugin.xml file, you are greeted with this Welcome screen. It contains hints about how to work with the project, active links to different pages in the Plug-in Manifest Editor, and actions like starting the Run-time Workbench. You can turn off the page when you become more comfortable with the environment.

- *Extensions*—Lists all extension points used by this plug-in.

- *Extension Points*—Lists all extension points defined by this plug-in, along with a cross-reference of who is using those extension points.

- *Source*—A raw XML editor for the plugin.xml file. Often it is useful to make a change in one of the other pages of the editor and then switch to the Source page to see what effect the change had.

8.3.2 *The Run-time Workbench*

Once you have created a plug-in project, you could compile it, package up a JAR file, copy it to the plugins directory as you did in section 8.1.3, and restart Eclipse. But the PDE provides an easier way in the form of the *Run-time Workbench,* a temporary Eclipse installation created automatically for running and debugging plug-ins.

To run your new plug-in under the Run-time Workbench, select Run→Run As→Run-time Workbench (or use the Run toolbar button). If you haven't done this before, then you will get a notice that Eclipse is completing a new installation, and then a new Eclipse Workbench will appear. This is the Run-time Workbench; it includes all the plug-in projects you are working on in addition to the plug-ins that are part of the standard Eclipse installation. If you look carefully, you will notice a new menu named Sample Menu and a new button in the Eclipse toolbar (see figure 8.12).

Click the button, and Eclipse opens a dialog commemorating your second plug-in (see figure 8.13). We'll look at the Java code behind that button shortly.

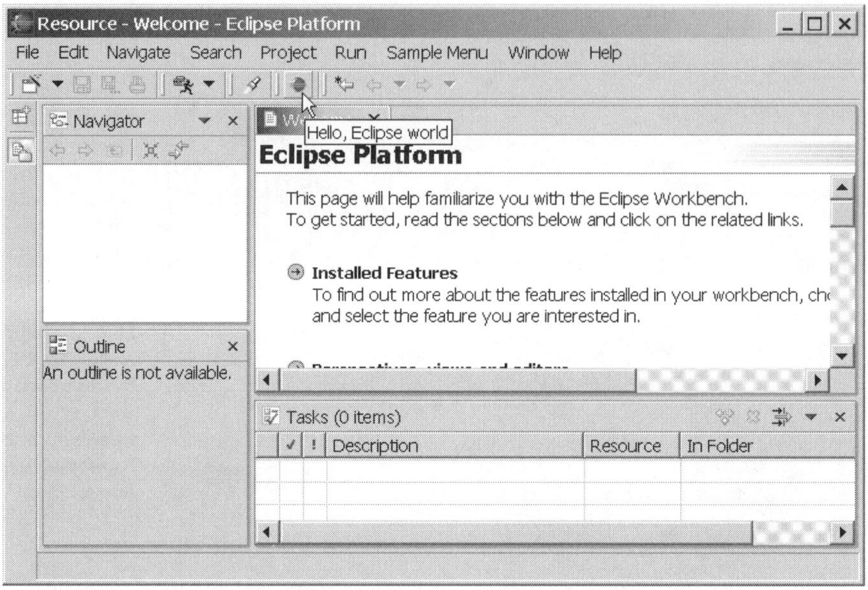

Figure 8.12   Starting the Run-time Workbench opens a new instance of Eclipse with all the plug-ins from your workspace installed. The "Hello, World" plug-in adds a Sample Menu and a toolbar button to the Workbench.

Debugging a plug-in is just as easy. Select Run→Debug As→Run-time Workbench. A second Eclipse Workbench starts up, containing your plug-ins. Debug this as you would any Java application (see chapter 3).

NOTE   If you are using JDK 1.4 or higher, you can make small changes to your source code and rebuild, and the changes will be instantly available in the Run-time Workbench. This is called *hot-swapping* or *hot code replace*. Substantial changes (such as adding a new class) may cause a warning to be displayed. If you get this warning, simply close the Run-time Workbench and run it again.

Figure 8.13
This dialog appears when you click the new toolbar button of the "Hello, World" plug-in.

Eclipse is *self-hosted*, which means it is used to develop itself. The concept of self-hosting got its start in compiler technology. The first version of a compiler is written in a simpler language, such as assembler, or perhaps using a competitor's product. But once the compiler is working, the developer rewrites it in the language being compiled, using the first version to build the second version, the second version to build the third, and so forth. Eclipse developers use Eclipse the same way, and created its plug-in development environment to support this process.

Compilers, being fairly complex programs in their own right, make excellent test cases for compilers. Likewise, by writing Eclipse with Eclipse, the developers can discover and correct any shortcomings in the handling of large projects and optimize the environment for extending the Eclipse Platform.

8.3.3 Plug-in class (AbstractUIPlugin)

The Hello, World Wizard created three files for you: a plug-in manifest (plugin.xml) and two source files (HelloPlugin.java and SampleAction.java). Because all Eclipse plug-ins and extensions follow this pattern (references in the XML file with Java classes to back them up), it's important to understand how it works. Open the Plug-in Manifest Editor and select the Overview page (figure 8.14).

XML

Switch to the Source page. You should see something like this:

```
<plugin
   id="org.eclipseguide.helloplugin"
   name="Hello Plug-in"
   version="1.0.0"
   provider-name="Eclipse in Action"
   class="org.eclipseguide.helloplugin.HelloPlugin">
...
</plugin>
```

Note that the link to the code is provided by the `class` attribute. When the plug-in is activated, this class will be instantiated and its constructor called.

Java

The class that backs up the plug-in definition in the manifest is `HelloPlugin`, contained in the source file HelloPlugin.java (see listing 8.1). In this section, we'll examine this code and explain how all the pieces fit together.

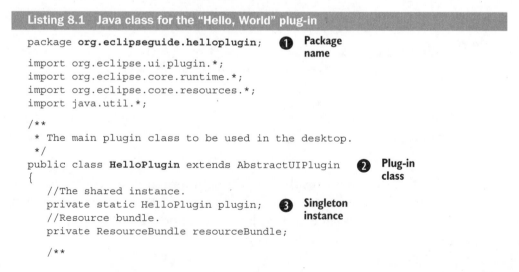

Figure 8.14 The Overview page of the Plug-in Manifest Editor is the central control panel for your plug-in. From here you can get a summary of the plug-in at a glance and access the other pages for more detail.

Listing 8.1 Java class for the "Hello, World" plug-in

```
package org.eclipseguide.helloplugin;        ① Package
                                                name
import org.eclipse.ui.plugin.*;
import org.eclipse.core.runtime.*;
import org.eclipse.core.resources.*;
import java.util.*;

/**
 * The main plugin class to be used in the desktop.
 */
public class HelloPlugin extends AbstractUIPlugin  ② Plug-in
{                                                       class
    //The shared instance.
    private static HelloPlugin plugin;         ③ Singleton
    //Resource bundle.                            instance
    private ResourceBundle resourceBundle;

    /**
```

```
 * The constructor.
 */
public HelloPlugin(IPluginDescriptor descriptor)        4   Plug-in
{                                                             constructor
   super(descriptor);
   plugin = this;
   try
   {
      resourceBundle =                                 Get a resource   5
         ResourceBundle.getBundle(                          bundle
            "org.eclipseguide.helloplugin.HelloPluginResources");
   }
   catch (MissingResourceException x)
   {
      resourceBundle = null;
   }
}

/**
 * Returns the shared instance.
 */
public static HelloPlugin getDefault()
{
   return plugin;
}

/**
 * Returns the workspace instance.
 */
public static IWorkspace getWorkspace()                 6   Return
{                                                             Workspace
   return ResourcesPlugin.getWorkspace();                     handle
}

/**
 * Returns the string from the plugin's resource bundle,
 * or 'key' if not found.
 */
public static String getResourceString(String key)     7   Look up key
{                                                             in resource
   ResourceBundle bundle =                                    bundle
      HelloPlugin.getDefault().getResourceBundle();
   try
   {
      return bundle.getString(key);
   }
   catch (MissingResourceException e)
   {
      return key;
   }
}
/**
```

```
 * Returns the plugin's resource bundle,
 */
public ResourceBundle getResourceBundle()
{
   return resourceBundle;
}
}
```

❶ The package name should be the same as the plug-in name, which should be the same as the project name. Packages in the Eclipse Platform start with `org.eclipse`. Although the convention is not always followed, user interface packages generally have `ui` in their name, and non–user interface packages include `core`. If you see a package with `internal` in the name, it is not intended to be used outside the package itself. Internal packages and interfaces can, and often do, change between releases (and even builds of the same release), so stay clear of them.

❷ This is where the plug-in class is created. There are two types of plug-ins: those with user interfaces and those without. `AbstractUIPlugin` is the base class for all UI type plug-ins, and `Plugin` is the base class for the rest.

❸ A Singleton pattern is used to ensure there will be only one instance of the plug-in's class.

❹ The plug-in's constructor is passed an `IPluginDescriptor` object, which has methods such as `getLabel()` that return information from the plug-in registry. You can get a reference to this descriptor later by using the `getDescriptor()` method. Note that all Eclipse interfaces begin with the letter `I`.

❺ See the name of the bundle in the `getBundle()` call? Once created, the properties file for this bundle goes in your org.eclipseguide.helloplugin project and is named HelloPluginResources.properties. You can manage it by hand or by using the Externalize Strings Wizard (Source→Externalize Strings).

❻ The `IWorkspace` interface is the key to the Eclipse Platform's resource management. It has methods to add, delete, and move resources; most important, it has the `getRoot()` method to return the *workspace root* resource, the parent of all the projects in the workspace. This is a Singleton object (only one in the system).

❼ The wizard has created a standard Java resource bundle for you to look up natural language strings. For example, to get the translated string for a greeting, you could call the method `HelloPlugin.getResourceString("%greeting")`.

Actually, two bundles are at work. The first one is associated with the plug-in externally and may be referenced in the plug-in manifest, plugin.xml. Properties for the external bundle are kept in the file plugin.properties. Generally speak-

ing, you will never use that one in the plug-in code. The second bundle, referenced here, is internal to the plug-in and is kept in the plug-in's JAR file.

8.3.4 Actions, menus, and toolbars (IWorkbenchWindowActionDelegate)

An *action* is the non–user interface part of a command that can be run by a user,
usually associated with a UI element like a toolbar button or menu. Actions are
referenced in the plug-in manifest and defined as Java classes. Figure 8.15 shows
what this extension looks like in the manifest editor's Extensions page.

You will probably find using the Extensions page more convenient and less
error-prone than editing the XML in the Source page. However, because XML is
a more compact representation than a series of screenshots of property pages, we
will show the raw XML for most examples in this chapter and the next. Keep in
mind, though, that there is a one-to-one correspondence between the two. Also,
you can switch back and forth between the pages of the manifest editor at any
time; a change in one is reflected in all the others.

XML

The first extension defined by the plug-in is an action set. An *action set* is a menu,
submenu, or draggable group of toolbar buttons that appears in the user interface.

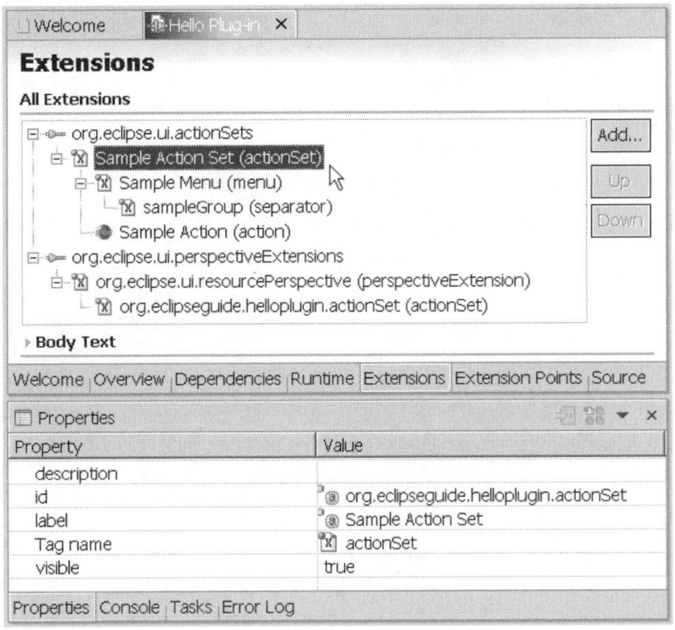

Figure 8.15
You can use the Extensions page of the Plug-in Manifest Editor to add new extensions to your plug-in. Properties and their values are viewed and modified through the Properties view. Required properties such as `id` and `label` are marked with an icon. If you prefer, you can edit the raw XML representation in the Source page.

Listing 8.2 shows the definition in the plug-in manifest (compare this to figure 8.15).

Listing 8.2   The actionSet extension

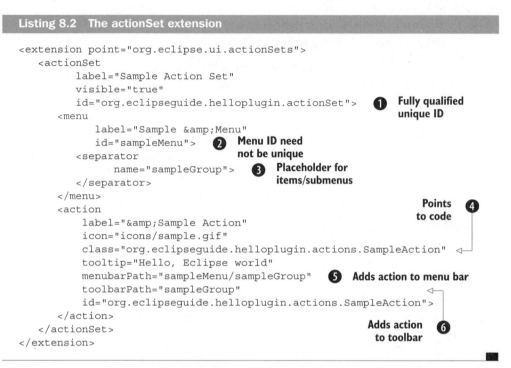

```
<extension point="org.eclipse.ui.actionSets">
    <actionSet
        label="Sample Action Set"
        visible="true"
        id="org.eclipseguide.helloplugin.actionSet">        ❶ Fully qualified
    <menu                                                        unique ID
        label="Sample &amp;Menu"
        id="sampleMenu">        ❷ Menu ID need
        <separator                 not be unique
            name="sampleGroup">    ❸ Placeholder for
        </separator>                  items/submenus
    </menu>
    <action                                              Points  ❹
        label="&amp;Sample Action"                       to code
        icon="icons/sample.gif"
        class="org.eclipseguide.helloplugin.actions.SampleAction"  ◁
        tooltip="Hello, Eclipse world"
        menubarPath="sampleMenu/sampleGroup"  ❺ Adds action to menu bar
        toolbarPath="sampleGroup"                              ◁
        id="org.eclipseguide.helloplugin.actions.SampleAction">
    </action>                                        Adds action  ❻
    </actionSet>                                     to toolbar
</extension>
```

❶ Each extension, and indeed just about everything in the plug-in manifest, has a *fully qualified ID* that, by convention, starts with the plug-in ID. It doesn't matter what you call these IDs, as long as you pick unique names.

❷ Of course, there are exceptions, such as menus. They typically use short names like `group1` to achieve some level of consistency between menus. For example, a File menu might have a `group1` section and a Windows menu might also have a `group1` section.

❸ Menus can contain *groups* and *separators*. Separators are simply groups that are drawn with thin lines between them. All menus have a section named `additions`, which is the default place new items are added if you don't specify a location. This particular menu has two levels: `sampleMenu` (the parent menu) and `sampleGroup` (the child group).

❹ As with plug-ins, the `class` property points to the code.

➎ The `menubarPath` property indicates the action is being added to a menu bar (in this case, the top-level bar of the Workspace). The paths look like directories, going from higher-level parent menus or groups to lower-level child ones.

➏ The `toolbarPath` property indicates that this action is also being added to a toolbar. There is one toolbar called `Normal`, but the name is usually omitted from the path.

Java

Now let's move over to the Java side and dig into the code for the `SampleAction` class, shown in listing 8.3.

Listing 8.3 The SampleAction class

```
package org.eclipseguide.helloplugin.actions;

import org.eclipse.jface.action.IAction;              ➊ JFace and
import org.eclipse.jface.viewers.ISelection;              UI imports
import org.eclipse.ui.IWorkbenchWindow;
import org.eclipse.ui.IWorkbenchWindowActionDelegate;
import org.eclipse.jface.dialogs.MessageDialog;

/**
 * Our sample action implements workbench action delegate.
 * The action proxy will be created by the workbench and
 * shown in the UI. When the user tries to use the action,     ➋ Code
 * this delegate will be created and execution will be            pointed to
 * delegated to it.                                               by manifest
 * @see IWorkbenchWindowActionDelegate
 */
public class SampleAction implements IWorkbenchWindowActionDelegate
{
    private IWorkbenchWindow window;     ➌ Main
    /**                                      Workbench
     * The constructor.                      window
     */
    public SampleAction()
    {
    }

    /**
     * The action has been activated. The argument of the
     * method represents the 'real' action sitting
     * in the workbench UI.
     * @see IWorkbenchWindowActionDelegate#run
     */
    public void run(IAction action)     ➍ Perform
    {                                       action
        MessageDialog.openInformation(  ➎ Open
            window.getShell(),              dialog
```

```
        "Hello Plug-in",
        "Hello, Eclipse world");
}

/**
 * Selection in the workbench has been changed. We
 * can change the state of the 'real' action here
 * if we want, but this can only happen after
 * the delegate has been created.
 * @see IWorkbenchWindowActionDelegate#selectionChanged
 */
public void selectionChanged(
    IAction action,
    ISelection selection)
{
}

/**
 * We can use this method to dispose of any system
 * resources we previously allocated.
 * @see IWorkbenchWindowActionDelegate#dispose
 */
public void dispose()        ⑥   Can be used
{                                    to free system
}                                    resources

/**
 * We will cache window object in order to
 * be able to provide parent shell for the message dialog.
 * @see IWorkbenchWindowActionDelegate#init
 */
public void init(IWorkbenchWindow window)
{
    this.window = window;
}
}
```

❶ JFace is a high-level wrapper on top of the Standard Widget Toolkit (SWT) used for the Eclipse UI. JFace deals in concepts like dialogs and viewers, whereas SWT deals in windows, canvases, and buttons. (For more details on SWT and JFace, see appendixes D and E.)

❷ A *proxy* stands in for an object until the real object is available. In this case, there is a proxy for the toolbar button (not seen here) created by the Workbench based solely on the information in the plug-in manifest. Remember that the plug-in (including this code) isn't even loaded until after the button is clicked. When the user finally clicks the button, this *delegate* is created and passed the action to run. It works just like a relay race. The first runner is the proxy, and the baton he carries is the action. The baton is passed to the second runner, the delegate, who finishes the race.

Because the "Hello, World" button is in the Workbench toolbar and the menu item is in the main Workbench menu, this code implements the Workbench window action delegate interface. There are similar interfaces for View, Editor, and Object action delegates, which are all based on `IActionDelegate`. `IActionDelegate` only has two methods—`run()` and `selectionChanged()`—which you will implement a little further down in this class.

3 `IWorkbenchWindow` is an interface used for the top-level window of the Workbench. It contains a collection of `IWorkbenchPages` that in turn hold all the views, editors, and toolbars. Some common methods you'll use in `IWorkbenchWindow` include `close()` and `getWorkbench()`.

4 The `run()` method is where the actual work gets done. The `IAction` interface has methods for getting and setting the user interface style of the button or menu it is associated with, and maintains a list of *listeners* that are called when any of its properties change.

5 `MessageDialog` is one of a group of JFace utility classes that perform common operations. The static method `openInformation()`, as you might guess, opens an information dialog (as opposed to an error, warning, question, or other type of dialog). Its first argument is a *shell*, which is a low-level SWT window. (You'll find that many classes have a `getShell()` method, and you will use it often.) The `openInformation()` method's second argument is the title of the dialog that will be shown, and the final argument is the text that will be displayed on the main area of the dialog.

6 Because SWT works more closely to the underlying window system than other APIs (notably Swing), it is sometimes necessary to free up system resources in `dispose()` methods that are explicitly called. Garbage collection cannot be relied on for this purpose because it is run at unpredictable times. This is one of the more controversial requirements of SWT, but it is not as painful as you might think.

8.3.5 *Plug-ins and classpaths*

One "gotcha" that continues to bite plug-in developers (new and old alike) is the way plug-in classpaths work. Plug-ins can only use classes exported by other plug-ins. For security reasons, plug-ins ignore the normal classpath settings at runtime, causing `ClassNotFound` exceptions even when the code compiled just fine.

Because of this restriction, if you want to use an external JAR file (one that is not in your workspace) inside a plug-in, you must bring it into your workspace.

Typically you do so by wrapping the JAR file in its own plug-in and making any other plug-ins that need the library depend on the new plug-in. The Eclipse Platform includes many examples, such as the `org.junit`, `org.apache.ant`, and `org.apache.xerces` plug-ins, which are simple wrappers around the JUnit, Ant, and Xerces libraries, respectively.

Wrapping a JAR file is one of the simplest plug-ins you can create, because no code is involved. The next example walks you through the necessary steps.

8.4 *The log4j library plug-in example*

As you recall from chapter 3, log4j is a free logging API created for the Apache Jakarta project. When you wanted to use it in a normal Java program from within Eclipse, you created a classpath variable for it and then referenced that variable inside the Java Build Path for the project. But let's say you need to use the library inside a plug-in, so you need to create a wrapper plug-in for it. To create the wrapper for log4j, start with a blank template from the New Plug-in Project Wizard:

1 Select File→New→Project to bring up the New Project Wizard (figure 8.3).

2 Select the Plug-in Project Wizard and click Next to open the New Plug-in Project Wizard.

3 Enter the name for the plug-in, **org.apache.log4j**, and click Next.

4 Leave the fully qualified ID as it is, making sure the option to Create a Java Project is selected, and click Next again.

5 Select the option to Create a Blank Plug-in Project (see figure 8.6). Click Finish to generate the plug-in.

Now, you need to customize the plug-in to contain the log4j library and include the proper export instructions so other plug-ins can use it. To do this, follow these steps:

1 In the new project directory, delete the src directory (right-click on it and select Delete), because there will be no source code in the project itself.

2 Copy the log4j JAR file (for example, log4j-1.2.8.jar) from the place you installed it in chapter 3 into the top level of the project directory. To do this, you can use File→Import→File System or, if you're using Windows, drag the file from your file explorer into the project.

3 Rename the JAR filename to remove the version number by right-clicking on it, selecting Refactor→Rename, and entering the new name, **log4j.jar**. The version number is specified in the plug-in manifest and is

appended to the plug-in directory name, so you don't also have to append it to the JAR filename.

4   Edit the project properties (right-click on the project and select Properties). Select Java Build Path, and then select the Libraries tab. Click Add Jars, navigate into the project, and select log4j.jar. Click OK.

5   While still in the project properties dialog, select the Order and Export tab. Put a check mark next to log4j.jar and click OK to save. This setting lets other plug-ins use this library at compile time.

6   Open the Plug-in Manifest Editor (double-click on plugin.xml) and switch to the Overview page. Set the Plug-in Name to **Apache Log4J**, change the Version to match the version number of the log4j package (for example, **1.2.8**), and fill in the Provider Name with **Eclipse in Action**.

7   Still in the manifest editor, switch to the Runtime page. Verify that log4j.jar is in the library list. Select it and turn on the option to Export the Entire Library. This setting lets other plug-ins use the library at runtime. You can also use this trick to make it look like classes from many other plug-ins come from a single plug-in.

8   Delete the reference to the src/ folder on the Runtime page under Library Content by right-clicking on it and selecting Delete. Again, because you are not building the plug-in from source code, you don't need a source folder.

9   Switch to the Source page of the manifest editor and admire your handiwork. When you are done, the XML in the Source page should look like this:

```
<?xml version="1.0" encoding="UTF-8"?>
<plugin
   id="org.apache.log4j"
   name="Apache Log4J"
   version="1.2.8"
   provider-name="Eclipse in Action">

   <runtime>
      <library name="log4j.jar">
         <export name="*"/>
      </library>
   </runtime>
</plugin>
```

10 Press Ctrl-S to save, and then close the Plug-in Manifest Editor.

8.4.1 *Attaching source*

Users of your plug-in will undoubtedly want to view log4j's source code at some point, perhaps while debugging or in order to understand how to use its classes. To make that functionality available, you have to place a zip file containing the source in the top-level directory of the plug-in (zip is used even on UNIX). In order for Eclipse to find the zip file automatically, it must have same name as the JAR file, but with src.zip appended to the end (for example, foosrc.zip goes with foo.jar). In normal plug-ins, the PDE makes this file for you from your own source code. But because you are not building the code for this library, you must make other arrangements:

1 Create a log4jsrc.zip file containing the source. The log4j distribution doesn't include a source zip file, but it does have a directory containing the source. Locate the top of the source tree in the distribution's src/java directory and put the org subdirectory and everything under it into the zip using the `jar` utility (`jar -cvf log4jsrc.zip`) or your favorite zip program, such as WinZip. When you're done, the zip file must have an internal structure like this:

```
org
+---apache
    +---log4j
        +---chainsaw
        +---config
        +---helpers
        +---etc...
```

2 Copy the new log4jsrc.zip file into your project (using File→Import→File System).

3 Associate the source zip to the log4j JAR file by right-clicking on log4j.jar and selecting Properties→Java Source Attachment (see figure 8.16). Click the Workspace button to locate the zip file. Doing so lets you view the source in your own plug-in projects.

8.4.2 *Including the source zip in the plug-in package*

When the time comes to make your plug-in available for other people to use, you need to package it in a zip file organized exactly as it should be organized under the plugins directory. Eclipse uses the properties in build.properties to tell it which files should be packaged and which ones should be ignored. Obviously, you want the source zip to be included, so follow these steps:

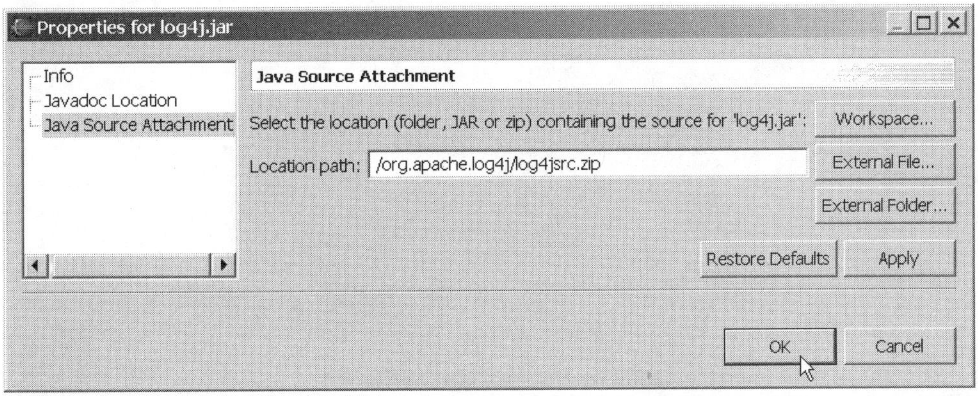

Figure 8.16 **Set the Java Source Attachment property on a JAR file to make its source visible in Eclipse. The recommended method is to click the Workspace button to locate a path relative to the workspace, as shown here.**

1   Open the Properties Editor on build.properties by double-clicking on it. Note that you can't edit build.properties and plugin.xml at the same time, because the manifest editor needs to write the properties file. So if you get an error that the file is in use or read only, close the manifest editor and try opening build.properties again.

2   Add the zip file to the `bin.includes` property. To do this, select the `bin.includes` property on the left to display the values for that property on the right. Click the Add button under Replacement Values and type **log4jsrc.zip**. Later, when it's time to deploy the plug-in, this property will be used to pick which files from your project are included. Internally, `bin.includes` is a variable name used in an Ant script that does the deployment.

TIP   You can use Ant patterns to include many files at once. For example, use a wildcard like ***.jar** to include all files ending with *.jar*. The pattern ****** (for example, ****/*.gif**) matches any number of directory levels, and a trailing slash (for example, **lib/**) matches a whole subtree.

---

3   While you're editing the properties file, remove the `source.log4j.jar` property by right-clicking on it and selecting Delete. Because there is no source code in the project except the zip file you just imported, this property is unnecessary. Press Ctrl-S to save. The build.properties file should now look like figure 8.17.

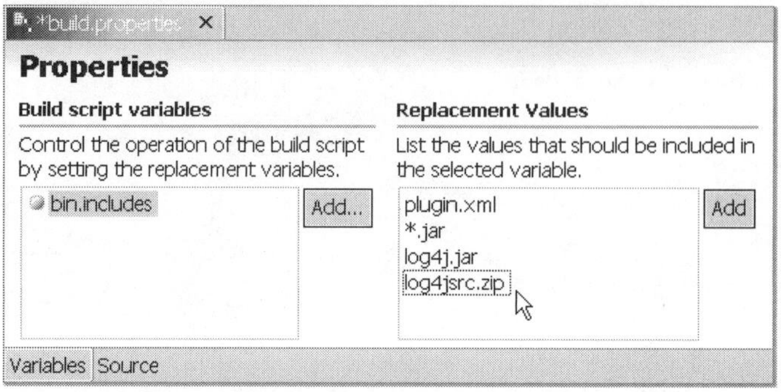

**Figure 8.17   Add the zip file containing the source to the
`bin.includes` property. Everything listed here will be included in
the final plug-in package when the time comes to deploy it.**

There you have it—a plug-in that wraps the log4j JAR file and that can be referenced from other plug-ins. You'll use this plug-in for the examples in chapter 9.

8.5 *Deploying a plug-in*

Once you've created a plug-in in your workspace, you can run and debug it using
the Run-time Workbench. But how do you install the plug-in or give it to someone else so they can install it? This process is called *deployment*. You can create
deployable zip files with Ant, but the PDE supplies an Export Wizard to make it
even easier. To demonstrate this process, let's create the zip file for the log4j
library plug-in you just built:

1   Select File→Export to start the Export Wizard, and then select Deploy-
    able Plug-ins and Fragments and click Next. The Export dialog shown in
    figure 8.18 opens.

2   Select the plug-in(s) to export and enter the filename of the zip file you
    want to create.

3   Click Finish to create the file.

Now you have a plug-in zip file that others can install.

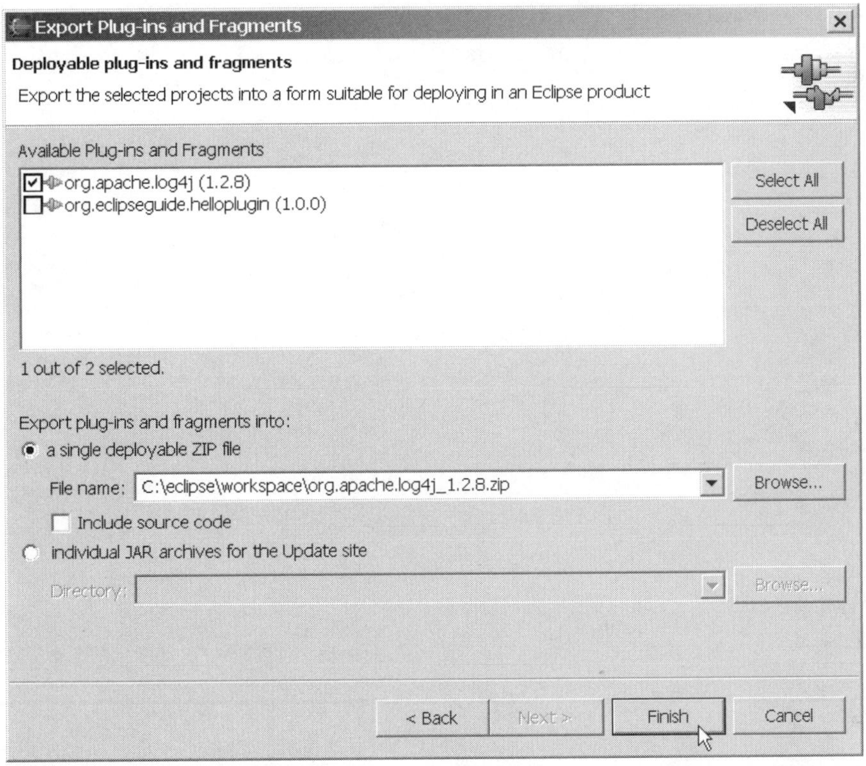

Figure 8.18   You can use the Deployable Plug-ins and Fragments Wizard to create zip files that others can install. Specify the plug-in and the name of the zip file to create and click Finish to create the file.

8.6 *Summary*

Every component of the Eclipse Workbench—every view, every editor, every menu—is defined in a plug-in. The Eclipse designers took great care to expose a fully functional public API for all plug-in writers to use. Because of this even playing field, high quality plug-ins you provide cannot be distinguished from plug-ins that were originally part of the Platform.

The convergence of an object-oriented polymorphic introspective language (Java), a universal data exchange format (XML), open-source tools (Ant, JUnit), design patterns, and agile programming techniques (such as refactoring) make Eclipse a unique and fun environment in which to program. Wizards and templates greatly lessen the learning curve, and the open source community built around Eclipse provides plenty of examples (and support) for the Eclipse programmer.

9

Working with plug-ins in Eclipse

In this chapter...

- Using extension points to add functionality to Eclipse
- Developing editors with syntax highlighting and code assistance
- Creating new views and pop-up menus
- Designing tables and filling them with data

Every component of the Eclipse Workbench—be it a view, editor, or menu—is defined by a plug-in. Using the plug-in architecture, you can customize Eclipse and extend it in ways the designers never envisioned.

Although Eclipse's wizards can make writing plug-ins easier, an understanding of the Platform APIs is essential to plug-in development. The best way to understand it is to see it in action, so in this chapter we'll explore a single, fairly complex example that demonstrates the most common APIs you're likely to use in your own projects.

9.1 *The log4j integration plug-in example*

Building on the log4j library wrapper from chapter 8, the example presented in this chapter adds log4j integration into Eclipse. To get an idea of what you need to do, consider how the integration of Ant is accomplished:

1   A wrapper plug-in, `org.apache.ant`, works just like the log4j wrapper. It contains only the Ant JAR files, which are exported in the plug-in manifest.

2   The integration plug-in, `org.eclipse.ant.core` (with support from the external tools plug-in, `org.eclipse.ui.externaltools`), provides the actual integration with Eclipse—the views, menus, and so forth.

Just to be clear, these are separate plug-ins: one for wrapping the open source library and one (or more) for Eclipse integration. The latter depends on the former.

Your first step will be to prepare a detailed requirements document and identify which user pains you want to solve with this project. Write use-case scenarios showing how the new software will address those pains, and use a storyboard or war-room setting to prioritize the features. After 6 to 12 months and several dozen committee meetings, you can then start coding....

Just kidding! In keeping with our philosophy of agile development, you would probably start by creating a basic plug-in and add functionality a bit at a time, testing and refactoring as you go. That is how we developed this example, but because the process was covered in previous chapters, we'll skip those stages and present you with the final product.

Figure 9.1 shows what the final plug-in looks like. The log4j integration plug-in adds the following features to Eclipse:

■   An editor for log4j.properties files, including syntax coloring and code assistance. To use this editor, simply open one of the files.

■   A view that listens on a socket for logging events and displays them in a table. To see the view, go to the Java perspective and then select Window→Show

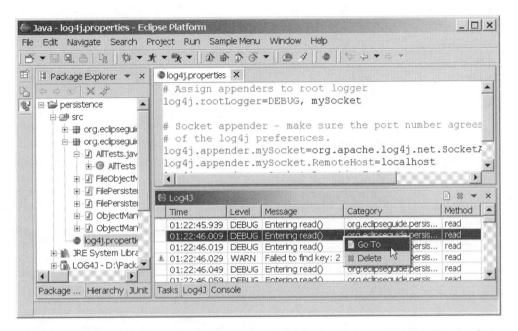

Figure 9.1   The log4j integration plug-in example demonstrates many common plug-in extensions such as syntax coloring, editors, views, tables, and pop-up menus. Full source code is available on the book's web site.

view→Log4J. To use it, specify a Socket appender with the same port used by the view (default 4445). See listing 9.1 for an example log4j.properties file.

- A decorator that marks all Java files currently using logging. To turn on the decorator, select Window→Preferences→Workbench→Label Decorations, check Log4J, and then click OK.

- A pop-up menu item for Java files to automatically add logging to the source code. To use this menu item, right-click on a Java file that doesn't already use a logger in the Package Explorer and select Add Logger.

- Preferences pages for all the aspects of the plug-in. Select Window→Preferences→Log4J to see them.

Listing 9.1   Sample log4j.properties file

```
# Assign appenders to root logger
log4j.rootLogger=DEBUG, mySocket

# Socket appender - make sure the port number agrees with the
# setting of the log4j preferences.
log4j.appender.mySocket=org.apache.log4j.net.SocketAppender
```

```
log4j.appender.mySocket.RemoteHost=localhost
log4j.appender.mySocket.LocationInfo=true
log4j.appender.mySocket.port=4445
```

9.1.1 Project overview

The full source code for this example is available on the book's web site. The following is an overview of all the packages, classes, and interfaces that make up the plug-in. Most of the code for the example is discussed throughout this chapter, in the sections noted.

Package org.eclipseguide.log4j

- Interface `ILoggingEventListener` (§9.3.3)—Interface for getting notifications of new log records
- Class `Log4jPlugin` (§9.5)—Main class for the plug-in
- Class `Log4jUtil`—Utility functions for log and JDT manipulation
- Class `LoggingModel` (§9.3.6)—Stores log records
- Class `ReceiverThread` (§9.3.7)—Receives log records from the running program

Package org.eclipseguide.log4j.decorators

- Class `Log4jDecorator`—Draws a special icon for classes that use logging

Package org.eclipseguide.log4j.editor

- Class `PropertiesConfiguration` (§9.2.7)—Source configuration settings for the properties editor
- Class `PropertiesDocumentProvider` (§9.2.7)—Provides input for the properties editor
- Class `PropertiesEditor` (§9.2.7)—Main class for the log4j properties editor
- Class `PropertiesPartitionScanner` (§9.2.4)—Splits the document into partitions
- Class `TokenManager` (§9.2.5)—Keeps track of all the colors used in the editor

Package org.eclipseguide.log4j.editor.contentassist

- Class `ConfigurationModel` (§9.2.6)—Representation of the log4j settings in the properties file
- Class `PropertiesAssistant` (§9.2.6)—Content assist processor for the properties editor

Package org.eclipseguide.log4j.editor.scanners

- Class `CommentScanner` (§9.2.4)—Parses comments into tokens
- Class `DefaultScanner` (§9.2.4)—Parses property names into tokens
- Class `FormatRule` (§9.2.4)—Custom parsing rule for log4j formats
- Class `ValueScanner` (§9.2.4)—Parses property values into tokens
- Class `WhitespaceDetector` (§9.2.4)—Helper class to tell what characters are whitespace
- Class `WordDetector` (§9.2.4)—Helper class to tell what characters are parts of words

Package org.eclipseguide.log4j.popup.actions

- Class `AddLoggerAction`—Rewrites the selected Java class to support logging

Package org.eclipseguide.log4j.preferences

- Class `EditorPreferencePage` (§9.4)—Settings for the log4j.properties editor
- Class `MainPreferencePage` (§9.4)—Settings for the log4j view

Package org.eclipseguide.log4j.views

- Class `Log4jView` (§9.3.3)—Main class for the log4j view
- Class `TableViewPart` (§9.3.4)—Helper class for views consisting of only a table
- Class `ViewLabelProvider` (§9.3.5)—Returns text or icons that describe logging records in a table

9.1.2 Preparing the project

It is not necessary to follow along in Eclipse to get the benefit of this chapter, but if you are doing that, then you begin by creating a new project for the plug-in. You'll have to do this for your own plug-ins too, of course.

You want a Java plug-in that uses the Default Plug-In Structure to provide a stable base of functionality on which you can add your own extensions. Here are the steps to accomplish that:

1. Select File→New→Project to bring up the New Project Wizard.
2. Select the Plug-in Project Wizard and click Next to open the New Plug-in Project Wizard.
3. Enter the name for the plug-in, **org.eclipseguide.log4j**, and click Next.
4. Leave the fully qualified ID, JAR file, and so forth unchanged. Click Next.

5 Select the Default Plug-In Structure option. Click Next.

6 Make sure the Plug-in Name is set to **Log4J Plug-in**, the Version Number is **1.0.0** (remember, this is the version of the integration plug-in and not the log4j library itself), and the Provider Name is **Eclipse in Action**. Click Finish to create the plug-in.

7 Open the Plug-in Manifest Editor (double-click on plugin.xml if it's not already open). Switch to the Dependencies page, click Add, and select `org.apache.log4j` (the plug-in from chapter 8) in the Workspace Plug-ins list. Doing so makes `org.apache.log4j` a requirement for this plug-in and adds it to the project's classpath. Save the manifest (press Ctrl-S).

The skeleton for the log4j integration plug-in is now complete. If you like, you can try out the plug-in with the Run-time Workbench and verify it exists by using Help→About Eclipse Platform.

NOTE   The Run-time Workbench lists all the plug-ins you have written up to this point. This is usually what you want, but if necessary, you can control which plug-ins are included in the Plug-ins and Fragments tab of the Launch Configuration options (select Run→Run or Run→Debug to edit launch configurations).

9.2 *Editors (TextEditor)*

The Eclipse Workbench window is made up of a number of *parts*. Parts can be either *editors* or *views*. The difference between editors and views is that editors are created from documents, they have a dirty flag, and they can be saved.

Modifications in editors can be undone or reverted to the original input. Views, on the other hand, display some sort of internal data structure (model), and any modifications you make in a view are immediate and cannot be undone. Editor inputs can only be edited in one editor part, but view models can be displayed in any number of related view parts.

So, the first addition to the log4j integration plug-in will be an editor for log4j.properties files. Eclipse provides a rich framework of classes and extensions for plug-in authors to write custom editors for any types of files. In fact, it can be a bit overwhelming, so the Platform SDK provides two editor examples: an XML editor and a simple Java editor. You won't use them here, but if you'd like to take a look, you can add the XML editor to your plug-in through the Extension Templates Wizard (edit plugin.xml, click Add on the Extensions page, select Extension Templates, and pick Editor).The sample Java editor is part of the highly recommended plug-in examples package available from http://www.eclipse.org. Once it's installed, you can read about it in the online help in the Platform Plug-in Developer Guide under Examples Guide→Workbench→Java editor.

One approach to learn about editors is to study these two examples (especially the Java editor). However, in this section, we have taken the approach of creating a simple editor from scratch and explaining each component as we go.

9.2.1 Preparing the editor class

Like most editors, the log4j.properties editor is text based, so it subclasses the `TextEditor` class (which ultimately subclasses `EditorPart`). `TextEditor` takes care of most of the mundane tasks of an editor, such as reading and writing from the file, breaking the file into lines, insertion, deletion, cut and paste, and so forth. The default Text editor is an unadorned instance of the `TextEditor` class.

If you would like to follow along in Eclipse and create a new editor class, do this:

1 In the Package Explorer, right-click on the `org.eclipseguide.log4j` project and select New→Class.

2 Use the dialog to change the Package Name to **org.eclipseguide.log4j. editor**, the Class Name to **PropertiesEditor**, and the Superclass to **org. eclipse.ui.editors.text.TextEditor**. Turn off the option to create a method stub for `main`, let the other options default, and click Finish to generate the class code.

9.2.2 Defining the editor extension

To add an extension to the plug-in for the new editor, follow these steps:

1 Open the plugin.xml manifest file and switch to the Extensions page. Select Add to add a new extension. This will bring up the Extension Wizard (figure 9.2).

2 Select Generic Wizards and Schema-based Extension and click Next. A *schema* is a definition of correct XML that can be inserted into the plug-in manifest. There is one for every extension point; if you want to define your own extension points, you will need to create a schema yourself. Schemas are written in XML and have a .xsd, .mxsd, or .exsd extension.

3 On the second page (figure 9.3), select `org.eclipse.ui.editors`. If you have imported the Workbench plug-ins, you may see all the extension points twice; select the first one. No ID or Name is necessary, so click Finish.

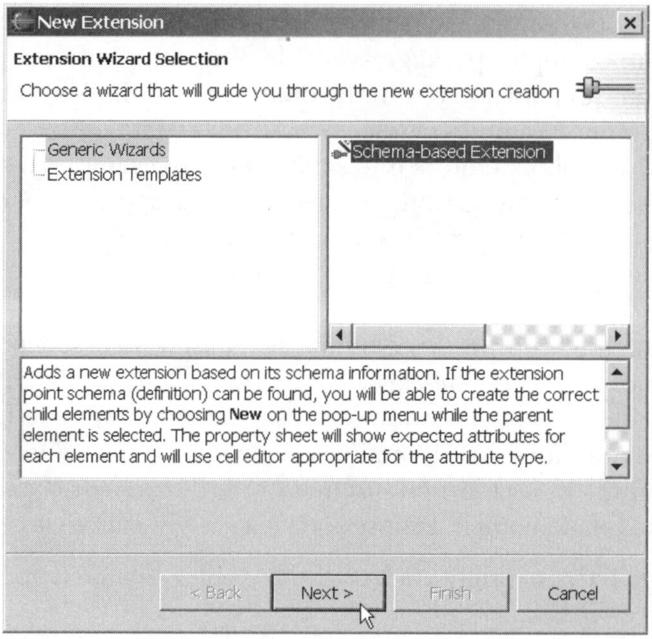

Figure 9.2
You can use the Extension Wizard to add new extensions through hand-crafted templates, but only a few are available. For most extensions you'll need to use the Generic Schema-based Extension Wizard. An experimental interface is available in 2.1 for adding new templates to this dialog. We hope it will be officially supported in the next version.

To see the online help for an extension point, select it and click the Details button. For your convenience, a list of all the supported extension points and what they do is provided in appendix C.

NOTE   If you don't see the extension point you need, turn off the Show Only Extension Points from the Required Plug-ins option. Doing so will show all extension points, but you may not be able to use some of them until you add the plug-ins they require to the Dependencies page of the Plug-in Manifest Editor. You may also need to add them to the Target Platform list (Windows→Plug-In Development→Target Platform). How can you tell what plug-in defines what extension point? The plug-in name is always the prefix of the extension point—for example, `org.eclipse.ui` is the plug-in for `org.eclipse.ui.editors`.

4   You should now see the `org.eclipse.ui.editors` extension point listed in your Extensions page. Right-click on it and select New→Editor. Doing so creates an `editor` object under the extension with a default name like `org.eclipseguide.log4j.editor1` (see figure 9.4).

5   View the properties for the editor by double-clicking on it. Set the `name` to **Log4J Properties Editor** and change the `id` to **org.eclipseguide.log4j.**

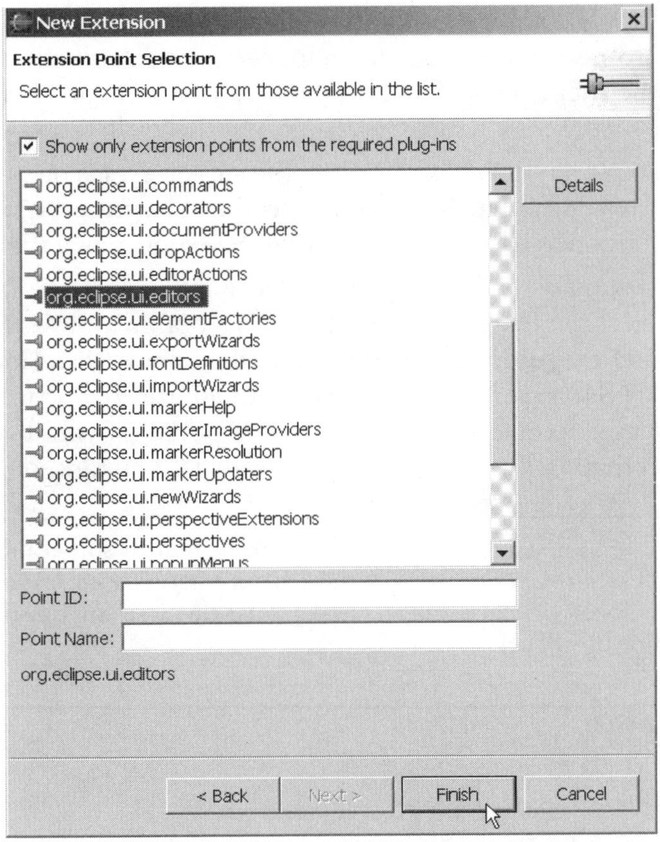

Figure 9.3
You use this dialog to select an extension point to use in your plug-in. Only the extensions that are defined by plug-ins you depend on are shown by default. Select an extension point and click Details to see its online help.

editor.properties. You may need to reposition the Properties view first so you can see it better, for example by stacking it with the Tasks view. Drag its title bar where you want it to go.

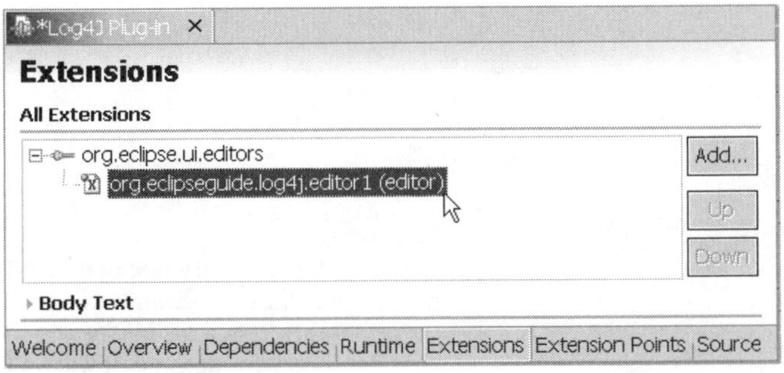

Figure 9.4
Adding the `editor` extension using the Plug-in Manifest (plugin.xml) Editor. Double-click on any of these objects to view the object's properties.

6   This editor is only for log4j.properties files, so set the `filenames` property to **log4j.properties** and set `default` to **true**. The default editor is executed when the user double-clicks on the file. The user can change this setting later.

7   So far you haven't made the link between the `editor` extension point and the class you created earlier. To do this, select the `class` property and click the Selection button to bring up the Java Class Selection dialog (figure 9.5).

8   The Class Selection dialog allows you to select any existing class or create a new one. Select the Use an Existing Java Class option and set the Class Name to **org.eclipseguide.log4j.editor.PropertiesEditor**. Click Finish, and then press Ctrl-S to save. Creating a class through this dialog would not work in this case, because current versions do not allow you to subclass `TextEditor`. Perhaps a future version will provide that enhancement.

NOTE   In Eclipse 2.1, the Class Selection dialog has a bug: It sometimes incorrectly switches to Generate a New Java Class when you click the Browse button. Before you click Finish, make sure the Use an Existing Java Class option is still set.

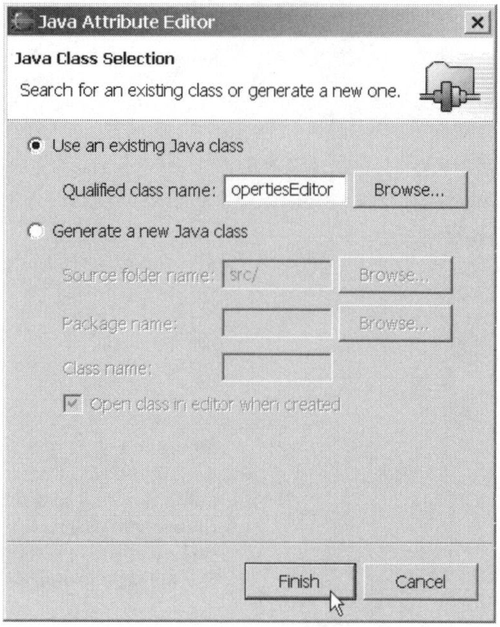

Figure 9.5
This troublesome little dialog is used to select an existing class or generate a new Java class. Unfortunately, it is a bit buggy and incomplete in Eclipse 2.1, but perhaps it will be fixed in future versions.

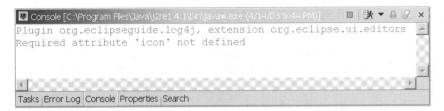

Figure 9.6 Watch the console window for runtime errors like this one. Often, if something in your plug-in isn't working, an error message about a missing attribute, an invalid menu path, or similar problems will appear here. Any logging you do in your plug-in also appears here.

9.2.3 *Adding an icon*

One more thing is missing; can you tell what it is? (Looking at the title of this section is cheating.) Yes, it's the icon. Just for an exercise, try to run the plug-in without defining an icon. If you leave out any required properties, your plug-in will not load, and you will get an error message in the console like the one shown in figure 9.6.

Follow these steps to add the `icon` property:

1 Right-click on the project, select New→Folder, enter the folder name **icons**, and click Finish. By convention, icons go in the icons folder.

2 Right-click on the new folder and select Import→File System to copy the icon there. You could create a new 16x16 pixel GIF format icon in a paint program, but for now just copy the sample.gif file from the `org.eclipse-guide.hello` project you created in section 8.2.3.

3 In the manifest editor, select the `editor` object again and view its properties. Click on the `icon` property and then the selection button, navigate down to where your icon is located, and put a check mark next to the GIF file (see figure 9.7). Click OK and then press Ctrl-S.

Figure 9.7
The Resource Selection dialog is used to select files in your project to refer to in the plug-in manifest. Using it is optional, but doing so is less error-prone than typing file paths by hand.

That's it! Now save all the files, select the project, and start the Run-time Workbench (select Run→Debug As→Run-time Workbench). In the new Workbench window, create a new Java project that uses logging (or just copy the one from chapter 3). Right-click on its log4j.properties file and select Open With. The Open With menu shows the new Log4J Properties Editor as an option, with a marker indicating it is the default editor. Select it, and voila—your new editor will open.

TIP   If you rename or move anything such as a class, an icon, or another object referred to in the plugin.xml file, that reference will not be updated by default and you will begin getting runtime errors. However, most of the refactoring menus have an option to update fully qualified names in non-Java files. Select this option, type **plugin.xml** as the filename, and then click Preview before accepting the change. This will usually take care of the updates for you.

XML

The Extension Wizard created an extension in your plugin.xml file that references the editors extension point. Here is the XML code it created:

```
<extension
    point="org.eclipse.ui.editors">
  <editor
      name="Log4J Properties Editor"
      default="true"
      icon="icons/sample.gif"
      filenames="log4j.properties"
      class="org.eclipseguide.log4j.editor.PropertiesEditor"
      id="org.eclipseguide.log4j.editor.properties">
  </editor>
</extension>
```

Java

The New Class Wizard created a skeletal class for PropertiesEditor that simply extends TextEditor. You'll expand this class later; here is its initial state:

```
package org.eclipseguide.log4j.editor;

import org.eclipse.ui.editors.text.TextEditor;

public class PropertiesEditor extends TextEditor
{
}
```

9.2.4 *Adding color*

Once you have the basic text editor functioning, the next thing you'll add is syntax coloring. In Eclipse text editors, coloring works at the highest level through *partitions*: non-overlapping regions of text in the document being edited. The text editor calls a *partition scanner*, which you provide, to decide what text is in what partition. Every character in the file belongs to one of the partitions you define or to the default partition (IDocument.DEFAULT_CONTENT_TYPE).

Consider a Java source file. The Java editor's partition scanner breaks the document into these partitions:

- Single-line comment
- Multiline comment
- Javadoc comment
- Character string
- Single character
- Default partition (contains everything else; i.e., the code)

How do you decide what your partitions should be? As a rule of thumb, you should only use partitions to differentiate sections that are grossly different in syntax. For example, if you have a source file that can contain two or more different languages, like a JSP file, you should put text from the different languages in different partitions. Comments generally belong in their own partition, because text inside a comment is freeform. The number of partitions is typically between two to five, but it's up to you.

Next, within the partitions, the editor calls a *token scanner* (which you also provide) to break the text into tokens. A *token* is the smallest unit of text that can be colored, so if you want every other character to be a different color, then every other character must be a different token (don't try this at home).

SIDEBAR   One thing to note about tokens in the editor is that there is not a unique token for every word in the file. For example, if you were tokenizing the previous sentence, you wouldn't generate a new token for *One*, another for *thing*, another for *to*, and so forth. Instead, you would generate several references to the same token—perhaps a default token, because the default should be the most common. If you're familiar with design patterns, you might recognize this as an example of the Flyweight pattern. It's a way to use the advantages of object-oriented coding without getting buried under millions of tiny objects.

The token scanners are unique to each partition. For example, in the Java code partition, the editor uses a Java keyword scanner that looks for words like `abstract` and `null` and returns a keyword token for those and a default token for everything else. Inside a Javadoc partition, however, the editor uses a Javadoc token scanner that looks for keyword tokens like `@author` and `@see`, HTML tag tokens like `<b>`, and link tokens like `@link`. All the other text in the Javadoc comment is assigned a default token. Some partitions may consist of one big token that spans the whole partition.

Partition scanners (*RuleBasedPartitionScanner*)

To see how you apply all this to the log4j.properties editor, let's look at an example properties file that you need to color:

```
# Assign one appender to root logger
log4j.rootLogger=DEBUG, myConsole

# Console appender
log4j.appender.myConsole=org.apache.log4j.ConsoleAppender
log4j.appender.myConsole.layout=org.apache.log4j.PatternLayout
log4j.appender.myConsole.layout.ConversionPattern=%5p %m - %l%n
log4j.appender.myLogFile.threshold=WARN
```

One thing that jumps out right away is the comments, which should go in their own partition. Next, notice that the remaining lines all follow the format *name=value*. The syntax of the names and values is quite different, so they each get their own partition. Somewhat arbitrarily, we picked names to go into the default partition, and the equals sign is considered part of the value. So, there are three partitions:

- Comments
- Values
- Everything else

To parse the text into partitions and tokens, you use the JFace base classes for *rule-based scanning*. A rule-based scanner walks through a list of parsing rules you supply (for example, to recognize a comment or a string), trying each one until it produces a match. Rule-based scanners provide an extremely easy, though somewhat inefficient, way to parse text. Listing 9.2 shows the partition scanner class, `PropertiesPartitionScanner`, responsible for breaking the text into partitions. (To save space, the rest of the listings in this chapter won't include the `package` or `import` statements at the top.)

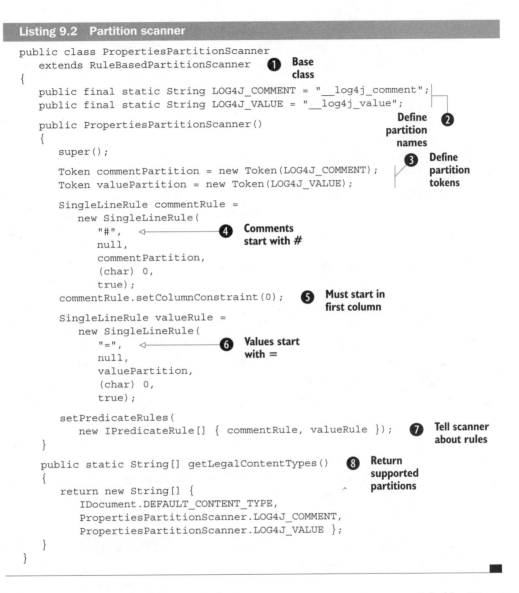

Listing 9.2   Partition scanner

```
public class PropertiesPartitionScanner
    extends RuleBasedPartitionScanner        ❶  Base
{                                                class
    public final static String LOG4J_COMMENT = "__log4j_comment";
    public final static String LOG4J_VALUE = "__log4j_value";
                                                     Define
    public PropertiesPartitionScanner()             partition  ❷
    {                                                names
        super();
                                                          ❸  Define
        Token commentPartition = new Token(LOG4J_COMMENT);   partition
        Token valuePartition = new Token(LOG4J_VALUE);       tokens

        SingleLineRule commentRule =
            new SingleLineRule(
                "#",         ◄────────────❹  Comments
                null,                         start with #
                commentPartition,
                (char) 0,
                true);
        commentRule.setColumnConstraint(0);  ❺  Must start in
                                                 first column
        SingleLineRule valueRule =
            new SingleLineRule(
                "=",         ◄────────────❻  Values start
                null,                         with =
                valuePartition,
                (char) 0,
                true);

        setPredicateRules(
            new IPredicateRule[] { commentRule, valueRule }); ❼  Tell scanner
    }                                                            about rules

    public static String[] getLegalContentTypes()  ❽  Return
    {                                                  supported
        return new String[] {                          partitions
            IDocument.DEFAULT_CONTENT_TYPE,
            PropertiesPartitionScanner.LOG4J_COMMENT,
            PropertiesPartitionScanner.LOG4J_VALUE };
    }
}
```

❶ This class extends a base class called RuleBasedPartitionScanner provided by JFace.
Rule-based scanners are used for both partition and token scanners. The scanner
works by reading the text and feeding it to a list of rules, which you supply in a
moment. It evaluates the rules, one at a time in the order specified, until one
matches. All scanning rules follow a simple pattern. Either they fire or they don't.
If they fire, they return the token you passed them, and the scanner stops there

and returns the token. If they don't fire, they return the `Token.UNDEFINED` token, and the scanner continues with the next rule in the list.

❷ For each partition type (sometimes called *content type*), you define a constant string. These are used for keys in a hash table later.

❸ Each partition also gets its own unique token object. These tokens don't have a color associated with them—that will wait until the token scanning within the partition is done.

❹ The `SingleLineRule` class is for text sequences that can't cross line boundaries. Here you use it for comments that begin with #. You don't specify an ending string, so the comment can continue until the end of the line. You also tell the rule there is no escape character ((char) 0). The last parameter tells the rule that an end of file can also terminate the sequence (for example, if the user is typing on the last line of the file).

❺ Here you constrain the rule so it only matches comments that start in the first column. Columns are zero based, like most things in Eclipse.

❻ The second rule for values is similar to the first one for comments. Values start with an equals sign and run to the end of the line or file, whichever comes first.

❼ Here you provide the scanner with the list of rules to evaluate.

❽ During refactoring, we discovered a couple of places that needed to know the list of supported partition types, so we combined the code here. This list must be complete and cover every character of the text.

Token scanners (RuleBasedScanner)

Now you need to write a token scanner for each of the three partitions. Let's begin with the easiest one: the scanner for the comment partition. Everything in the comment partition is a comment, so it doesn't have to do any real parsing. All it needs to do is return a token that is unique to comment text. Listing 9.3 shows the `CommentScanner` class.

Listing 9.3 The CommentScanner class

```
public class CommentScanner extends RuleBasedScanner
{
   public CommentScanner(TokenManager tokenManager)
   {
      IToken commentToken =
         tokenManager.getToken(Log4jPlugin.PREF_COMMENT_COLOR);
      setDefaultReturnToken(commentToken);
   }
}
```

For all the token scanners, you'll use the `RuleBasedScanner` base class. It works in a fashion similar to the `RuleBasedPartitionScanner` class you used in the last section. A token manager is used to keep track of tokens and colors (discussed shortly). A token is assigned to each section of text within the partition. Because there is only one type of text inside the comment partition, you don't need to supply any rules. The code just sets the default token that will always be returned.

Next, let's look at the scanner for the default partition (listing 9.4). This scanner is only slightly more complicated. You want all the words to be considered part of a property name, except for whitespace (blanks, tabs, and so forth).

Listing 9.4 The DefaultScanner class

```
public class DefaultScanner extends RuleBasedScanner
{
    public DefaultScanner(TokenManager tokenManager)
    {
        IToken propertyToken =
            tokenManager.getToken(Log4jPlugin.PREF_PROPERTY_COLOR);

        setDefaultReturnToken(propertyToken);
        setRules(
            new IRule[] {
                new WhitespaceRule(new WhitespaceDetector())});
    }
}
```

If no rules match, the default token is returned—in this case, the property token. A single rule is added to match whitespace characters.

The `WhitespaceDetector` class is one you must provide. Here's a simple definition that returns `true` for blanks, newlines, tabs, and other types of whitespace characters:

```
public class WhitespaceDetector implements IWhitespaceDetector
{
    public boolean isWhitespace(char c)
    {
        return Character.isWhitespace(c);
    }
}
```

Finally, the scanner for the value partition is shown in listing 9.5. This one is much more complicated because it has to handle keywords and formats like `%m` and `%d{hh:mm:ss a}`.

Listing 9.5 The ValueScanner class

```
public class ValueScanner extends RuleBasedScanner
{
    String[] keywords =          ❶  Define keywords
        {                            that can appear
        "ALL",                       in values
        "DEBUG",     .
        "ERROR",
        // ...
        };
    public ValueScanner(TokenManager tokenManager)
    {
        IToken defaultToken =
            tokenManager.getToken(Log4jPlugin.PREF_DEFAULT_COLOR);
        IToken formatToken =
            tokenManager.getToken(Log4jPlugin.PREF_FORMAT_COLOR);   ❷  Rule for
        IToken keywordToken =                                           braces
            tokenManager.getToken(Log4jPlugin.PREF_KEYWORD_COLOR);

        IRule braceRule =
            new SingleLineRule("{", "}", formatToken, (char) 0, true);

        WordRule keywordRule = new WordRule(new WordDetector());
        for (int i = 0; i < keywords.length; i++)    Rule for    ❸
        {                                            keywords
            keywordRule.addWord(keywords[i], keywordToken);
        }

        IRule formatRule = new FormatRule(formatToken);   ❹  Rule for
                                                              formats
        IRule whitespaceRule =
            new WhitespaceRule(new WhitespaceDetector());  ❺  Rule for
                                                              whitespace
        setDefaultReturnToken(defaultToken);
        setRules(
            new IRule[] {                        ❻  Everything
                braceRule,         ❼  Tell base     else gets
                formatRule,           class about   default color
                keywordRule,          all rules
                whitespaceRule,
                });
    }
}
```

❶ In order to recognize what is a keyword and what is not, you need a list of the keywords. This example code requires the case of the keyword to match, which may or may not be appropriate for your application.

❷ Log4j formats are a little tricky to parse because they can contain modifiers in braces. Here you get the brace part out of the way by marking everything between braces (including the braces themselves) as a format.

❸ You use a `WordRule` class to match all the keywords. The keywords are added to the rule one at a time with the `addWord()` method. If any of them match, then the rule as a whole matches. For coloring purposes, you don't need to distinguish between the keywords; just note that one of many keywords occurred. `WordRule` uses a class that implements the `IWordDetector` interface to tell which characters are part of a word and which are not. This is a class you supply. Here's the example you use:

```
public class WordDetector implements IWordDetector
{
    public boolean isWordStart(char c)
    {
        return Character.isLetter(c);
    }
    public boolean isWordPart(char c)
    {
        return Character.isLetterOrDigit(c);
    }
}
```

❹ The third rule is a custom one that matches log4j formats starting with a percent sign. This rule is discussed in the next section.

❺ You need a whitespace rule to match any blanks and tabs in the file. The whitespace rule generally comes last.

❻ Any text not covered by one of the rules is assigned a default token and color.

❼ Finally, you feed all the rules you created to the base class. The order is important, because the scanner tries the rules in the given order until one matches.

Custom rules (IRule)

The Platform doesn't supply a rule for log4j formats, so you have to create your own. Rules are pretty simple—they have one method, `evaluate()`, which is passed an `ICharacterScanner` class. You read a character at a time as long as the characters are matching the rule, and back up if you go too far. `evaluate()` returns `true` if there's a match and `false` otherwise. Listing 9.6 shows the source for the `FormatRule` class.

| Listing 9.6 The FormatRule class |

```
public class FormatRule implements IRule
{
    private final IToken token;

    public FormatRule(IToken token)
    {
        this.token = token;        ❶ Remember what
    }                                 token to return
```

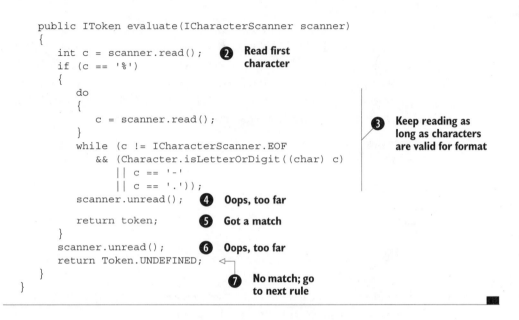

```
public IToken evaluate(ICharacterScanner scanner)
{
    int c = scanner.read();              ❷ Read first
    if (c == '%')                          character
    {
        do
        {
            c = scanner.read();
        }
        while (c != ICharacterScanner.EOF   ❸ Keep reading as
            && (Character.isLetterOrDigit((char) c)   long as characters
                || c == '-'                           are valid for format
                || c == '.'));
        scanner.unread();  ❹ Oops, too far

        return token;      ❺ Got a match
    }
    scanner.unread();      ❻ Oops, too far
    return Token.UNDEFINED;
}                          ❼ No match; go
}                            to next rule
```

❶ The constructor saves the token so you can return it if there is a match.

❷ You read the stream one character at a time using `ICharacterScanner.read()`. If the first character is a percent sign, it indicates the start of a format token.

❸ This loop keeps consuming characters as long as they are valid for a format. For this example, you don't check to see if the format is really valid; you just make sure it contains valid characters. You might want to be a little more picky in your code.

❹ One nice thing about using `ICharacterScanner` is that you can back up. This relieves you from having to keep track of the last character read. Here you've read a character that doesn't belong in a format, so you call the `unread()` method to stuff it back for the next consumer to examine.

❺ You've matched a valid-looking format, so you return the format token.

❻ In this case the first character was not a percent sign, so you stuff it back for the next consumer.

❼ When rules don't match, they should return `Token.UNDEFINED` so the rule scanner continues with the next rule, if there is one.

9.2.5 *Token manager*

If you look at the editor samples provided with Eclipse, you'll see they use a *color manager* class to keep track of all colors used in the editor. You need to keep track of colors because they (specifically instances of the SWT `Color` class) are limited operating system resources. You need to make sure you don't allocate more than you need, and that you release them when you're done with them. The easiest way to do this is to dedicate a class to keep track of them.

A *token manager,* on the other hand, keeps track of both tokens and the colors that go with them. We designed this after refactoring the color manager a few times to add support for user-settable colors in the preferences. For example, you want to be able to support going into the Preferences dialog and changing the color for all keywords, and have the editor be affected immediately.

Preferences are covered more in section 9.4, but basically the editor listens for preference changes by registering a function that is called when a change occurs. When this happens, the editor tells the token manager about the change by calling the `handlePreferenceStoreChanged()` method. If the color for a token was changed in the preferences, this lets it be changed in the real token as well. Next, the editor needs to know if the change affected how the text being edited looks on the screen (in other words, its *presentation*). To do this, it calls `affectsTextPresentation()`. If that method returns `true`, then the editor knows it needs to redraw some of the text.

Listing 9.7 shows the `TokenManager` class for the log4j editor. This class, or something like it, will be very useful in all your editor projects.

Listing 9.7 The TokenManager class

```
public class TokenManager
{
    private Map colorTable = new HashMap(10);        ❶ Colors and
    private Map tokenTable = new HashMap(10);           tokens managed
    private final IPreferenceStore preferenceStore;     by this class

    public TokenManager(IPreferenceStore preferenceStore)
    {
        this.preferenceStore = preferenceStore;
    }

    public IToken getToken(String prefKey)
    {
        Token token = (Token) tokenTable.get(prefKey);  ❷ Look up in
        if (token == null)                                 hash table
        {
            String colorName = preferenceStore.getString(prefKey);  ❸ Create
            RGB rgb = StringConverter.asRGB(colorName);                new
            token = new Token(new TextAttribute(getColor(rgb)));      token
            tokenTable.put(prefKey, token);
        }
        return token;
    }
```

```
public void dispose()
{
    Iterator e = colorTable.values().iterator();
    while (e.hasNext())
        ((Color) e.next()).dispose();
}

private Color getColor(RGB rgb)
{
    Color color = (Color) colorTable.get(rgb);
    if (color == null)
    {
        color = new Color(Display.getCurrent(), rgb);
        colorTable.put(rgb, color);
    }
    return color;
}

public boolean affectsTextPresentation(PropertyChangeEvent event)
{
    Token token = (Token) tokenTable.get(event.getProperty());
    return (token != null);
}

public void handlePreferenceStoreChanged(PropertyChangeEvent event)
{
    String prefKey = event.getProperty();
    Token token = (Token) tokenTable.get(prefKey);
    if (token != null)
    {
        String colorName = preferenceStore.getString(prefKey);
        RGB rgb = StringConverter.asRGB(colorName);
        token.setData(new TextAttribute(getColor(rgb)));
    }
}
}
```

❹ Release all colors back to OS

❺ Look up in hash table

❻ Create new color

❼ See if it's one of ours

❽ See if it's one of ours

❾ Replace color

❶ You keep a list of all the tokens and colors managed by this class. Each list is a hash table.

❷ The key for the token table is a constant string, the name of the token. The token name also happens to be the name of a preference setting you'll use to keep track of colors later.

❸ The key was not found, so a new token needs to be created and recorded. The color name is looked up in the preference store (more on that in the next section), the name is converted to an RGB (red, green, blue) format, and a new color is allocated and assigned as the foreground color for the token. This example only supports setting the foreground color, but you could also set the background color and the style (for example, bold or italics) of the text.

❹ The `dispose()` method returns all colors back to the operating system. Colors are a limited system resource, so it's very important to return each one or eventually your program will fail.

❺ The key for the color table is the RGB value for the color.

❻ The color has not been seen before, so you need to create a new one. Colors are Standard Widget Toolkit (SWT) resources based on the current `Display`.

❼ This routine is called to see if a property change (for example, the user changing a setting in the Preferences dialog) could affect the way the text looks in the editor. You take a conservative approach: If the property is the name of one of your tokens, then you say yes, it did change the way the text looks. In your own applications, you may want to be a little smarter about the test.

❽ This routine is called to apply the property change to your tokens after the preference store has been changed but before the editor decides whether it needs to redraw text. The first step is to see if the property name is one of your tokens. If not, you don't have to worry about it.

❾ If the property changed is the name of one of your tokens, then you replace the color with a new color allocated from the new value specified in the preferences.

9.2.6 *Content assist (IContentAssistProcessor)*

When you're typing in Eclipse's Java editor and you press Ctrl-Space, the editor makes some suggestions for you about what comes next. For example, if you type the first half of a class name, the editor pops up a small window showing all the classes that start with that string. This functionality is known as *content assist*, or sometimes *code completion*. In addition, when you type a variable name and then press the period key, the Java editor pops up the assist window showing all the members and methods of that variable. This is called *auto activation*.

You want the log4j.properties editor to do something similar (see figure 9.8). The `TextEditor` class provides support by working with a content assist processor, which you provide. You can provide a different assist processor for each partition. For the purposes of this example, you'll only do content assist in the default partition, for property names. Listing 9.8 shows the `PropertiesAssistant` class that implements this functionality for the log4j.properties editor.

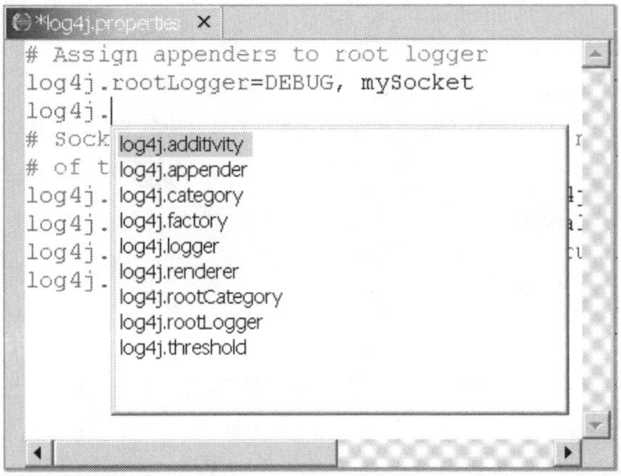

Figure 9.8
When you type a period, the log4j properties editor takes a guess at what comes next. As you type more characters, the list of guesses is narrowed down.

Listing 9.8   The PropertiesAssistant class

```
public class PropertiesAssistant implements IContentAssistProcessor
{
    public ICompletionProposal[] computeCompletionProposals(
        ITextViewer viewer,
        int documentOffset)
    {
        ICompletionProposal[] proposals = null;
        try
        {
            IDocument document = viewer.getDocument();
            IRegion range =
                document.getLineInformationOfOffset(documentOffset);
            int start = range.getOffset();
            String prefix =
                document.get(start, documentOffset - start);

            ConfigurationModel model =
                new ConfigurationModel(document.get());
            List completions = model.getCompletions(prefix);

            proposals = new CompletionProposal[completions.size()];
            int i = 0;
            for (Iterator iter = completions.iterator();
                iter.hasNext();)
            {
                String completion = (String) iter.next();
                proposals[i++] =
                    new CompletionProposal(
                        completion,
                        start,
                        documentOffset - start,
                        completion.length());
            }
```

1 Editor calls this to create proposals

2 Get text before cursor

3 Get list of possible completions

4 Create array of proposals

5 Add proposal

```
        }
        catch (Exception e)
        {
            DebugPlugin.log(e);      ❻ Report
        }                              exceptions
                                       to error log
        return proposals;
    }

    public char[] getCompletionProposalAutoActivationCharacters()
    {
        return new char[] { '.' };   ❼ Period
    }                                   activates
                                        assist
    public String getErrorMessage()
    {
        return "No completions available.";
    }

    // unused methods omitted...
}
```

❶ The editor calls the `computeCompletionProposals()` method when it needs the list of proposals, and takes care of drawing the list and managing the assist window for you. It passes in the viewer, which is the user interface part of the editor, and a document offset, which tells you where the cursor is located relative to the text being edited.

❷ The `IDocument` interface, provided by JFace, is used for classes that hold the actual text being edited. The `get()` method retrieves part or all of the document. In this snippet, you get the starting and ending offset of the current line, and then extract the text from the start of the line to the current cursor position into the `prefix` variable.

❸ `ConfigurationModel` is a class specific to log4j that parses the properties file and suggests appropriate strings that could appear at the current location.

❹ This function is supposed to return an array of `CompletionProposal` classes, so you allocate one for each completion suggested by the `ConfigurationModel`.

❺ Here is the heart of the method: the part that fills in the proposals. The editor's mission, should you decide to accept the proposal, will be to substitute all the text from the beginning of the line to the current cursor position with one of the suggested completion strings.

❻ Unexpected exceptions should be logged so your users can report errors. The `DebugPlugin.log()` method puts a record into the .log file, located in the workspace's

.metadata subdirectory. This file can be read with a text editor or by using the PDE Runtime Error Log view.

❼ There are two steps to make code assist automatically activated. The first step is performed here by defining the character or characters that trigger the activation. The second step is to call the content assistant's `enableAutoActivation()` method (see the `PropertiesConfiguration` class later in this section).

The `ConfigurationModel` class is specific to log4j. It gets a list of appenders from the `rootLogger` property; for example, if `log4j.rootLogger` is "DEBUG, one, two, three" then the appenders are `one`, `two`, and `three`. In the interests of brevity we won't reprint the whole thing here, but this is the most important part—the `getCompletions()` method:

```
public List getCompletions(String prefix)
{
    List completions = new LinkedList();

    for (int i = 0; i < appenders.length; i++)
    {
        if (testCompletion(appenders[i], prefix))
            completions.add(appenders[i]);
    }
    for (int i = 0; i < baseProps.length; i++)
    {
        if (testCompletion(baseProps[i], prefix))
            completions.add(baseProps[i]);
    }
    return completions;
}
```

`testCompletion()` is a private method that takes a possible completion string and tests it against the string the user has typed up to the cursor. It returns `true` or `false`, depending on whether the completion string matches the string typed so far:

```
private boolean testCompletion(String completion, String prefix)
{
    return completion.toLowerCase().startsWith(
        prefix.toLowerCase())
        && (completion.lastIndexOf(".")
            == prefix.lastIndexOf("."));
}
```

In case you're wondering, the tests with `lastIndexOf()` simply make sure the completion string has the same number of periods as the prefix string. For example, if the user typed **log4j.**, then `log4j.appenders` would be a valid completion, but `log4j.appenders.MySocket` would not.

9.2.7 *Putting it all together*

So far we've refrained from showing you the glue that binds all this code together—but now it's time. The first class, PropertiesDocumentProvider (see listing 9.9), is the *document provider* for log4j.properties files. Given an object, in this case a file, a document provider's job is to create an IDocument. An IDocument is a JFace interface that represents a document (for example, a piece of text). It also creates the partition scanner and assigns it to the document, and just to be fair it also assigns the document to the scanner. PropertiesDocumentProvider subclasses FileDocumentProvider, a JFace class that does most of the work for you.

Listing 9.9 The PropertiesDocumentProvider class

```
public class PropertiesDocumentProvider
   extends FileDocumentProvider
{
   protected IDocument createDocument(Object element)
      throws CoreException
   {
      IDocument document = super.createDocument(element);
      if (document != null)
      {
         IDocumentPartitioner partitioner =
            new DefaultPartitioner(
               new PropertiesPartitionScanner(),
               PropertiesPartitionScanner.getLegalContentTypes());
         partitioner.connect(document);
         document.setDocumentPartitioner(partitioner);
      }
      return document;
   }
}
```

The PropertiesConfiguration class, shown in listing 9.10, subclasses the JFace class SourceViewerConfiguration. This class acts as the central repository for all information about the editor. It consists of a series of getXXX() methods to get the different parts of the editor, such as the content assist processor.

Listing 9.10 The PropertiesConfiguration class

```
public class PropertiesConfiguration
   extends SourceViewerConfiguration
{
   private final TokenManager tokenManager;

   public PropertiesConfiguration(TokenManager tokenManager)
```

```
   {
      this.tokenManager = tokenManager;
   }

   public String[] getConfiguredContentTypes(        ❶ Return all
      ISourceViewer sourceViewer)                        partition types
   {
      return PropertiesPartitionScanner.getLegalContentTypes();
   }

   public IPresentationReconciler getPresentationReconciler(  ◁
      ISourceViewer sourceViewer)
   {                                                     Get damagers   ❷
      PresentationReconciler reconciler =               and repairers ...
        new PresentationReconciler();
      DefaultDamagerRepairer dr;

      dr = new DefaultDamagerRepairer(             ... for default   ❸
            new DefaultScanner(tokenManager));         partition
      reconciler.setDamager(dr, IDocument.DEFAULT_CONTENT_TYPE);
      reconciler.setRepairer(dr, IDocument.DEFAULT_CONTENT_TYPE);

      dr = new DefaultDamagerRepairer(
            new CommentScanner(tokenManager));      ❹  ... for
      reconciler.setDamager(dr,                          comment
         PropertiesPartitionScanner.LOG4J_COMMENT);      partition
      reconciler.setRepairer(dr,
         PropertiesPartitionScanner.LOG4J_COMMENT);

      dr = new DefaultDamagerRepairer(
            new ValueScanner(tokenManager));        ❺  ... and
      reconciler.setDamager(dr,                          for value
         PropertiesPartitionScanner.LOG4J_VALUE);        partition
      reconciler.setRepairer(dr,
         PropertiesPartitionScanner.LOG4J_VALUE);

      return reconciler;
   }

   public IContentAssistant getContentAssistant(
      ISourceViewer sourceViewer)
   {
      ContentAssistant assistant = new ContentAssistant();  ❻ Use base
      assistant.setContentAssistProcessor(                     assistant and
         new PropertiesAssistant(),                            plug in
         IDocument.DEFAULT_CONTENT_TYPE);                       processor
      assistant.enableAutoActivation(true);      ❼ Typing a period
      assistant.enableAutoInsert(true);     ◁       brings up assist
      return assistant;
   }                                       ❽  If there is one
}                                             proposal, do it
```

1 The base class calls this method to get all the partition types supported by the editor. Be sure to include the default partition in the list.

2 Damagers and repairers; oh, the horror. These guys always come in pairs. Damagers are like the insurance adjusters that assess what the falling tree did to your house. Repairers are the contractors that come in later to fix what the adjusters approved.

3 Each partition gets its own damager and repairer. Most of the time you can use the DefaultDamagerRepairer class and plug in a few values. This is the where your token scanners get associated with your partition types. Here, you set up the default partition.

4 Next you set up the comment partition. The order is not important.

5 Finally, you set up the value partition.

6 Here you plug in the content assist processor. The base class, ContentAssistant, handles the grunt work.

7 You turn on auto activation so that typing in a period (or whatever character is set in the content assist processor class) brings up the assist window.

8 If you press Ctrl-Space to bring up content assist but there is only one proposal, turning on this option causes the editor to immediately pick that proposal for you. Both this option and auto activation should really be controlled by a preference setting, but that's left as an exercise for the reader.

Now you're cooking with gas. One more class left to go—the PropertiesEditor class (subclassing TextEditor) is upgraded to set the editor's source configuration, its document provider, its preferences store, and so forth. See listing 9.11 for the final version.

Listing 9.11 Final PropertiesEditor class

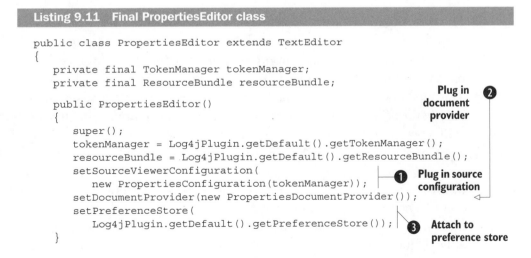

```
public class PropertiesEditor extends TextEditor
{
    private final TokenManager tokenManager;
    private final ResourceBundle resourceBundle;

    public PropertiesEditor()                                    Plug in       2
    {                                                            document
        super();                                                 provider
        tokenManager = Log4jPlugin.getDefault().getTokenManager();
        resourceBundle = Log4jPlugin.getDefault().getResourceBundle();
        setSourceViewerConfiguration(
            new PropertiesConfiguration(tokenManager));    1  Plug in source
        setDocumentProvider(new PropertiesDocumentProvider());     configuration
        setPreferenceStore(
            Log4jPlugin.getDefault().getPreferenceStore());  3  Attach to
    }                                                             preference store
```

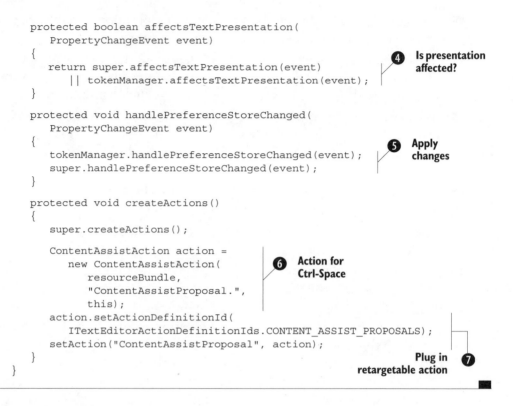

```
protected boolean affectsTextPresentation(
   PropertyChangeEvent event)
{
   return super.affectsTextPresentation(event)            Is presentation
      || tokenManager.affectsTextPresentation(event);     affected?
}

protected void handlePreferenceStoreChanged(
   PropertyChangeEvent event)
{
   tokenManager.handlePreferenceStoreChanged(event);      Apply
   super.handlePreferenceStoreChanged(event);             changes
}

protected void createActions()
{
   super.createActions();

   ContentAssistAction action =
      new ContentAssistAction(                             Action for
         resourceBundle,                                   Ctrl-Space
         "ContentAssistProposal.",
         this);
   action.setActionDefinitionId(
      ITextEditorActionDefinitionIds.CONTENT_ASSIST_PROPOSALS);
   setAction("ContentAssistProposal", action);
}                                                          Plug in
}                                              retargetable action
```

❶ This code creates your source configuration class and associates it with the editor.

❷ The same thing is true for the document provider. Now the editor knows how to read files.

❸ The editor needs to be attached to the plug-in's *preference store*, a logical object managed by the workspace that holds all the plug-in's options.

❹ The token manager is called upon to decide whether the editor's text needs to be redrawn (that is, it's damaged) due to a preference change.

❺ This method is called to handle the preference changes. The token manager must handle them before the editor gets a chance, so it can update the tokens and their colors before the editor starts using them to redraw text.

❻ Content assist gets its own special action type here. It's a little strange because this is a *retargetable action*, which means each editor or view can redefine what the action means. Another example of a retargetable action is the Copy command on the Edit menu. The meaning of Copy varies, depending on what kind of window you are in; in a text editor it might copy some text, but in the Resource view it would copy a file. Content assist works the same way.

❼ This code does the retargeting. Content assist is one of the special predefined actions like Copy and Paste that the text editor classes all know about.

The `ContentAssistAction` helper class requires some resources to be present in your plug-in's resource bundle, and they all must start with the same string (passed to the constructor). Here are the properties used for the log4j preferences editor, from the file Log4jPluginResources.properties:

```
# Required for content assist (see PropertiesEditor.java)
ContentAssistProposal.label=Content Assist@Ctrl+Space
ContentAssistProposal.tooltip=Content Assist
ContentAssistProposal.image=
ContentAssistProposal.description=Content Assist
```

Congratulations! You now have a fully functioning, color-coding, content-assisting editor to show the neighbors. Won't they be jealous?

9.3 *Views (ViewPart)*

As we mentioned earlier, a *view* is a type of Workbench part, just like an editor. Views provide a presentation of some underlying model and often give you the ability to modify it. For the next example, you'll develop a view that displays log4j logging records.

Log4j can send its output to a number of different destinations, including the console, flat files, databases, and sockets. If you've used log4j for long, you may be familiar with the Chainsaw and LogFactor5 programs. These programs listen on a socket for log4j output and present it in a convenient tabular format. As Swing clients, they cannot be directly integrated into the Eclipse environment, which relies on native SWT widgets. So, what you want is an Eclipse view with similar functionality that can fit well inside the Workbench. Figure 9.9 shows the view you'll create.

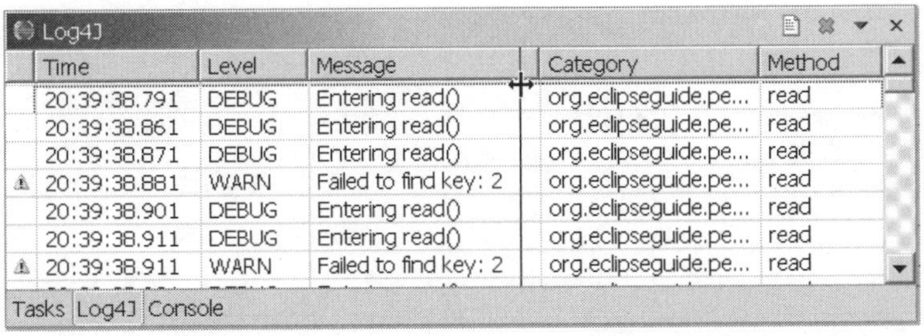

Figure 9.9   The Log4j view developed in this chapter has columns for the most useful columns in logging records. The columns are resizable (except the first one), and the view remembers their sizes when you close Eclipse.

This view is typical of the kind you might need in your applications. It has a number of resizable columns for different fields in the log, a couple of buttons on its toolbar, a drop-down menu, and a pop-up menu. This is probably overkill for this particular application, but it allows us to demonstrate some important functionality.

SIDEBAR   While creating the examples for this book, the authors took full advantage of the open source nature of Eclipse by examining similar code inside the Eclipse platform. In particular, the Task List view uses a table just like this one to show compiler errors and other tasks. If you'd like to look at Eclipse internals such as the Task List view, the easiest way is to go to the Java perspective and select Navigate→Open Type (or press Ctrl-Shift-T). Begin typing your best guess for the class name (for example, **task**) and watch as the selection of classes and interfaces is narrowed down. When you find the one you want (in this case, TaskList), select it and click OK (or just press the Enter key). Then you can use the powerful Java navigation features of the JDT to explore the source code. If you have trouble finding the right class, see the tips in section 8.2 to include more plug-ins in your search.

9.3.1 *Adding the view*

If you look in appendix C, you'll find a table with all the extension points defined by Platform plug-ins. One of these, org.eclipse.ui.views, is described this way: "Defines additional views for the Workbench." That sounds like what you want, so on the Extensions page, add the extension for org.eclipse.ui.views; under that extension, create a category object and a view object. The properties for these objects should be filled in as shown in the following XML:

```
<extension
    point="org.eclipse.ui.views">
  <category
      name="Log4J"
      id="org.eclipseguide.log4j">
  </category>
  <view
      name="Log4J"
      icon="icons/sample.gif"
      category="org.eclipseguide.log4j"
      class="org.eclipseguide.log4j.views.Log4jView"
      id="org.eclipseguide.log4j.views.Log4jView">
  </view>
</extension>
```

Figure 9.10
Views are added to the Show View dialog
through the `org.eclipse.ui.views`
extension point. You can organize them into
groups using the `category` property.

(If you're following along with this example in Eclipse, you'll need to leave off the class field at first, or create a skeleton class as you did for the editor example in section 9.2.1 until you put the final one in place.)

Notice how you set the view's `category` property to the category's `id` property. Doing so makes the view appear under the category in the Show View dialog (Window→Show View→Other) as shown in figure 9.10. The exact spelling and capitalization are important.

9.3.2 *Modifying perspective defaults*

To make a view even easier for the user to discover, you may want to add it to the view shortcuts (Window→Show View) or make it come up as part of an existing perspective like the Java perspective. You can do both by adding `org.eclipse.ui.perspectiveExtensions` to your plugin.xml file, as shown here:

```
<extension
    point="org.eclipse.ui.perspectiveExtensions">
  <perspectiveExtension
      targetID="org.eclipse.jdt.ui.JavaPerspective">
    <view
        relative="org.eclipse.ui.views.TaskList"
        relationship="stack"
        id="org.eclipseguide.log4j.views.Log4jView">
    </view>
    <viewShortcut
```

```
                        id="org.eclipseguide.log4j.views.Log4jView">
          </viewShortcut>
        </perspectiveExtension>
      </extension>
```

The `targetID` property tells Eclipse you're adding something to the Java perspective. The `view` element adds your new view to this perspective, stacked underneath the Task List. `viewShortcut` adds the log4j view to the view shortcut list for this perspective. Notice how each element refers back to the ID of the view defined earlier.

NOTE   The `perspectiveExtensions` settings only modify the defaults for the perspective. If the user customizes the Java perspective (for example, by moving the views around) and then installs your plug-in, they won't see the new view unless they either add it manually or perform a Window→ Reset Perspective to cause Eclipse to reload the perspective from its default settings.

9.3.3 *View class*

Eclipse views can contain anything, but the Log4j view has just one table in it. To make the code a little more understandable and flexible, you'll break the code into two pieces: a `TableViewPart` class that provides generic support for views that consist only of a table; and a `Log4jView` class that extends `TableViewPart`, hooks up with the input source, and presents the log4j-specific rows and columns.

Defining columns

Let's look at the `Log4jView` class first, starting with the definitions of the table columns:

```java
public class Log4jView extends TableViewPart
{
    public static final int COL_IMAGE = 0;
    public static final int COL_TIME = 1;
    public static final int COL_LEVEL = 2;
    public static final int COL_MESSAGE = 3;
    public static final int COL_CATEGORY = 4;
    public static final int COL_METHOD = 5;

    private String columnHeaders[] =
        { "", "Time", "Level", "Message", "Category", "Method", };

    private ColumnLayoutData columnLayouts[] =
        {
            new ColumnPixelData(19, false),
```

```
       new ColumnWeightData(75),
       new ColumnWeightData(50),
       new ColumnWeightData(200),
       new ColumnWeightData(100),
       new ColumnWeightData(75),
   };
```

You define six columns and hard-code their names and positions. In a production-quality view, you would load the names from resources and allow the user to add and delete columns and move them around, but this code will suffice for the example.

`ColumnLayoutData` is a JFace class that supplies data for the Table layout. A *layout* is an algorithm that arranges SWT widgets on the screen. Layouts are discussed in more detail in appendix D.

`ColumnPixelData` and `ColumnWeightData` are subclasses of `ColumnLayoutData`. The former is used for fixed-width columns and the latter for variable-width columns. Variable-width columns are a nice alternative to hard-coding pixel widths in your code. When it's first sizing the table, the layout algorithm lets the columns expand according to their weight until they fill all the available space. Column weights are relative to the total of all weights. In this example the total is 500, so column 3 takes up 200/500 (two fifths) of the available space. Because the first column will contain an icon, it doesn't need to shrink or grow; in fact, you don't want it to shrink, or the user might not be able to see your icon.

Listening for model changes

The `LoggingModel` class is one we made up to store a list of all the log4j records. It will be covered in section 9.3.6. `LoggingListener` is a private class defined shortly that lets the view know about model changes:

```
   private LoggingModel model;
   private LoggingListener modelListener;

   private Action deleteAction;
   private Action gotoAction;
```

Like tables in Swing, JFace tables use a Model-View architecture. Unlike Swing, however, JFace does not automatically keep up with changes in the underlying model the views are displaying. This is fine for short lists that don't change often, such as the Task List, but in the Log4j view, you need a table that is continually updated as new records are received from the running program.

`ILoggingEventListener` is an interface we made up that has one method: `handleEvent()`. You hook this class into the model so the method is called whenever the model gets a new log4j record. `LoggingEvent` is a standard log4j class that encapsulates a logging record (its level, location, message, and so forth):

```
private class LoggingListener implements ILoggingEventListener
{
    public void handleEvent(final LoggingEvent event)
    {
        getSite().getShell().getDisplay().asyncExec(new Runnable()
        {
            public void run()
            {
                getViewer().add(event);
            }
        });
    }
}
```

The code inside the `handleEvent()` method introduces a very important concept: the *user interface thread*. SWT, and thus Eclipse, dedicates one thread for the entire user interface. Using the `Display.asyncExec()` method, you can make your own code run in that thread. `asyncExec()` adds your code to a queue and returns immediately; there is also a `syncExec()` method that waits for the code to run before returning. Just be careful not to wait on any locks or perform any long-running operations in this thread, or the UI responsiveness will suffer. Both of these methods have been heavily optimized, so you don't have to worry about calling them often. If you have used Swing before, the methods are analogous to Swing's `invokeAndWait()` and `invokeLater()` methods. For more information on the UI thread, see appendix D.

Inside the `Runnable`, you call `getViewer().add()` to add the event to the end of your table view. In most applications, this call isn't needed because the view can be refreshed at any time from the model. However, using `add()` here lets log lines show up immediately in the table view. You could also set up a thread that refreshes the view every so often with a batch of incoming lines.

SIDEBAR   SWT tables have gotten a bad reputation for being slow compared to Swing tables. There is some truth to this, because Swing tables can be *virtual*, meaning they can do only the work necessary to show a small window onto potentially millions of table items. As of this writing, SWT does not include a virtual table widget. One could argue that a table with millions of lines is not a good user interface, but that's really for you to decide.

For non-virtual tables, the authors of this book and others have contributed code to the next version of Eclipse that will significantly speed up adding and removing table items. So, we hope performance will not be an issue for most table sizes you are likely to need in the future.

Constructing and creating

Continuing with the `Log4jView` class, the constructor for this view simply gets a few values for later use and tells the superclass about the column definitions:

```
public Log4jView()
{
    super();
    model = Log4jPlugin.getDefault().getLoggingModel();
    modelListener = new LoggingListener();
    setColumnHeaders(columnHeaders);
    setColumnLayouts(columnLayouts);
}
```

At the point where the constructor is called, you can't do anything else, because the view's user interface doesn't exist yet—not until `createPartControl()` is called, that is:

```
public void createPartControl(Composite parent)
{
    super.createPartControl(parent);

    TableViewer viewer = getViewer();
    viewer.setContentProvider(model);
    viewer.setLabelProvider(new ViewLabelProvider());
    viewer.setInput(ResourcesPlugin.getWorkspace());

    setDoubleClickAction(gotoAction);

    model.addListener(modelListener);
}
```

`createPartControl()` is a common method that you'll see in every view and editor. It's called by the Framework to create the SWT widgets that make up the part. The parent of the view, an SWT `Composite` class, is passed in so all the subwidgets can be added to it. SWT implements the Composite design pattern, and the `Composite` class is the superclass of most SWT widgets. Composites can contain other composites, leading to a great deal of flexibility in the widget hierarchy.

In this example, the widgets are created in the superclass, so the code calls that first. Next you get a reference to the `TableViewer` class, which is the JFace wrapper for the SWT `Table` class. SWT tables are bare bones—you add text and/or graphics at specific rows and columns. `TableViewer` adds the concept of a *content provider* (otherwise known as a *model*). In addition, in JFace, tables are made up not of text but of arbitrary objects that are rendered by a *label provider*. A label provider, as the name implies, makes up the text labels and icons for the underlying SWT widget to use.

In this example, the `TableViewPart` superclass takes care of registering the double-click action for you. So, the only thing left to do is hook your listener into the model so you can be notified of new log lines.

Adding menus and toolbar buttons

Now let's see how you add menus and toolbar buttons:

```
protected void fillLocalPullDown(IMenuManager manager)
{
    super.fillLocalPullDown(manager);
    manager.add(gotoAction);
    manager.add(new Separator());
    manager.add(deleteAction);
}

protected void fillContextMenu(IMenuManager manager)
{
    super.fillContextMenu(manager);
    manager.add(gotoAction);
    manager.add(deleteAction);
    manager.add(new Separator("Additions"));       ❶ Menu
}                                                       placeholder

protected void fillLocalToolBar(IToolBarManager manager)
{
    super.fillLocalToolBar(manager);
    manager.add(gotoAction);
    manager.add(deleteAction);
}
```

The superclass calls the `fillXXX()` methods to add items to the menus and toolbars specific to this view. `fillLocalPullDown()` creates the view's pull-down menu (figure 9.11a), `fillContextMenu()` is for the pop-up (context) menu inside the view (figure 9.11b), and `fillLocalToolBar()` is for the view's toolbar (figure 9.11c).

 The `Additions` separator provides a placeholder in case another plug-in wants to add items to this context menu. If any were added they would appear at the end, after a separator line.

Defining actions

When you select one of the menus or click the toolbar button, it runs the action specified. Here's where the actions are defined:

```
protected void createActions()
{
    super.createActions();
```

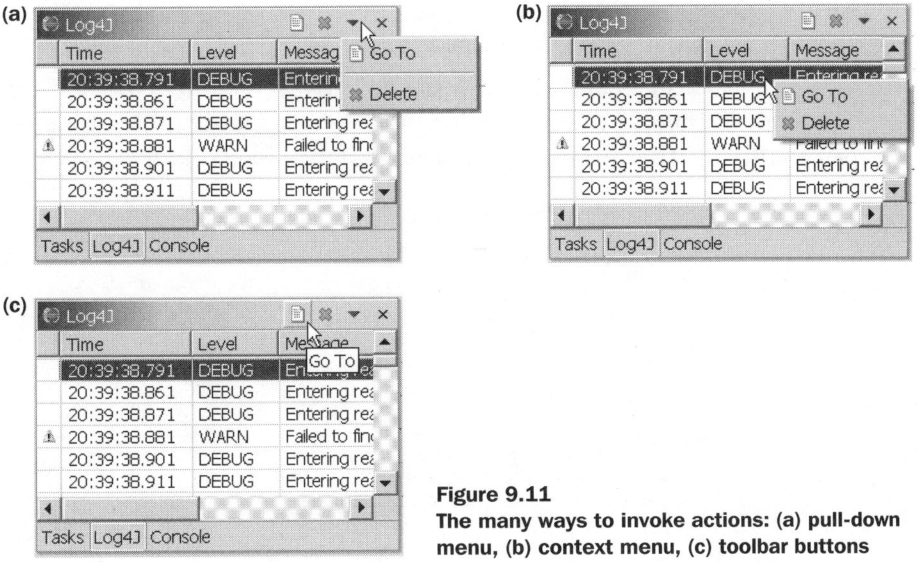

Figure 9.11
The many ways to invoke actions: (a) pull-down menu, (b) context menu, (c) toolbar buttons

The superclass calls the `createActions()` method to define any actions specific to log4j. You define two: `delete` and `goto`. The `delete` action is as follows:

```java
deleteAction = new Action()
{
   public void run()
   {
      getTable().setRedraw(false);
      model.clear();
      getViewer().refresh(true);
      getTable().setRedraw(true);
   }
};
deleteAction.setText("Delete");
deleteAction.setToolTipText("Delete log");
deleteAction.setImageDescriptor(
   PlatformUI
      .getWorkbench()
      .getSharedImages()
      .getImageDescriptor(
      ISharedImages.IMG_TOOL_DELETE));
```

This action is used to clear the model and update the view. To prevent the "rows being sucked down the drain" visual effect, you turn off redraw in the SWT table until all the items can be removed.

In this example, you reuse one of the Platform's shared images (a small X icon), but you could just as easily create your own GIF and load it here. And again, in a production application you should use resources instead of the hard-coded strings shown.

The goto action demonstrates working with selections. When executed, the goto action examines the record currently selected in the table of log output and jumps to the line that produced the record in the Java editor:

```
gotoAction = new Action()
{
   public void run()
   {
      ISelection selection = getViewer().getSelection();      ❶ Get
      Object obj =                                               selection
         ((IStructuredSelection) selection).getFirstElement();
      if (obj != null)
      {
         LoggingEvent event = (LoggingEvent) obj;      ❷ Pick log4j
         LocationInfo location =                            record
            event.getLocationInformation();
         if (location != null)
         {
            Log4jUtil.linkToSource(location);
         }
      }
   }
};
gotoAction.setText("Go To");
gotoAction.setToolTipText("Go To");
gotoAction.setImageDescriptor(
   PlatformUI
      .getWorkbench()
      .getSharedImages()
      .getImageDescriptor(
      ISharedImages.IMG_OBJ_FILE));
}
```

❶ JFace keeps track of the currently selected table item(s) for you, so you just need to call getSelection() to retrieve the object(s) selected. The JFace interface IStructuredSelection is used to store zero or more items selected. To make programming easier, selections are never null, but instead can be empty. For this example, you only need the first item selected. The superclass sets up the table to support single selections only, but it's good defensive programming practice to expect either single or multiple selections in the code.

❷ Table items are raw log4j LoggingEvent objects that contain, among other things, the location of the source code line that wrote the logging record. The Log4jUtil class, available from the web site, contains a utility function (linkToSource) to open a Java editor on the source file and scroll down to the line.

Cleaning up

Wrapping up the class is the `dispose()` method:

```
public void dispose()
{
    model.removeListener(modelListener);
    super.dispose();
}
}
```

It's the responsibility of `dispose()` to disconnect listeners and free up any windowing system resources. `dispose()` is the counterpart to `createPartControl()`. For the Log4j view, you need to remove the listener from the model and dispose of any system resources allocated in the superclass (such as the table widget).

9.3.4 Table framework

Next let's examine the `TableViewPart` class that is subclassed by `Log4jView`. It is generic enough that you can use it in your own projects with minimal change.

`TableViewPart` extends `ViewPart`, the superclass of all Eclipse views. `ViewPart` is an abstract Platform class (not part of JFace). Its subclasses must implement the following:

- `createPartControl()`—To create the view's controls
- `setFocus()`—To accept focus

In addition, a number of optional methods can be provided, including:

- `init()`—To initialize the view when it is first opened
- `saveState()`—To remember view settings before it is closed
- `dispose()`—To free up any resources the view was using

Constructing and creating

You don't need a constructor for this class, because the base class's constructor is sufficient. So, let's begin with `createPartControl()`. The Platform calls `createPartControl()` to create the SWT widgets in the part, in this case a JFace table viewer:

```
public class TableViewPart extends ViewPart
{
    private Table table;
    private TableViewer viewer;

    public void createPartControl(Composite parent)
    {
        viewer = new TableViewer(
            parent,
```

```
            SWT.SINGLE | SWT.FULL_SELECTION      ❶  SWT style
                | SWT.H_SCROLL | SWT.V_SCROLL);       bits
    table = viewer.getTable();                   ❷  Set options
    table.setHeaderVisible(true);                    on SWT
    table.setLinesVisible(true);                     widget

    createColumns();
    createActions();                             ❸  Finish setup
    hookMenus();                                     of viewer
    hookEvents();
    contributeToActionBars();
}
```

❶ The SWT style bits are defined as follows:

- SWT.SINGLE—Single selection only
- SWT.FULL_SELECTION—Makes the entire row selectable (not just the first column)
- SWT.H_SCROLL—Adds a horizontal scrollbar when needed
- SWT.V_SCROLL—Adds a vertical scrollbar when needed

❷ JFace does not hide the underlying SWT widgets, so when you want to do something like turn on the grid lines, you go directly to the Table widget to do it.

❸ Methods in this class and the subclass are called to create columns, define actions, and so forth.

Defining columns

If you recall from the last section, the subclass passed the list of columns and other information to this class through some set*XXX*() methods. These are defined here:

```
private String columnHeaders[];
private ColumnLayoutData columnLayouts[];
private IAction doubleClickAction;

public void setColumnHeaders(String[] strings)
{
    columnHeaders = strings;
}

public void setColumnLayouts(ColumnLayoutData[] data)
{
    columnLayouts = data;
}

public void setDoubleClickAction(IAction action)
{
    doubleClickAction = action;
}
```

Initializing and saving state

Now we get into the view lifecycle. init() is called when the view is opening, and saveState() is called when the Workbench (not the view) is closing:

```
private IMemento memento;

public void init(IViewSite site, IMemento memento)
    throws PartInitException
{
    super.init(site, memento);
    this.memento = memento;
}
public void saveState(IMemento memento)
{
    if (viewer == null)
    {
        if (this.memento != null)
            memento.putMemento(this.memento);
        return;
    }
    saveColumnWidths(memento);
}
```

❶ **Handle view opening**

❷ **Remember state**

❸ **Handle case where viewer not yet created**

❹ **Record column widths**

Memento is another design pattern that offers an alternative to serializing. The problem with serializing is that it's fragile—if you serialize a class, add a field, and then try to deserialize it, you're hosed. Under the covers, mementos use XML snippets to store only the most important information, but you don't need to deal with the XML directly. In your table, you use it to hold the width of each column.

❶ The Eclipse Platform remembers the state of a view from the last time the view was opened and passes the memento to the init() method so it can reopen it in the same state.

❷ Just before closing down, the Platform calls saveState() on all open views to give them an opportunity to save their state into the memento provided.

❸ If the Workbench is shut down before the viewer control is created, then you need to resave any memento that was passed to init() without modifying it.

❹ Otherwise, you call a function to save the widths of all your columns into the memento.

Creating columns

Now let's see how the tables are created. createColumns() is called right after the Table widget is created, to populate it with the table's columns:

```
protected void createColumns()
{
    if (memento != null)          ❶ Restore previous
    {                                settings
        restoreColumnWidths(memento);
    }

    TableLayout layout = new TableLayout();   ❷ Create layout
    table.setLayout(layout);                     for table

    for (int i = 0; i < columnHeaders.length; i++)
    {
        TableColumn tc = new TableColumn(table, SWT.NONE, i);   ❸ Create
                                                                   column
        tc.setText(columnHeaders[i]);
        tc.setResizable(columnLayouts[i].resizable);
        layout.addColumnData(columnLayouts[i]);
    }
}
```

❶ First you check to see if there are any previous settings on the column widths that you need to apply.

❷ You create a `TableLayout` algorithm to plan where all the columns go based on the column data provided by the subclass.

❸ Notice how the table columns are created. You don't call a method on the table to create a column; you instantiate a `TableColumn` class, passing it a reference to the table. This is a common pattern seen throughout SWT. `TableColumn` and `Table` handshake with each other to do the right thing.

Creating menus

Next is the function that creates your menus. In the `hookMenus()` method, you create a new `MenuManager` and fill it with menu items. Well, that's not quite true. Really, you tell the menu manager that when it's about to create this menu, delete everything in it, and call a function (`menuAboutToShow()`) to fill it back up again. This is the recommended approach, because it makes the menu completely dynamic:

```
protected void hookMenus()
{
    MenuManager menuMgr = new MenuManager("#PopupMenu");
    menuMgr.setRemoveAllWhenShown(true);
    menuMgr.addMenuListener(new IMenuListener()
    {
        public void menuAboutToShow(IMenuManager manager)
        {
            TableViewPart.this.fillContextMenu(manager);   ❶ Fill in
        }                                                      menu
```

```
      });
      Menu menu = menuMgr.createContextMenu(viewer.getControl());
      viewer.getControl().setMenu(menu);                          Hook    ❷
      getSite().registerContextMenu(menuMgr, viewer); everything
   }                                                              together
```

 menuAboutToShow() turns around and calls the fillContextMenu() function (which is just a stub in the superclass).

❷ This is boilerplate code to create the menu, associate it with the viewer, and register it with the Workbench so it can be extended by other plug-ins.

Handling mouse events

How do you handle mouse clicks in the view? Glad you asked:

```
protected void hookEvents()
{
   viewer.addSelectionChangedListener(
      new ISelectionChangedListener()
   {
      public void selectionChanged(SelectionChangedEvent event)
      {
         if (event.getSelection() != null)
            TableViewPart.this.selectionChanged(event);
      }
   });
   viewer.addDoubleClickListener(new IDoubleClickListener()
   {
      public void doubleClick(DoubleClickEvent event)
      {
         doubleClickAction.run();
      }
   });
}
```

hookEvents() adds two listeners to the JFace table viewer. The first one is notified whenever the user's selection changes (for example, when they click on a row), and the second one is notified when the user double-clicks on a row. Of course, to double-click, you first have to click, so rows that are double-clicked get both notifications.

Handling focus events

The Platform calls setFocus() when the user clicks anywhere in the view for the first time. In your application, you might want to highlight or recalculate some value being displayed, but in this example you just pass the call on to the table viewer:

```
public void setFocus()
{
    viewer.getControl().setFocus();
}
```

Accessing the underlying widgets

Two getter functions are used in the subclass:

```
public Table getTable()
{
    return table;
}

public TableViewer getViewer()
{
    return viewer;
}
```

Filling menus and toolbars

An *action bar* is a combination toolbar and pull-down menu. The `TableViewPart` class doesn't define any buttons or menu items on its own:

```
protected void contributeToActionBars()
{
    IActionBars bars = getViewSite().getActionBars();
    fillLocalPullDown(bars.getMenuManager());
    fillLocalToolBar(bars.getToolBarManager());
}
```

Because this class is not abstract, you need to stub out a few methods called in the superclass for the subclass to override:

```
protected void fillContextMenu(IMenuManager manager)           { }
protected void fillLocalPullDown(IMenuManager manager)         { }
protected void fillLocalToolBar(IToolBarManager manager)       { }
protected void selectionChanged(SelectionChangedEvent event)   { }
protected void createActions()                                 { }
```

You could avoid using stubs by making the `TableViewPart` class abstract, but then all subclasses would be forced to override all the abstract methods whether they need them or not. In addition, if you added a new abstract method, it would break all the subclasses.

Remembering column widths

Perhaps the hardest part in the class is the code that saves and restores column widths, shown next. Here you get another example of how to use mementos. As mentioned earlier, mementos are implemented with XML, but you won't see a single angle bracket here:

```
protected static final String TAG_COLUMN = "column";    ❶  XML
protected static final String TAG_NUMBER = "number";        element
protected static final String TAG_WIDTH = "width";          names

protected void saveColumnWidths(IMemento memento)
{                                                        ❷  Get list of
    Table table = viewer.getTable();                        current
    TableColumn columns[] = table.getColumns();             columns

    for (int i = 0; i < columns.length; i++)
    {
        if (columnLayouts[i].resizable)
        {
            IMemento child = memento.createChild(TAG_COLUMN);
            child.putInteger(TAG_NUMBER, i);
            child.putInteger(TAG_WIDTH, columns[i].getWidth());
        }
    }                                                    Save column  ❸
}                                                            width
```

❶ First you define the names of the XML elements used to store the width data.

❷ Then you reach down to the SWT `Table` class to get a list of its current columns.

❸ Saving data in a memento is easy; you just call `createChild()` for each piece of data, and under that child you can place whatever other children you want. When you're done, the XML stream looks something like this:

```
<column number="1" width="490" />
<column number="2" width="64" />    ...
```

The Workbench state is stored in .metadata/.plugins/org.eclipse.ui.workbench/ workbench.xml in your workspace directory.

For more complicated states, mementos can have other mementos as children, to an arbitrary depth. The following code reads the memento and regenerates the layout data that specifies the column widths:

```
protected void restoreColumnWidths(IMemento memento)
{
    IMemento children[] = memento.getChildren(TAG_COLUMN);  ❶  For all
    if (children != null)                                       columns ...
    {
        for (int i = 0; i < children.length; i++)
        {
            Integer val = children[i].getInteger(TAG_NUMBER);  ❷  Get
            if (val != null)                                       column
            {                                                      number
                int index = val.intValue();
                val = children[i].getInteger(TAG_WIDTH);
                if (val != null)
                {
```

```
                    columnLayouts[index] =
                        new ColumnPixelData(val.intValue(), true);
                }
            }
        }
    }
}
```

Apply width to column ❸

❶ First the code gets a list of all the column elements from the memento.

❷ Then, for each one, it retrieves the column number and width.

❸ Finally, it creates new table layout data that makes the column fixed width (but resizable).

That's the end of the `TableViewPart` class. Next let's look at how the items in the table are drawn.

9.3.5 *Label providers (LabelProvider)*

As we mentioned earlier, JFace provides an abstraction on top of SWT tables. Instead of containing an array of strings and icons, JFace tables contain arbitrary objects. But at some point, the objects must be turned into strings and icons for display. That's the job of a *label provider*. Given an object, the label provider returns a `String` and an `Image` that represents that object. Think of it as the `toString()` method on steroids.

`ITableLabelProvider` is an interface that adds the concept of columns to a plain old, run-of-the-mill label provider. Now, instead of asking for one string/icon per object, the caller can ask for a pair for each column.

If you look back at figure 9.9, you'll see that the first column (column 0) has an image and no text, whereas the others have text and no image. This is implemented by the `ViewLabelProvider`, explained in listing 9.12.

Listing 9.12   The ViewLabelProvider class

```
class ViewLabelProvider
    extends LabelProvider
    implements ITableLabelProvider
{
    private static final DateFormat DATE_FORMATTER =      ❶  Formatter for
        new SimpleDateFormat("HH:mm:ss.SSS");                   record's time

    public String getColumnText(Object obj, int index)   ❷  Get text for
    {                                                          specified
        LoggingEvent event = (LoggingEvent) obj;               column
        LocationInfo locationInfo;
        switch (index)
```

```
        {
            case Log4jView.COL_TIME :
                return DATE_FORMATTER.format(new Date(event.timeStamp));
            case Log4jView.COL_LEVEL :
                return event.getLevel().toString();
            case Log4jView.COL_MESSAGE :
                return event.getRenderedMessage();
            case Log4jView.COL_CATEGORY :
                return event.getLoggerName();
            case Log4jView.COL_METHOD :
                locationInfo = event.getLocationInformation();
                if (locationInfo != null
                    && locationInfo.getMethodName() != null)
                {
                    return locationInfo.getMethodName();
                }
                break;
        }
        return "";
    }

    public Image getColumnImage(Object obj, int index)       ❸ Get icon for
    {                                                            given column
        if (index == Log4jView.COL_IMAGE)
            return getImage(obj);
        else
            return null;
    }

    public Image getImage(Object obj)       ❹ Get error/
    {                                           warning icon
        LoggingEvent event = (LoggingEvent) obj;
        Level level = event.getLevel();

        ISharedImages sharedImages =          ◁──────── ❺ Borrow
            PlatformUI.getWorkbench().getSharedImages();       one from
                                                               Platform
        return sharedImages.getImage(
            (level == Level.ERROR
                ? ISharedImages.IMG_OBJS_ERROR_TSK
                : (level == Level.WARN
                    ? ISharedImages.IMG_OBJS_WARN_TSK
                    : null)));
    }
}
```

❶ The Java base library provides a nice, locale-specific date/time formatter with a bewildering array of options. Luckily you just need to print the time, in the format *hours:minutes:seconds.milliseconds*.

❷ The `getColumnText()` method takes one row of the table and the column number (zero based) and renders that cell into a `String`.

NOTE   SWT will be very displeased if you pass it a null when it is expecting a string. Use an empty string instead, to avoid a null pointer exception.

---

❸ This method is similar to `getColumnText()`, except it returns an `Image` instead of a `String`. Null images are OK.

❹ The `getImage(Object)` method comes from the `LabelProvider` class. By returning an error or warning icon here, you satisfy both callers that expect a `Label-Provider` and callers that expect an `ITableLabelProvider`.

❺ Where possible, we like to borrow predefined images from the Platform. There are several reasons, but the main two are that the images are already loaded into memory, so they're faster to use; and they're prettier than most programmers can create.

9.3.6 *Models*

The `LoggingModel` class (listing 9.13) is simple, but it demonstrates a couple of useful concepts—*listener lists* and *structured content providers*:

- A *listener list* is a list of listeners (well, what did you expect?). More specifically, it's an array used to store objects that want to be notified of particular events. It is guaranteed not to have any duplicates, so if you add a listener twice and remove it once, it doesn't appear in the list any more. It's very important not to leave stale listeners in the list (to do so would cause a memory leak or worse), so don't be shy about removing them. The best place is in a `dispose()` method.

- A *structured content provider* provides content to structured viewers (you saw that coming, didn't you?). A structured viewer is a class like `TableView`, which uses a Model-View architecture—that is, it separates the data from the presentation of the data. These classes need to get their data (content) from somewhere (the provider). So, the model class (`LoggingModel`) implements `IStructuredContentProvider`.

TIP   Whatever you do, *do not* remove listeners or release any other type of resource in `finalize()`. The Java `finalize()` method is completely useless, because you can't predict when, or even if, it will run. Avoid it. 'Nuff said.

Listing 9.13 The LoggingModel class

```
public class LoggingModel implements IStructuredContentProvider
{
    private ListenerList listenerList = new ListenerList();    ❶ Interested
    private List events = new ArrayList();    ❷ All log4j records      parties

    public void addListener(ILoggingEventListener listener)    ❸ Opt in to
    {                                                               model
        listenerList.add(listener);                                 changes
    }
    public void removeListener(ILoggingEventListener listener)  ❹ Opt out
    {                                                               of model
        listenerList.remove(listener);                              changes
    }

    public void addEvent(LoggingEvent event)    ❺ Add new
    {                                               record; notify
        events.add(event);                          listeners
        Object[] listeners = listenerList.getListeners();
        for (int i = 0; i < listeners.length; i++)
        {
            ((ILoggingEventListener) listeners[i]).handleEvent(event);
        }
    }

    public void clear()    ❻ Remove all
    {                          records
        events.clear();
    }

    public Object[] getElements(Object inputElement)    ❼ Get all
    {                                                       records
        return events.toArray();
    }

    public void dispose()    ❽ Clean up
    {
    }

    public void inputChanged(    ❾ Switch
        Viewer viewer,              inputs
        Object oldInput,
        Object newInput)
    {
    }
}
```

❶ A ListenerList class (from JFace) is used to hold all parties interested in model changes. Although you know that, for this example, there will only ever be one interested party, it's good to get in the habit of using this kind of boilerplate code, because it reduces errors.

❷ You keep a complete list of all the log4j records ever written. In a real application, you would probably want to have some kind of cap on this list—say, the last 50,000 records or so. Or, you could spool them out to disk.

❸ If a view is interested in keeping up with every single model change, it can register itself by calling this method. Many views are content with getting all the elements at once, using the getElements() method.

❹ As noted, it's the view's responsibility to remove itself from the interested parties list.

❺ The addEvent() method is called from the receiver thread (see the next section) whenever a record comes in from the log4j socket. Its first job is to keep the model up to date, and then it notifies any interested parties about the addition.

❻ clear() is called in the delete action (see section 9.3.3) when the user clicks the Delete button or selects the item from one of the view's menus or toolbars. It erases all records in the model. If you wanted to get fancy, you could notify the viewers about that, too; but in this example the viewer tells the model to clear, so it already knows.

❼ Here you return all the records in the model.

❽ This code releases any resources.

❾ This method could be used to handle gross input changes, but is not needed in this example. You have to define it, though, because it's an abstract method of ViewPart.

9.3.7 Receiver thread

In the plug-in, a thread is started that listens for log records and adds them to the model. The full code for the ReceiverThread class can be found in the examples on the web site, but here are the essentials.

The thread creates a new server socket and accepts a connection on it from the log4j client (the program being debugged):

```
ServerSocket server = new ServerSocket(port);
Socket client = server.accept();
```

Then it deserializes LoggingEvents from the socket stream until end of file is reached. As it pulls each one out, it sends it off to the model to be added to the list. The loop ends when the socket gets an end of file exception (not shown):

```
ObjectInputStream ois =
    new ObjectInputStream(client.getInputStream());
while (true)
```

```
{
    LoggingEvent event =
        (LoggingEvent) ois.readObject();
    model.addEvent(event);
}
```

9.4 *Preferences (FieldEditorPreferencePage)*

No plug-in discussion would be complete without an explanation of *preferences*. We've mentioned them a few times in this chapter, but now it's time to look at them in more detail and show how to design preference pages.

You've used preference pages like the one in figure 9.12 many times during the course of this book. But how are they created, and where do they save their options? How do the plug-ins read and use those options, and where do the defaults come from? We'll answer these questions in this section.

Like editors and views, preference pages are defined in the plug-in manifest (plugin.xml). This section defines the two pages in the log4j integration plug-in:

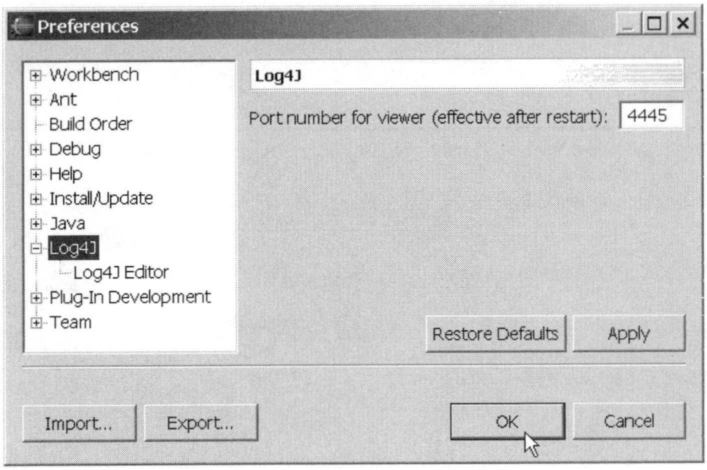

Figure 9.12
Main Preferences page for the Log4J plug-in. This page has a single field, which is constrained to be a number in a certain range.

```
<extension
     point="org.eclipse.ui.preferencePages">
  <page
    name="Log4J"
    class="org.eclipseguide.log4j.preferences.MainPreferencePage"
    id="org.eclipseguide.log4j.preferences.MainPreferencePage">
  </page>
  <page
    name="Log4J Editor"
    category="org.eclipseguide.log4j.preferences.MainPreferencePage"
    class="org.eclipseguide.log4j.preferences.EditorPreferencePage"
```

```
        id="org.eclipseguide.log4j.preferences.EditorPreferencePage">
    </page>
</extension>
```

Notice how the hierarchy of pages is established through the `category` property, similar to the view categories you set up earlier.

9.4.1 *Main preference page*

Listing 9.14 shows the code for the `MainPreferencePage` class. A preference page can use a number of superclasses, but the most convenient one is `FieldEditor-PreferencePage`. This class lets you make a page with fields tied directly to the underlying preference store. Changing the field in the preference page automatically updates the store, and vice versa. So, if you can design your preference page in terms of these fields, as in this example, it will save you quite a bit of time.

Listing 9.14   The MainPreferencePage class

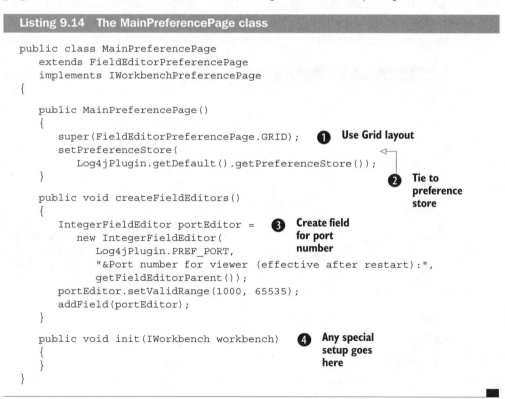

```
public class MainPreferencePage
    extends FieldEditorPreferencePage
    implements IWorkbenchPreferencePage
{

    public MainPreferencePage()
    {
        super(FieldEditorPreferencePage.GRID);        ❶ Use Grid layout
        setPreferenceStore(
            Log4jPlugin.getDefault().getPreferenceStore());
    }                                                 ❷ Tie to
                                                         preference
                                                         store
    public void createFieldEditors()
    {
        IntegerFieldEditor portEditor =     ❸ Create field
            new IntegerFieldEditor(           for port
                Log4jPlugin.PREF_PORT,        number
                "&Port number for viewer (effective after restart):",
                getFieldEditorParent());
        portEditor.setValidRange(1000, 65535);
        addField(portEditor);
    }

    public void init(IWorkbench workbench)   ❹ Any special
    {                                           setup goes
    }                                           here
}
```

❶ The Grid layout provides the most flexibility, so you should almost always use that.

❷ This is how the field editor page is tied to your preference store, so it can change the preferences automatically.

❸ This page has only one field, which takes an integer value. The value must be between 1000 and 65535. JFace provides many different types of fields, including strings, booleans, fonts, lists, radio buttons, and colors. You can also create your own field types if you like.

❹ `init()` is a required method from `IWorkbenchPreferencePage`. Here you don't have any initialization code, so you just leave it empty.

The `FieldEditorPreferencePage` class and its superclasses provide the banner graphic, the Restore Defaults button, and the Apply button.

9.4.2 *Editor preference page*

The editor preference page is similar, except it has a list of colors to choose from, one for each token type that the editor knows about (see figure 9.13). Listing 9.15 shows the code for the `EditorPreferencePage` class.

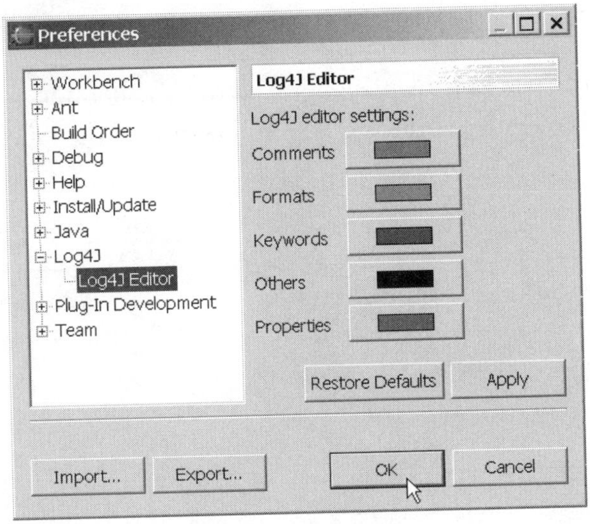

Figure 9.13
Log4J editor preferences control the colors of various tokens. The changes take effect immediately when you click Apply or OK.

Listing 9.15   The EditorPreferencePage class

```
public class EditorPreferencePage
    extends FieldEditorPreferencePage
    implements IWorkbenchPreferencePage
{
```

```
public EditorPreferencePage()
{
   super(GRID);
   setPreferenceStore(
      Log4jPlugin.getDefault().getPreferenceStore());
   setDescription("Log4J editor settings:");      ❶  Set description
}
public void createFieldEditors()
{
   addField(                                        ❷  Create color
      new ColorFieldEditor(                             field for each
         Log4jPlugin.PREF_COMMENT_COLOR,                token type
         "&Comments",
         getFieldEditorParent()));
   addField(
      new ColorFieldEditor(
         Log4jPlugin.PREF_FORMAT_COLOR,
         "&Formats",
         getFieldEditorParent()));
   // etc...
}
// ...
}
```

❶ This page sets a description, which is displayed just under the banner.

❷ Here is an example of the color field editor. The ampersands in the labels set up keyboard shortcuts.

9.5 *Plugin class*

To wrap up the log4j integration example, you need to add a few things to the plug-in class (Log4jPlugin) originally defined in section 9.1.2. First, you define a few static strings for preference names:

```
public static final String PREF_COMMENT_COLOR =
   "log4j_comment_color";
public static final String PREF_PROPERTY_COLOR =
   "log4j_property_color";
// etc...
public static final String PREF_PORT = "log4j_view_port";
```

Next you have to create defaults for the colors and the port number. These defaults are applied the first time the plug-in is run, and are also used if the user clicks the Restore Defaults button on the Preferences page:

```
protected void initializeDefaultPreferences(
   IPreferenceStore store)
```

```
{
    super.initializeDefaultPreferences(store);

    store.setDefault(
        Log4jPlugin.PREF_COMMENT_COLOR,
        StringConverter.asString(new RGB(63, 127, 95)));
    store.setDefault(
        Log4jPlugin.PREF_FORMAT_COLOR,
        StringConverter.asString(new RGB(255, 0, 42)));
    // etc...

    store.setDefault(Log4jPlugin.PREF_PORT, 4445);
}
```

Finally, you have a method that starts up the receiver thread:

```
private void setupReceiver()
{
    int port = getDefault().getPreferenceStore().getInt(
        Log4jPlugin.PREF_PORT);
    try
    {
        ReceiverThread lr =
            new ReceiverThread(loggingModel, port);
        lr.start();
    }
    catch (IOException e)
    {
        DebugPlugin.log(e);
    }
}
```

Whew! That completes the log4j integration example. Just a reminder: You can find all the source code for this example, including a few extra features we didn't have room to show in this book (such as decorations and JDT integration), at the book's web site. Feel free to use any of the code in your own projects.

9.6 *Summary*

Eclipse is often viewed as just a Java IDE, but as you've seen in the past two chapters, that's just the tip of the iceberg. The same interfaces used to develop the Platform plug-ins is available for you to use to create customized editors and views for your own plug-ins. All the source code is available, too. As a result, your plug-ins can integrate seamlessly with and extend the Java development environment, or you can write entirely new environments to support other languages and applications.

We hope you've enjoyed your exploration of Eclipse as much as we've enjoyed being your guide. Be sure to check out the extended examples for this book at http://www.manning.com/gallardo. Further adventure and rewards await the dedicated traveler, so keep pushing the boundaries of your knowledge and experience. The only limit is your imagination.

Java perspective menu reference

Looking at Eclipse's menus, which can have more than 100 options, can be daunting. Many options, such as File→Save, are familiar and do what you expect. Others, such as Source→Generate Delegate Methods, may leave you wondering. This appendix describes them all for you, with special attention to those that may not be obvious or that perform complex tasks, such as refactoring. The available menus and their contents change from perspective to perspective; here we list those found in the Java perspective, which are generally a superset of the other perspectives' menus.

Table A.1   File menu options

New	Creates projects (Java, Simple, Plug-in), folders within projects, and resources within folders and projects.
Close [Ctrl-F4]	Closes the current editor.
Close All [Ctrl-Shift-F4]	Closes all editors.
Save [Ctrl-S]	Saves the resource currently being edited.
Save As	Saves the resource currently being edited with a new pathname or filename.
Save All [Ctrl-Shift-S]	Saves all resources that have been changed in the editor.
Revert	Reverts the resource being edited to its last saved state.
Move	Moves resource to a new location. Not semantically aware; see Refactoring→ Move for moving Java elements.
Rename	Renames a resource. Not semantically aware; see Refactoring→Rename for moving Java elements.
Print [Ctrl-P]	Prints the resource currently being edited. Only available if the editor supports printing.
Import	Brings resources or projects into the workspace. Options include: ■ *Existing Project into Workspace*—Can be used to copy a project from another Eclipse workspace or to add a project that has been deleted from the current workspace, providing the contents have not been deleted (see Edit→Delete). ■ *File System*—Adds resources such as files and Java packages from outside the present project into the current project. ■ *Zip File*—Allows you to select and import resources from inside a zip file.
Export	Makes resources or projects in the workspace available outside Eclipse. Options include: ■ *File System*—Copies resources out of Eclipse; destination cannot be inside workspace. ■ *JAR file*—Archives selected resources into a JAR file. ■ *Javadoc*—Creates a Javadoc from selected resources. (Identical to Project→Generate Javadoc.) ■ *Zip File*—Archives selected resources into a zip file.
Properties [Alt-Enter]	Opens the Properties dialog for a selected resource or project.

Table A.2 Edit menu options

Undo [Ctrl-Z]	Undoes the last action.
Redo [Ctrl-Y]	Undoes the last undo.
Cut [Ctrl-X]	Copies the currently selected text, resource, or project to the clipboard and deletes it from its current location.
Copy [Ctrl-C]	Copies the currently selected text, resource, or project to the clipboard.
Paste [Ctrl-V]	Pastes the clipboard contents to the current location in a file, workspace, or project.
Delete	Deletes the selected text, resource, or project. When you're deleting a project, a dialog box presents the options of deleting the project's contents or preserving the contents. If the contents are preserved, the project can be restored using File→Import→Existing Project into Workspace. Note, however, that you will not be able to create a new project with the same name unless you delete the contents.
Select All [Ctrl-A]	Selects the entire contents of the currently selected resource in the editor.
Find/Replace [Ctrl-F]	Presents a dialog box for finding and, optionally, replacing text in the currently selected resource in the editor. See Search→Search for locating text in multiple files.
Find Next [Ctrl-K]	Searches forward (from the current cursor location) for the next occurrence of the previously found text.
Find Previous [Ctrl-Shift-K]	Searches backward for the previous occurrence of the found selected text.
Incremental Find Next [Ctrl-J]	Searches forward for text as it is typed incrementally (letter by letter). Search text appears in the status bar at the bottom of the Workbench. (For example, if the cursor in the editor is located before the text *doe, a deer*, pressing *d* will locate and highlight the *d* in *doe*; continuing by pressing *e* will locate and highlight the *de* in *deer*. Pressing Backspace will delete the *e* in the status bar and return the cursor to the *d* in *doe*.)
Incremental Find Previous [Ctrl-Shift-J]	Searches backward for the text as it is typed, letter by letter.
Add Bookmark	Adds a bookmark (a named tag) to the current line in the resource currently selected in the editor. The line can then be located by marks in the margin of the editor when the file is open. A bookmark can also be added to a file selected in the Package Explorer. A Bookmark view, similar to the Task view, is available to make it easier to navigate between different bookmarks.
Add Task	Adds a task to the selected resource.
Expand Selection To	Selects text in a semantically aware way. Note that the associated shortcut keys in particular provide a convenient way to select expressions, lines, methods and classes. Options include: ■ *Enclosing Element* [Alt-Shift-Up Arrow] ■ *Next Element* [Alt-Shift-Right Arrow] ■ *Previous Element* [Alt-Shift-Left Arrow] ■ *Restore Previous Selection* [Alt-Shift-Down Arrow]

Table A.2 Edit menu options *(continued)*

Show Tooltip Description [F2]	Provides information, as a tooltip, about the element at the current cursor location. Note that the F2 shortcut is significantly more convenient than the menu selection.
Content Assist [Ctrl-Space]	Provides context-sensitive code completion. Typing (or clicking) on an object name, for example, and then selecting Edit→Content Assist (or pressing Ctrl-Space) displays a pop-up window with a list of available methods and attributes. Content Assist will also create variable, method, and field names; for example, typing **String** followed by a space and then selecting Content Assist provides the variable name string.
Quick Fix [Ctrl-1]	Suggests fixes for an error. Suggestions are available when a yellow light bulb appears in the left margin of the editor. Clicking the corresponding line and selecting Edit→Quick Fix (or clicking on the light bulb) brings up a list of suggestions. For example, if there is an undefined identifier on the line, suggestions might include creating a local variable, creating a class field, or adding a parameter to the method. Additionally, if a variable with a similar name is defined, it offers to change the undefined name.
Parameter Hints [Ctrl-Shift-Space]	Displays the parameters a method accepts. If the method is overloaded, a list of the overloaded methods is shown instead. For example, suppose a method Strings has been defined. Typing **s.equals(** and selecting Edit→Parameter Hints will display *Object anObject*.
Encoding	Changes the encoding the editor uses to display the file.

Table A.3 Source menu options. This menu is also available from the context menu in the Java editor.

Comment [Ctrl-/]	Comments out selected lines with //.
Uncomment [Ctrl-\]	Removes comment marks (//) from selected lines.
Shift Right	Indents the selected text. You can also select text in the editor and press Tab
Shift Left	Outdents the selected text. You can also select text in editor and press Shift-Tab.
Format [Ctrl-Shift-F]	Applies formatting (as defined using Windows→Preferences→Java→Code Formatter) to the selected text or to the whole file if no text is selected.
Sort Members	Sorts class members by type and name in the file currently selected in the editor. To view or change this order, select Windows→Preferences→Java→Appearance→Member Sort Order.
Organize Imports [Ctrl-Shift-O]	Sorts the import statements by package name prefix in the file currently selected in the editor. To view or change this order, select Windows→Preferences→Java→Organize Imports.
Add Import [Ctrl-Shift-M]	Adds an import statement to the file for the type at the cursor.
Override/Implement Methods	Generates stubs for methods in a superclass—either abstract methods that need to be implemented or concrete methods that can be overridden.

Table A.3   Source menu options. This menu is also available from the context menu in the Java editor. *(continued)*

Generate Getter and Setter	Creates methods for accessing and setting class fields. A dialog box presents available fields, together with the options to create getter and setter methods for each.
Generate Delegate Methods	Creates methods that delegate to a class field's methods. A dialog box presents available fields and the available methods for each. For example, if a class has a field `myString`, delegate methods can be added to the class for any method applicable to `myString`. Assuming `myString` is of type `String`, any of the `String` class's methods can be delegated. Selecting `equals(Object)` in the dialog box would generate the following: ```\npublic boolean equals(Object obj)\n{\n return myString.equals(obj);\n}\n```
Add Constructor from Superclass	Adds unimplemented constructors from a superclass.
Add Javadoc Comment	Adds a Javadoc comment to a method or class.
Surround with try/ catch Block	Surrounds the selected lines with a `try` block and adds `catch` clauses for each type of exception thrown. One of Eclipse's handiest features.

Externalize Strings	Replaces all hard-coded strings with a key referring to key-value pairs in a property file and creates a class for retrieving the values by referencing the key. Suppose a class contains this line:
	
	```\nSystem.out.println("Hello, world!");\n```
	
	Assuming you accept the defaults in the Externalize Strings Wizard that is launched, this line will be changed to:
	
	```\nSystem.out.println(\n Messages.getString(\n "HelloWorld.Hello,_world_!_1")); //$NON-NLS-1$\n```
	
	The comment `$NON-NLS-1$` indicates that this string should not be externalized. If you try to select Externalize Strings again, you'll get a message that says no strings were found to externalize.
	    A `Messages` class is created, containing the following method for retrieving strings from the property file:
	
	```\npublic static String getString(String key)\n{\n // TODO Auto-generated method stub\n try\n {\n return RESOURCE_BUNDLE.getString(key);\n }\n catch (MissingResourceException e)\n```

Table A.3   Source menu options. This menu is also available from the context menu in the Java editor. *(continued)*

<table>
<tr><td></td><td>

```
    {
        return '!' + key + '!';
    }
}
```

A properties file named test.properties by default is created with the following entry:

```
HelloWorld.Hello,_world_!_1=Hello, world\!
```

This feature is especially useful when you're internationalizing applications, because separate properties files can be provided for different languages. Note that this is a refactoring, and as such can only be undone using Refactor→Undo.</td></tr>
<tr><td>**Find Strings to Externalize**</td><td>Finds files in a selected package, folder, or project that contain hard-coded strings. A dialog box listing these files allows you to externalize the strings in each file using the same Externalize Strings Wizard launched by Source→Externalize Strings.</td></tr>
<tr><td>**Convert Line Delimiters**</td><td>Allows you to select the line delimiters to use. The default is the platform default: CR/LF on Windows; LF on Unix, Mac OS X, and Linux. Java tools are generally tolerant of any line delimiter (or mix of delimiters).</td></tr>
</table>

Table A.4   Refactorings menu options. This menu is also available from the context menu in the Java editor. References to modified elements (method or class names, signatures, and so on) throughout the workspace will be updated, if appropriate, unless you veto them individually by clicking the Preview button in the Refactoring Wizard. See section 4.2 for an introduction to Eclipse's refactoring features.

<table>
<tr><td>**Undo** [Alt-Shift-Z]</td><td>Undoes a refactoring. Refactoring can only be undone using this command, in place of the standard Undo command. Normally, only a single complete refactoring can be undone; in addition, if you make further changes to any of the files involved in the refactoring, you may not be able to undo the refactoring.</td></tr>
<tr><td>**Redo** [Alt-Shift-Y]</td><td>Redoes a refactoring that was undone with Refactoring→Undo.</td></tr>
<tr><td>**Rename** [Alt-Shift-R]</td><td>Renames Java elements, including attributes, methods, classes, and package names in a semantically aware way (updates all references correctly).</td></tr>
<tr><td>**Move** [Alt-Shift-V]</td><td>Moves Java elements, including static fields and methods, to other classes, and classes to other packages in a semantically aware way.</td></tr>
<tr><td>**Change Method Signature**</td><td>Changes parameters, return types, and visibility of methods.</td></tr>
<tr><td>**Convert Anonymous Class to Nested**</td><td>Moves an anonymous inner class to a nested class. Anonymous classes are a way of defining and instantiating a class inside a method, in the place where it is used. The semantics require that this class either implement an interface or extend a superclass.

Anonymous classes are a common and convenient shorthand for creating listeners for GUI elements, for example. When the class gets too large, however, anonymous classes make for code that is hard to read and understand.

For example, the following method instantiates and returns an anonymous class implementing an interface `Bag` that has two methods, `get()` and `set()`:</td></tr>
</table>

Table A.4 Refactorings menu options. This menu is also available from the context menu in the Java editor. References to modified elements (method or class names, signatures, and so on) throughout the workspace will be updated, if appropriate, unless you veto them individually by clicking the Preview button in the Refactoring Wizard. See section 4.2 for an introduction to Eclipse's refactoring features. *(continued)*

```java
public class Example
{
    public Bag getBag()
    {
        return new Bag()
        {
            Object o;
            Object get()
            {
                return o;
            }
            void set(Object o)
            {
                this.o = o;
            }
        };
    }
}
```

After you place the cursor inside the anonymous class and select this refactoring from the menu, the Refactoring Wizard (not surprisingly) asks for a name for the new nested class. If you enter `BagImpl`, it modifies the code as follows:

```java
public class Example
{
    private final class BagImpl implements Bag
    {
        Object o;
        Object get()
        {
            return o;
        }
        void set(Object o)
        {
            this.o = o;
        }
    }
    public Bag getBag()
    {
        return new BagImpl();
    }
}
```

Table A.4 Refactorings menu options. This menu is also available from the context menu in the Java editor. References to modified elements (method or class names, signatures, and so on) throughout the workspace will be updated, if appropriate, unless you veto them individually by clicking the Preview button in the Refactoring Wizard. See section 4.2 for an introduction to Eclipse's refactoring features. *(continued)*

Convert Nested Type to Top Level	Converts a nested class to a top-level class in its own file. One of the benefits of a nested class is that it has access to the outer class's attributes and methods. This refactoring preserves this capability by adding an instance variable of the outer class's type to the new top-level class. Consider a class `Example`, with a nested class called `NestedClass`:

```
public class Example
{
    class NestedClass
    {
        String attribA;
    }

    NestedClass getNestedClass()
    {
        return new NestedClass();
    }
}
```

Refactoring moves `NestedClass` to its own file, NestedClass.java; adds a field of type `Example`; and adds a constructor to set that field:

```
class NestedClass
{
    private final Example example;

    NestedClass(Example example)
    {
        this.example = example;
    }
    String attribA;
}
```

In the outer class, a reference to the outer class, `this`, is passed to the constructor when `NestedClass` is instantiated:

```
public class Example
{
    NestedClass getNestedClass()
    {
        return new NestedClass(this);
    }
}
```

(In this trivial example, the nested class doesn't access any of the outer class members, so you could simplify the code by removing the `Example` instance variable and making the corresponding change to the constructor.)

Table A.4   Refactorings menu options. This menu is also available from the context menu in the Java editor. References to modified elements (method or class names, signatures, and so on) throughout the workspace will be updated, if appropriate, unless you veto them individually by clicking the Preview button in the Refactoring Wizard. See section 4.2 for an introduction to Eclipse's refactoring features. *(continued)*

Push Down	Moves methods or attributes from a class to a subclass. For example, suppose a class `Person` includes a field `job` and a method `getJob()` and has a subclass `Employee`. This refactoring can be used to move `job` and `get-Job()` to the `Employee` class.
	Before using this refactoring, you must first select a member. Selecting `job` followed by Push Down displays a dialog box that lists class members, with the `job` field selected. Other members can be selected here, too; clicking the Add Required button adds members required by the `job` field, which in this case is the `getJob()` method.
	(Note that the Add Required feature doesn't always work correctly in version 2.1, so you may need to verify that all necessary fields and methods are selected; otherwise an error will occur and you'll have to return to this screen to correct it.)
Pull Up	The complement of Push Down. Moves class members from a class to its superclass. The caveat about Push Down also applies here: you need to verify that all associated members are selected in the Refactoring Wizard.
Extract Interface	Uses a class as a template to create an interface. See section 4.2.2 for an example.
Use Supertype Where Possible	Changes references from a class to its superclass. This refactoring is useful when the exact type of a concrete class is not important—only the fact that it implements a particular abstract class. For example, you might use this option if you've written code using the concrete class `GregorianCalendar`, a subclass of `Calendar`, but decide you want to generalize your code to use `Calendar`; this way, your program can use other subclasses of `Calendar`, such as (potentially) one that implements the traditional Chinese calendar.
Inline [Alt-Shift-I]	Replaces a method call with the method's code, a variable with the expression that was assigned to it, or a constant with the constant's hard-coded value. These options are the complements of Extract Method, Extract Local Variable, and Extract Constant, respectively.
Extract Method [Alt-Shift-M]	Creates a method from a section of another method. This refactoring is arguably the most useful and powerful that Eclipse provides. You can use it when a method gets too long and a subsection can logically be separated. It can significantly improve code reuse if the subsection can be used by other methods. For example, consider the following method (a simplified version of code introduced in section 4.2.7), which obtains a record from a file in the form of a vector and converts it into an object:

```
String fileName;
Class type;

public Object get(int i)
   throws InstantiationException,
   IllegalAccessException
```

Table A.4   Refactorings menu options. This menu is also available from the context menu in the Java editor. References to modified elements (method or class names, signatures, and so on) throughout the workspace will be updated, if appropriate, unless you veto them individually by clicking the Preview button in the Refactoring Wizard. See section 4.2 for an introduction to Eclipse's refactoring features. *(continued)*

```java
    {
        FilePersistence persistence =
                new FilePersistence(fileName);
        Vector v = persistence.read(i);
        Object o = type.newInstance();
        Iterator vIter = v.iterator();
        while (vIter.hasNext())
        {
            // Use Reflection API to populate
            // Object o with elements from Vector
        }
        return o;
    }
```

This code does two logically distinct things: It obtains a record in the form of a vector and performs a conversion from a vector to an object. By separating the two steps, the conversion can be reused for vectors obtained in other ways, such as by retrieving them from a database. To extract the vector to object code, select the lines beginning with

```java
        Object o = type.newInstance();
```

and ending with

```java
        return o;
```

Select Refactor→Extract Method and provide a method name such as `vector2Object`. The wizard in this case correctly determines that it should take a parameter of type `Vector` and return an `Object`. (In other cases, you may need to move variable declarations and adjust parameters so the extraction can be performed more cleanly. You may also want to reorder and rename parameters and change the methods' visibility.) When you are satisfied with the dialog box settings, click OK. The refactored code then looks like this:

```java
    String fileName;
    Class type;

    public Object get(int i)
        throws InstantiationException,
        IllegalAccessException
    {
        FilePersistence persistence =
                new FilePersistence(fileName);
        Vector v = persistence.read(i);
        return vector2Object(v);
    }

    private Object vector2Object(Vector v)
        throws InstantiationException,
```

Table A.4   Refactorings menu options. This menu is also available from the context menu in the Java editor. References to modified elements (method or class names, signatures, and so on) throughout the workspace will be updated, if appropriate, unless you veto them individually by clicking the Preview button in the Refactoring Wizard. See section 4.2 for an introduction to Eclipse's refactoring features. *(continued)*

	``
	    IllegalAccessException
	{
	    Object o = type.newInstance();
	    Iterator vIter = v.iterator();
	    while (vIter.hasNext())
	    {
	        // Use Reflection API to populate
	        // Object o with elements from Vector
	    }
	    return o;
	}
	``

Extract Local Variable
[Alt-Shift-L]
	Converts an expression that is used directly to a local variable. In the previous example, the `get()` method has the following `return` statement:
	
	``
	return vector2Object(v);
	``
	
	With the expression `vector2Object(v)` selected, this refactoring asks you to provide a variable name, adds a statement assigning the value of the call to a variable, and then returns the variable as follows:
	
	``
	Object o = vector2Object(v);
	return o;
	``

Extract Constant	Converts a hard-coded constant (and, optionally, all occurrences of that constant in a class) to a final static field. For example, if you select `3.141592654` in the following example
	
	``
	double radius(double diameter)
	{
	    return(diameter * 3.141592654);
	}
	``
	
	and provide the name `PI` as the constant name in the Refactoring Wizard, the class is modified as follows:
	
	``
	private static final double PI = 3.141592654;
	double radius(double diameter)
	{
	    return(diameter * PI);
	}
	``

Convert Local Variable to Field	Converts a variable declared in a method to a class field.

Table A.5 Navigate menu options. Three types of commands appear in the navigation menu: commands that alter the way resources are displayed, such as Go Into and Open Type Hierarchy; commands that navigate between resources, such as Open Type Hierarchy and Open Resource; and commands that navigate within a file, such as Show Outline and Go to Last Edit Location. Some commands (in particular, the Next and Previous commands) change, depending on the context.

Go Into	Makes the current selection the root of the display in hierarchical views, such as Package Explorer and the Navigator view. For example, if you are viewing a project in the Package Explorer and select a package, only the selected package will be visible in the Package Explorer. After you select Go Into, the Up tool button becomes active in the view's toolbar; you can click it to return to viewing the whole project.
Go To	Has various options, including Up One Level, which is equivalent to the Up tool button mentioned in Go Into. Other options allow you to locate packages, types, and unit tests; to move from one class member to the next or to a previous class member; or to locate a matching brace in code.
Open Declaration [F3]	Locates the file where the type of Java element selected in the editor is declared, and displays the declaration in the editor.
Open Type Hierarchy [F4]	Displays the class hierarchy containing the Java element selected in the editor in the Hierarchy view.
Open Super Implementation	Locates the implementation of the selected method in the superclass and displays it in the editor.
Open External Javadoc [Shift-F2]	Opens the Javadoc entry for the currently selected element.
Open Type [Ctrl-Shift-T]	Opens a dialog box that lets you locate a class by typing the first few letters of its name. The class is opened in the editor.
Open Type in Hierarchy [Ctrl-Shift-H]	Opens a dialog box that lets you locate a class by typing the first few letters of its name. The class is opened in the editor and in the Hierarchy view.
Open Resource [Ctrl-Shift-R]	Opens a search dialog box that lets you locate a resource by typing the first few letters of its name.
Show In	Locates and displays the currently selected resource in another view. For example, if a Java source file is selected in the editor, you can use Show In to locate the file in the Package Explorer view.
Show Outline [Ctrl-O]	Provides an outline view as a pop-up window in the editor that can be used to navigate inside the currently selected file.
Next [Ctrl-.] **Go to Next Problem** **Next Match**	Depending on context, locates the next item in a list or in the current file. For example, if you are editing a source file that contains errors, this menu item appears as Go to Next Problem and takes you to the next error in the file.
Previous [Ctrl-,] **Go to Previous Problem** **Previous Match**	Depending on context, locates the previous item in a list or current file. While you're editing a source file that contains errors, this menu item appears as Go to Previous Problem and takes you to the previous error in the file.

Table A.5   Navigate menu options. Three types of commands appear in the navigation menu: commands that alter the way resources are displayed, such as Go Into and Open Type Hierarchy; commands that navigate between resources, such as Open Type Hierarchy and Open Resource; and commands that navigate within a file, such as Show Outline and Go to Last Edit Location. Some commands (in particular, the Next and Previous commands) change, depending on the context. *(continued)*

Go to Last Edit Location [Ctrl-Q]	Moves to the location of the last edit in the current file in the editor.
Go to Line [Ctrl-L]	Locates a specific line number.
Back [Alt-Left Arrow]	Locates the previously selected resource (similar to a web browser's Back button).
Forward [Alt-Right Arrow]	Locates the resource that was selected before you chose the Back command (similar to a web browser's Forward button).

Table A.6   Search menu options

Search [Ctrl-H]	Opens the Search dialog box, which has separate tabs for the File, Help, and Java search options, plus a plug-in search.
File	Opens a dialog box you can use to search for text in files. The files can be all files in the workspace or restricted by file pattern or working set.
Help	Opens a dialog box you can use to search for text in the Eclipse documentation. The documents searched can be limited to those defined in a working set.
Java	Opens a dialog box you can use to search for text in Java files. Files can be all files in the workspace or restricted to a working set.
References [Ctrl-Shift-G]	Searches for references to a selected Java element. The menu option can be used to search the workspace or to limit the search to the element's class hierarchy or a working set. The shortcut Ctrl-Shift-G only searches the workspace.
Declarations [Ctrl-G]	Searches for declarations of a selected Java element's type. The menu option can be used to search the workspace or to limit the search to a working set. The shortcut Ctrl-G only searches the workspace.
Implementors	Searches for implementations of the selected Java interface. Options are available to search the workspace or to limit the search to a working set.
Read Access	Searches for statements or expressions that reference the selected class field. Options are available to search the workspace or to limit the search to the class hierarchy or a working set.
Write Access	Searches for statements or expressions that modify the selected class field. Options are available to search the workspace or to limit the search to the class hierarchy or a working set.
Occurrences in File [Ctrl-Shift-U]	Finds all occurrences of the selected text in a file.

Table A.7   Project menu options

Open Project	Opens a project that has previously been closed.
Close Project	Closes a project's resources. A closed project is made unavailable in the workspace, but its contents are left in the workspace directory on disk. Closing unused projects saves memory and can reduce build time.
Rebuild Project	Forces a complete rebuild of the selected project, including resources that have not changed.
Rebuild All	Forces a complete rebuild of all open projects, including projects and resources that have not changed.
Generate Javadoc	Opens the Javadoc Wizard, which allows you to select projects and resources and generate Javadocs for them.
Properties	Opens a Properties dialog for the currently selected project (or the project to which the currently selected resource belongs).

Table A.8   Run menu options. Note that in the Debug perspective, this menu has additional options for controlling execution of code in the debugger.

Run Last Launched [Ctrl-F11]	Reruns the application that was most recently run. (This is the same as the Run button on the main toolbar.)
Debug Last Launched [F11]	Re-debugs the application that was most recently debugged. (This is the same as the Debug button on the main toolbar.)
Run History	Displays a list of recently run applications, from which you can select an application to run again.
Run As	Runs an application with the default settings. Options are available for standard Java applications, unit tests, or applets. An option is also available for launching a special runtime instance of the Eclipse Workbench, which is useful for developing plug-ins.
Run	Opens a dialog box that lets you configure and launch an application.
Debug History	Displays a list of recently debugged applications, from which you can select an application to debug again.
Debug As	Debugs an application with the default settings. Options are available for standard Java applications, unit tests, or applets. An option is also available for launching a special runtime instance of the Eclipse Workbench.
Debug	Opens a dialog box for configuring and launching an application using the debugger.
Watch	Displays the selected variable or expression in the Expressions view. The value is updated whenever the program is suspended.
Inspect	Displays the selected variable or expression in the Expressions view. The value displayed is a snapshot and is not updated.

Table A.8   Run menu options. Note that in the Debug perspective, this menu has additional options for controlling execution of code in the debugger. *(continued)*

Display [Ctrl-D]	Displays the result of evaluating the selected variable or expression in the Display view, where it can be edited and reevaluated.
Execute [Ctrl-U]	Executes the selected code in a Java scrapbook page.
Run to Line [Ctrl-R]	Runs the application and suspends it at the selected line.
Step into Selection [Ctrl-F5]	Steps into the selected method. The method must be in the line of code where execution is currently suspended. This command is valuable because it allows you to step into a single method when multiple (and possibly nested) methods are called in the single line of code.
Add/Remove Breakpoint [Ctrl-Shift-B]	Adds or removes a breakpoint on the currently selected line, which must be executable. You can configure the breakpoint's properties by right-clicking on it in the editor or by using the Breakpoints view in the Debug perspective. Options include stopping according to hit count or when a condition is met. The breakpoint can also be set to suspend either the JVM or just the thread being debugged.
Add Java Exception Breakpoint	Sets a breakpoint that suspends execution when the selected exception is thrown. This option can be configured to break when the exception is caught, uncaught, or both.
Add/Remove Method Breakpoint	Sets a breakpoint that suspends execution when a selected method is entered. (You can use the breakpoint properties to select whether to suspend when the method is entered, exited, or both.) This type of breakpoint is intended to be used with a method for which you don't have the source code. You can set the breakpoint using the Java class file editor or in the Outline view.
Add/Remove Watchpoint	Sets a breakpoint on a class field. By default, execution is suspended whenever the field is accessed or modified; you can change this setting using the Breakpoint Properties dialog box. You can also enable suspension based on hit count or limit the breakpoint to a specific thread.
External Tools	Selects an external tool to run, such as an Ant build.

Table A.9   Window menu options

New Window	Opens a new Eclipse window. This option is useful for working with two perspectives at the same time.
Open Perspective	Allows you to open a new perspective from a submenu.
Show View	Opens a new view in the current perspective.
Hide Editors **Show Editors**	Toggles between hiding and showing the editor pane in the current perspective.
Lock the Toolbars	When selected, toolbars cannot be rearranged.

Table A.9   Window menu options *(continued)*

Customize Perspective	Allows you to select the items that are available in the current perspective's main menu (such as resource types that can be created using the File→New menu selection) and the toolbar (for instance, tool buttons contributed by plug-ins).
Save Perspective As	Saves the current perspective (perhaps with added and rearranged views) as a custom perspective. To open a custom perspective, use Window→Open Perspective→Other.
Reset Perspective	Resets the current perspective to its default.
Close Perspective	Closes the current perspective.
Close All Perspectives	Closes all perspectives.
Keyboard Shortcuts	Displays shortcut keys for navigating between perspectives, view and editors.
Switch to Editor [Ctrl-Shift-W]	Opens a dialog box that allows you to easily select an open editor.
Preferences	Opens a dialog box that lets you change Eclipse settings and preferences. See section 2.4 for an introduction to configuring Eclipse to your preference.

Table A.10   Help menu options

Welcome	Displays the welcome page for the Eclipse platform, the JDT, or the PDE.
Tips and Tricks	Displays tips and tricks for the Eclipse platform, the JDT, or the PDE. This page contains useful information about recently added or lesser-known features.
Help Contents	Displays online documentation. If you've downloaded the Eclipse SDK, guides available include the Workbench User Guide, Java Development User Guide, Platform Plug-in Developer Guide, JDT Plug-in Developer Guide, and PDE Guide.
Software Updates	Obtains updates from the Eclipse web site and manages configuration information (allowing a previous configuration to be restored). This option is also used to install plug-ins from Eclipse update sites.
About Eclipse Platform	Displays the Eclipse version number and information about installed features and plug-ins.

CVS installation procedures

Concurrent Versions System (CVS) can be deployed several ways. The simplest approach, called *local access*, is to put the repository on a disk that is shared by everybody on the team. The CVS client (which can be either a command-line or a GUI application) uses lock files to synchronize access to the files. No special server is required. This approach isn't recommended, because nothing prevents users from damaging the repository—especially if they inadvertently read or write to the repository directly without using the CVS client.

A much better way is to use a CVS server that prevents direct access to the repository. Officially, Eclipse only supports CVS version 1.11.1p1 or higher on UNIX and Linux. However, a port of CVS, CVSNT, is available for Windows NT/2000/XP; even though it isn't officially supported, CVSNT version 1.11.1.1 and greater generally work well with Eclipse. If you must use Windows, another option is to install Cygwin, a UNIX emulator that runs on Windows platforms.

If you will be using CVS for serious development, you should have a machine dedicated as a CVS server, and you should consider using UNIX or Linux on this machine. One major advantage of using CVS on UNIX or Linux is that you have a better choice of authentication methods—SSH in particular is recommended. CVSNT only supports the pserver protocol, which, like Telnet, sends the password over the network in clear text, and is therefore unsuitable for use on the Internet. The other Windows alternative, Cygwin, is more difficult to install but does support SSH.

The major disadvantage of using UNIX or Linux is that they require an understanding of system administration and security issues, especially if you will be connecting the machine to the Internet. However, if you are part of a large team, you likely will have someone responsible for setting up and maintaining this server.

B.1 Installing CVS on UNIX and Linux

Most UNIX and Linux distributions include the two packages—CVS and the SSH server—required to set up the system as a CVS server using SSH authentication. CVS is a single executable that contains code for running both as a client and as a server; it is usually located in the /usr/bin directory. You may wish to verify that you can run CVS by entering `cvs --help` at a command prompt:

```
[user@cvsserver user]$ cvs --help
```

This command should display a concise list of CVS options. If instead you get the error *Command not found*, you need to locate the CVS executable and add its directory to your path. One way to do this for all users is to add it to the path defined in the /etc/profile file.

If CVS is not installed (or if you have a version older than 1.11), you can download the latest version from http://www.cvshome.org. Binaries are available for popular distributions of Linux, but it is easy to download the sources and build a version for other UNIX and Linux versions as well.

B.1.1 *Creating the CVS repository*

Once you have CVS installed, you can create your CVS repository. Follow these steps:

1 Log in as superuser.

2 Create a group named cvs and a user named cvs who belongs to the cvs group, by modifying the /etc/group and /etc/passwd files. At this time, you can also add to the cvs group any users who will be using CVS.

3 Create a directory for the repository. This directory can be virtually anywhere, but /usr/local/repository is a typical location:

```
[root@cvsserver local]# cd /usr/local
[root@cvsserver local]# mkdir repository
```

4 Initialize the directory as a CVS repository using the following cvs command:

```
[root@cvsserver local]# cvs -d /usr/local/repository init
```

In Linux, files and directories are associated with both an owner and a group. In order to allow everyone in the cvs group access to the repository, you need to make sure the repository and all the files in it belong to the cvs group, and that the group has full access to the repository. To ensure this, first change the ownership and group of the repository and its subdirectories to cvs:

```
[root@cvsserver local]# chown -R cvs.cvs repository
```

Next, change the permissions:

```
[root@cvsserver local]# chmod -R 4774 repository
```

This command, which assigns permissions, might need a little explanation. chmod often takes symbolic values, but it can also take a three- or four-digit absolute value. As you may know, the last three digits determine the permissions granted to the file owner, the members of the group, and everyone else; in this case, the two 7s allows full access to owner and group, respectively, and the 4 allows read-only access for everyone else.

If there are four digits, as there are here, the first one specifies how user and group IDs will be set when the user creates a new file; setting this digit to 4 means the group will be set according to the parent subdirectory. You need to do this because otherwise, when a cvs user creates a new file, the group will be set to a user's default group rather than cvs. That would mean other members of the cvs group couldn't access the file unless they also belonged the creator's default group. (To learn more about the chmod command, check out its manual page: Type `man chmod` at a UNIX/Linux prompt.)

That is all you need to do to set up a repository. If you were using local access, as described earlier, you could begin creating modules—the CVS equivalent of a project—and checking code in and out, using the command-line version of CVS. But, as we warned, this is not a reliable way to use CVS; and more to the point here, this approach is not supported by Eclipse. Instead, you need a way to access this repository using some form of remote access.

B.1.2 *Setting up SSH remote access*

There are several different options for accessing CVS remotely, but here we will consider only the two options supported directly by Eclipse: SSH and pserver. SSH (Secure Shell) is recommended because it is the most secure; it's also the easiest to set up, assuming you already have SSH installed on your machine. Of the two versions of SSH, SSH1 and SSH2, Eclipse only supports SSH1 by default; but this shouldn't cause a problem, because newer SSH servers supporting SSH2 usually provide backward compatibility for SSH1.

The major drawback to using SSH is that Windows clients other than Eclipse (such as standard command-line clients or GUI clients) may not support SSH without additional software and configuration. In this case, as long as your server is on an internal network and you aren't overly concerned about security, pserver is a reasonable option.

To use SSH, the only thing you need to do is make sure the SSH server is running on your CVS server machine. Eclipse will take care of all the details of logging in and executing CVS commands for you on the client side. You can verify that SSH is running by typing the following command at the command prompt:

```
[user@cvsserver user]$ ps cax | grep sshd
```

The ps cax command normally displays all the programs that are currently running on the system, but here the pipe command (|) causes the output from ps to be sent as input for the grep program. There it is searched for the text *sshd*, the name of the SSH daemon (or server) executable. Any line including this text is printed out. If this command doesn't print out anything, you probably don't have SSH running—one possibility is that it has a different name.

If sshd is not running, search your system to see if SSH is installed. Normally, the sshd executable is found in the /usr/sbin directory. You can start it manually, but a better option is to modify the system startup files (for example, /etc/rc) to start sshd automatically when the system boots. If SSH is not installed on your system, you can download a free version from http://www.openssh.com.

B.1.3 *Setting up pserver remote access*

Using pserver is only a little more involved than using SSH. You need to set up your machine to listen for incoming pserver requests and pass them to CVS. Two steps are required to set this up: associating the symbolic name cvspserver with the default pserver port, 2401; and configuring your port-mapping service—either inetd or xinetd—so that it forwards requests from this port to CVS. To find out whether you are using inetd or xinetd, enter the command **ps cax** to list all the processes running on your machine; then see which appears in the list. When you do this, note the process id (PID) associated with inetd or xinetd; you'll need it later.

The first step, defining the symbolic name, has probably already been done for you: The file /etc/services should contain the following lines for cvspserver, but if doesn't, add them:

```
cvspserver        2401/tcp              # CVS client/server operations
cvspserver        2401/udp              # CVS client/server operations
```

If you are using inetd, you don't call CVS directly; instead you call tcpd, the TCP wrappers program, and have it call CVS. Doing so provides a little extra security, because tcpd uses the configuration files /etc/hosts.allow and /etc/hosts.deny to determine which machines (by IP address or IP address range) are allowed to access CVS. Add the following line to inetd.conf:

```
cvspserver stream tcp nowait root /usr/sbin/tcpd /usr/bin/cvs -f --
➡    allow-root=/usr/local/repository pserver
```

To allow everyone with an IP address beginning with 192.168.1 access, the hosts.allow file should contain the following line:

```
ALL: 192.168.1.
```

This overrides any settings in the hosts.deny file, so you can prohibit everyone else by having this line in hosts.deny:

```
ALL: ALL
```

If you are using xinetd instead of inetd, there's no need to use tcpd. You can call CVS directly, because the TCP wrapper's functionality is built into xinetd; it automatically uses the /etc/hosts.allow and /etc/hosts.deny files. For xinetd, rather than adding a line to an existing file, you need to create a new configuration file called cvspserver in the /etc/xinet.d directory, with the following contents:

```
service cvspserver
{
    disable = no
    socket_type = stream
    protocol = tcp
    wait = no
    user = root
    server = /usr/sbin/cvspserver
    server_args = -f --allow-root=/usr/local/repository
}
```

If this file already exists, you probably only need to change the value of `disable` from `yes` to `no`.

To have the changes take effect, you need to send inetd or xinetd a hangup signal, using the `kill` command. To do this, you need to determine the process ID of inetd or xinetd using the `ps cax` command, as mentioned earlier, and enter the following command, substituting the appropriate value for *pid*:

```
[root@lx01 local]# kill -SIGHUP pid
```

Note that on some UNIX systems the appropriate symbolic constant for the hangup signal is `HUP`, rather than `SIGHUP`. You can find out the constant on your system by running the `kill` command with the `-l` option, which lists all valid signals.

If you've created a repository and set up your system to use either SSH or pserver, you are ready to begin checking code into and out of CVS using Eclipse.

B.2 *Installing CVS on Mac OS X*

The Apple Macintosh OS X operating system is based on BSD UNIX. So, installing CVS is similar to doing so on UNIX and Linux, as described in section B.1, with the following differences:

- CVS for Macintosh is available as part of the Mac OS X Developer Tools. At this writing, however, the latest release of Developer Tools (December 2002) includes CVS version 1.10, which does not work properly with Eclipse. You need to download the source for the latest version from http://www.cvshome. org and build it yourself. This is surprisingly easy to do, because OS X is based on a fairly standard version of BSD UNIX. After decompressing the source, refer to the file INSTALLING in the root directory of the distribution.

- SSH comes as part of Mac OS X, but it is not enabled by default. To start it, open a Terminal window and edit the file /etc/hostconfig using your favorite UNIX text editor, such as vi or pico. (If you haven't enabled root access, you'll need to use the `sudo` command to perform administrative chores. Instead of typing **vi /etc/hostconfig**, type **sudo vi /etc/hostconfig**.) Change the value of SSHSERVER from -NO- to -YES-.

- You create and manage users and groups using the NetInfo utility.

B.3 *Installing CVSNT on Windows*

If you are only interested in learning how to use CVS, having CVS running on your Windows NT/2000/XP machine may be the most convenient option—especially if you don't have access to a Linux, UNIX, or Mac OS X machine. Or perhaps, despite advice to the contrary, you really do want to use a Windows-based CVS server. You need CVSNT, a version of CVS that is being developed separately from the main CVS version. This version of the CVS server runs as an NT service and can perform authentication using Windows usernames and passwords.

The main complaint about CVSNT is that it is less mature than the mainstream CVS code base and, with fewer developers working on it, it tends to have more bugs. Nonetheless, many people are working quite happily with CVSNT, despite the occasional glitch.

To install CVSNT, download the latest version from http://www.cvsnt.org and run the executable (for example, cvsnt-1.11.1.3-69.exe). Then, follow these steps:

1   On the opening screen, click Next to start installation.

2   You are given the opportunity to accept the license under which CVSNT is released—the Gnu Public License (GPL)—and asked to agree to its terms. To proceed, select I Accept the Agreement and click Next.

3   Select the folder where CVSNT should be installed; the default is C:\Program Files\cvsnt. Click Next.

4   A screen appears, warning you to turn off Filesystem Realtime Protection. Click Next.

5   In the Select Components window, make sure Server Components is checked. The remaining default selections should be fine. Under Protocols, make sure the Password Server (pserver) protocol is checked. Click Next.

6   Select a Start Menu folder (such as CVSNT) and click Next.

7   In the Select Additional Tasks window, make sure Install Cvsnt Service and Cvsnt Lock Service are checked. Click Next.

8 In the Review Options window, click Install.

9 When you're finished, click OK.

After you install CVSNT, start it by choosing Start Menu→Programs→CVSNT→Service Control Panel. Create a repository as follows:

1 Click the Repositories tab. Make sure Repository Prefix is not checked. (Eclipse does not support this option.)

2 Click Add to add a repository, and enter a path such as **c:\repository**. A message will appear, saying the path does not exist and asking if you want to create it. Click Yes.

3 Click Apply.

4 Return to the Service Status dialog box and click Stop for both CVS Service and CVS Lock Service. After they are stopped (the Start buttons are no longer be grayed out), click Start for each.

Check the new directory's permissions and make sure all users who will be using the CVS repository have full control.

B.4 *Installing Cygwin CVS and SSH on Windows*

Cygwin is a free UNIX emulation environment that runs inside all versions of Windows beginning with Windows 95 (with the exception of Windows CE). It provides many standard UNIX packages, and most UNIX programs compile and run without change, including CVS and SSH. Because of the added step of installing and configuring a UNIX-like environment, setting up CVS with Cygwin is more complex than the self-contained CVSNT server, but it is much more secure.

Before you can download Cygwin, you must first download a small installation program, setup.exe, from http://www.cygwin.com/setup.exe. This program lets you select and download the core Cygwin package and the packages you need for CVS and SSH. On Windows NT, 2000, and XP machines, make sure you are logged in as administrator and perform the following steps:

1 Run setup.exe and click Next to leave the introductory dialog box.

2 Select Install from Internet and click Next.

3 Accept the default destination for Cygwin, c:\cygwin, or enter another location if you prefer.

4   Assuming you are using a dedicated server for CVS as recommended, under the option Install For select Just Me. (If you or others will also using the machine for other purposes, you can select All Users, but again, this is not recommended.)

5   Make sure Default Text File Type is set to UNIX. If you don't do this, some programs won't behave correctly. Click Next.

6   Enter a download location for the files and click Next.

7   The next screen allows you to set up your Internet connection. Fill it in appropriately and click Next.

8   Setup.exe downloads a list of mirror locations from which you can get the files. Choose one close to you and click Next.

9   A list of the packages available is downloaded, and the Select Packages screen appears. Initially the screen shows all the package categories, but this isn't very helpful. Click the View button until the text beside it says *Full*.

10 Scroll down the list until you find CVS listed on the right-hand side; click the Skip column entry on the left. Doing so displays the version of CVS to be downloaded.

11 Similarly, select the packages CYGRUNSRV (which you need to install SSH as a service, if you are using Windows NT, 2000, or XP) and OpenSSH.

12 Click Next, and installation begins.

13 Once Cygwin has finished installing, you are asked to create an icon on your desktop, Start menu, or both. Choose as you see fit.

You now have a working installation of Cygwin. You can select the desktop icon or the menu item, or run bash.bat in the Cygwin bin directory to get to a bash shell prompt. You next need to configure SSH and start it at the shell prompt as follows:

1   To configure SSH, enter the command `ssh-host-config`.

2   You are presented with several options. Answer **yes** to allow privilege separation and **yes** to install SSH as a service; this will register SSH as a service to be started automatically when the system is started. Enter **ntsec** for the CYGWIN environment variable.

3   To start SSH as a service immediately, without rebooting, enter the command `cygrunsrv -S sshd`.

The final step is to create a CVS repository. To do this, follow the steps described in section B.1.

B.5 *Troubleshooting the CVS installation*

If you've followed the instructions in this appendix carefully and set up groups and users as described, chances are you won't have any problems. However, if you do, the best source of information is the http://www.cvshome.org site. We can cover only a few common issues here.

The most common error you are likely to experience is the message *cvs error: cannot open /root/.cvsignore: Permission denied* when you try to connect from Eclipse using the pserver protocol. In Linux, this error can be caused by stopping and restarting the inetd or xinetd daemon while logged in as root, rather than sending the daemon a hangup signal to re-read the configuration file. This happens because the daemon inherits root's environment when started this way. (This doesn't happen when it is started normally at startup.) You may be able to fix the problem by stopping the daemon again, unsetting the environment variable HOME (the way to do this depends on which shell you are using), and restarting the daemon. Another possible cause is omitting -f from the cvspserver line in the inetd.conf file.

A problem that may occur on Windows is a failure to create a directory when you first try to add a new project from Eclipse, using the Team→Share Project option from the Package Explorer context menu. As a workaround, you can add the directory to the CVS repository manually. You can then repeat the steps for sharing a new project. Eclipse will notify you that the project already exists and ask if you want to synchronize your local project with the remote module. Click Yes. In the next message, Eclipse will ask which branch tag you would like to synchronize with; leave HEAD selected and click OK.

B.6 *Backing up the CVS repository*

One of the incidental benefits of using a source control system like CVS, which creates a central repository for your source code, is that it simplifies making backups. There are many backup schemes, manual and automated, but the most important thing is to choose one, do it regularly, and keep some of the backups off-site. Also, test your backups to make sure you are able to recover in the event of a disaster.

There is nothing special about the CVS files; you can copy them to tape or burn them on a CD. It's a good idea to schedule backups when people won't be using the system, and it's an even better idea to disable logins while performing backups to prevent saving the repository in an inconsistent state—which could occur if someone checks in files while the backup is going on.

Plug-in extension points

The plug-ins that form the Eclipse Platform define numerous extension points your plug-ins can use to add functionality to Eclipse. Typically, every major new Eclipse project adds its own plug-ins to the list. This appendix's table C.1 summarizes the extension points in the Platform SDK, including the JDT and Team plug-ins.

Treat this appendix like a ball of threads—you simply have to grab the one you want and start following where it leads. Often the biggest hurdle to getting started with something like this is finding out where to begin. This appendix provides that starting point for extensions.

Once you've picked an extension point, you can read its detailed documentation by going to the Plug-in Manifest Editor's Extension page, clicking the Add button, selecting Schema Based Extensions, selecting an extension point, and then clicking Details. See also chapters 8 and 9, which provide examples of using some of these extension points.

The id attribute

We have worked extensively with the Eclipse development team to improve the quality of the online documentation on extension points. However, one detail that is not covered well is the use of the id attribute. Some extension points need the id attribute to be specified on the extension itself (for example, the markers extension); some need it to be specified on elements within the extension (for example, editors); and others need something different. This is likely due to the evolution of the Eclipse API over time. Generally speaking, once an API has been released it cannot be changed, so we are stuck with a few kinks in the thread. We've examined each extension point to see how you are supposed to use the id attribute and added a few notes to help you out.

Deprecated, obsolete, and internal extension points

The Extension page shows a few extension points you should not use in your plug-ins. In the descriptions in table C.1, we use the following designations:

- *Deprecated* means the extension point still works in the current version but will become obsolete in a future version. Avoid it in any new code.

- *Obsolete* means the extension has been removed from the current version. Although the syntax is accepted, it has no effect.

- *Internal* or *experimental* means the extension point is documented but is marked as internal so it is likely to change in future releases. The ones marked *experimental* are more likely to be supported in an official way based on user feedback.

- *Unimplemented* indicates an extension that was not yet ready at the time of the 2.1 release but may be supported in future releases.

Release introduced

The Since column in table C.1 indicates the Eclipse Platform version number in which the extension point was first introduced. If this column is blank, the extension point has existed since version 1.0.

Table C.1 Extension points supported in the Eclipse Platform SDK

Extension point	Description	Since	Notes
org.eclipse.ant.core. antTasks	Associates Ant tasks with classes in your plug-in, to extend what Ant can do when run inside Eclipse.		3
org.eclipse.ant.core. antTypes	Associates Ant data types with classes in your plug-in.		3
org.eclipse.ant.core. extraClasspathEntries	Supplies extra class libraries (JAR files) for Ant to use.		3
org.eclipse.compare. contentMergeViewers	Provides a compare/merge viewer factory for one or more file types.		2
org.eclipse.compare. contentViewers	Provides a viewer factory for one or more file types.		2
org.eclipse.compare. structureCreators	Provides a class to create a tree structure for one or more file types.		2
org.eclipse.compare. structureMergeViewers	Provides a viewer factory for one or more structured file types.		2
org.eclipse.core. resources.builders	Registers an incremental builder under a symbolic ID and human-readable name.		1
org.eclipse.core.resources. fileModificationValidator	Provides a class for team providers to handle the validate-save and validate-edit operations.	2.0	3
org.eclipse.core.resources. markers	Registers a custom marker with optional super-types and attributes, including some already-defined supertypes.		1
org.eclipse.core.resources. moveDeleteHook	Provides a class for resource move and delete operations. Only one hook is allowed.	2.0	3
org.eclipse.core.resources. natures	Installs a custom nature that can be used in user projects.		1
org.eclipse.core.resources. teamHook	Registers a class for team providers to handle specialized events like verifying link creation.	2.1	3

Table C.1 Extension points supported in the Eclipse Platform SDK *(continued)*

Extension point	Description	Since	Notes
`org.eclipse.core.` `runtime.applications`	Defines a top-level application that can be invoked on the Eclipse command line with the `-application` option.		1
`org.eclipse.core.` `runtime.urlHandlers`	Adds URL handlers to the Platform search path.		3
`org.eclipse.debug.core.` `breakpoints`	Defines custom breakpoints.		2

`org.eclipse.debug.core.`
`launchConfigurationCompar-`
`ators`
	Declares specialized Java comparators to compare attributes.		2

`org.eclipse.debug.core.` `launchConfigurationTypes`	Specifies the class used to run and debug applications of various types.		2
`org.eclipse.debug.core.` `launchers`	*Obsolete* in 2.0: Use the `launchConfigura-` `tionTypes` extension point.	n/a	n/a
`org.eclipse.debug.core.` `sourceLocators`	Specifies classes to help the debugger locate source code.		2
`org.eclipse.debug.core.` `statusHandlers`	Registers error handlers for debugger status codes.		2
`org.eclipse.debug.ui.` `consoleColorProviders`	Supplies code to manage the color of console output.	2.1	2
`org.eclipse.debug.ui.` `consoleLineTrackers`	Supplies code to listen for lines written to the console.	2.1	2
`org.eclipse.debug.ui.` `debugActionGroups`	Groups several actions together so they can be made visible or invisible together.		2
`org.eclipse.debug.ui.` `debugModelPresentations`	Defines classes to render and present the labels, icons, and editors for the specified debug models.		2

`org.eclipse.debug.ui.`
`launchConfigurationTab-`
`Groups`
	Contributes a group of tabs for specific launch configuration types (for both run and debug).		2

`org.eclipse.debug.ui.`
`launchConfigurationType-`
`Images`
	Associates images with the specified launch configuration types.		2

`org.eclipse.debug.ui.` `launchGroups`	Defines a group of launch configurations to be displayed together.	2.1	2
`org.eclipse.debug.ui.` `launchShortcuts`	Adds shortcuts to the Run and/or Debug menus in one or more perspectives.		2

Table C.1   Extension points supported in the Eclipse Platform SDK *(continued)*

Extension point	Description	Since	Notes
org.eclipse.help.appserver.server	*Internal.* Adds an application server for help and other plug-ins.		1
org.eclipse.help.browser	Registers HTML browsers.		2
org.eclipse.help.contexts	Defines context-sensitive (F1) help for a plug-in.		3
org.eclipse.help.luceneAnalyzer	Registers natural-language text analyzers used for indexing and searching the help.		3
org.eclipse.help.support	Defines a help system to replace the built-in one. Not recommended except for custom applications.		3
org.eclipse.help.toc	Contributes one or more tables of contents files for this plug-in.		3
org.eclipse.help.webapp	*Internal.* Registers the name of the help web application plug-in.	2.1	3
org.eclipse.jdt.core.classpathContainerInitializer	Declares lazily loaded custom classpath containers.	2.0	2
org.eclipse.jdt.core.classpathVariableInitializer	Declares lazily loaded custom classpath variables for use in Java build paths.	2.0	3
org.eclipse.jdt.core.codeFormatter	Defines new code formatters.	2.0	3
org.eclipse.jdt.debug.ui.vmInstallTypePage	Provides the JRE launch configuration pages for custom VM types.		2
org.eclipse.jdt.junit.testRunListeners	Registers code to be notified about the execution of a test.	2.1	3
org.eclipse.jdt.launching.classpathProviders	Registers custom source and classpath providers.	2.1	2
org.eclipse.jdt.launching.runtimeClasspathEntryResolvers	Provides classes to look up classes and source files for the given classpath variables and/or containers.		2
org.eclipse.jdt.launching.vmConnectors	Provides custom ways to connect to the JVM for debugging and launching.		2
org.eclipse.jdt.launching.vmInstallTypes	Defines new types of Java virtual machine installations.		2
org.eclipse.jdt.ui.classpathContainerPage	Adds wizard pages to create or edit classpath container entries.		4

Table C.1   Extension points supported in the Eclipse Platform SDK *(continued)*

Extension point	Description	Since	Notes
org.eclipse.jdt.ui. javadocCompletionProcessor	Defines Javadoc completion processors (for example, to suggest xdoclet tags).		2
org.eclipse.jdt.ui. javaEditorTextHover	Defines new types of hovering behavior in Java editors.		2
org.eclipse.jdt.ui. javaElementFilters	Adds custom filters for views that show Java elements (such as the Package Explorer).		2
org.eclipse.pde.ui. newExtension	*Experimental.* Defines wizards to create new extensions in the PDE's manifest editor.		2
org.eclipse.pde.ui. projectGenerators	*Experimental.* Defines wizards to create the initial content of the PDE plug-in projects.		2
org.eclipse.pde.ui. templates	*Experimental.* Defines templates that are used to generate code for new extensions.		2
org.eclipse.search. searchPages	Adds tabs to the Search dialog.		2
org.eclipse.search. searchResultSorters	Provides custom sorting options in the Search view.		2
org.eclipse.team.core. fileTypes	Declares files as being either text or binary, based on their extension.		3
org.eclipse.team.core.ignore	Adds patterns to the version control ignore list.		3
org.eclipse.team.core. projectSets	Provides handlers for reading and writing project sets (collections of team-shared projects).		2
org.eclipse.team.core. repository	Defines new team providers.	2.0	2
org.eclipse.team.ui. configurationWizards	Supplies wizards that take care of associating projects with team providers.		2
org.eclipse.ui. acceleratorConfigurations	*Deprecated in 2.1: Use the commands extension instead.* Defines accelerator configurations that the user can choose from the Preferences page.	2.0	2
org.eclipse.ui. acceleratorScopes	*Deprecated in 2.1: Use the commands extension instead.* Defines scopes that limit where accelerator sets can be active.	2.0	2
org.eclipse.ui. acceleratorSets	*Deprecated in 2.1: Use the commands extension instead.* Defines collections of keyboard shortcuts for workspace actions.	2.0	4
org.eclipse.ui. actionDefinitions	*Deprecated in 2.1: Use the commands extension instead.* Defines actions.	2.0	2

Table C.1 Extension points supported in the Eclipse Platform SDK *(continued)*

Extension point	Description	Since	Notes
org.eclipse.ui. actionSetPartAssociations	Associates action sets with Workbench parts that are visible when the Workbench part is active.		4
org.eclipse.ui.actionSets	Defines action sets (menu or toolbar items) that appear in a view that the user has customized.		2
org.eclipse.ui.capabilities	*Unimplemented in 2.1.* Registers new project capabilities.	n/a	n/a
org.eclipse.ui.commands	Defines commands, command categories, and default key bindings.	2.1	4
org.eclipse.ui.decorators	Adds decorators that modify the icon or label of items in a view depending on its state.	2.0	2
org.eclipse.ui. documentProviders	Registers document provider classes for the given extensions or input types. These are used when opening editors.		2
org.eclipse.ui.dropActions	Defines a handler so that objects from this plug-in can be dropped into views of other plug-ins.		2
org.eclipse.ui. editorActions	Adds actions to editor menus and toolbars that were registered by other plug-ins.		2
org.eclipse.ui.editors	Adds new editors to the Workbench.		2
org.eclipse.ui. elementFactories	Defines element factories, which are used to recreate objects saved to disk when Eclipse is shutting down.		2
org.eclipse.ui. exportWizards	Creates wizards that appear in the Export dialog.		2
org.eclipse.ui. fontDefinitions	Registers new fonts for use by the Workbench.	2.1	2
org.eclipse.ui. importWizards	Creates wizards that appear in the Import dialog.		2
org.eclipse.ui.markerHelp	Provides a way to get help on markers.	2.0	3
org.eclipse.ui. markerImageProviders	Provides images for new marker types.	2.1	2
org.eclipse.ui. markerResolution	Adds classes that propose quick fixes for problems that are marked with a specific marker type.	2.0	3
org.eclipse.ui. markerUpdaters	Defines marker update strategies that are used to update the marker's attributes based on its position and text when its resource is saved.	1.0	2
org.eclipse.ui.newWizards	Adds wizards to the New dialog, optionally creating categories for them to go in.		2

Table C.1 Extension points supported in the Eclipse Platform SDK *(continued)*

Extension point	Description	Since	Notes
org.eclipse.ui. perspectiveExtensions	Extends perspectives defined by other plug-ins. This allows you to add menu and toolbar items, shortcuts, views, and so on.		4
org.eclipse.ui. perspectives	Defines new perspectives.		2
org.eclipse.ui.popupMenus	Adds items to pop-up menus tied to objects, views, or editors defined by other plug-ins.		2
org.eclipse.ui. preferencePages	Adds pages to the Preferences dialog.		2
org.eclipse.ui. projectNatureImages	Defines small icons used to decorate project images, based on their nature.		2
org.eclipse.ui. propertyPages	Adds property pages for workspace objects of a given type.		2
org.eclipse.ui. resourceFilters	Adds predefined filters to views that display resources (such as the Navigator view).		3
org.eclipse.ui.startup	Marks the plug-in for loading when Eclipse is started.	2.0	3
org.eclipse.ui.viewActions	Adds items to a view's menu or toolbar.		2
org.eclipse.ui.views	Defines additional views for the Workbench.		2
org.eclipse.ui.workingSets	Defines working set wizard pages.	2.0	2
org.eclipse.update.core. featureTypes	Creates a new feature type for alternate packaging and verification schemes.		1
org.eclipse.update.core. installHandlers	Defines a global install handler that features being updated can reference.		1
org.eclipse.update.core. siteTypes	Defines a custom update site layout.		1
org.eclipse.update.ui. searchCategory	*Internal.* Adds new search categories in the Update Manager.		2

Notes

1   The id attribute is specified on the <extension> tag using a relative ID, and the extension can contain only one element. Eclipse prepends the ID with the plug-in's ID. For example:

```
<extension point="org.eclipse.core.resources.builders"
        id="mybuilder"
```

```
              name="My Builder">
      <builder>
        <run class="com.example.builders.MyBuilder" />
      </builder>
</extension>
```

2   The `id` attribute is specified on the object inside the `<extension>` tag, and the extension can contain more than one object. The ID must be fully qualified. For example:

```
<extension point="org.eclipse.ui.views">
   <view id="com.example.viewone"
         name="One"
         class="com.example.views.One" />
   <view id="com.example.viewtwo"
         name="Two"
         class="com.example.views.Two" />
   ...
</extension>
```

3   The `id` attribute is not used at all, so it can be omitted.

4   This involves some other, nonstandard use of the `id` attribute (consult the online documentation).

Introduction to SWT

This appendix introduces the Standard Widget Toolkit (SWT) and specifically covers:

- What SWT is
- SWT architecture
- SWT with events and threads
- How to run SWT code

SWT was developed by IBM as a replacement toolkit for the Abstract Window Toolkit (AWT) and Swing. IBM's goal was to create a GUI toolkit that would look and behave like the natural OS widgets and perform with the same speed. In this appendix we will look at what AWT and Swing did and compare the approach taken by IBM. After that, we will discuss how to use SWT, pointing out important concepts and topics along the way.

D.1   *What is the Standard Widget Toolkit?*

The Eclipse Platform Technical Overview (http://www.eclipse.org/whitepapers/eclipse-overview.pdf) describes SWT as a "widget set and graphics library integrated with the native window system but with an OS-independent API." Before analyzing this statement further, let's look at the first graphical API offered in Java version 1.0: the Abstract Window Toolkit (AWT). AWT provided an API for building graphical components such as labels, text boxes, buttons, lists, and menus and delegated to the operating system the task of providing its specific implementation of the component. When you build an AWT text box, the operating system constructs its text box and displays it on the application's window—a Java text box on Windows looks like a Windows text box, and a Java text box on Macintosh looks like a Macintosh text box.

The problem with AWT is that Sun only implemented the widgets that were common among all platforms that supported Java. To address this issue, Sun, working with Netscape, introduced Swing, which was an attempt to make a wholly cross-platform widget set. To achieve this goal, they wrote everything in Java, rather than delegating to the OS. This approach helped Java become more useful in terms of UI, but at a cost:

- The controls did not match the look of the platform on which they where run.
- The controls performed much worse compared to the native implementations.

Sun tried to address the first issue by developing what it called a *pluggable look-and-feel* for each OS. However, although this approach addressed part of the problem, Sun was unable to keep up with changing operating systems. For instance, a Windows look-and-feel looks the same on Windows 95, Windows 98, Windows ME, Windows 2000, and Windows XP, whereas the native applications look differently depending on which version is running.

Sun has made great strides in addressing the performance issues, but ultimately an emulated component can never perform as well as its native equivalent. A translation phase always occurs in the Java Virtual Machine (JVM), which converts the emulated component to a set of native painting instructions.

During the development of Eclipse, IBM developed a new approach to the problem, which is something of a hybrid of the two Sun approaches. SWT is a set of widgets that accesses the native controls through the Java Native Interface (JNI). Only those few controls that are not present on a particular OS are emulated. The downside of this approach is that a native library is required for each platform on which Eclipse/SWT is deployed. However, the benefit is that applications look and perform as well as native applications. And, as of the 2.1 release of Eclipse, SWT is supported on most major desktop operating systems and on the Pocket PC.

D.2 *SWT architecture*

Having talked a little about what SWT is, let's look at it graphically. As you can see in figure D.1, SWT is built up of three basic components: A *native library* that talks to the OS; a `Display` *class* that acts as an interface through which the SWT talks to the GUI platform; and a `Shell` *class* that acts as the top-level window of the application, which can contain *widgets* (another term for *controls* and *composites*).

Before we continue, let's explore some of the terms we just introduced:

- *Display*—The best way to think of the `Display` class is as a butler. It carries out all the important tasks and saves you from dealing with them. One of

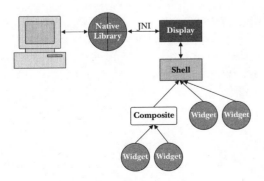

Figure D.1
How the SWT widgets fit together in regard to each other and the underlying OS

the most important jobs the class does is to translate the native platform's events into those suitable for use within SWT and vice versa. When developing your own application, you will normally have little to do with the Display class, other than to create it before all other windows.

- *Shell*—Basically, a window the user sees that is ultimately controlled by the OS's Window Manager. Shells are used for two different types of windows. The first is the top-level window of your application, upon which the rest of your GUI is built. In this case, Shell is created as a child of the Display class. The other type is a window that is the child of another window; for instance, dialog boxes. In this case, Shell is created as a child of the Shell upon which it is to appear.

- *Widget*—This term refers to *controls* and *composites*; you will notice throughout the SWT documentation that the three terms are used interchangeably. At its simplest, a widget is a GUI object that can be placed inside another widget.

- *Control*—A GUI item that has an OS counterpart; for instance, a button, text area, or menu.

- *Composite*—A widget that can have children; examples are toolbars and trees. The best example is the canvas, which you use to build up complex user interfaces with the help of sub-canvases using different layouts.

The SWT architecture was designed to mimic the platform application structure, so it has an important effect on the creation of widgets and disposal of resources.

D.2.1 *Widget creation*

When you're creating a widget in SWT, you need to take into account how it is also created in the underlying OS. Every control has a similar constructor that takes two arguments: the first specifies what the parent widget is, and the second specifies what the style of the widget should be. This is a requirement of how many underlying OSs work. When the SWT object is created, the equivalent OS object is also created, and it needs to know what the parent is. This also applies to the style settings for a number of widgets; once they are created, the style cannot be changed. (A *style* is a hint to the OS about how a widget looks. For instance, when you're creating a Button, the style defines what type of button it is: radio, push, checkbox, and so on.)

D.2.2 *Resource disposal*

Normally, when you're using Swing/AWT, you simply create your widgets, images, fonts, and so on without worrying about disposing of them, because you know the JVM will take care of them when garbage collection runs. However, when you're using SWT, you have to be more careful about how you use OS GUI resources, because only a limited supply is available.

When you create a resource-based object in SWT (for instance, Color, Cursor, Font, or Image), you must dispose of it. If you don't dispose of those you no longer need, a resource leak will occur and you will end up in a situation where you will not be able to create any more objects, nor will any other application running in the OS.

The following code snippet allocates a Color resource and then disposes of it:

```
Color blue = new Color (display, 0, 0, 255);
blue.dispose()
```

D.3 SWT and events

The most common piece of code you will see in all SWT programs is the following:

```
while (!shell.isDisposed ())
{
   if (!display.readAndDispatch ())
      display.sleep ();
}
```

This is commonly referred to as the *message pump* or *event dispatching loop*. Its job is to receive events from the OS (for instance, the user moving the mouse) while the top-level application window is open, dispatch them to the appropriate SWT widget, and then sleep until there is another event to process. You're required to have at least one of these in your program; otherwise, your application won't receive any events from the OS, which won't make the user very happy.

This approach is quite different than that used for AWT and Swing; there, this mechanism is hidden from the developer. It isn't hidden in SWT because if you create SWT code as part of a plug-in for Eclipse, you don't need a message pump—you automatically use the one provided by the Workbench.

The remainder of the event-handling mechanism is similar to that used for AWT and Swing. A number of basic event types and their respective listeners and adapters are declared in the org.eclipse.swt.events package. Consult the online documentation for a complete list. The following code snippet demonstrates how to create an event listener and how to add it to an object:

```
Button button = new Button(display, SWT.PUSH);
button.addSelectionListener(new SelectListener()
{
   public void widgetDefaultSelected( SelectionEvent e ) {}
   public void widgetSelected( SelectedEvent e )
```

```
    {
        System.out.println("Button Pressed");
    }
});
```

For those unfamiliar with handling events, don't worry, it's simple. As we've mentioned, an event correlates to an action such as a user moving a mouse or a window being maximized. For every type of event that can be received, there is an interface called a *listener*. A listener is a class that knows how to handle the particular event and do something useful based on it. To create a listener class, you have to create a class that implements the particular listener interface that matches the event you want to handle.

Looking at the previous snippet, we are interested in the `SelectionEvent` that is sent when a button is clicked. If you look at the Javadoc for that event, you will see that the appropriate listener is the `SelectionListener`. To add a listener to a widget class, you call one of its `addXXXListener()` methods, as in the earlier code that used `addSelectionListener()`.

TIP   Rather than spend time repeating what the Javadoc says, we encourage you to examine the online help. There you will find a complete list of the available event types, along with descriptions for them and the widgets that handle/generate those events. To see the help, select Help→Help Contents→Platform Plug-in Developers Guide→Programmers Guide→Standard Widget Toolkit→Widgets→Events.

D.4 *SWT and threads*

When you're building an SWT application using the SWT, an important factor to consider is how all the widgets interact with threads. If you're familiar with AWT and Swing programs the following will seem familiar, but there are some important differences to notice.

A single important thread referred to as the *UI thread* is responsible for processing events, dispatching them to appropriate widgets, and carrying out window painting. Without it, your application would do nothing. You may be thinking that we said something about this before, and we did.

With AWT and Swing, the UI thread or event dispatching thread is hidden from the developer; with SWT, the thread that creates the message pump becomes the UI thread. This design decision makes it possible to plug SWT plug-ins into Eclipse. In another departure from Sun's approach, SWT was designed to be able to have more than one event dispatching thread. (This functionality is rarely used, and we mention it only for completeness.)

The main thread is the UI thread, so you should not carry out any complex or time-consuming tasks (such as database access) or anything that might block the thread. Instead, you should spin off another thread to carry out those operations. Not doing so will seriously affect the responsiveness of your UI and inconvenience the user, which is never a good thing to do. Tied in with this is the fact that the only thread allowed to make calls to the SWT widgets without raising an `SWTException` is the UI thread.

You may wonder how you update the UI when your spun-off thread is complete. To do this, you use two helper methods that are part of the `Display` class: `asyncExec()` and `syncExec()`. (Note to Swing users: These methods are synonymous with the `invokeLater()` and `invokeAndWait()` methods of the `SwingToolkit` class. And yes, if you think Sun's methods are more clearly named, we agree.) These methods work as follows:

- `asyncExec(Runnable)`—Should be used when you want to update the UI but you don't really care when it happens. Remember that using this method means no guaranteed relationship exists between the processing in the background thread and the UI updates.

- `syncExec(Runnable)`—Should be used when your background thread needs a UI update to occur before it can continue processing. Note that your background thread will be blocked until the UI update has occurred.

Both of the methods take classes that implement the `Runnable` interface. The following snippet shows how you would typically use those methods:

```
Display.getDefault().asyncExec(new Runnable()
{
    public void run()
    {
        button.setText(new Date().toString());
    }
});
```

The `asyncExec()` method is part of the `Display` class, so you need to first retrieve the present instance of the Display class; doing so saves having to pass a reference to the `Display` class throughout your program. To the `asyncExec()` method, you pass a class that implements the `Runnable` interface. Typically you create an anonymous class, as in the previous example, to do the update.

D.5 *Building and running SWT programs*

You probably want to start coding, or at least look at some proper SWT code—and we will in just a moment. However, before we do, let's address how you build and run the code.

This book is about using Eclipse, so we will focus first on setting up Eclipse so you can do SWT development. Then we'll look at what you need to do to run code. After that, we'll explain the steps to run your SWT program from the command line.

To set up Eclipse, follow these steps:

1 Select your project in the package view, right-click, and select Properties.

2 Select Java Build Path and then click on the Libraries tab.

3 Select Add External JARs. Note that you might wish to create a variable if you are likely to use SWT a lot.

4 Locate the swt.jar file appropriate for your platform, as shown in figure D.2 (*<eclipse-root>* is the parent directory where Eclipse is located):

- *Linux GTK*—*<eclipse-root>*/plugins/org.eclipse.swt.gtk_2.1.0/os/linux/x86
- *Linux Motif*—*<eclipse-root>*/plugins/org.eclipse.swt.motif_2.1.0/os/linux/x86
- *Solaris Motif*—*<eclipse-root>*/plugins/org.eclipse.swt.motif_2.1.0/os/solaris/sparc
- *AIX Motif*—*<eclipse-root>*/plugins/org.eclipse.swt.motif_2.1.0/os/aix/ppc
- *HPUX Motif*—*<eclipse-root>*/plugins/org.eclipse.swt.motif_2.1.0/os/hpux/PA_RISC
- *Photon QNX*—*<eclipse-root>*/plugins/org.eclipse.swt.photon_2.1.0/os/qnx/x86
- *Mac OSX*—*<eclipse-root>*/plugins/org.eclipse.swt.carbon_2.1.0/os/macosx/ppc

5 Click OK.

NOTE For some platforms, such as GTK, more than one JAR is required to run SWT (GTK uses swt.jar and swt-pi.jar files). In this case, you must add all the required JARs to the classpath. To do so, repeat the previous steps for each JAR file. All JAR files are located in the same directory/folder.

To run your code, you need to follow these steps:

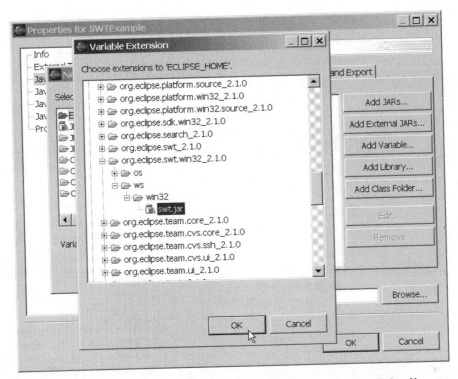

Figure D.2 Add swt.jar to your classpath through the Project Properties dialog. You can use either the Add External JARs button or the Add Variable option to locate it.

1 In the Package Explorer view, select the class that contains the `main` you wish to run.

2 Select Run→Run.

3 In the Run dialog, select Java Application and click New.

4 Select the Arguments tab and click the cursor in the VM Arguments text box.

5 Enter `-Djava.library.path=<path>`, where `<path>` is one of the following, based on your OS (see figure D.3):

- Win32—<*eclipse-root*>\plugins\org.eclipse.swt.win32_2.1.0\os\win32\x86

- Linux GTK—<*eclipse-root*>/plugins/org.eclipse.swt.gtk_2.1.0/os/linux/x86

- Linux Motif—<*eclipse-root*>/plugins/org.eclipse.swt.motif_2.1.0/os/linux/x86

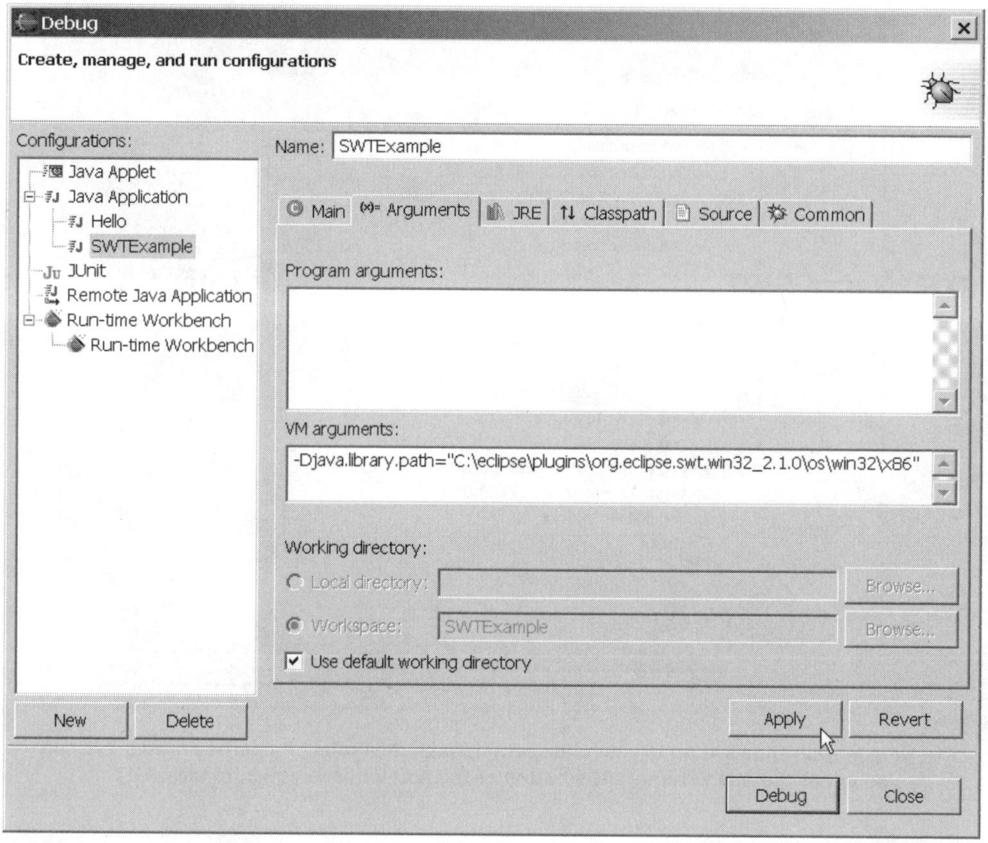

Figure D.3 **To let your program find the native SWT DLL, you need to add it to your Java library path through the Launch Configuration dialog.**

- Solaris Motif—<*eclipse-root*>/plugins/org.eclipse.swt.motif_2.1.0/os/solaris/sparc
- AIX Motif—<*eclipse-root*>/plugins/org.eclipse.swt.motif_2.1.0/os/aix/ppc
- HPUX Motif—<*eclipse-root*>/plugins/org.eclipse.swt.motif_2.1.0/os/hpux/PA_RISC
- Photon QNX—<*eclipse-root*>/plugins/org.eclipse.swt.photon_2.1.0/os/qnx/x86
- Mac OSX—<*eclipse-root*>/plugins/org.eclipse.swt.carbon_2.1.0/os/macosx/ppc

6 Click Apply and then click Debug.

Your application is now running. Remember to terminate the example; to do this, you can click on the square in the console view.

Running your code from the command line is similar:

1 Ensure that the appropriate JAR files for your platform are in the classpath.

2 Call `java` with the `-Djava.library.path` argument (as per the previous steps) and the name of your program.

D.6 Using SWT

We've covered the concepts of what SWT is and how to set up Eclipse so you can build and run examples. It's now time to take a look at a simple SWT example.

Rather than dump the code on you, we will lead you through the classes that form this example. If you wish to follow the code using Eclipse, make sure Eclipse is set up as described in section D.5. Then, create two Java classes (File→ New→Class): `BasicFramework` and `MainApp`. Be sure you create them with the package set to `org.eclipseguide.swt`.

D.6.1 The BasicFramework class

Let's first look at `BasicFramework`. The first part defines the package in which this class is located and then imports the required classes for this example:

```
package org.eclipseguide.swt;

import org.eclipse.swt.SWT;
import org.eclipse.swt.events.*;
import org.eclipse.swt.widgets.*;
```

`BasicFramework` is declared Abstract to ensure that whoever subclasses this class provides implementations for the `dispose()` and `displayHelpAboutDialog()` methods. In this basic framework, these methods are used as a reminder that resources should be disposed of and you need to provide your own About dialog. The remainder of the code is holders for the widgets you will use shortly:

```
public abstract class BasicFramework
{
    protected Display display;
    protected Shell shell;
    protected Menu menuBar, fileSubMenu, helpSubMenu;
    protected MenuItem fileSubMenuHeader;
    protected MenuItem fileExit, helpSubMenuHeader;
    protected MenuItem helpAbout;

    public abstract void dispose();
    public abstract void displayHelpAboutDialog();
```

The following inner class implements the `SelectionLister`, so it will deal with `Selection` events. It will be attached to the Exit menu item (defined in a moment). The basic principal is that it closes the window, which terminates the message pump, and then it calls `dispose()` to ensure that the two actions are tied together:

```
class FileExitListener implements SelectionListener
{
    public void widgetSelected(SelectionEvent event)
    {
        shell.close();
        dispose();
    }
    public void widgetDefaultSelected(SelectionEvent event)
    {
        shell.close();
        dispose();
    }
}
```

Similarly, the next inner class deals with selection events for the About button on the Help menu:

```
class HelpAboutListener implements SelectionListener
{
    public void widgetSelected(SelectionEvent event)
    {
        displayHelpAboutDialog();
    }
    public void widgetDefaultSelected(SelectionEvent event)
    {
        displayHelpAboutDialog();
    }
}
```

NOTE   In the two listener classes, the two methods `widgetSelected` and `widgetDefaultSelected` cover different event types. `widgetSelected` processes events from widgets the user has selected with a pointer—for instance, clicking on a button. `widgetDefaultSelected` processes events that are generated when the user presses the Space or Enter key and the button has focus.

Next you begin creating the hierarchy of the SWT architecture:

```
public BasicFramework(String windowTitle)
{
    display = new Display();
```

```
shell = new Shell(display);
shell.setText(windowTitle);
```

Remember that the `Display` widget is the object through which your application will talk to the OS. `Shell` is then created and passed the `display` as its parent. This `shell` acts as your top-level window, upon which everything else goes. Finally, `Shell` has a number of helper methods: `setMinimized()`, `setMaximized()`, and so on. Here you set the title of the window.

Building a fully featured menu bar in SWT is a complicated process. Rather than simply having some simple classes like `MenuBar`, `Menu`, `MenuItem`, and `Sub-Menu`, the designers have gone for two classes that carry out multiple roles, depending on what style they are passed:

```
menuBar = new Menu(shell, SWT.BAR);
fileSubMenuHeader = new MenuItem(menuBar, SWT.CASCADE);
fileSubMenuHeader.setText("&File");
```

The first step is to create the menu bar upon which all the other menus hang. You do this by passing in the style argument `SWT.BAR`. You then create a *hang point*, which is basically a placeholder for where the menu will be attached. Finally, you set the text that appears on the menu bar for the placeholder. The `&` symbol beside the letter *F* indicates that F should be treated as a *mnemonic* (a keyboard shortcut for accessing the menu). To use it, you press the Alt key to activate the menu and then press the F key to select that menu. You can then use the cursor keys to explore the menu.

The next part of building the menu requires you to create the menu that appears when you click on the File text. You create it to be a drop-down menu by specifying the `DROP_DOWN` style. (The other possible style option is `POP_UP`, which creates a pop-up menu that is useful for right-click selections and so forth.) Then, you attach the menu to the placeholder:

```
fileSubMenu = new Menu(shell, SWT.DROP_DOWN);
fileSubMenuHeader.setMenu(fileSubMenu);
```

In the last stage of building a menu, you create items to go on the menu. As before, you need to specify the style of the menu items, but you have more choices—in addition to creating a pushbutton menu item, you can also create a check-boxed item, a radio item, or a separator (used to create sections in your menus):

```
fileExit = new MenuItem(fileSubMenu, SWT.PUSH);
fileExit.setText("E&xit");
```

These are written the same way as the File menu:

```
helpSubMenuHeader = new MenuItem(menuBar, SWT.CASCADE);
helpSubMenuHeader.setText("&Help");

helpSubMenu = new Menu(shell, SWT.DROP_DOWN);
helpSubMenuHeader.setMenu(helpSubMenu);

helpAbout = new MenuItem(helpSubMenu, SWT.PUSH);
helpAbout.setText("&About");
```

Next you attach the listener classes to the menu items. From this point on, when you click the File menu's Exit option or the Help menu's About option, those events will be dealt with:

```
fileExit.addSelectionListener(new FileExitListener());
helpAbout.addSelectionListener(new HelpAboutListener());
```

The following line attaches the menu bar to the top-level `shell`:

```
shell.setMenuBar(menuBar);
}
```

The following is the last section of code for the `BasicFramework` class. It is an important section; not only does it make the top-level window (`shell`) appear on the screen, it also creates the message pump, which is the heart of this example. When you're developing a standalone application, remember that without this part, your program will do very little:

```
public void mainLoop(int hSize, int vSize)
{
    shell.setSize(hSize, vSize);
    shell.setVisible(true);
    shell.open();

    while (!shell.isDisposed())
    {
        if (!display.readAndDispatch())
            display.sleep();
    }
}
}
```

D.6.2   *The MainApp class*

Now let's look at the `MainApp` class, which extends the `BasicFramework` and does something useful with it. As before, you declare that this class is a member of the `org.eclipseguide.swt` package and then import all the classes used in this example:

```
package org.eclipseguide.swt;

import java.util.*;
```

```
import org.eclipse.swt.SWT;
import org.eclipse.swt.events.*;
import org.eclipse.swt.layout.FillLayout;
import org.eclipse.swt.widgets.*;
```

Rather than using a thread to set up a timer, you use the `java.util.Timer` class. If you haven't used Java 1.3 and beyond before (1.3 is the minimum Eclipse needs to run), you may not have come across this class. It is a simple convenience class that provides a dedicated timer thread:

```
public class MainApp extends BasicFramework
{
    Timer timer;
    Button button;
```

The button is placed in the main window of the example and displays the time. When clicked, it prints the time to the console.

The following inner class extends the abstract `TimerTask` class. Basically, a timer task is a `Runnable` that is passed to the `Timer` and executed at a desired interval. Inside the `run` method, you add an anonymous `Runnable` to the event queue, which updates the button text with the current time. You don't care when the UI thread processes this, so you add it using the `asyncExec` method:

```
private class ClockUpdateTask extends TimerTask
{
    public void run()
    {
        Display.getDefault().asyncExec(new Runnable()
        {
            public void run()
            {
                button.setText(new Date().toString());
            }
        });
    }
}
```

This is the constructor of the `MainApp` class. Here you call the constructor of your parent class `BasicFramework`, passing the title text:

```
public MainApp()
{
    super("SWT Example Framework");
```

Every window can have a layout manager that controls the placement and sizes of the widgets:

```
shell.setLayout(new FillLayout(SWT.VERTICAL));
```

Five layouts are already defined: FillLayout, StackLayout, GridLayout, FormLayout, and RowLayout. There is also a CustomLayout you can use to better control the widget placements.

TIP   To learn more about layouts, we recommend that you read the article "Understanding Layouts in SWT" (available from the Articles section of the Eclipse website: http://www.eclipse.org/articles/).

The next part of the code creates and adds a pushbutton to the shell window. You're using the fill layout, so there is no point in specifying the size of the button. It will simply expand to fill all available space:

```
button = new Button(shell, SWT.PUSH);
```

The following code shows an alternate way of adding a listener to a widget by connecting an anonymous class to it. It is preferable to use anonymous classes for short classes. Otherwise, it is recommended that you use a proper class (be it an inner class, or package friendly):

```
button.addSelectionListener(new SelectionListener()
{
    public void widgetSelected(SelectionEvent event)
    {
        System.out.println(
            "Button clicked - time is: " + button.getText());
    }
    public void widgetDefaultSelected(SelectionEvent event)
    {
        System.out.println(
            "Button pressed with default key - time is: "
                + button.getText());
    }
});
```

Next you create the timer and schedule that your ClockUpdate task will start after a 0 millisecond delay; it will be called every 1000 milliseconds (1 second) thereafter:

```
timer = new Timer();
timer.scheduleAtFixedRate(new ClockUpdateTask(), 0, 1000);
```

You don't have to tell the timer to start—as soon as the app is created, it is running.

The following code calls the mainLoop of the parent class BasicFramework, where you enter the event loop and don't return until the shell is closed. When it is, you exit the JVM in which the app is running:

```
        this.mainLoop(300, 200);

        System.exit(0);
    }
```

This is called to create the `MainApp` class and start the whole ball running:

```
public static void main(String[] args)
{
    new MainApp();
}
```

Now you implement the abstract methods of the parent class; however, the code doesn't do anything useful with them. It is designed so you can put all resources you declare into the `dispose()` method, so you can easily locate everything that needs to be disposed of:

```
public void dispose()
{
    System.out.println("Disposing of Resources");
}

public void displayHelpAboutDialog()
{
    System.out.println("Display Help About Dialog");
}
}
```

We also envisioned that you would put whatever logic you need for creating your About dialog in the `displayHelpAboutDialog()` method.

D.6.3 *Trying the example*

With the code complete, you can run the example to give it a test drive. If you're simply following the text, figure D.4 shows what the example looks like.

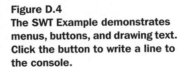

Figure D.4
The SWT Example demonstrates menus, buttons, and drawing text. Click the button to write a line to the console.

Introduction to JFace

In this appendix, we will examine a higher-level GUI toolkit created by IBM, called JFace. We will discuss what it is, what it's for, and how it interacts with the Standard Widget Toolkit (SWT).

E.1 Architecture

JFace is a platform-independent toolkit built on SWT. It provides convenience classes for many typical application features and simplifies a number of common UI tasks. It enhances and works with SWT without ever hiding it from the developer.

Figure E.1 shows the relationship between SWT, JFace, and Eclipse. As you can see, JFace is completely dependent on SWT, but SWT is not dependent on anything. Furthermore, the Eclipse Workbench is built on both JFace and SWT and uses them both as needed.

Some of the common tasks JFace addresses include the following:

- It provides *viewer* classes that handle the tedious tasks of populating, sorting, filtering, and updating widgets.

- It provides *actions* to allow users to define their own behaviors and to assign them to specific components, such as menu items, toolbar items, buttons, and so on. Actions are designed to be shared among different widgets. Rather than duplicate code, the same action can be used for a menu item and an entry on a toolbar.

- It provides *registries* that hold images and fonts. These registries are intended to provide a mechanism to more easily look after limited OS resources. Images and fonts that are used often should be put in these registries.

- It defines standard *dialogs* and *wizards* and defines a framework that can be used to build complex interactions with the user. Some of the dialog types that have been implemented include `MessageDialog`, `InputDialog`, and `PreferenceDialog`.

JFace's primary goal is to free you to focus on the implementation of your specific application without having to solve problems that are common to most GUI applications.

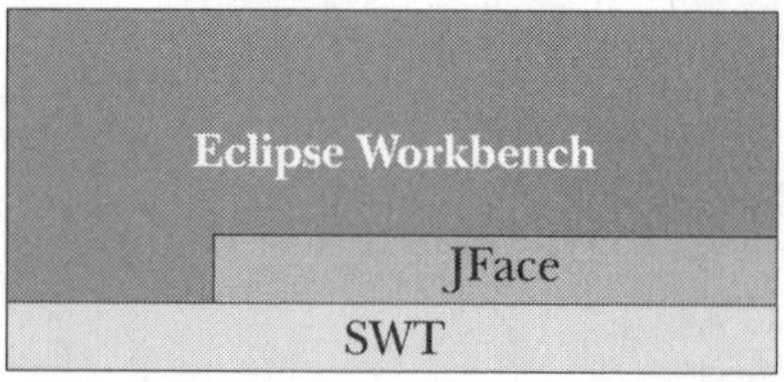

Figure E.1
JFace integration with other Eclipse technologies

Before you can compile and run the example in this appendix, you need to add a few more JAR files to your classpath or Eclipse project library:

- *<eclipse-root>*\plugins\org.eclipse.jface_2.1.0\jface.jar
- *<eclipse-root>*\plugins\org.eclipse.core.runtime_2.1.0\runtime.jar
- *<eclipse-root>*\plugins\org.eclipse.ui.workbench_2.1.0\workbench.jar
- *<eclipse-root>*\plugins\org.eclipse.core.boot_2.1.0\boot.jar

Remember that you need to have the appropriate SWT library in your Java library path, as shown in appendix D.

E.2 *Building a JFace application*

Building applications using JFace is different from building pure SWT applications. To begin with, you don't have to worry about implementing the message pump, and you don't work directly with the `Display` or `Shell` class. Instead, you derive your main class from `org.eclipse.jface.window.ApplicationWindow`. This class has full support built into it for menu bars, toolbars, and a status line.

Through the course of this example, we will show you how to build a simple application that has a menu bar, a toolbar, and a status line. Before we walk through the code, we'd like to show you what you will be creating. Figure E.2 shows the final example: E.2a shows the main window with a menu, a toolbar with a button on it, and a status line. E.2b shows the same action used for the button, but this time on the menu.

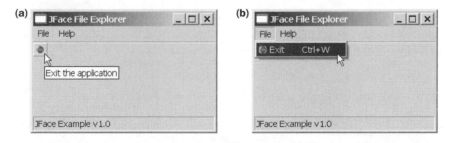

Figure E.2   Using JFace, it's easy to create buttons and menus that perform the same action. (a) shows the button and (b) shows the menu. Notice that the icon in the menu is the same as the icon in the button.

NOTE   We highly recommend examining the following articles, which discuss building a JFace-based standalone application (a limited clone of the Windows Explorer window) from the ground up:

- http://www-106.ibm.com/developerworks/opensource/library/os-ecgui1/
- http://www-106.ibm.com/developerworks/opensource/library/os-ecgui2/
- http://www-106.ibm.com/developerworks/opensource/library/os-ecgui3/

E.2.1 *JFaceExample class*

First let's walk through the main class that builds the screen (JFaceExample). The code begins by importing the packages required for this example:

```
package org.eclipseguide.jface;

import org.eclipse.jface.action.*;
import org.eclipse.jface.window.ApplicationWindow;
import org.eclipse.swt.SWT;
import org.eclipse.swt.widgets.*;
```

The ExitAction class extends Action and provides a common class that can be shared between certain widgets:

```
public class JFaceExample extends ApplicationWindow
{
    private ExitAction exitAction;
```

A null parent is passed to the ApplicationWindow class to indicate that it should be created as a top-level window. If you wanted to create it as a child window, you would pass an existing Shell instance instead:

```
public JFaceExample()
{
    super(null);
```

You create an instance of the ExitAction class, passing an instance of the ApplicationWindow class as an argument. The argument is later used by the ExitAction class to close the main window:

```
    exitAction = new ExitAction(this);
```

The following methods are part of the ApplicationWindow class:

```
    this.addMenuBar();
    this.addStatusLine();
    this.addToolBar(SWT.FLAT | SWT.WRAP);
}
```

When they are called, they in turn call the methods createMenuManager(), createStatusLineManager(), and createToolBarManager(). If you wish to have a menu, status line, or a toolbar, then you need to override those methods, ensuring that they return the correct type. We will look at the implementations of those methods shortly.

The `createContents()` method is one you should override when building your application, in order to create and place your widgets. For this example, you simply set the application window's title and status line:

```
protected Control createContents(Composite parent)
{
    getShell().setText("JFace File Explorer");
    setStatus("JFace Example v1.0");
    return parent;
}
```

Note that the application window calls this method after all other widgets have been created but before the window has been displayed on the screen.

The size of the application window is set by the `initializeBounds()` method:

```
protected void initializeBounds()
{
    getShell().setSize(300, 200);
}
```

Building menus in SWT was a painful process, but thankfully JFace makes the process somewhat easier. To create a set of menus, you must first create a menubar that is an instance of `MenuManager`. Then, for each submenu, you create another instance of the `MenuManager` class and add it to the menu bar. The final step is to add a class that extends the `Action` class:

```
protected MenuManager createMenuManager()
{
    MenuManager menuBar = new MenuManager("");
    MenuManager fileMenu = new MenuManager("&File");
    MenuManager helpMenu = new MenuManager("&Help");
    menuBar.add(fileMenu);
    menuBar.add(helpMenu);
    fileMenu.add(exitAction);
    return menuBar;
}
```

The `StatusLineManager` class provides methods for setting the text of the status line, for controlling a progress bar displayed on the status line, and for displaying error text and images:

```
protected StatusLineManager createStatusLineManager()
{
    StatusLineManager statusLineManager = new StatusLineManager();
    statusLineManager.setMessage("Hello, world!");
    return statusLineManager;
}
```

Creating a toolbar is simply a matter of creating an instance of `ToolBarManager`, passing in a style, and then adding any actions:

```
protected ToolBarManager createToolBarManager(int style)
{
    ToolBarManager toolBarManager = new ToolBarManager(style);
    toolBarManager.add(exitAction);
    return toolBarManager;
}
```

Note that the styles allowed are the same as those for the SWT `Toolbar` class—those that affect the orientation of the toolbar (`SWT.VERTICAL` and `SWT.HORIZONTAL`) and those that affect the look of the toolbar (`SWT.FLAT` and `SWT.WRAP`).

The next part is basically the same as when you're working with SWT. You create the main window, set it to keep running until the user closes it, open the window, and then finally dispose of the `Display` when `open()` returns:

```
public static void main(String[] args)
{
    JFaceExample fe = new JFaceExample();
    fe.setBlockOnOpen(true);
    fe.open();
    Display.getCurrent().dispose();
}
}
```

E.2.2 *ExitAction class*

That wraps up the `JFaceExample` class. Now let's examine the `ExitAction` class. Again you import the required packages:

```
package org.eclipseguide.jface;

import java.net.*;
import org.eclipse.jface.action.Action;
import org.eclipse.jface.resource.ImageDescriptor;
import org.eclipse.jface.window.ApplicationWindow;
```

As we mentioned at the beginning of this appendix, an action lets you define what behavior should occur when it is activated and to share that behavior with other widgets. In this case, you create an action that begins the process of stopping the application by closing the main window:

```
public class ExitAction extends Action
{
```

Being able to share this behavior between different widgets is useful because it lets you create a single area of code rather than causing problems through duplication. With some careful effort, you will be able to create common actions that you can share among your programs.

The text is passed as appropriate to the widget connected to this `Action`:

```
ApplicationWindow window;

public ExitAction(ApplicationWindow w)
{
    window = w;
    setText("E&xit@Ctrl+W");
    setToolTipText("Exit the application");
```

As mentioned in appendix D, the & symbol before a letter indicates that the letter should be treated as a mnemonic. (If a menu is open and has keyboard focus, you can press the appropriate key to execute the action.) The @ symbol defines a keyboard accelerator; in this case, pressing Ctrl-W directly calls the `Action`.

The following code sets the image associated with this `Action`, which appears to be placed on a toolbar or menu. The image is loaded from a directory called icons, which must be located in the same place as the example's class files.

```
    try
    {
        setImageDescriptor(
            ImageDescriptor.createFromURL(
                new URL("file:icons/sample.gif")));
    }
    catch (MalformedURLException e)
    {
        e.printStackTrace();
    }
}
```

`Action`'s `run` method needs to be overridden to provide the behavior you desire, in this case to close the window and effectively cause the program to end:

```
public void run()
{
    window.close();
}
}
```

index

Symbols

\# (number) 129
${ and } 126
% (percent sign) 72
(\) backward slashes 119
(/) forward slashes 119
* (asterisk) 129
** (double asterisk) 129
*.jar file 221
*lib file 221
? (question mark) 129
~ (tilde) 129

Numerics

1.5.2 ant.jar 117

A

About button 354
About Eclipse Platform
    option 322
about.html file 221
ABSOLUTE format 73
absolute paths118 127
abstract TimerTask class 357
Abstract Window Toolkit
    (AWT) 344
AbstractUIPlugin 233, 236
accelerator configurations 338
Action class 365
ACTION parameter 214
action sets 238, 339
actions 237, 238, 239, 240, 362

adding to editor menus and
    toolbars 339
defining 286, 287
JSP 180
actionSet extension 238
Add Bookmark option 309
Add Constructor from
    Superclass option 311
Add External JARs option 350
Add Folder option 106
Add Import option 310
Add Jars option 243
Add Java Exception Breakpoint
    option 321
Add Java Projects to Tomcat
    Classpath section 184
Add Javadoc Comment
    option 311
Add Task option 309
Add to Version Control
    option 190
add() method 84
Add/Remove Breakpoint
    option 321
Add/Remove Method
    Breakpoint option 321
Add/Remove Watchpoint
    option 321
addEvent() method 300
additions section 238
Additions separator 286
AddLoggerAction class 253
add*XXX*Listener() method 348
Advanced option 188
affectsTextPresentation()
    method 269

agile methodology 40
agile programming 145
AllTests class 89
ALT attribute 194
alternate packaging 340
Always Save All Modified
    Resources Automatically
    Prior to Refactoring
    option 155
anonymous classes 358
Ant (build tool) 112, 116, 126,
    128, 131, 138, 141
    associating data types with
        classes in plug-ins 335
    associating tasks with classes
        in plug-ins 335
    benefits of 112, 140
    extension points used
        with 335
    file sets and path
        structures 129, 130
    Java Development Kit (JDK)
        required 112
    plug-in for 221
    projects 118, 119
    properties 126
    reducing redundant code 131
    running outside
        Eclipse 116, 117
    sample build 131, 136
        debugging the build 138
        overview 131
        performing a build 136
        simple example 115–118
    targets 119
    tasks 119–127

Ant library 242
ant-project help command 138
Apache Organization's Jakarta
      project 178
Apache Software
      Foundation 116
append attribute 121, 123
appenders 71, 74, 75
-application option 336
ApplicationWindow
      class 363, 364
Apply Patch option 169
architecture of Eclipse 8, 9, 10
Arguments tab 351
assert methods 50
assertEquals() method 50
assertFalse() method 50
assertNotNull() method 50
assertNotSame() method 50
assertNull() method 50
assertSame() method 50
assertTrue() method 50, 88
astronomy classes 85, 86, 87, 88
asyncExec() method 284,
      349, 357
attributes
      of value objects 85–86, 91
      XML 114, 115
author attribute 125
auto activation 271
automated refactoring 96

B

Back option 319
backing up CVS (Concurrent
      Versions System) 332
backslashes (\) 119
base directory 118
basedir attribute 118, 122
basedir property 127
Beck, Kent 43
bin directory 108, 112, 117
bin.includes property 245
binary files 338
binary imports 225
Binary Plug-in Projects
      decoration 224
binary plug-ins 225
Board of Stewards 5

braces 266
branches 171
      creating and using 172–173
      difference from versions 152
branching 145
breakpoint properties 64, 66
breakpoints, custom 336
browsers, HTML 337
BSD UNIX 328
BufferedReader class 66
BufferedWriter class 58, 66
build directory structure
      creating 105, 107, 108
      separating source and build
            directories 105, 107
build order 198
Build Order option 198
build paths 198, 337
build process
      creating build directory
            structure 105, 107, 108
      need for 104
build tools 110. *See also* Ant
      (build tool)
build.properties file 133, 244
build.xml file 115, 116, 118,
      132, 150, 158
BuildAll target 136, 158
builds 14
buttons
      adding to toolbars 286
      defining own behaviors
            for 362
      for shortcuts 18

C

C Development Toolkit (CDT) 8
C source files 109
Cactus tool 193
canvases 346
category property 302
CDT (C Development
      Toolkit) 8
CelestialBody equals()
      method 87, 88
CelestialBody.java superclass 85
Chainsaw program 279
Change ASCII/Binary Property
      option 190

Change Method Signature
      option 155, 312
Check Out as Project
      option 153
class attribute 233
class files 107, 227
Class Name 229
class property 238
Class Selection dialog 258
class variables 43, 44
classes
      anonymous 358
      compiling in Java 111
      containing collections 112
      renaming 96, 97, 98
      to look up classes and source
            files for classpath
            variables 337
      viewer 362
ClassMappingFailure
      exception 95
classname attribute 123
ClassNotFound exceptions 241
classpath, specifying 115
classpath attribute 115, 123, 125
classpath element 115, 128
.classpath file 150
CLASSPATH environment
      variable 112
classpath variables 36, 133,
      153, 337
CLEAN command 110
CLEAN target 110
CLEANALL command 110
clear() method 300
ClockUpdate task 358
Close All option 308
Close All Perspectives
      option 322
Close option 308
Close Perspective option 322
Close Project option 320
close() method 241
closing tags 113
cmpStrings() method 87, 88
code assistant 24
code completion 271
code generation
      templates 34, 35
code-completion feature, of Ant
      editor 116

code-generation dialog 229
collaboration. *See* source
    control 144
collections, classes
    containing 112
color field editor 304
color manager classes 269
colors
    adding 261, 264, 267
    of console output 336
ColumnLayoutData class 283
ColumnPixelData subclass 283
columns
    creating 291, 292
    defining 282, 283, 290
    remembering
        widths of 294, 296
ColumnWeightData
    subclass 283
comma separated values
    (CSV) 54
Command not found error 325
command prompt 104,
    138, 140
commands, defining 339
Comment option 310
comment partitions 277
comments
    for CVS repository 151
    HTML 114
    in changed files 160
    Javadoc 97, 108, 135
    partitions for 264
CommentScanner
    class 253, 264
Common Public License (CPL) 7
Commons Logging 185
Company class 112
compare/merge viewer
    factory 335
compilation 111
compilation unit 21
compilers 233
Compilers option 224
CompletionProposal class 273
composites 346. *See also* widgets
computeCompletionProposals()
    method 273
Concurrent Versions System
    (CVS). *See* CVS (Concur-
    rent Versions System)

Conf folder 189
ConfigurationModel class 252,
    273, 274
conflicts in updated files 160
console, color of output 336
Console view 138, 149
ConsoleAppender 71
    constructors 236, 285
container, servlet 178, 179
content assist 271, 274
Content Assist function 58
Content Assist option 310
content provider 285, 298
content type 264
ContentAssistAction class 279
ContentAssistant class 277
context-sensitive (F1) help 337
Controller component 178
controls 345, 346. *See also*
    widgets
conversion of data 199
conversion specifiers 72, 73
Convert Anonymous Class to
    Nested option 312
Convert Line Delimiters
    option 312
Convert Local Variable to Field
    option 317
Convert Nested Type to Top
    Level option 314
Copy command 278
Copy option 309
Copy Plug-in Contents into the
    Workspace Location
    option 225
CPL (Common Public License) 7
Create a Blank Plug-in Project
    option 228, 242
Create a Java Project
    option 226, 242
Create Class FieldMapEntry
    option 92
Create Patch option 168
Create Selected Folders Only
    option 81
createActions() method 287
createChild() class 295
createMenuManager()
    method 364
createObjectManager() factory
    method 90

createObjectManager()
    method 100
createObjectManager(Class
    type) method 84
createPartControl()
    method 285, 289, 290
createStatusLineManager()
    method 364
createToolBarManager()
    method 364
creating
    Java classes 22, 24
    Java projects 20, 21
    shortcuts 15
    CSV (comma separated
        values) 54
Ctrl-Space key sequence 16, 198,
    271, 277
Ctrl-W key sequence 367
Ctrl-Z key sequence 165
custom breakpoints 336
custom markers 335
Custom Plug-in Wizard 228
custom rules 267
Customize Perspective
    option 322
CustomLayout 358
Cut option 309
CVS (Concurrent Versions
    System) 144–167, 174
    and SSH 324
    backing up 332
    checking in to 158, 160
    creating and applying
        patches 167, 169
    creating CVS repository 325
    installing 324, 325, 327, 328,
        329, 330, 332
        CVSNT on Windows 329
        Cygwin and SSH installa-
            tion on Windows 330
        on Mac OS X 328
        on UNIX and Linux 324,
            325, 327
    overview 324
    troubleshooting problems
        with 332
    placing Tomcat project under
        control of, 190
    sharing project with 146,
        147, 149, 152

CVS *(continued)*
 adding and committing
  files 149
 checking project out of
  CVS 152
 creating repository
  location 146
 synchronization modes 165
 synchronizing with
  repository 162
 versions and branches 171,
  172, 173
CVS console view 149
CVS diff utility 169
CVS label decorators 149
CVS Repository Exploring
 option 147
CVS server 324
CVS Synchronize view 148
.cvsignore file 151
CVSNT 324
CVSROOT directory 152
cygrunsrv -S sshd command 331
CYGRUNSRV package 331
Cygwin 324, 330

D

-D option 133
DailyRollingFileAppender 71
damagers 277
-data option 226
data validation and
 conversion 199
DatabaseObjectManager
 class 96, 168
databases, providing persistence
 with 101
DATE format 73
date format specifiers 73
Debug As option 320
debug attribute 123
Debug History option 320
Debug Last Launched
 option 320
Debug menu 336
debug models 336
Debug option 320
Debug perspective 18
Debug view 27, 28
debug() method 70

debugger
 helping locate source
  code 336
 status codes 336
debugging 17, 62, 64
 as collaborative effort 145
 finding and fixing bugs 66,
  67, 68
 in Ant (build tool) 138
 Java program 27, 28, 29, 30
 JSPs 207
 plug-ins 232
 servlets 204, 208, 209
 setting breakpoint properties
  in 64, 66
 with aid of branching 145
DebugPlugin.log() method 274
Declarations option 319
default key bindings 339
Default Plug-In
 Structure 228, 253
Default Text File Type
 option 331
DefaultDamagerRepairer
 class 277
defaultexcludes attribute 129
DefaultScanner class 253, 265
defining properties 126
delegates 241
delete action 287
Delete option 309
delete() method 60, 61, 67,
 154, 155
delete(int key) method 84
deleting
 directories 121, 136
 files 121
 reference to src/ folder 243
dependencies
 defined 109
 evaluation of 111
 Dependencies page 230, 256
depends attribute 119
Deployable Plug-ins and
 Fragments 246
deploying plug-ins 246
deprecated extension
 points 334
description attribute 119
Deselect Working Set
 option 186

desktop, dragging shortcuts
 to 15
destdir attribute 123, 125
destfile attribute 122
destPage variable 215
Details button 150
dialogs, defining 362
diff utility, 169
dir attribute 121, 126, 129
Direction setting 156
directories
 containing plug-ins 220
 deleting 121, 136
 for distributable files,
  creating 108
 importing external
  directories 80, 81, 82, 83
 web application directory
  structure 191, 192
directory attribute 121
directory structure, build 105
Display class 345, 346, 349
Display option 321
display resources, predefined
 filters for 340
Display view 30
Display.asyncExec()
 method 284
displayHelpAboutDialog()
 method 353, 359
dispose() method, 241, 271,
 289, 353, 354, 359
disposing of resources, 347
distributable files, creating
 directory for, 108
-Djava.library.path
 argument 353
document provider classes 339
document providers 275
documentation 108
 benefits of source control
  for 145
 for Ant (build tool) 120
 help, 10
doGet() method 181, 198, 199
domain names 22
do-nothing constructor 84
doPost() method 181, 198, 200,
 204, 209
Double.parseDouble()
 method 199

downloading Eclipse 14, 15
drag-and-drop, importing
        external projects with 83
drop() method 60, 154, 155
DROP_DOWN style 355
drop-down menus 355
dropObjectTable() method 84, 88
DSTAMP property 126, 132
DynamicMBean interface 238,
        239, 266, 277

E

Eclipse
    architecture of 8, 9, 10
    code-generation feature 24, 25
    downloading 14, 15
    future of 11
    installing 15
    origin of 4, 5, 6
    overview 15–20
    preferences 32, 33, 35, 37
    versions of 14, 15
    what it is 7
    Workbench 16, 18, 19, 20
Eclipse Community page 215
Eclipse organization 5
Eclipse Platform 7, 8
Eclipse Platform Technical
        Overview 344
Eclipse Software Development
        Kit (SDK) 11
Edit menu options 309
editor menus, adding
        actions 339
editor preference page 303
EditorPreferencePage class 253
editors 16–18, 254–278
    adding an icon 259, 260
    adding color 261, 264, 267
    adding to Workbench 339
    content assist 271, 274
    defining editor
        extension 255, 256
    difference from views 254
    preparing editor class 255
    token manager 269
element factories 339
elements, XML 114, 115
enableAutoActivation()
        method 274

Encoding option 310
environment attribute 128
environment variables 128,
        133, 153
equals() method 86, 87
Equinox project 222
error handlers 336
error handling 95
error() method 70
evaluate() method 267
event dispatching loop 347
event listeners 347
events, and SWT (Standard
        Widget Toolkit) 347
.exe file 109
exception handling 95
excludes attribute 122, 123,
        129, 130
executable file 15
Execute option 321
execution order 110
Exit menu item 354
ExitAction class 364, 366
Expand Selection To
        option 309
Export dialog 339
Export option 308
Export the Entire Library
        option 243
Export Wizard 246
exporting preferences 37
Expression view 30
expressions 29, 30, 180
.exsd extension 255
extending persistence
        component 83–95
    creating factory method 84
    creating test suite 89
    creating unit test class 84
    implementing ObjectManager
        class 90–95
    Star test case 88–89
extensibility of Eclipse 12
extensible architecture 220
Extensible Markup
        Language 113
Extension page, of Plug-in
        Manifest Editor 334
extension points
    discussion of 220
    for plug-ins 334, 340, 341

    deprecated, obsolete, and
        internal 334
    id attribute 334, 340, 341
Extension Points page 231
Extension Templates
        Wizard 255
Extension Wizard 260
Extensions page 231
External Plug-ins and Fragments
        option 225
external projects,
        importing 80–83
External Tools option 321
Externalize Strings option 311
Externalize Strings Wizard 236
Extract Constant option 317
Extract Interface option 315
Extract Local Variable
        option 317
Extract Method option 315–317
extracting interfaces 99–101
eXtreme Programming (XP) 40
extssh option 147

F

F1 (context sensitive help) 337
factory method 84
failonerror attribute 120–125
Fast View 19
fatal() method 70
Feature Project 223
Field methods 95
FieldEditorPreferencePage
        class 301–304
File Associations dialog box 116
file attribute 120, 121, 127
File menu options 308
File option 319
File System box 189
File System option 81, 242, 244
FileAppender 71
filename parameter 155
filenames, setting 127
FileObjectManager class 96,
        101, 154, 157, 201
FilePersistenceServices class 41,
        42, 57, 83, 84, 93, 154,
        160, 202
FilePersistenceServices.vec-
        tor2String() method 203

FilePersistenceServicesTest class 46, 156, 157
FilePersistenceServicesTest test case 89
files, adding and committing to CVS 149
  defining as text or binary 338
  deleting 121
  distributable 108
  history of changes to 144
  importing external files 80, 81, 82, 83
  locking 145, 174
  outdated 105
  specifying for Ant 129, 130
  updated, resolving conflicts in 160
FileSave All option 82
Filesystem Realtime Protection 329
filesystems 15, 16
fillContextMenu() method 286
FillLayout layout 358
fillLocalPullDown() method 286
fillLocalToolBar() method 286
fillXXX() methods 286
filtering widgets 362
finalize() method 298
Find Next option 309
Find Previous option 309
Find Strings to Externalize option 312
Find/Replace option 156, 157, 309
floppy disk icon 18
flow of control 110
Flyweight pattern 261
focus events 293
folders 15, 16
followsymlinks attribute 129
fonts 339, 362
fork attribute 123
Format option 310
format styles 33
FormatRule class 253, 267
FormLayout layout 358
Forward option 319
forward slashes (/) 119
Fragment Project 223
From Directory text box 81
future of Eclipse 11

G

Gamma, Erich 6, 43
garbage collection 241
Generate Delegate Methods option 311
Generate Getter and Setter option 86, 205, 311
Generate Javadoc option 320
Generic Wizards option 255
GET requests 193
get() method 84, 91, 93, 273
get(int key) method 83
getAttribute() method 208
getBundle() method 236
getCollection() method 210
getColumnText() method 298
getCompletions() method 274
getElements() method 300
getFields() method 91
getImage(Object) method 298
getNextKey() method 201
getRoot() method 236
getSelection() method 288
getShell() method 241
Getter and Setter dialog box 86
getter methods 86
getViewer() method 284
getWorkbench() method 241
getXXX() methods 85, 86, 205, 275
global install handlers 340
Gnu make (build tool) 109
Gnu Public License (GPL) 329
Go Into option 318
Go to Last Edit Location option 319
Go to Line option 319
Go to Next Problem option 318
Go To option 318
Go to Previous Problem option 318
goto action 288
GPL (Gnu Public License) 329
GridLayout layout 358
grouping actions 336
groups, in menus 238
GTK platform 350
GUI builder 11

H

handleEvent() method 284
handlePreferenceStore-Changed() method 269
handlers 339, 340
hang point 355
HEAD entry 152
HELLO attribute 163, 164
Hello project 111, 116
Hello World Wizard 228
HelloPlugin class 233
HelloPlugin.getResourceString method 236
HelloPlugin.java file 233
HelloPluginResources.properties 236
help, online 319, 348
  context-sensitive (F1) 337
Help Contents option 3, 22
Help menu 322, 354
  indexing files 337
  overview 10
  searching 337
Hide Editors option 321
hiding plug-ins from Package Explorer menu 226
history of Eclipse 4, 5, 6
history, revision 145
HOME environmental variable 332
Home.jsp 195
hookEvents() method 293
hot-swapping 232
hovering behavior in Java editors 338
HTML (Hypertext Markup Language) 113, 178
HTML browsers 337
HttpJspBase subclass 207
HttpServlet class 181, 207
Hypertext Markup Language (HTML) 113, 178

I

IAction interface 241
IActionDelegate 241
IBM 5, 7, 12
IBM's Websphere Studio Application Developer 11

ICharacterScanner class 267, 268
ICharacterScanner.read()
    method 268
icons 18, 259, 260, 340
icons file 221
IContentAssistProcessor 271, 274
ID plug-ins 238
id attribute 334, 340, 341
IDocument interface 273, 275
if attribute 119
ILoggingEventListener
    interface 252, 283
images
    associating with specific launch
        configuration types 336
    registries for 362
Implementors option 319
Import dialog box 81, 339
Import feature 80, 82, 83
Import option 308
importing
    external projects 80–83
    preferences 37
    SDK plug-ins 224, 226
includeEmptyDirs
    attribute 120, 121
includes attribute 122, 123,
    129, 130
incoming mode 162, 165
incoming/outgoing mode 165
incremental builders 335
incremental compilation 111
Incremental Find Next
    option 309
Incremental Find Previous
    option 309
indexing help files 337
info() method 70
-Init target 136
init() method 289, 291, 303
initializing state 291
Inline option 315
Inspect option 320
installing CVS (Concurrent
    Versions System) 324–332
    CVSNT on Windows 329
    Cygwin and SSH installation
        on Windows 33
    on Mac OS X 328
    on UNIX and Linux 324,
        325, 327

overview 324
troubleshooting problems
    with 332
Tomcat 182
Integer.parseInt() method 62
integration build 14
interfaces, extracting 99,
    100, 101
internal extension points 334
internal targets 136
"internal," use of word in
    package name 236
invokeAndWait() method 349
invokeLater() method 349
IOExceptions 70
IPluginDescriptor object 236
IRule 267
ISO8601 format 73
IStructuredSelection 288
ITableLabelProvider
    interface 296
IWordDetector interface 267
IWorkbenchWindow
    interface 241
IWorkbenchWindowActionDel-
    egate 237, 238, 239, 240
IWorkspace interface 236

J

Jakarta project 178
jar -cvf log4jsrc.zip utility 244
jar attribute 123
jar command 183
JAR filename 243
JAR files
    specifying which to search
        for 130
    wrapping in plug-in 242
Jar target 135
Java
    classes 22, 24
    code completion
        features 24, 25
    evaluation of
        dependencies 111
    projects 20, 21
    using Make (build tool)
        with 111
Java Build Path Control
    option 224

Java Build Path option 198,
    243, 350
Java build paths 337
Java Builder Output option 227
Java Class Selection dialog 258
Java comparators 336
Java compiler (javac.exe) 112
Java Development Kit
    (JDK) 112
Java Development Toolkit
    (JDT) 6, 7, 16
Java editors 16, 255, 338
.java files 227
Java keyword scanner 262
Java Native Interface
    (JNI) 345
Java option 319
Java perspective 18
Java program
    debugging 27–30
    running, 26
Java projects, creating 20, 21
Java Runtime Environment
    (JRE) 112
Java scrapboook page 31
Java Snippet Imports dialog
    box 31
Java Source Attachment
    option 244
Java Structure Compare
    section 163
Java virtual machine
    (java.exe) 112
Java Virtual Machine
    (JVM) 345
java.exe (Java virtual
    machine) 112
java.util.Timer class 357
JavaBean, using with JSP 205
javac (Java compiler) 111
javac.exe (Java compiler) 112
Javadoc, defining completion
    processors 338
Javadoc comments 32, 33, 97,
    108, 135
Javadoc partition 262
Javadoc target 135
javax.servlet.http.HttpServlet
    superclass 198
JDBCAppender 71
JDK (Java Development Kit) 112

JDT (Java Development Toolkit) 6, 7, 16
JFace 362, 363, 364, 366
  architecture of 362
  building applications using 363, 364, 366
JFace utility classes 241
JFace wrapper 240
JRE (Java Runtime Environment) 112, 337
JSP directives 181
JSP expressions 180
JSP scriptlets 179
JSP tags 180
JSPs
  overview 179, 180, 181
  programming with 198, 199, 202, 205, 207
    data validation and conversion 199
    debugging JSPs 207
    multiproject build settings 198
    robust string handling 202
    using JavaBean with JSP 205
JUnit library 242
junit property 126
JUnit testing framework 43, 44
  implementing public methods in 58–62
  method stubs 44–46
  test cases 49, 50–52, 54
  testing in 54–57
  unit tests 44–46
JUnit TestRunner classes 134
JUnit tests 84, 85, 134
JUNIT variable 153
JUnit Wizard 46
JVM 122, 134
JVM (Java Virtual Machine) 337

K

keyboard shortcuts 338, 355
Keyboard Shortcuts option 322
keyword scanner 262
kill command 328

L

Label Decorations option 224
label decorators 149
label providers 285, 296
LabelProvider class 296, 297
language neutrality 10
lastIndexOf() method 274
Launch Configuration options 254
launch configurations 336
layout manager 357
layouts 72, 73, 358
lazy loading 222
lib directory 117
Libraries tab 243, 350
licenses, open source 6, 7
lightweight methodology 40
Link to Folder option 189
linked folders, editing web.xml with 188
Linux, installing CVS on 324, 325, 327
listener list 298
ListenerList class 300
listeners, creating 347
listeners list, of IAction interface 241
lists, pattern 122
local access 324
local history 52, 54
location attribute 127, 130
Lock the Toolbars option 321
locking files 145, 174
log4j
  configuring 74, 75
  logging with 68, 69
  using with Eclipse 75–77
log4j configuration file 150
log4j JAR file 242
log4j library 242, 243, 244
log4j logger 95
LOG4J variable 153
log4j.rootLogger 274
Log4jPlugin class 252, 304
Log4jPluginResources.properties file 279
Log4jUtil class 252
Log4jView class 253, 282, 285
LogFactor5 program 279
Logger.getLogger() method 70

Logger.getRootLogger() static method 70
loggers 70, 71
logging
  Tomcat 185
  with log4j 69
LoggingEvent objects 288
LoggingListener class 283
LoggingModel class 252, 298, 300
Long.parseLong() method 199
lowercase, forcing classpath to 128

M

Mac OS X, installing CVS on 328
main menu 18
main preference page 302
main toolbar 18
main() method 68, 164
mainLoop method 358
MainPreferencePage class 253, 302
Make (build tool) 109–112, 140
man chmod command 326
Manifest Editor 254, 256
Mark as Merged option 164, 166
markers 335, 339
MCV architecture 178
memento 291, 294, 295
menuAboutToShow() function 292, 293
menubarPath property 239
MenuManager class 365
menus 18, 237–240
  adding 286
  bars for additional menus 355
  creating 355
  defining own behaviors for items on 362
  drop-down 355
  filling 294
  quick reference tables 308
message attribute 121
message pump 347
MessageDialog class 241
messages, of Ant (build tool) 138
method stubs 44, 45

methods
  renaming 96, 97, 98
  stubs for 84
mnemonics 355, 367
mock objects 193
model changes 283
Model component 178
models 298
Model-View architecture 283
Modify Attributes and Launch
  dialog box 158
modifying
  files, permission for 145, 174
  perspective defaults 281
monumental methodology 40
More Info button 222
mouse events 293
Move option 308, 312
multiple developers. *See* team
  development
multiple files, deleting 121
multiproject build settings 198
multithread debugging 208, 209
myenv prefix 128
myMethod() method 155
.mxsd extension 255

N

name attribute 114, 119, 209
native library 345
natural-language text
  analyzers 337
Navigate menu options 318
Navigator view 18, 19
nested elements 114, 115
nesting, in XML vs. HTML 113
NetInfo utility 329
New Class Wizard 34, 260
new code formatters 337
New dialog box 84, 339
New Editor option 256
New File dialog box 132
New Folder dialog box 188
New Java Class dialog 187
New Java Class Wizard 23
New Java Project Wizard 21
New Make (NMAKE build
  tool) 109
New option 308
New Plug-in Project Wizard 242

New Project Wizard 226, 253
New Window option 321
Next Match option 318
Next option 318
nightly build 14
NMAKE (New Make build
  tool) 109
No ID or Name Is Necessary
  option 256
nonvirtual tables 284
Normal toolbar 239
Notepad 222
NTEventLogAppender 71
ntsec authentication option 331
number (#) symbol 129
NumberFormatException 67

O

object files 109
Object Technologies
  International (OTI) 5
object2Vector() method 92
ObjectManager class 168
  and value objects 86
  implementing 90–95
ObjectManager factory
  method 91
ObjectManager update()
  method 95
ObjectManager.java option 97
ObjectManagerTest test case 89
obsolete extension points 334
om.save() method 209
online help 348
Open Declaration option 318
Open External Javadoc
  option 318
Open Perspective option 321
Open Project option 320
Open Resource option 318
open source 6, 7
Open Super Implementation
  option 318
Open Type Hierarchy
  option 318
Open Type in Hierarchy
  option 318
Open Type option 318
Open With menu 260
open() method 366

openInformation() method 241
opening tags 113
OpenSSH package 331
operating system 15
optimistic locking 145
optimize attribute 124
optional.jar 117
Order and Export tab 243
Order button 136
order of execution 110
Order Targets dialog box 136,
  137, 138
org subdirectory 244
org.apache.ant classpath 242
org.apache.ant wrapper
  plug-in 250
org.apache.xerces plug-in 242
org.eclipse.... extension
  points 335
org.eclipse.ant.core plug-in 221
org.eclipse.swt.events
  package 347
org.eclipse.ui.perspectiveExten-
  sions 281
org.eclipse.ui.views extension
  point 280
org.eclipseguide.astronomy
  package 134
org.eclipseguide.helloplugin
  project 236
org.eclipseguide.helloplugin.
  HelloPlugin 229
org.eclipseguide.log4j
  package 252
org.eclipseguide.log4j.decora-
  tors package 252
org.eclipseguide.log4j.editor
  package 252
org.eclipseguide.log4j.edi-
  tor.contentassist
  package 252
org.eclipseguide.log4j.edi-
  tor.scanners package 253
org.eclipseguide.log4j.popup.
  actions package 253
org.eclipseguide.log4j.prefer-
  ences package 253
org.eclipseguide.log4j.views
  package 253
org.eclipseguide.persistence
  package 89, 134

org.eclipseguide.simpleplugin_
  1.0.0 subdirectory 222
org.eclipseguide.swt Java
  class 353
org.junit plug-in 242
Organize Imports option 310
origin of Eclipse 4, 5, 6
OTI (Object Technologies
  International) 5
outdated files 105
outgoing mode 165
Outline view 19, 21
output attribute 123
output folder 106
Override and Update option 166
Override/Implement Methods
  option 310
Overview page 230, 233
overwrite attribute 120

P

package attribute 125
Package Explorer 21, 83, 255
  defining class variables
    with 43, 44
  hiding plug-ins from menu
    of 226
  revealing plug-in source code
    with 224
Package Explorer view 149, 351
Package Name 255
package name 236
Package Navigator 80
pair programming 40, 80
paragraph tags 113
Parameter Hints option 310
parameters, removing 155
parsing text 262
partition scanners 261, 262, 264
partitions 261
parts 254
Password Server (pserver) 329
Paste option, 309
patches, 167 169
path attribute 130
PATH environment variable 112
paths
  absolute 118, 127
  in UNIX 120
  relative 118, 127

specifying for Ant (build
  tool) 129, 130
pattern lists 122
patterns
  adding to version control
    ignore list 338
  wildcards in 129
PDE (Plug-in Development
  Environment) 223
  importing SDK plug-ins 224
  preparing Workbench 224
  using Plug-in Project
    Wizard 226, 228
PDE Runtime Error Log view 274
percent sign (%) 72
permission, to modify
  files 145, 174
Persistence class 85
persistence component,
  extending 83–95
  creating factory method 84
  creating test suite 89
  creating unit test class 84
  implementing ObjectMan-
    ager class 90–95
  Star test case 88, 89
  working with astronomy
    classes 85–88
persistence components 41, 42
Persistence project 80, 105, 153
Persistence/bin setting 107
PersistenceServices class 101
perspective defaults,
  modifying 281
perspectiveExtensions
  settings 282
perspectives 16–18
  changing 19–20
  defining new 340
pessimistic locking 145, 174
platform neutrality 10
Platform Plug-in Developer
  Guide 255
Platform runtime 9
Platform search path 336
pluggable look-and-feel 344
Plug-in Details option 222
Plug-in Development
  option 226
Plug-in Manifest
  Editor 230, 254

Dependencies page 256
Extension page 334
plug-in manifest file
  (plugin.xml) 221–244
Plug-in Name 243
Plug-in perspective 229
Plug-in Project 223
Plug-in Project Wizard 226,
  228, 253
plug-in registry 222
Plug-in Runtime Library 227
plugin.properties file 221, 236
plugin.xml (plug-in manifest
  file) 230, 244
plugin.xml (plug-in
  manifest) 221, 222, 228
plugin.xml file 255, 260
plug-ins 3, 177, 219–306
  Hello, World 228, 230, 231,
    233, 237
  anatomy of 220
  and editors 254–269, 271, 275
    adding an icon 259, 260
    adding colors 261, 264, 267
    content assist 271
    defining editor
      extension 255, 256
    preparing editor class 255
    token manager 269
  and extension points 220
  binary 225
  creating 20, 222
  debugging 231
  defined 220
  deploying 246
  extension points for 334,
    340, 341
    deprecated, obsolete, and
      internal 334
    id attribute 334, 340, 341
  ID of 227, 238
  lifecycle of 222
  loading 222
  log4j library 242–244
  overview 3, 177, 219, 220
  plug-in class 304
  Plug-in Development Envi-
    ronment (PDE) 223, 224,
    226, 228
    importing SDK plug-ins 224
    preparing Workbench 224

plug-ins *(continued)*
    Plug-in Development Envi-
        ronment (PDE) *(continued)*
        using Plug-in Project
            Wizard 226, 228
        See also PDE
    plug-in fragments 10
    preferences 301–303
        editor preference page 303
        main preference page 302
    source code for 224
    views 279–300
        label providers 296
        models 298
        modifying perspective
            defaults 281
        overview 279
        receiver thread 300
        table framework 289–294
        View class 282–283, 286, 289
    wrapping JAR files in 242
Plug-ins and Fragments tab 254
PMC (Project Management
    Committee) 6
POP_UP option 355
populating widgets 362
pop-up menus 340
POST requests 193
predefined properties 127
preference store 278
preferences 301–303
    editor preference page 303
    handling changes 278
    main preference page 302
    when using PDE 224
Preferences dialog 269, 340
Preferences option 322
Preferences page, accelerator
    configurations 338
Preferences pages 251
-Prep target 136
Preview button 98
Preview option 155
Previous Match option 318
Previous option 318
Print option 308
Printer.class 111
Printer.java 111
printf() function 72
private attribute 125
.project file 150, 153

Project Management Committee
    (PMC) 6
Project menu options 320
project nature 9
project sets, handlers for reading
    and writing 338
projects 15, 16
    Ant (build tool) 118, 119
    sharing with CVS (Concur-
        rent Versions System)
        146–149, 152
        adding and committing
            files 149
        checking project out of
            CVS 152
        creating repository
            location 146
    wizards for associating with
        team providers 338
Projects tab 198
projects, external 80
properties
    Ant (build tool) 126
    of projects, editing 243
Properties dialog box 43
Properties Editor 245
properties file 133
Properties option 308, 320
PropertiesAssistant class 252,
    271, 273
PropertiesConfiguration
    class 252, 275–277
PropertiesDocumentProvider
    class 252, 275
PropertiesEditor class 252,
    260, 277
PropertiesPartitionScanner
    class 252
property build.number 120
property pages 340
protected attribute 125
Provider Name 229, 243
proxies 240
ps cax command 326, 327–328
pserver 147
pserver (Password Server) 329
pserver remote access 327
pseudo-targets 110
public attribute 125
public methods,
    implementing 58, 60–62

Pull Up option 315
Push Down option 315

Q

Quick Fix option 45, 310
quotation marks 114

R

RandomAccessFile class 66
Read Access option 319
read() method 46, 50–59,
    154, 155
Rebuild All option 320
Rebuild Project option 320
rebuilds, forcing 110
receiver thread 300
ReceiverThread class 252, 300
red, green, blue (RGB)
    format 271
Redo option 309, 312
redundant code, reducing 131
RefactorExtract Interface
    option 99
refactoring 154, 156, 157,
    95–102, 264
Refactorings menu
    options 312, 319
RefactorRename option 97
RefactorUndo option 98
References option 319
Reflection Tutorial 90
registries 15, 222, 362
relative paths 118, 127
relpersistencepath 132
remote access 326, 327
removing
    parameters 155
    source.log4j.jar property 245
Rename dialog box 97
Rename option 308, 312
renaming
    classes 96–98
    JAR filename 243
    methods 96–98
repairers 277
repository location 146
reproducibility 104
request.getParameter()
    method 199

Required Plug-in Entries folder 225
Reset Perspective option 322
resource disposal 347
resource move operation 335
Resource perspective 17–19
Resource(s) by Name option 151
Restore Defaults button 304
retargetable action 278
retrieving versions 172
Revert option 308
Review Options window 330
revision history 145
RGB (red, green, blue) format 271
RollingFileAppender 71
root loggers, specifying 74
RowLayout layout 358
rule-based scanning 262
RuleBasedPartitionScanner class 262–264
RuleBasedScanner class 267
rules, custom 267
defined 109
Run Ant option 116
Run As option 320
Run dialog 351
Run History option 320
Run Last Launched option 320
Run menu 336
Run menu options 320, 321
Run option 320
Run to Line option 321
run() method 241, 357
Runnable 357
Runtime option 117
Runtime page 230
Runtime page, of manifest editor 243
Run-time Workbench 231, 260

S

Sample Menu 231
SampleAction class 239–241
sampleGroup level 238
sampleMenu level 238
Save All option 308
Save As option 308
Save option 308
Save Perspective As option 322

save() method 88, 91, 92, 201
save(Object o, int key) method 83
saveState() method 289, 291
saving state 291
say() method 27
schemas 255
scopes 338
script editor 115
scriptlets, JSP 179
SDK (Software Development Kit) 11
SDK plug-ins, importing 224, 226
search and replace feature 156
Search dialog, adding tabs to 338
Search menu options 319
Search option 319
Search view, custom sorting options in 338
searching help 337
Select Additional Tasks window 329
Select All option 309
Select Components window 329
Select Packages screen 331
SelectionEvent 348
SelectionListener 348
SelectionLister 354
self-hosted, defined 233
separating source and build directories 105, 107
separators, in menus 238
serializing 291
Server Components 329
server.xml file 191
Service Status dialog box 330
servlet container 178, 179
servlets
    creating and testing 187, 188
    overview 181
    programming with 198, 199, 202, 204, 208, 209
        data validation and conversion 199
        debugging servlets 204, 208, 209
        multiproject build settings 198
        robust string handling 202
setFieldMap() method 91, 92

setFocus() method 289, 293
setMaximized() method 355
setMinimized() method 355
setter methods, generating automatically 86
setUp() method 46, 49, 59
setXXX() methods 86, 205
SGML (Standard Generalized Markup Language) 113
Share Project with CVS Repository dialog box 147
Shell class 345, 346
shell window 358
shells 241
Shift Left option 310
Shift Right option 310
shortcut toolbar 18
shortcut 15, 18
Show Editors option 321
Show In option 318
Show in Resource History option 159
Show Only Extension Points from the Required Plug-ins option 256
Show Outline option 318
Show Tooltip Description option 310
Show View dialog 281
Show View option 321
simple projects 20
SingleLineRule class 264
Singleton pattern 236
Smalltalk 5
SMTPAppender 71
SocketAppender 71
Software Development Kit (SDK) 11
Software Updates option 322
Sort Members option 310
sorting widgets 362
source code
    creating executable program from 109
    extending persistence component 83–95
    creating factory method 84
    creating test suite 89
    creating unit test class 84
    implementing ObjectManager class 90–95

source code *(continued)*
  Star test case 88, 89
  working with astronomy
    classes 85–88
  for plug-ins 224
  helping debugger locate 336
  hot-swapping 232
  importing external
    project 80–83
  open 6, 7
  refactoring 95–102
    extracting an
        interface 99–101
    future refactoring 102
    renaming a class 96–98
source control
  See also CVS (Concurrent
    Versions System)
  need for 144
source directory, separating from
    build directory 105, 107
Source Folder 227
Source Folder option 107
Source menu options 310
Source page 106, 231
Source page, of manifest
    editor 243
source.log4j.jar property 245
sourcefiles attribute 125
sourcepath attribute 125
sourcepathref attribute 125
SourceViewerConfiguration
    class 275
specialized events 335
src directory 106, 150, 242
src/java directory 244
srcdir attribute 123
SSH, installing on Windows 330
SSH remote access 326
SSH server 147
ssh-host-config command 331
stable build 14
StackLayout layout 358
Standard Generalized Markup
    Language (SGML) 113
Standard Widget Toolkit
    (SWT) 240, 344
  See also SWT
Star test case 88, 89
Star.java class 85
Start Menu folder 329

Start Tomcat tool button 184
Start Working in the Branch
    box 173
state, initializing and saving 291
static factory method 100
status codes, for debugger 336
status messages, of Ant (build
    tool) 138
StatusLineManager class 365
step filters 29
Step Into button 29
Step into Selection option 321
Step Over button 29
Step Return button 29
Step With Filters button 29
String equals() method 87
string handling 202
string2Vector() method 203
StringTokenizer class 202
Structure Compare outline
    view 162
structured content provider 298
stubs for methods 84
styles 346
sub-canvases 346
subdirectories, for plug-ins 222
Submit button 194
Sun Microsystems 344
Sun's Java Development Kit
    (JDK) 112
Sun's Reflection Tutorial 90
Surround with try/catch Block
    option 311
Swing 344
SwingToolkit class 349
Switch to Editor option 322
SWT (Standard Widget Tool-
    kit) 344–350, 353, 356, 357
  and events 347
  and threads 348, 349
  architecture of 345, 346, 347
  building and running SWT
    programs 350
  overview 9
  relationship with JFace 362
  resource disposal 347
  tables 284
  using 353, 356, 357
  what it is 344
  widget creation 346
SWT Toolbar class 366

SWT.BAR style argument 355
SWT.FULL_SELECTION style
    bit 290
SWT.H_SCROLL style bit 290
swt.jar 350
SWT.SINGLE style bit 290
SWT.V_SCROLL style bit 290
SWTException 349
swt-pi.jar file 350
syncExec() method 349
synchronization modes 165
Synchronize Repository
    feature 158
Synchronize with Repository
    feature 162
synchronizing
  local files with latest on CVS
    server 153, 154
  with repository 162
syntax coloring 261, 264, 267
Sysdeo Tomcat plug-in 183, 185
system tray 15
Systems applet 118

T

table framework 289–294
table of contents files 337
TableColumn class 292
TableLayout algorithm 292
tables 284
TableViewer class 285
TableViewPart class 253, 282,
    289, 294, 296
tabs
  adding to Search dialog 338
  configuring group of for spe-
    cific launch configuration
    types 336
tags 119
  HTML 113
  JSP 180
  XML 113
Target Platform list 256
targetID 282
targets 109
  Ant (build tool) 119, 136
  internal 136
  Make (build tool) 109
Task List view 280
Task List.viewShortcut 282

tasks, Ant (build tool) 119–126
Tasks view 21
team development, 140 141
  See also CVS (Concurrent Versions System)
  source control 144, 145
tearDown() method 46, 49
templates
  defining 338
  for wrapping log4j library 242
  to create plug-ins 228
test cases, creating 49, 50, 52
test suite, creating 89
TestCase option 84
test-driven development 41
testing 53–55, 57
  servlets 187, 188
  Tomcat 182
  web applications 192–196
testRead() method 46, 54, 67
TestRunner classes 134
testStar() test method 89
testString2Vector() method 203
testVector2String() method 203
testWrite() method 46, 60
text, parsing 262
text editors 16, 222
text files 338
TextEditor class 254–264, 267, 269, 271, 275, 278
  adding an icon 259, 260
  adding color 261, 264, 267
  content assist 271, 274
  defining editor extension 255, 256
  preparing editor class 255
  token manager 269
threads, and SWT (Standard Widget Toolkit) 348, 349
tilde (~) 129
timer, creating 358
timer tasks 357
Tips and Tricks option 322
TODAY property 126, 132
todir attribute 120
tofile attribute 120
token manager 269, 278
token scanners 261, 264, 267
Token.UNDEFINED token 264
TokenManager class 252, 269

tokens 261
Tomcat 182, 185
  creating and testing servlets 187, 188
  creating project with JSP file 185
  placing project under CVS control 190
tomcatPluginV21.zip file 183
toolbarPath property 239
toolbars 18, 19, 237, 238, 239, 240
  adding actions 339
  adding buttons 286
  defining own behaviors for items on 362
  filling 294
  shortcut 18
tooltip 18
toString() method 70
tree structures 335
troubleshooting CVS installation problems 332
TSTAMP property 126, 132
typeMap() method 93, 94
types 129

U

UI thread 348, 349
Uncomment option 310
Undo feature 86
Undo option 309, 312
undoing actions 165
unimplemented extension points 335
unit test class 84
unit tests 44, 45, 134
UNIX
  file paths in 120
  installing CVS on 324–325, 327
unless attribute 119
unread() method 268
Update feature 158, 164
Update from Repository option 166
Update Manager 340
Update Site Project, 223
update() method 91, 154, 155

update(Object o, int key) method 83
updated files, resolving conflicts in 160
updating widgets, classes for 362
upgrading Ant in Eclipse 117
Use an Existing Java Class option 258
use attribute 125
Use Classpath Containers for Dependent Plug-ins option 224
Use Default Port option 147
Use Specified Module Name option 148
Use Supertype Where Possible option 315
user interface thread 284
utility programs 111

V

VA4J (Visual Age for Java) 5
Validate Connection on Finish option 147
validate-save and validate-edit operations 335
validation of data 199
value build.number+1 120
value objects 86, 91
value partitions 277
ValueScanner class 253, 266, 267
variables 29, 30
  classpath 36, 133, 153
  environment 153
  environmental 128
Variables view 30
Vector class 45
vector2String() method 204
vectors 91
verbose attribute 120, 121, 124
verification schemes 340
version attribute 125
version control ignore list 338
version control. *See* source control
versions 14, 171–173
  adding labels 171
  difference form branches 152
  retrieving 172
vi (text editor) 222
View class 282, 283, 286, 289

View component 178
viewer classes 362
viewer factories 335
ViewLabelProvider class 253, 296, 297
ViewPart class 289
views 16–19, 279–283, 286, 289, 296, 298, 300
    changing 19, 20
    difference from editors 254
    label providers 296
    models 298
    modifying perspective defaults 281
    overview 279
    receiver thread 300
    table framework 289–294
    View class 282, 283, 286, 289
Visual Age for Java (VA4J) 5
VM Arguments text box 351

W

WAR file 191
warn() method 70, 76
watch expression 30
Watch option 320
waterfall methodology 40
web development tools 178–16
    building web application 191–209
        See also JSPs, programming with; servlets, programming with
    design and testing 193, 196
    web application directory structure 191, 192
Sysdeo Tomcat plug-in 183, 185

Tomcat 182, 185
    creating and testing servlets 187, 188
    creating project with JSP file 185
    placing project under CVS control 190
web sites
    development schedule 15
    downloads 14
web.xml file 188
WEB-INF directory 192
Websphere Studio Application Developer 11
Welcome option 322
Welcome page 230
Which Method Stubs Would You Like to Create option 85
whitespace rule 267
WhitespaceDetector class 253, 265
widgetDefaultSelected method 354
widgets 345, 346
    See also SWT (Standard Widget Toolkit)
    creating 346
widgetSelected method 354
wildcards, in patterns 129
Window menu options 321
Windows
    installing CVSNT on 329
    installing Cygwin and SSH on 330
WinZip 244
wizards 21
    defining 338, 362
    in Export dialog 339
    in Import dialog 339

in New dialog 339
    Plug-in Project Wizard 226, 228
    that associate projects with team providers 338
WordDetector class 253
WordRule class 267
work directory 192
Workbench 9, 16–20, 162, 224
working sets 42
workspace 9
Workspace Plug-ins list 254
workspace root resource 236
wrapping JAR files 242
Write Access option 319
write() method 46–54, 58, 154, 155
writeBytes() method 66
writeChars() method 66

X

Xerces library 242
XML (Extensible Markup Language) 233, 238
    code created by Extension Wizard 260
    overview 113–115
XML editor 185, 231, 255
XMLBuddy 185
XMLBuddy plug-in 194
XP (eXtreme Programming) 40
.xsd extension 255

Z

zip files 246